More praise for

NEW AMERICANS

"Each story is unique. . . . A reminder to those who were born in the United States that not everyone has been as fortunate, and that for many recent arrivals the welcome mat has appeared threadbare.."

The Christian Science Monitor

"Timely. . . . A sobering and provocative analysis."

Houston Chronicle

"An upbeat book. . . . *New Americans'* mission is to update mainstream America's picture of immigrants huddled on Ellis Island waiting to be free. And it does this well."

The Nation

"Compelling. . . . The most gripping of these narratives bring into sharp focus the suffering, severing of family ties and the struggle to rebuild shattered lives that are so much a part of the immigrant experience."

Constitution

"Fascinating reading. . . . Lets longtime residents see the country with fresh eyes, as a challenging, inconsistent, but amazingly strong nation that still offers unique opportunities."

Booklist

Also by Al Santoli

EVERYTHING WE HAD

TO BEAR ANY BURDEN

NEW AMERICANS

AN ORAL HISTORY

Immigrants and Refugees
in the U.S. Today

AL SANTOLI

Ballantine Books • New York

Library of Congress Catalog Card Number: 89-91492

ISBN: 0-345-36455-4

This edition published by arrangement with Viking Penguin, a division of Penguin Books USA, Inc, New York.
Cover design by James R. Harris

Cover photographs, clockwise from upper left: © Index/Stock International Inc.,
© 1990 Hugh Brown, © 1990 Al Santoli; The Image Bank/
© 1987 Sobeliklonsky; The Image Bank/© 1989 Margaret W. Peterson

Manufactured in the United States of America

First Ballantine Books Edition: June 1990

10 9 8 7 6 5 4 3 2 1

To my parents, with love and respect

The bosom of America is open to receive not only the opulent and respectable stranger, but the oppressed and persecuted of all nations and religions whom we shall welcome to participate in all of our rights and privileges, if by decency and propriety of conduct they appear to merit the enjoyment.
—*George Washington*

This was the secret of America: a nation of people with the fresh memory of old traditions who dared to explore new frontiers.
—*John F. Kennedy*

The people I knew believed that America was the last place in the world where we could find freedom.
—*Rod Zdvoracek*
  Czech refugee, San Francisco

Freedom is nothing else
but a chance to be better.
—*Albert Camus*

ACKNOWLEDGMENTS

During a year of travel throughout the United States while researching this book and meeting the people in it, my wife, Phuong—herself a new American who is still learning English—persevered in New York City by her own wit and resourcefulness. Her courage and warmth are an important influence on this work. And although my journalistic pursuits have often kept me apart from my parents, their love and encouragement have been an important source of inspiration.

I am deeply grateful to Gerry Howard, my editor, who believed in this project from its conceptualization and challenged me to keep going at times when I stumbled; to my agents, Anne Sibbald and Mort Janklow, for being there when their expertise is needed; and to Walter Anderson and Herb Kupferberg at *Parade*, for their friendship and guidance.

Although not in the best health, Jack Bloomfield and his wife, Shirley, helped to transcribe a mountain of interview tapes. My travel was expertly budgeted by Gabriella Kaufman at Best in Travel. And Dr. and Mrs. Benjamin Levine allowed extra time to pay the rent when my advance disappeared.

Since I am not much of a linguist, the many languages spoken by the immigrants and refugees I encountered posed no small problem. Sincere thanks to my translators at home and on the road: Sandra Izquierdo, Claire Honorat, Akbhar Andkhoie, Zung Dao, Helena Herzberg, Antonio Silvestre, Julie Padilla and Marta Silva, Nasar Tahmass, and my wife.

Through my journalistic involvement in immigration and refugee issues I met a number of generous activists and caseworkers, who helped introduce me to newcomers whom they have been involved with or helped to resettle. Friends and associates in communities around the country also introduced me to additional new arrivals. Among these invaluable guides were, in New York: Robert DeVecchi, Charles Sternberg, and Barbara Nagorski at the International Rescue Committee; Vacek Adamczak at the Committee for Solidarity; Arie Bierman, Mary Ellen Rhindress, Mark Handelman, and Edna Rosenman at the New

York Association for New Americans; Larry Epstein; Imelda Cancio; Sally Sommer; Hugh and Penny Brown; Roseanne Klass at Freedom House; Rahin Abedi at the Afghan Mutual Assistance Association; Mohammad Sarvar Akbari; Hakjong Andrew Riew, Peter Nahm, Don Ha, and Jong Sik Lee at the Korean Association of New York; Kenny Sang Soo and Nam Sun Kim; Jerry Goodman at the National Coalition on Soviet Jewry; Karl Zuckerman at the Hebrew Immigrant Aid Society; Mira Wolfe at the Jewish Community House of Bensonhurst; Pauline Bilus at Project ARI; Michael Hooper at the National Coalition for Haitian Refugees; and Arthur Helton and Mitchell Hartman at the Lawyers Committee for Human Rights.

In Washington, D.C.: Susan Goodwillie and Kyle Horst at Refugees International; Le Xuan Khoa, Carol Leviton Wetterhahn, and Diana Bui at the Indochina Resource Action Center; Lionel Rosenblatt at the Department of State; Mac Thompson; Ray Evans and Nguyen Van Canh at the International Rescue Committee; Berta Romero and Dale "Rick" Schwartz at the National Immigration, Refugee, and Citizenship Forum; Roger Winter and Joseph Cerquone at the U.S. Committee for Refugees; Vaughn Forrest and Kristin Foskett; James Webb; and Dr. Tsehaye Teferra at the Ethiopian Committee Development Council.

In Atlanta: Sokhan and Souvannary Ket; Marge Flaherty, Charlie Cowden, and Phung Quang Chieu at the International Rescue Committee; and Joan Kimball, Kim Grady, and Robert Barnett at the Atlanta Ballet. In St. Paul: Chue Xiong and Sue Xiong at the Midwestern Asian Food Company; Mrs. Mee Xiong, and the International Institute. In Maine: Donald Scott. In Greensboro, North Carolina: Rollie Bailey at the Lutheran Immigration and Refugee Service.

In Chicago: John Wright; Anne Keegan at the *Chicago Tribune*; Randy Pauley and Hayelom Ayele at the city's Commission on Human Relations; Ed Silverman at the Illinois Refugee Resettlement Program; Howard Patinkin, police official; Ngoan Le, Ha Nguyen, and Lou Berkman at the Vietnamese Association of Illinois; Zung Dao, Edgewater Beach Café; Lam Ton, Mekong Restaurant; Tuan Nguyen, Pasteur Restaurant; Juju Lien and Trudy Langendorf at the Chinese Mutual Assistance Association.

In Boston: Nicole Candine at the International Rescue Committee.

In San Francisco: Don Climent and Leslie Peterson at the International Rescue Committee; Ctirad "Rod" Zdvoracek; and Vaclav Sabata. In Los Angeles: Diane Rudolph, Robbie Long, and Pat Duncan. In Long Beach: Vora and Rochelle Huy Kanthoul, Than Pok, Chantara Nop, Prany Sananikone, and Thiem Ung at the United Cambodian Community.

In Indiantown, Florida: Christine Power; Sister Kathy Komarek; Claire Siefker; Joan Flocks; Antonio Silvestre and Jeronimo Camposeco at the Holy Cross Service Center; Jerry Upton of the American Friends Service Committee; Rob Williams; Sister Teresa Auad at the Indios Cooperative; and Sister Esperanza Jassa at the Hope Rural School. In Miami: Cheryl Little and Neils Frenzen at the Haitian Refugee Center; Ray Flores, a volunteer for the United Way; Richard Druks of the City Attorney's Office; and Rafael García-Toledo.

An expert on Mexican-American affairs is Aurora Camacho de Schmidt in Philadelphia. In El Paso: Pablo Salcido and Alfonso Romo at KITV; Dave García at NBC-TV; Manny de la Rosa and Patricia Roybal at the Trinity Coalition; Javier Colmenero at the Catholic Pastoral Center; José Rodríguez at Texas Rural Legal Aid; Pete Duarte and Dr. Domingo Reyes at Centro de Salud Familiar La Fe Health Center; Phylis Armijo at Thomason Hospital; Pat Ayala at the city's Health and Human Services; Mario Órtiz, INS (U.S. Immigration) regional director (in Dallas); Al Giugni, the INS director in El Paso, and his assistant, Tim Pastor; Mike Williams, chief, U.S. Border Patrol in El Paso, and Patrolman Robinson; Robert Mellado, INS; and Claudio Sánchez, KXCR Radio.

A special thanks to the countless persons, individuals and families, who shared their experiences with me. Although their stories may not appear here, their grit and spirit are very much a part of this book.

CONTENTS

NEW AMERICANS

AN ORAL HISTORY

INTRODUCTION

Since the 1960s, American society has been undergoing a transformation that is dynamic and at the same time challenges the very ideals that the nation was founded and built upon. We are a culture of immigrants whose sweat, visions, and schemes have fueled the evolution of industry and technology and augmented the freedoms of faith, enterprise, and expression still denied to most areas of the world. We are now experiencing the most awesome surge of immigrants and refugees in modern times. The newcomers, mostly Asians, Latins, Creoles, Africans, Moslems, Jews, and Slavs, are not only changing the ethnic makeup of America, but also creating a dramatic impact in many communities.

More than six hundred thousand legal immigrants arrive in this country each year, and at least that number of illegal entrants. Most simply walk, swim, or drive across the wide-open two-thousand-mile Mexican border. The newcomers, alien in language and culture, are settling in large cities, rural towns, and affluent suburbs. They have caused fear and concern in many native-born Americans, sentiments that have been echoed by congressional leaders and transposed into legislation.

On the floor of the U.S. Senate, Senator Alan Simpson has stated, "If . . . these new persons and their descendants do not fully integrate into American society, they may create in America some of the same social, political, and economic problems that exist in the countries that they have chosen to depart. Furthermore, if language and cultural separatism rise above a certain level, the unity and political stability of our nation will, in time, be seriously eroded."

This fear of erosion of the American language and culture, and loss of jobs to newcomers, has led to "English Only" ballots in state elections, boycotts of Asian businesses in black communities in New York and Washington, D.C., and an exodus of the middle class from cities experiencing heavy Hispanic influx like Miami and Los Angeles. This is not the first time that America's tolerance toward newcomers has been at a crossroad.

"To live within one of these foreign communities [within American cities] is to actually live on foreign soil. The thoughts, feelings and traditions are often entirely alien to an American. The newspapers, the literature, the ideals, the passions, the things which agitate the community are unknown to us except in fragments." This observation, from the book *Poverty* by the progressive reformer Robert Hunter, was not about Cuban-dominated Miami, or the Vietnamese community in Orange County, or San Francisco's Chinatown, or Spanish Harlem, or the Soviet Jewish "Little Odessa" in Brooklyn. Rather, he was describing Eastern European sections of Chicago and Italian neighborhoods in New York in 1904. Less than a generation later, a Czech, Anton Cermak, was mayor of Chicago and Fiorello La Guardia, an Italian, was mayor of New York for three terms.

There have been winners and losers, regardless of nationality, in every wave of immigrants. Some have come with title or wealth to expand their fortune. Many others have fled poverty, war, persecution, or natural disaster in their ancestral lands. Survivors, they arrive with little more than dreams of a brighter future—if not for themselves, then for their children. They have often encountered ambivalence or social discrimination upon reaching America's shores.

Although seventeenth-century British merchants outmaneuvered French and Spanish rivals to dominate the New World, a large number of English colonists were indentured servants, convicts, and the dregs of English society, who suffered something akin to the bondage endured by African slaves.

Four Scots-Irishmen were among the signers of the Declaration of Independence in Philadelphia, but after a million impoverished survivors of the Irish potato famine reached these shores in disease-ridden, overcrowded "coffin ships" between 1845 and 1850, anti-Catholic riots broke out in Philadelphia and other cities. A political party called the Know-Nothings elected governors in six out of thirty-one states in 1855 on an anti-Catholic, anti-German immigration platform. Uncomfortable on the Atlantic Coast, German and Scandinavian families loaded into horse-drawn covered wagons and journeyed into the Midwestern prairie. They built log cabins and sod houses and developed the grain farms that now feed much of the world.

Jews fleeing Portuguese and Spanish inquisitions arrived in the Dutch New Amsterdam colony—New York—in the mid-seventeenth century and helped to develop America's seagoing trade. More than one hundred years later, Jewish merchants helped finance George Washington's revolutionary forces. At the turn of the twentieth century, during the peak years of European immigration, Jews fleeing pogroms in Russia constituted nearly twenty percent of total arrivals. But Jews faced a variety of social restrictions in all areas of American society until after World War II.

The New World was discovered by an Italian sea captain, Christopher Columbus, and America was named after another Italian explorer, Amerigo Vespucci. Between 1880 and 1924 more than four million Italian immigrants arrived, including my father and my mother's family, and helped to build America's cities. But until recent years, many Italians, like New York's Governor Mario Cuomo, were told to change their names to sound more Anglo-Saxon if they wanted to get ahead in American life.

In 1924, to halt the massive immigration of Italians, Poles, Slavs, and Eastern European Jews, Congress passed a law, The National Origins Act, based on ethnic and racial quotas. This law, combined with the Chinese Exclusion Act of 1882 and a 1917 law that exempted only Filipinos, effectively prohibited Asian immigration. And the U.S. Border Patrol was created in 1924 to provide a token enforcement presence at key crossing points on the Mexican border. However, Mexico's population at the time was small, and thousands of Mexican laborers were still needed to develop agriculture in the Southwest and California.

During the Great Depression of the 1930s and World War II, legal immigration slowed to a trickle. Throughout this period, dominated by the brutal rule of Stalin and Hitler, when millions of Russians and Jews perished and eventually all of Europe was in flames, a total of only 250,000 refugees were accepted. There was a chauvinist backlash even to this small number. When Albert Einstein escaped the Nazis and came to Princeton University in 1933, he was picketed by the Women's Patriotic Corps.

After the war, millions of Europeans were homeless. Many had fled the Soviet takeover of Eastern Europe. More than three million Russians, refugees and prisoners of war, were returned to suffer persecution, Gulag incarceration, and in some cases death. But only a handful of refugees were accepted in America until the Displaced Persons Act of 1948 permitted four hundred thousand to enter over a four-year period. Still, the discriminatory quotas of the National Origins Act kept down the number of legal entrants. Ellis Island was permanently closed in 1954, symbolizing the end of mass migration from Europe. America was in the midst of a baby boom, and the return of GIs from World War II and Korea combined with an expanded role for women in the workplace to fill the nation's job demands. As a result, more than two million Mexicans, mostly laborers and their families, were deported.

Through the 1950s, special provisions were granted for Hungarian refugees after the Soviets crushed a 1956 rebellion, a small number of Chinese who fled Mao Tse-tung's takeover in China, and some Mexicans and West Indians needed for low-paying domestic labor. However, more than seventy-five percent of the annual 250,000 annual newcomers still came from Europe and Canada.

The revolution in American immigration began after Fidel Castro seized power in Cuba in 1959. During the next three years, more than 250,000 Cuban refugees made the 150-mile journey to Florida's southern coast. The first wave, mostly the cream of Havana's educated and business circles, were welcomed by Floridians. But as thousands continued to arrive, jobs became scarcer, schools more crowded, and the Spanish language dominant in many neighborhoods.

During this period, mass communications and international transportation began to transform the globe into a tighter, more homogeneous community. More significantly, as the populations of the United States and Europe became static, that of the Third World began exploding, to the point where it will grow to an estimated five billion people by the year 2000. Latin America's combined population, less than 165 million in 1950, was 405 million in 1985—nearly twice as large as that of the United States. Within forty years, it is projected to top eight hundred million. And in Asia, India is now surpassing China in population, with more than a billion inhabitants. As a result of overpopulation, widespread poverty, and regional conflicts that have created eleven million refugees in the eighties, Third World migrants have eclipsed Europeans as America's most numerous new arrivals.

The 1965 Immigration and Nationality Act eliminated ethnic bias and expanded yearly quotas by giving priority to family reunification, which works in favor of large close-knit Asian and Latin families. In 1966, the percentage of legal entrants from Europe fell to thirty-eight percent, while Hispanics jumped to thirty-nine percent and Asians to thirteen percent. In 1985, only eleven percent were Europeans, Hispanics were forty percent, and Asians tripled to forty-five percent. The sixty thousand legal Mexicans alone equaled the total of Europeans accepted. The largest European group, thirteen thousand British, was far behind the forty-eight thousand Filipinos, thirty-five thousand Koreans, twenty-six thousand Indians, twenty-four thousand Dominicans, twenty thousand Cubans, nineteen thousand Jamaicans, sixteen thousand Iranians, and fifteen thousand Taiwanese. Added to this were from five hundred thousand to two million illegal aliens, mostly from Mexico and Latin countries.

With the low American birth rate, immigrants and illegal aliens accounted for nearly twenty-six percent of America's population growth in 1986. That percentage may become even higher by the turn of the century. Experts predict that by the middle of the next century Americans of European ancestry will no longer be the majority.

While America was proudly celebrating the centennial of the Statue of Liberty, a national debate was raging over whether the republic can continue the present immigration trend and yet retain cultural, linguistic, and democratic stability. Can these newcomers from all corners of the earth assimilate into a cohesive yet pluralistic society? Or will ethnic rivalries eventually fragment communities into Lebanon-like cauldrons of discontent and secessionist movements? Will Spanish replace English as the dominant language in large areas of the Southwest?

Some experts point out that the number of Americans between the ages of fifteen and twenty-nine years has declined by 2.3 million since 1980, a trend that may continue into the twenty-first century. At the same time, around forty-five percent of the 4.5 million legal immigrants since 1980 are of this job entry-level age, a cohort necessary to sustain the country's economic growth. Some of these immigrants have created independent small businesses that have revitalized inner cities in New York, Chicago, and Washington, D.C. Others, like low-paid garment workers in Los Angeles and assembly-line workers in New England and Minneapolis, have by their very presence prevented entire industries from moving abroad. These workers patronize local merchants and pay taxes, and the relatively low cost of their labor has kept consumer prices low for fresh foods and basic products.

However, communities heavily impacted by illegals are strapped with a financial burden. Los Angeles County, where at least 1.5 million illegals from Mexico and Central America reside, paid out an estimated $92 million in support for around fifty thousand children of alien parents in 1984. Another $100 million went into health-care costs, and an estimated $100 million was paid in benefits to unemployed illegals.

Thanks to the thriving economy, Los Angeles can shoulder this outlay of public funds without spiraling into a crisis. But communities along the Texas-Mexico border, traditionally plagued with poverty and high unemployment, are severely strained by their large illegal populations, which have grown significantly since Mexico's economy collapsed in 1982. And throughout the country, economists and labor organizers claim that illegal workers are pulling down wages and displacing American workers, not only in low-paying jobs like farm labor, but in higher-paying fields like construction and manufacturing as well. However, in Boston an illegal construction worker from Ireland responds, "Some native American workers, including Irish Americans, call us 'donkeys' and say we're taking jobs away. But if they want work, I'm sure they can get it instead of hanging around doorsteps."

Black immigrants from the West Indies earn an average family income that is now forty percent higher than American-born blacks, and their children—even Haitian illegals—have a much higher rate of high-school graduation. Refugees from Ethiopia, largely from Africa's elite educated minority, are making strong efforts to attend college, even though they start out at entry-level jobs like taxi driving and hotel housecleaning.

Many Koreans are college graduates excluded from white-collar jobs by language differences, who have opened corner markets in run-down areas of inner cities. Thousands of Filipino medical professionals and around twenty-five thousand Indian physicians staff many American hospitals and clinics. In 1986, the average household income for the seven hundred thousand Indians in America and around the same number of Koreans is more than $25,000—almost $10,000 above the national average.

American scientific research programs and high-technology industries are bolstered by foreign students from Taiwan, Hong Kong, and Korea who choose to remain in the United States after they finish college. In recent years, close to half the recipients of America's prestigious high-school science awards have been Asian Americans. Cambodian and Hmong children have become finalists in national spelling-bee competitions, and Vietnamese boat refugees have become valedictorians. The reason for their success is not that they are inherently brighter than other ethnic groups. Rather, they are dedicated to long hours of study, are encouraged by their parents, and have a thirst to excel in learning that many American-born students have abandoned. Also, many refugee children are especially driven by the memory of the death and suffering they have left behind.

On the downside of the large influx of Asians are attempts by crime syndicates like the Japanese Yakuza and Chinese Triads to muscle into the lucrative American underworld. They are joined by smuggling rings from West Africa, Jamaica, and Latin America, who now dominate much of the narcotics trade.

During the 1986 fiscal year, U.S. Border Patrol agents made more than twelve hundred drug seizures along the Mexican frontier, worth about $150 million. Drug-enforcement officials claim that heroin is increasingly brought into the country by illegal aliens and migrant workers. Half of all crack arrests in southern California are of illegal aliens, who also constitute fifteen percent of all felony arrests and twenty-five percent of auto-theft arrests. In New York City, one in ten felons arrested is an alien. And Miami suffered a devastating crime wave after hard-core Cuban criminals arrived in the 1980 Mariel boatlift. However, they were a minority among the 125,000 Mariel refugees who came to America largely to join hardworking relatives who have helped to transform Miami from a backwater tourist town into a dynamic metropolitan trade center.

In October 1986, the Congress passed a new Immigration Reform and Control Act to attempt to stem the tidal wave of illegal immigrants and establish a fair and orderly entry process. During congressional deliberations, Theodore Hesburgh, the president of Notre Dame university and a member of the U.S. Select Commission on Immigration and Refugee Policy, testified as to the results of the Commission's research: "[Today's] immigrants work hard, save and invest, and create more jobs than they take. The children of immigrants acculturate well to American life. They seem to be healthier and do better in school than native-born Americans. Therefore . . . it is in the national interest to accept a reasonable number of immigrants and refugees each year . . . regardless of color, nationality, or religion."

As the son of an immigrant who came from a small farming town in the mountains of Italy, the husband of an Asian refugee, and, foremost, an American citizen, I am deeply concerned about the quality of society our children and grandchildren will inherit. The purpose of this book is to explore the dynamic impact that the massive new wave of legal and illegal newcomers are having on American communities. I wanted to know more about where they came from and why they are coming to this country. Can they assimilate and truly embrace the ideals that most native-born Americans value?

For nine months—from July 1986 to March 1987—I traveled throughout the United States. On my journey I met an incredible spectrum of newcomers, from European royalty living in Beverly Hills to wretched Caribbean boat people living in a rat-infested Miami slum, to tribespeople from the mountains of Laos attempting to farm in Minnesota, to a hero of Poland's Solidarity Movement now working in a nonunion factory in Rhode Island, to a dance student from the Philippines who is now a prima ballerina in Atlanta, to former guerrilla fighters from Ethiopia trying to establish a life for their children on the outskirts of

Washington, D.C. Many of their stories are presented here in their own words.

Some, like Dr. Daud Nassery from Afghanistan, had harrowing journeys. He recalls trying to hide from Soviet gunships as he led his wife and children through the war-ravaged Hindu Kush Mountains.

> My wife rode one of the horses while she was nursing the baby. She held the child very tight so they wouldn't fall. We were concerned about the horses on the steep, narrow trails. . . . I carried one daughter on my back, a rifle over my other shoulder; a freedom fighter carried my other daughter.
>
> One of the horses, who was pregnant, just quit walking. Blood came out of her nostrils. I felt sorry for the poor animal. We all were pushing our bodies to the limits of endurance. On one mountain I thought, "There must be magnets in the ground," because we were so exhausted that our legs wouldn't move.

Paulette Francius, age twenty-seven, who lives alone with four small children in Miami, recalls leaving Haiti:

> It was dark night when we left. All together seventy-two people walked down to the harbor. We took turns getting into a small rowboat that quietly ferried us to a sailboat. . . . Our departure turned quite frightening. The Macoutes [police] saw us and came after us, shooting. Even on the ocean, they continued shooting. Our sailboat was too crowded and could hardly float. Everyone was crammed together on the boat's deck. . . . The weather turned bad—the wind became fierce, and there were very high waves. . . . The boat tipped over on its side. The boat was sinking quickly. We all dove into the sea.

Other newcomers arrive in comfortable commercial flights. Maniya Barredo, a former child television star in the Philippines, recalls:

> I arrived in New York from Manila, alone but exhilarated. I was seventeen, on my first big trip away from home. My uncle was to meet me at the airport. . . . The next day, I was scheduled to audition at the Joffrey School's American Ballet Center . . . in Manhattan. Well, my uncle put me on a subway in Queens. . . . I had never ridden on public transportation. . . . I was petrified. And I was too shy to ask anyone for directions. I missed my exit and went all the way to God knows where.
>
> At the end of the line, I was the only person left on the train. I pulled my rosary out of my purse and began praying.

Unlike most immigrants, refugees don't have a home to return to. When bewildered Vietnamese refugees began arriving in Chicago's Uptown area in 1975, it was a hard-core dumping ground for derelicts, mental-hospital rejects, and drug addicts in the midst of a high-crime ghetto. At first victimized, the refugees learned to work with local officials and began to fend for themselves. They started opening small shops and family-owned restaurants. Today Uptown is a thriving community that attracts tourists and shoppers from other areas. Trong Nguyen, a social worker who helped organize the refugee community, says,

> When the refugees first began arriving . . . in Uptown, we felt like we were thrust from one war zone to another. Local community organizations strongly opposed the refugees. People talked about a "Yellow Horde invasion." . . . My goal was to help those in need . . . I never thought about making a lot of money for my own use. Sometimes my wife says, "It seems that you care more about the community than your own family." But I explain to [my children] that when you have a bowl of rice, no matter how small, you have to think about those people who don't have any rice to eat.

Through my previous work as a journalist, I have spent considerable time in Southeast Asian refugee camps and in conflict areas where former Americans allies are still being slaughtered. In congressional debate on whether the United States should continue to accept a yearly quota of Southeast-Asian refugees (now less than five percent of legal entrants), one prominent Senator stated, "The most durable solution for refugees since World War II has been repatriation." This is deeply questionable.

Oleg Jankovic, a naval aviator during the Vietnam War and in the Persian Gulf during the hostage crisis, is now an assistant to the Secretary of the Navy. He was born in a European refugee camp to Russian parents at the end of World War II. Only the courageous action of his mother saved him from being repatriated to the Soviet Union. He remembers when American authorities handed over his stepfather, a decorated partisan who fought under the British, to Soviet authorities:

> While my mother was cooking dinner on the wood burning stove, American MPs came . . . to prepare [Mikhail] for repatriation. . . . She took me to see him in the jail. I grabbed him around the leg and said, "Papa, come home. Come home." I was only two years old, going on three. . . . They had [him] in leg irons, and it seemed like the Soviets had him drugged after he was transferred to their zone. . . . We never heard from him again. Apparently he was executed.

The Soviets asked for my sister and me to be handed over to them, as children of a Russian father. . . . It was only because my mother pretended to be a Czech citizen that we were kept from them. Out of these circumstances grew a fiction that my mother maintained, even to her children, until near the end of her life.

The most lively hub of Russian culture outside the Soviet Union is the Shorefront area of Brooklyn, where thirty-thousand Soviet émigrés have settled in a neighborhood nicknamed Little Odessa. Mark Grottel, age sixty-two who has a Ph.D. in physics, and his wife, Irene, now a computer programmer for a corporate bank in the Wall Street area, came from Leningrad in 1979. After six years at a nuclear engineering firm, Mark was suddenly laid off. Worried that he may not find another job, he says:

For some Russians . . . the openness and mobility of American society has been difficult to adapt to. Freedom is a very high responsibility. In Russia, . . . the state decides everything for you: what kind of education you have, the job you get, your vacations, the apartment you live in. Medical care is provided, enough food to survive, and there is law and order in the streets.

When Russian émigrés arrive here, all of a sudden we are given the freedom to choose and make all of our own decisions. Some people are unable to go out on their own and make a life for themselves. They only see troubles—dirty subways, crime in the streets. Everything is very strange to them—the language and the pace people move at. . . . They get lost and want to run back to where life is familiar.

For many newcomers, adaptation to American life has not been easy. Even for those who have "made it," hard knocks have been part of the process. Language, style, and generation gaps between children who quickly adapt American ways, and their more socially isolated parents are common. Yet the courage and determination to overcome the many obstacles to assimilation make many immigrants and refugees role models that established Americans can learn from.

In El Paso, where the population is dominantly Mexican and Mexican American, the dropout rate for Spanish-speaking high-school students is around fifty-five percent. To try to remedy this problem, Mexican-American professionals in the community have formed an education-oriented voluntary project called El Paso Adelante (El Paso Forward). One of Adelante's members, Cesar Caballero, age thirty-eight, came from Mexico as a boy and grew up in a Spanish-speaking barrio. Today he is a library director for the University of Texas. He says:

> When I was a kid, there were some Chicano professionals, but they were so few in number that we didn't have them around as role models. Most of the members of El Paso Adelante are products of the local barrio who left to get an education. Now we are going back to tell the kids, "Stay in school, develop a career, pursue an education." . . .
>
> Our group is trying to make ourselves available to kids and encourage other Chicano professionals to be role models for the youths. They can be speakers in the school system. And we are trying to establish a scholarship fund for young people to return to high school or attend college. Hispanics can't expect America's major industries to come knocking on our doors if we are not trained, skilled, and educated. Our goal is to develop model programs that can be used throughout Texas.

In my travels I have seen both the positive and negative sides of the immigrant and refugee experience. Although today's newcomers are from extraordinarily diverse backgrounds and cultures, a common humanity transcends their differences. And, not unlike our own parents, grandparents, or ancestors, who journeyed from distant lands, new arrivals are motivated by a combination of ingenuity, self-sacrifice, grit, and fear. Through their personal stories and reflections—some exhilarating and others heartbreaking—they share with us a valuable reminder of how precious and rare is our freedom and our open society. Regardless of our shortcomings and uncertainty as we continue to evolve as a Nation made up of the people of many nations, America remains a beacon of hope to many peoples of the world.

MY BROTHERS' WAY

M. Daud Nassery
Refugee from Kabul, Afghanistan
Medical Doctor
Eastham, Massachusetts

The coastal lights of Cape Cod glowed softly through twilight fog. I entered the only hardware store in a small New England village. I was looking for a man named Mohammad who had come from a fierce tribal land halfway across the world. I was not prepared for his haunting green eyes, gentle voice, and slight build.

In a friendly Yankee manner, the store manager met me at the door. He introduced me to his assistant. Mohammad Daud Nassery (called Dowd by his American friends) had been a pediatrician in Afghanistan. Two years earlier, he twice had escaped from his ravaged homeland. After surviving a first dangerous journey across the Hindu Kush Mountains, he then had returned to Kabul with a small group of freedom fighters to rescue his wife and three small daughters.

They arrived penniless at the Pakistan frontier, joining three million other destitute Afghani refugees. Most live in windswept tent cities without hope. Of the sixteen million people in Afghanistan before the 1979 Soviet invasion, more than a million have been killed, and at least five million men, women, and children have fled—nearly half of the world's total refugee population through mid-1988. A select few—less than twenty thousand—have been allowed into the United States.

For Daud and his family, freedom has not come easily. Although he is a competent physician, refugee doctors are unable to practice in America until they complete a grueling series of medical examinations in the English language. While waiting to take the exams, Daud had taken a job in the hardware store to support his growing family.

At closing time, Daud put on a navy-blue jacket and invited me to spend the night at his home. He wanted to tell the story of his incredible journey, and how the people of this small American community rescued his family and gave them a new life.

His weathered gray wooden clapboard house is surrounded by a pine forest near the intersection of a graveled dirt road and a two-lane asphalt highway. Inside, a bright-red Afghan carpet with floral designs covers the floor of the front room, which is also the playroom for three active little girls. On lacquered paneling above a brick fireplace is a round metallic plaque inscribed with an Islamic prayer.

His two oldest girls, Roya (age eight) and Najilla (seven), dressed in preppy cotton sweaters, speak to each other in perfect English. But they answer their mother in their native tongue. Daud's wife, Aqela, was a high-school teacher in Kabul. Under thirty, she has curly brown hair prematurely streaked with gray. She is unable to speak

English, and isolated at home with the baby, Muska. Through Daud's translation, she explained her frustration that adult language classes are unavailable. Consequently, she is trying to learn English on her own. Comfortable in a green turtleneck shirt, a wool sweater, and loose-fitting slacks, she has gracefully adapted to the Western style of dress.

After a delicious dinner of sweet rice with carrots and raisins, and broiled chicken, we all sat together around the Afghan carpet. Daud showed me photos of loved ones left behind. He described children, victims of the war, that he had tried to heal in a refugee hospital near the Khyber Pass. Still shaken by what he remembered, Daud hushed his voice to a near-whisper as he began his story.

It was Friday, November 1, 1984, when I left Kabul. Before leaving, I wrote a letter to my American family, Edward and Bernice Brown, in Massachusetts. Fifteen years earlier, I had lived with them as a foreign-exchange student. In the letter I explained that the government drafted me out of the Child Health Hospital to be a doctor in the Communist army. Rather than reporting for duty, I was choosing "my brothers' way." I had to escape as my brothers had done. My wife had just given birth to a beautiful girl with blue eyes. We named her Muska, which means "a smile."

I found an old bicycle and cut my hair short to look like a soldier, so the police would be less suspicious of me. I filled an old sack with hay and groceries. Inside I hid my doctor's certificate, my American high-school yearbook, and other documents that I would need in Pakistan. And I put a bundle of old clothes on the back of the bicycle. This was to give the appearance that I was on leave from military service and going home to the countryside.

Another doctor, my former classmate, came with me. Our plan was to ride our bicycles to the foot of the mountains, near a freedom fighters' camp. There we would meet my contact, a college student who was the freedom fighters' liaison with Kabul.

It was very difficult to get out of the city, because all major roads are controlled by the army. A half-hour after we started cycling, we came upon a group of soldiers searching a bus. As we neared the roadblock, I tried to keep my composure. They called to me and joked. They thought we were fellow soldiers and didn't stop us.

Afghanistan was invaded by the Soviets in 1979, but it is still primarily a Moslem country. Most men have "Mohammad" or "Allah" at the beginning or end of their name, but they are usually called by their middle name. For example, my name is Mohammad Daud Nassery. You can call me Daud.

I was born on April 18, 1952, in the capital, Kabul. The city was built from stone more than thirty-five hundred years ago, where two valleys intersect a mile high in the Hindu Kush Mountains. My wife, Aqela, and our three daughters were all born in Kabul as well. Our oldest girl, Roya, was born in 1978 and our second, Najilla, in 1979. The youngest, Muska, was born on September 4, 1984.

My parents have six children, five brothers and a younger sister. Now we are scattered all around the world. Three of my brothers are in India, one in Austria; my sister is in New Zealand; I am in Massachusetts; and my parents are still in Afghanistan. We are kind of an international family.

A very formative part of my high-school education was in Massachusetts, where I lived with an American family during my senior year. Afghanistan was not a country that had many foreign-exchange students. I entered a nationwide competition for a scholarship. We took a series of intensive exams and were interviewed by American and Afghan officials.

In August 1969, I was sent to Eastham, Massachusetts, a small working-class town on Cape Cod. It's very Americana, settled in the 1600s by the Pilgrims. The local people are very friendly.

Edward and Bernice Brown treated me like one of their own children. I still call them Mom and Dad. The youngest of their three sons, Peter, was in the same class as me. We played soccer on the same team. David, who was in college out of the state, would visit once in a while on weekends and at Christmas. The oldest son, Edward, was in his second or third year of medical school.

One of the first differences I noticed in America is the size of families. In Afghanistan, even the smallest family has five or six kids. And extended-family members are very close-knit: brothers- and sisters-in-law, aunts and uncles, and grandparents all live together or nearby.

Only the father works and takes the responsibility to provide for the family. Even if he doesn't make a large amount of money, he shares whatever he earns with the extended family. Even in households where people are hungry most of the time, everybody shares what little food they have.

I saw in America that everyone in the family works to pay for his or her life. Even teenage children like my American brother worked part-time in the summer to pay for college and contribute some rent to his parents. Mom and Dad were teaching the children responsibility. From an American point of view, that's good. But from my cultural point of view, it was shocking and strange.

In Kabul, I knew families who had stores. Nephews and nieces worked for them, but none of them got paid. They believed that it was their duty to help the family business.

The first weeks that I lived with the Browns, while everyone in the family went out to their jobs, I stayed alone at home and felt kind of bored. One morning, while we were having breakfast, I asked my American mother if I could work in their grocery store.

What I meant by "work" was that I wanted to help them. I didn't know that there is a difference between "work" and "help" in this country. If you say "help," it means you don't expect to get paid. I said, "Mom, I'd like to work with my brothers in your store." She said, "I'm sorry, how much money do you want?"

My face got red. I was kind of embarrassed. I said, "Why is money being mentioned? I don't want money. I just want to help you, because I am a member of the family."

Mrs. Brown said okay. I worked in the store until school began at Nauset High, which was the only high school for three or four towns: Eastham, Orleans, Brewster, and Wellfleet. American high school was something really new. It was especially hard for me to see a boy and girl holding hands and kissing in school—I thought that I was dreaming. Having girlfriends, dating, and dances were something new to me. For a while I thought that it was not a nice way to behave in public. It was the 'sixties. To see girls dressed in short dresses, miniskirts, was strange and frustrating. But after a while I got used to it.

In Afghanistan, there is no such thing as dating, especially in high school. If a boy and a girl liked each other, they would try to keep it secret. Almost all marriages were arranged by the families. Even today, in the countryside, nobody can break the old rules. In the cities, traditions are changing. Some of the younger generation have their own way of life. But they are not as independent as children in this country. You cannot date or see each other without the parents' permission.

My marriage was arranged by our families, who are distant cousins. My wife, Aqela, and I were engaged from the time that she was two or three years old and I was six or seven. The reason for an early engagement is that families try to make their relationship stronger by sharing their children. My father worked in the Ministry of Finance, and Aqela's father was a schoolteacher. When I started high school, my parents told me that Aqela was going to be my wife.

Sometimes arranged marriages don't work. But divorces are very few, because in our culture and religion divorce is considered shameful. If a husband and wife are having problems, the family will try to discuss and resolve their differences. Both sets of parents try to mediate, even if it means that the wife must spend some time away, in her father's house. I was very surprised, when I came to America, to find out the number of families that are broken and divorced.

When I left high school in Afghanistan, I was in the middle of my junior year. At Nauset High, I was placed in the senior class. I was confident that I wouldn't have any difficulty with English, because I had taken language classes in Kabul. But people were talking so fast, I couldn't understand the New England accent. And my vocabulary was limited. For a few months, I had a terrible time. I forced myself to listen carefully.

In my country it was required to take seventeen different subjects during junior year. Every one was compulsory, including geography, history, geology, literature, chemistry, religion, trigonometry, and others. If you failed one, you failed the whole year.

I found the American school system to be much easier—only a few compulsory subjects like English, physical education, and American history. When I registered at Nauset High, I had to go through a list of subjects that my counselor gave me. I picked out fifteen or sixteen subjects. The principal was amazed. He thought that I was kidding. I said, "This is the way that we do it in my country. The schedule is staggered so that we can take many courses."

The principal said, "Even if you are capable of taking that many courses, our curriculum couldn't fit you into our timetable." So I cut it down to five or six subjects, including advanced biology. There were only four Americans in the class, and one of them dropped out. In calculus, also, there were only three of us.

The examinations system is easier here, too—the multiple-choice questions. Even if you read through the textbook once, it's easy to get a passing grade. Afghanistan's system is like that of the French. You have to memorize a thick book, and for the exam you write a long essay. If you were tired and missed a few pages of the text, or didn't have time to read them, you could fail the test and consequently the whole term.

My second semester here, after my English improved, I made the honor role. I became a member of the National Honor Society. The advanced biology course was a tough one—I got a C+ in the first semester. So the next semester, when they gave me the Honor Society membership card, I was surprised. I doubted myself and thought that I didn't deserve it. I learned that the American system is very fair. In Afghanistan, you can be an excellent student all through the year, but the final examination can break you. I liked school in America, because there wasn't that much pressure and students have a wider choice of subjects that they could enjoy.

After I graduated from American high school, I went back to Afghanistan in July 1970. I was happy to be returning to my family. But I felt sad that I had to say goodbye to my American friends. None of us could imagine what was about to happen in my country.

In Kabul, our school year begins in March and ends in November. So, even though I had an American diploma, I had to repeat senior year. Everybody was ahead of me, and I didn't have any notes. It was especially tough because I had become like an American. I had to pressure myself to act like my own countrymen. Without thinking, I would speak in English or use American slang. My classmates would laugh. The way we dress, everything, was very different.

The national costume for males is baggy trousers and a long shirt. But in schools and offices people wear Western clothes. Professionals like teachers, doctors, or officials wear white shirts and ties.

At the time, Afghanistan was a monarchy. Life in the cities and countryside was mostly peaceful. People, rich or poor, had enough to eat. My father had a secure job, and we owned some land in the eastern part of the country, where we got all of our rice and wheat and vegetables. It was more than what we needed, so each year we sold the surplus in the market.

In 1971, after high school, I began premedical studies at Kabul University. There were three professions that I always loved: medicine, law, and my secret dream—to become an airplane pilot. I chose medicine because of encouragement from my family and friends.

I spent seven years studying medicine and had one year of internship. During that time, everything in my country changed. In 1973, the King's cousin, Daoud, seized power. He proclaimed himself president and made the mistake of escalating the number of Soviet advisers to a dominant position in all departments of government and the army. And many members of Daoud's Cabinet were members of the Communist Party.

After a few years, as the standard of living in the country declined, Daoud realized that the Communists were detrimental to his government. So he began to throw them out, one at a time. This made the Soviet government angry. Then Daoud realized that he had taken so many loans from the Soviets that our economy would not be able to repay them. Daoud decided to discuss this with other Islamic countries. He traveled to Saudi Arabia. He met with Anwar Sadat in Egypt, the Shah in Iran, and President Bhutto in Pakistan. The Saudis told him, "We will provide a blank check without interest, so you can pay back the Russians and get them out of your country. They are a danger to your sovereignty and your Islamic faith."

But it was too late. The KGB was already very active in Afghanistan. Our Minister of Commerce, who was on the tour with Daoud, was a KGB agent. He reported directly to the Russians the results of Daoud's trip. The Russians responded swiftly.

Two Communist Afghan generals, Taraki and Amin, staged a violent coup, backed by the Russians, in April 1978. The Communists killed Daoud and his whole family on the same day. Even the little grandson, coming home from kindergarten.

Fighting began immediately against the Communist regime. Soldiers loyal to Daoud fought for about twenty-four hours. Daoud himself, up to his last minute, was reportedly fighting back against the Communists with a machine gun in his hands.

Immediately the new regime, supported by the Russians, imposed a curfew on the city. They tried to propagandize the idea that any person attached to religion was a "reactionary," and old-fashioned. They imprisoned and murdered many religious leaders, intellectuals, lawyers, and people with money or large land holdings. They especially tried to brainwash the children with constant propaganda in the schools. Many ordinary people became angry. The anti-Communist movement that had begun during Daoud's regime grew rapidly.

At the time of the coup, my first daughter, Roya, was about to be born. I was in the last year of medical school, and my wife, Aqela, was finishing her studies to become a high-school teacher. We lived in my parents' house with my brothers and sister.

In America, people always telephone first to ask to visit. If you go to an Afghan's house, people are happy to have a guest and will offer you whatever they have. If a guest goes happy from our home, we take pride. Because we believe that a guest is a friend of God.

Before the Communists, life wasn't hard in Kabul city. There were no food shortages, and family life was very affectionate. But the Communists created a secret-police network by recruiting ordinary people. It could be a child the age of one of my daughters. Maybe a shopkeeper. At the university it could be a fellow student or a teacher. It could be an old man in the street. A waitress in a restaurant, a household servant, or a janitor at the university.

In any school, from elementary to college level, there is a secret-police or Russian KGB office. Teachers at school ask kids to talk about what goes on in their homes, what their parents say, and if they have any visitors. Sometimes they even pay the kids for information.

In one family, a young teen-age girl, a high-school student, sent a report to the government: "My father is saying prayers. He's speaking against the government." The next day, the poor father was put in jail, nobody knows where. His daughter was rewarded for this—maybe a scholarship to Russia, money, or a prize.

When I began medical school, there were 250 students in my class. Only seventy-seven students graduated. It wasn't because the others failed. Many disappeared. Sometimes I would be in a classroom, sitting through a lecture; secret police would come into the room and grab a student by the arm. They would tell him, "Let's go to the principal's office." Those students never came back.

I was the top student in my class. But I was not a Communist Party member, so I was denied permission to become a staff member at Kabul University Hospital. And I had studied in the United States, so I would never be trusted. The government assigned me to Infectious Diseases Hospital in Kabul.

My second daughter, Najilla, was born on September 18, 1979. My wife went into labor in the early evening, just before the night's curfew was about to begin. I wanted to take her to the maternity hospital. But if anyone goes out of their home between 8:00 P.M. and 5:00 in the morning, Russian soldiers will shoot you without even asking what you are doing. And Afghan government soldiers stop people and ask "Do you know the secret code word?" Ordinary people have no idea what that is. They are shot right on the spot.

Everyone in the city is so afraid of the curfew that they rush home from work. Kabul is the most modernized city in the country. But each day it dies after 4:00 P.M. Every decent man tries to lock up his store and run away from the military patrols. If one of my patients had an emergency like a heart attack, or a woman is giving birth in the middle of the night, they could not call for a doctor or rush to the hospital until morning, when the curfew is over.

My wife was no exception. We couldn't risk a trip to the hospital, so I had to deliver the baby at home. Fortunately, I carried the right kind of equipment in my medical bag. There is always a chance of infection when you perform a medical procedure in an unsterile environment.

During this time, many people escaped from jails and joined the Mujahedin, our name for the freedom fighters. Even within the military government, although Taraki and Amin were members of the "Khalq" Communist wing, they fought for power among themselves. Amin's faction murdered Taraki in September 1979. The freedom fighters' movement continued to grow. It was apparent that the regime could not maintain power. That's why, during Chrismastime in 1979, the Russians sent their own army to take over Afghanistan.

The first night of the invasion, they murdered thousands, including Amin's entire family and all his government officials. The Soviets installed a new Communist leader, Babrak Kamal of the minority "Parcham" Communist wing. Within days, more than a hundred thousand Russian troops occupied all major cities and towns.

The Russians brought soldiers from Soviet Central Asia—Turkmenistan, Uzbekistan, Tadzhikistan—to serve as translators. But they hate the Russians, and so they told Afghan people to defend ourselves. They said that we shouldn't allow the Russians to take over our country the way that they lost theirs in the nineteenth century. My brothers were involved in protest marches. Two months after the invasion, a tremendous rally took place all over Kabul. The organizers were college students, but people of all ages, from children to grandparents, joined in.

The evening before the rally, people were chanting slogans against the invasion. The whole city was rocking like a cradle. We thought it would be the end of the Russian occupation, because the movement had such a strong spontaneous spirit. We thought that after the demonstration there would be no more Communist regime.

But the result was quite different. When soldiers opened fire, it turned into a sad, bloody event. Fighting erupted in the streets between the people and the army. The Russians used tanks and machine guns. Many people were killed. I lost a number of friends.

I was trapped inside the hospital, because the streets were in chaos. We didn't have enough food for the patients, so we sent the hospital ambulance to a grain silo to pick up some bread. But in a short while, the poor driver returned. The ambulance windshield was broken, and the vehicle was all banged up. It was a wild situation—gunshots and rocks flying. The driver hid beneath the steering wheel and said his prayers while fighting went on all around him. Many people were shot— high-school girls, religious people, college students, ordinary workers. And thousands were put in jail.

After the invasion, life in Kabul became very tough. Even during the day, every fifty feet, groups of secret police or soldiers asked for your ID. They searched your body. Even at the workplace, security guards who knew who you are searched you every day. Sometimes I'd get angry and think, "I am not a stranger, I am not a thief. This country is my home. Why should I be inspected all the time?"

Sometimes I was in a rush to get to work but police stopped the bus in the middle of the street. People were yelling and screaming, "We are late! We want to get to our jobs!" But the police searched everyone and demanded to see our ID cards. And they made us all open our briefcases or purses.

Since the occupation, Kabul's population has tripled to two million people. Thousands of villagers continue to pour into the city each month to escape Russian attacks in the provinces. Transportation in the city has become a big problem. Buses are so crowded that people must hang on to the outsides.

The Russians brag that they have built roads. But there is no guarantee that anyone will be allowed to travel on them. I have seen Russian troops stationed along the highways stop trucks or buses. The soldiers take whatever food or valuables they like. If they ask for money and you don't give it, you could get shot.

People from all parts of Afghanistan have told me of these same experiences: "I was beaten and robbed by Russian soldiers. They took my hat. . . . They took my watch. . . . They took my coat. . . . They took my shoes."

Sometimes farmers from the provinces would bring their children to the hospital in very critical condition. I would get mad and say, "Why did you wait so long? There is nothing I can do for the child." The parents would respond, "We knew that we should have brought her earlier. But there was no transportation. We spent two nights camped off the highway because of the curfew. We finally found transportation, but we were stopped by Russian soldiers. They made us wait for hours for no reason. We showed them that our child was deathly ill, but they wouldn't allow us to go."

In the countryside, everything that people own is being destroyed. Homes and fields are being systematically burned by the Russians. The people despair. I saw this all the time at the hospital. In one case, a family carried in a three-year-old child with severe pneumonia. On the way to the city, a Russian mine that was planted in the road exploded beneath the bus they were riding in. The blast killed two or three members of the family. Another had his arm cut off. Sometimes even a simple wound required amputation, because there was no medicine to stop infection.

Before the invasion there were around fifteen hundred doctors in Afghanistan. Now maybe two hundred remain, few of them in the countryside. And if there is a doctor, there is no medicine. If there is medicine, it is probably outdated.

I was transferred to the Institute of Child Health in Kabul to do my residency in pediatrics in 1982. We did research on how the Russian occupation had affected child mortality. The research was led by a senior consultant of our clinic. He was among the most respected Afghan doctors. He worked very hard on the study and presented the results at a symposium in honor of the International Children's Year. Do you know what happened to him? He was threatened by the top official in Kabul: "You are the most stupid person. You shouldn't say these things."

The doctor had presented the statistics very clearly. Child mortality had increased, first, for economic reasons: people could not afford to feed their children adequately because food production was targeted for destruction by the Russians. Second, there usually was no doctor or medicine in their towns, and no transportation into the cities. Third, abnormal psychological pressures were caused by war and economic hardship.

The doctor presented these data accurately, and he was scientific. But the authorities blamed us for telling the truth. We worked in one of the most sophisticated teaching hospitals in the region. We had doctors from India, Pakistan, Jordan, and other countries. But conditions in the hospital went from bad to worse, because most of the time we were so shorthanded. I had to run from ward to ward to find common supplies like a butterfly needle to start an IV. Or we would be out of simple IV packets.

The Russians only supply military hospitals. There, transfusions are readily available, with no limits on how many pints of blood you can give a military patient. But in our hospital, a family would bring in a child with gastroenteritis. A small amount of IV serum would save the child's life—water with a little sodium and glucose, which costs pennies. But there wasn't a single bag of serum. Or, if serum was available, there wasn't the plastic IV line to give the child the transfusion.

We had only a few butterfly needles that fit into a child's vein, so we had to use the same needles several times. We boiled them for sterilization. The needles became dull. The poor children—when we tried to puncture a vein, it would rupture and cause a great deal of pain. The parents got angry at us. They'd say, "You are so cruel, not compassionate." They didn't realize that those were the only devices we had.

In 1984, when I received my induction notice for the army, I knew that I had to escape. All of my brothers were already out of the country. They were afraid of being put back into prison.

My youngest brother, who is now in Austria, was jailed in 1981 for no reason. He disappeared from his high-school class. Somebody came from the principal's office to speak with him. He vanished, leaving all of his books in the classroom.

When my brother didn't come home that afternoon, we became very worried. He was the type of kid who always came home right after school and played soccer. The next morning I went to the school, which was my alma mater, and spoke with the science teacher. He told me that my brother was taken by the secret police. I went to offices all around the city to try to find some information, but I was given no response. Finally I found out that he was in the central jail. No reason was given.

My parents were worried sick. After four and a half months, my brother was released. They had beaten him badly. He told us that every time he was tortured he chewed on his shirtsleeve so that he wouldn't scream. They shocked him with electricity; doused him in cold water; then made him stand barefoot on ice; hung him upside down; and burned his body with a red-hot iron skewer. . . .

He said that other prisoners were accused of anti-government activity without trial. The police brought their wives, daughters, or fiancées to the prison. In front of the prisoner, the police tortured and sexually molested the women in order to force the prisoner to confess. This broke the nervous system of many men and caused them to lose their minds.

The walls and floors of the torture rooms were covered with the blood of victims. And hundreds of people were buried alive in ditches: the torturers tied their hands behind their backs and covered them with mud and dirt. Many more people have been shot.

After my brother was released, the police raided our house two or three times. In 1982, on the first day of the Ramadan religious period, our whole family was at home resting. Ramadan is a time of prayer, repentance, and fasting. People stay home from work and rest.

I told my wife, "I'd like to nap for a while." Suddenly I heard a loud voice. My father was asking men who entered our yard without permission, "What are you doing?" Our house was surrounded by secret police. They had Kalashnikov rifles. Some were dressed in ordinary clothes, others were in uniforms. My father argued with them.

The man in charge was the local head of the secret police. He didn't want to introduce himself. My father continued to challenge them. Getting angrier, he said, "How do I know who you are?" The chief took out his card to prove that he was a member of the KHAD [the state security service]. And he demanded to search our home.

The chief and his men searched through every book in the house, looked in every closet, bedroom, toilet. They grabbed my older brother and put him in their car. After fourteen months, he was given what the Communists call a "revolutionary trial." He still wouldn't admit to anything, so they gave him electric-shock torture and kept him awake for many nights, continually being beaten. When they finally released him, he was put under constant surveillance. They told him that, if he was suspected of any more anti-government activity, they would arrest him again. And it was just a matter of time before I would be drafted and sent to the front lines against the freedom fighters . . . or be put in jail. Some of the Mujahedin were my former classmates. I tried to send them medicines. And I occasionally made short field trips to treat their patients.

In mid-1984, I was preparing to qualify for my pediatrics certificate. I had passed the first exam, given by the Institute of Medical Science of India. And I had done two research papers. One, on diseases affecting Afghan children under the age of two, was published in *The All-India Journal of Medical Science*.

Only three weeks before I was to take my final certification board, the government dismissed me from the institute. They ordered me to prepare to go to the front lines with the army.

My wife, who was teaching high-school chemistry, was nearing the birth of our youngest child. My oldest daughter, Roya, was in first grade; and Najilla was in kindergarten. Even at that young age, the Communists had already started brainwashing the kids with Marxist-Leninist ideas. They were sometimes taken to demonstrations set up by the Russians. And they were taken to the Soviet cultural auditorium and other places for indoctrination. Thousands of elementary-school children, between seven and thirteen years old, are sent for ten-year periods to Russia for education and brainwashing. The Communists don't care about the parents' objections.

For the sake of my entire family, I made up my mind: "This is the best time to leave the country."

I had been corresponding with my American family, the Browns, from the time I finished high school in Massachusetts. I broke off communication with them for a few years after the Russian invasion: the mail was censored. But I took a chance and started writing to them again when I began to plan my escape.

I didn't leave immediately, because my wife was about to give birth. I feared that complications would make the delivery dangerous for both Aqela and the baby. I wanted to make sure that the procedure was

conducted safely. I wanted to know that my wife was alive, and I wanted
to see my child.

When the government called me for the army, I was given a temporary
deferment certificate with a specific date to report. So, for a couple
months, during the daytime I stayed out of sight at home; in the evenings
I secretly set up a private office to continue my medical practice and
earn a living.

After the birth of my little girl, Muska, I made contact with the
freedom fighters to arrange my escape to Pakistan. From Kabul, the
border is a seventy-five-mile journey through the mountains. We planned
that, when my wife and the baby were strong enough, the rest of the
family would join me.

I had saved enough money by working in my secret clinic to provide
for my family's needs for six months. I bought all the fuel, wood, and
canned food that they would need for winter, which was rapidly approaching. I wrote to the Browns to inform them of my daughter's birth
and to let them know that I would be escaping.

On November 1, a colleague and I disguised ourselves as soldiers and
bicycled out of the city. We negotiated our way through police and
military checkpoints and rode our bikes to where the mountains became
too steep to pedal. As we climbed higher on a rough trail, four or five
Mujahedin carrying rifles greeted us.

We spent around a week in the freedom fighters' zone, visiting villages
to give medical assistance to people in need. My friend, who is a surgeon,
performed minor surgery. The Soviets are bombing and burning most
agricultural areas, causing a tremendous number of civilian casualties
who have no access to medical aid.

The most horrible weapons the Russians use are tiny toy-shaped bombs,
designed so that children will pick them up. Kids are happy to grab
them, thinking that they've found a toy. The bombs are shaped like
butterflies, two or three inches long, with just enough explosive to blow
off a hand or foot. Sometimes children die from shock or loss of blood.
I photographed children I treated who lost their hands and arms from
these toy-shaped bombs.

As we went from village to village on the mountain trails, our freedom
fighter guides kept walking us away from the small bombs. They shot
their rifles to explode them.

The Mujahedin leader wanted us to stay in their zone for a while.
Not only was there a need for doctors, but we needed to get our bodies
adjusted to the high altitude before we began the dangerous journey
through the mountains to Pakistan. And, for survival, we needed to

learn how to hide from Soviet aircraft and blend into the environment like guerrillas. I also learned how to use a rifle.

After a week, a small group of freedom fighters were ready to travel to Pakistan for resupply. We began our journey. The weather was freezing. I only carried some clothing and light medical equipment like a stethoscope, blood-pressure apparatus, and first-aid materials.

We had a few packhorses that were loaded down with boxes. So we traveled on foot, south of the Khyber Pass, staying off the main trails to keep from being shot or bombed by Russian aircraft. Throughout our journey, we passed through villages reduced to rubble. Houses in ruins, mosques in ruins. Skeletons littered fields and the sides of trails. Bones of animals . . . bones of humans.

At times, we came across corpses of innocent civilians who had been recently shot. Their blood was still fresh on the ground. In other places, we found graves of refugees buried by freedom fighters along the trails.

On some days, the only thing we had to eat or drink was snow at the top of mountains. Mountain trails became so narrow and slippery that we had to crawl. I looked straight down sheer cliffs, at an altitude of more than ten thousand feet. Was I afraid? Definitely!

The higher altitudes were freezing cold. I've seen freedom fighters who lost their fingers and toes from frostbite: the toes turned black and fell off; the men didn't even realize it because they were frozen numb. Some Mujahedin wear light boots, but many others only have sandals. Out of a group of fifty men, possibly half will have boots.

After five days, we reached a place on the Pakistan border called Teri Mangal. We took a bus to a town around eighty miles inside Pakistan called Kohat. From there, I went north to Peshawar, a crowded, noisy bazaar of a city near the foot of the Khyber Pass. It is the capital of Pakistan's tribal Northwest Frontier. Half of the city's seven hundred thousand people are refugees from all parts of Afghanistan.

Most of the three million Afghan refugees in Pakistan live in primitive camps near the border. The areas given for the camps are barren moonscapes filled with tents, baking in the sun without grass, trees, or water.

For the first couple of months, I lived in a refugee camp with a group of freedom fighters. We didn't have much food. To sleep we huddled in a tent without enough room to stretch our legs.

To look for work I had to walk for miles and miles, because I didn't have the money for the bus. I carried my diplomas, certificates, and my documents from the United States in a paper folder. But every place where I applied as a pediatrician, they wouldn't accept me because I was a man. Arab people who work for agencies like the Red Crescent [the Muslim Red Cross] have an attitude that, since children are brought to a hospital by the mother, the pediatrician must be a woman. Unlike Afghanistan, where Islamic tradition was more relaxed, fundamentalists believe it's not nice for a man doctor to treat a female patient. And in the refugee hospitals the major need was for surgeons, because of the war. All the money that I brought from Afghanistan, I had already spent. I felt hopeless.

When I arrived in Peshawar, I wrote a letter to the Browns. From that point, we kept a steady correspondence. The Browns made copies of my letters and distributed them to my former classmates and friends in Eastham. Some were published in the *Cape Codder* newspaper. I was fortunate to have made a number of lasting friendships at Nauset High. Those friends and their parents helped to make my survival possible.

One day in December 1984, at the post office in Peshawar, I met an old friend from Kabul. He said, "Why don't you go to the U.S. refugee office? You can apply to live in the United States."

The next day, I went to Islamabad, the capital of Pakistan. I found that office and applied for the U.S.A. It's a good thing that I kept all my documents with me, including my yearbook from Nauset High, my transcripts, and my Honor Society card. When I showed all that, the American official said, "That's enough." He gave me a form to fill out and said that in two months I would receive a letter with the date of a further interview. I planned to have my family with me by then.

The Browns sent me enough money so that I could eat and have the strength to continue looking for work. I was fortunate to find a job at the Al Jihad Hospital. It was a good-sized facility built by the Mujahedin with money from Arabic countries. It had 160 beds and various departments: surgery, general medicine, and a polyclinic. We provided services for thousands of refugees.

I worked on a team of four pediatricians. We tried to make our children's service very effective. I was paid 4,100 Pakistan rupees, which is the equivalent of $250, each month. It doesn't seem like much, but in that environment it was a lot of money.

I constantly worried about how to get my family out of Afghanistan. After my escape, I knew how hard the journey would be for my wife and small daughters. But my overriding concern was the punishment they could receive from the Communists because of my departure.

Aqela and the children continued living with my parents. On two occasions, the secret police searched the house, looking for me. My parents told the police, "We don't know where he is. He was drafted by the army." This temporarily confused them.

I asked Mujahedin who traveled in and out of Pakistan to bring messages to my wife. But heavy winter snow made travel through the mountains impossible, so nobody could bring my family out. I had visions of them being caught by the army or fired on by helicopter gunships.

In the spring of 1985, I decided to sneak back into Afghanistan to rescue my family. On April 23, I left Peshawar in a small group of eight freedom fighters. In our group were four or five men from my hometown. We all played soccer together on the same team when we were in school. They were like family who wanted to help me to rescue my wife and children. We carried automatic rifles on our shoulders, wearing bandoliers of ammunition. It was very heavy and I wasn't used to it. We also had a caravan of horses and donkeys carrying supplies for Mujahedin inside of Afghanistan.

At Parchinar, a place on the border where the Mujahedin kept their weapons, we were attacked by Russian aircraft. Two jets violated Pakistani territory and tried to drop bombs. I could not believe what I saw:

The minute the jets came overhead, all of the freedom fighters spontaneously pointed rifles at them. And there was an anti-aircraft machine gun on top of a mountain. Everyone opened fire. It was actually kind of comical. We all knew that these small rifles couldn't be effective against the jets. But everyone on the ground kept shooting—thousands of bullets, completely harmless. But this may have caused the pilots to not drop their bombs.

There weren't just hundreds of freedom fighters at this camp, there were thousands. It was the time that the snow was thawing in the mountains, and everyone was packing up to go back into our country. We weren't sure of the safety of the trails, so the freedom fighters didn't go all at once. Instead, scouts who were very good at guerrilla tactics went ahead in groups of two or three. They left signals along the trails, as we followed some distance behind them.

I will never forget one evening of the journey. I met a refugee family from the northern part of Afghanistan who had been traveling thirty or forty days by foot and on donkeys. They were alone on top of a mountain when, out of nowhere, Russian jet fighters screamed toward them. The family scattered in all directions, diving for shelter behind rocks. After the jets bombarded them, they found their young daughter was dead. She was not wounded: she had become so frightened that her heart stopped. I questioned the father. He said his daughter didn't have a heart problem. But she was terrified because the jets flew so close and the explosions just missed them.

It was cold that evening. We had no food, nothing at all. The poor parents had their heads in their hands. There wasn't even a place to bury their daughter. It was just sheer rock, not even enough twigs to make a small fire to boil water to wash the child's body. (Part of our religious tradition is to wash a corpse before putting it in the coffin.)

I thank God for that group of freedom fighters. I don't know how, but they found some wood. And they found a big pan to boil water. With the bayonets of their rifles they chipped and dug into the hard ground to make a grave.

There was no place where the parents could wash the child's body in private, so the freedom fighters took off their shawls, which they wore as coats, and made a tent. The mother of the girl washed the body. Then they did the religious ceremony for the burial. There was not a lantern or a single candle. It was freezing cold. We held hands to keep warm. After a couple of hours, the girl was buried.

We traveled for five or six days to reach the county of Musahi, just outside of Kabul. We could only travel at night, so as to avoid the Russian helicopters and jets. Large numbers of soldiers patrolled the area. It was the anniversary of the 1978 Communist coup, so the Russians imposed a "security belt" around the capital. Helicopter gunships and artillery shot randomly all day. And all through the night they fired flares that made the area bright as day. We had to move our camp four or five times. They were shooting at the mountains, shooting at animals, shooting at any town. Their policy is to instill fear in the population.

I was able to get a message to my family in a very cunning way. I asked a very old lady to carry a note to my father in a bag of flour. Two days later, I was surprised to see my father in a nearby village. I was so happy to see him. He stayed overnight at the Mujahedin base. He went back to Kabul in the morning to prepare my family to leave.

That afternoon, my father left Kabul with my wife and children, my mother, and my sister. They were stopped by the police on the way out. The police asked my little daughters, "Where are you going? Are you supposed to be in school?" They almost answered yes, but my wife had warned them not to say anything. They pretended to be people from the countryside. Children in rural areas don't go to school at their young age. I thanked God when they arrived at the camp.

It was around eleven o'clock at night when we started our journey. My father and mother chose to stay in Afghanistan. The moment we said farewell, all of us were crying. I was trying to tell the children not to cry and to be strong. But it was tough. I didn't know if we would survive this journey.

My two oldest girls, Roya and Najilla, were six and five years old. The baby, Muska, was only six months. They were afraid of the horses. They had never ridden on animals before, and we had no saddles. It was hard for them to hold on, because they were tired and cold. Everyone but my wife and sister and I was a stranger to them. The children couldn't stop crying.

We walked for the first twenty-four hours. Night turned into morning and back into night again. The mountains seemed endless. The snow was melted at lower altitudes, but the peaks were still covered. The earth was muddy, and the steep trails were very slippery. The horses would almost panic when they stumbled.

I would look up at the mountains before us and think, "We can't make it." But we climbed higher and higher. Before I knew it, we'd be looking down on lesser peaks below. We were so exhausted.

My daughters lost their balance and fell off the horses, because they were so tired. My sister fell off and suffered a four-inch cut on her forehead. I put a dressing on it to stop the bleeding.

Around 8:00 A.M. on the second day, we were crossing a flat valley where there used to be a river. There was no longer any water, only small rocks and a smooth surface. Suddenly three Russian helicopter gunships appeared overhead. They saw us and circled back, lowering their altitude. I was so scared. I knew that we were going to be shot. And sometimes Russian pilots land their helicopters and grab refugee families. They take the refugees up to a high altitude. Then they push the poor people out of the aircraft.

As the three helicopters circled back toward us, we were too exhausted to run. There was no place to hide. The freedom fighters tried to find cover along a hillside for the ladies. But my five-year-old daughter, Najilla, and I were the last ones in the caravan. We were stuck in the middle of the open space. Even if I tried running, we would be caught.

I asked little Najilla to lie on the ground. I picked up my youngest child's blanket, which was the color of the earth, kind of gray. I placed it over Najilla to camouflage her. The problem was, the horse whose reins I held was very wild. If I let go, he would panic and run. So I had to keep the reins in my hand. I thought, "This is suicidal to just stand here. I should hide beneath the horse's body. When they shoot at us, at least I will have some cover." It was unrealistic, but I crawled beneath the horse's belly.

I could hear the rest of my family along the hillside, crying for me. Little Najilla was beneath the blanket, crying and asking what was going to happen to us. I just lay there waiting for the inevitable. The womp-

womp-womp sound of the helicopters was getting louder and closer.

The horse was petrified and began to urinate, giving me a shower. I started laughing and laughing. From under the blanket, Najilla asked, "Why are you laughing, Father? Is it time to laugh?" I told her, "Just be quiet."

The helicopters circled us two or three times and then, thank God, for whatever reason, moved on without firing. After that incident, we were so frightened that we kept moving for twenty-four hours.

My wife rode one of the horses while she was nursing the baby. She held the child very tight so they wouldn't fall. We were concerned about the horses on the steep, narrow trails. So we asked the women and children to dismount. I carried one daughter on my back, a rifle over my other shoulder, a freedom fighter carried my other daughter.

One of the horses, who was pregnant, just quit walking. Blood came out of her nostrils. I really felt sorry for the poor animal. We were all pushing our bodies to the limits of endurance. On one mountain I thought, "There must be magnets in the ground," because we were so exhausted that our legs wouldn't move. It felt like some type of force was pulling us down. Like being in a dream where you try to run and your legs won't go.

It's at impossible times like this that you realize that God helps you. I remember thinking, "God, I can't make it. I'm so tired that I can hardly move." But you keep trying. Because it is a question of life or your family dying.

When we passed through towns and villages that were destroyed by the Russians, my wife and children experienced a terrified feeling that is hard to describe. It was like seeing our own homes destroyed for no reason. Or like victims of violent crime—a stranger has destroyed their life who hasn't the right to do so.

Because we kept moving day and night, after the third day we reached Pakistan. As we neared the border, we were invited into the home of a friend of one of the freedom fighters. The man said, "Please do not go any farther without first stopping to rest in my home. The children are with you and the ladies."

The fireplace was warm. And the man was very kind to offer us good food. We slept all night. When we woke in the morning, our muscles were so tight and cramped, we couldn't move. Our entire bodies were in pain. We had pushed ourselves to the limit.

It is a queer feeling to leave your country. When we looked back at the mountains, I cannot express the feeling in words. I thought, "I've left my country. And I don't know if there will ever be a day when I can return." My face was chapped and peeling from windburn. My children's faces were also peeling badly. It was May 1985.

After we rested at the man's home, I chartered a pickup truck to take us to Peshawar. There are a number of truckers who earn their living by transporting refugees and freedom fighters from the border to Peshawar and other refugee-camp areas inside Pakistan.

Before I rescued my family, I was lucky to find a small house on the outskirts of Peshawar city. I gave a deposit to the owner before I went into Afghanistan. I asked him not to rent the house to anyone else. We estimated that it would take two to four weeks for my trip. He agreed to hold the house for that length of time.

I was grateful to have a home for my family when we arrived. But the rent was very high. I was able to afford the house because of the generosity of my friends in Massachusetts. The whole community in Eastham provided for my family.

The Browns and other friends created a fund in my name at one of the banks. People contributed $5 or $10 or more. The money that my American parents sent to me was from the fund.

When we arrived in Peshawar, it was very hot. The first night we didn't have a fan; it was unbearable. So, the next morning, I went out and with money from Eastham bought a ceiling fan. The next night we had a guest. We let him sleep in the room with the fan while we slept in the house's other room. My little child, Muska, got so bitten by mosquitoes, and the area is so dusty, that after a few days her face became infected with impetigo. It took more than a month to treat her with medicine.

I went back to work at Al Jihad Hospital. A minibus transported medical personnel back and forth from Peshawar to work in the refugee camp every day. I waited until July to get back in touch with the American embassy in Islamabad. I was busy in the hospital; then the month of June was the Ramadan holiday. And the immigration office had instructed me to bring passport-sized photos of all my family. I was afraid that, because my daughter's face was full of impetigo scabs, the refugee office would think that she had some type of serious disease. They would reject us. A refugee's life is full of fear.

When we were destitute, all the beautiful letters of support that we received from the Browns and the Eastham community were a great psychological lift. They persuaded us not to give up. They assured me that our problems would all be solved. This was a great gift to our emotional well-being. It makes a big difference when somebody on the outside cares. This doesn't happen with many refugees.

The Nassery family as refugees in Pakistan

In December 1985, I received notice from the American Immigration Service saying that our application was approved. It took another couple of months to go through intensive medical checkups. My sister's fiancé was already living in New Zealand. He returned to Pakistan to marry my sister, then took her to New Zealand. I continued to work in the hospital while we waited for final approval.

We left Pakistan at 2:00 A.M. on April 22, 1986. It was a commercial 747 aircraft. Of three hundred people on the flight, seventy were Afghan refugees. Because of the time change, we arrived at JFK Airport in New York at 4:00 P.M. on the same day. A lady from the International Rescue Committee was waiting for us. She assisted us through customs. We were told that our connecting flight to Boston would leave at 9:45 P.M. So we stayed by ourselves in that huge airport and waited.

When we left Pakistan, it was summertime, well over a hundred degrees every day. But in New York it was still spring and rather cool. All of our warm clothes were in our luggage, which was checked by Pakistan Airlines only as far as London. I didn't know to tell the clerk in Islamabad to send them all the way to New York. So we didn't have any extra clothes, only a little money, and we hadn't brought any food. We had to wait five hours for the next flight. We were so exhausted that one of the children dozed and fell off her chair.

Around 9:30 P.M. the lady from IRC appeared with our airline tickets. The flight to Boston was around forty-five minutes long. On that plane, I thought about our homeland and about rebuilding our lives. I didn't know whether we would be able to make a life here. I pledged to myself that I wouldn't give up.

The first night in Boston, we stayed in a hotel that IRC found for us. The next morning, the IRC representative brought us to Cape Cod. We agreed that my family would stay with my American parents for a week to make up our minds whether to live on the Cape or move into Boston.

After a week, we decided to stay in Eastham, because we had so many friends and our American family here. And life would be easier for the kids to adapt to here, rather than in a big city. The Browns had found a house for us, even before we arrived. It had been empty for a couple years, because the lady who owned it was very old and had moved into a nursing home.

The house was in pretty run-down shape. So the Browns made an agreement with the landlord that, in exchange for repairing the house, my family could live rent-free for twelve months. During the first three weeks, we lived with the Browns while our friends helped us to renovate our new home.

Some of my former classmates are still single. Others, who are married, brought their whole families to help. There was always someone there working. We had as many as twenty people working together. But it was expensive. It cost $350 to fix the oil heater. And in the kitchen there was a hole in the wall covered with boards that used to be a window. I discovered that there was something wrong with the electric water pump that provides well water to the house: it was running twenty-four hours a day for no reason. And the refrigerator was out of order.

We put in new windows, repaired the electrical and heating systems, replaced the water pump, painted the walls, and varnished the exposed wood. With the help of our friends, we put in hundreds of work hours. Truly a labor of love.

With money that was left in the fund, I bought a refrigerator, a television, a gas stove, and other appliances. Mrs. Brown was just like a mother to us. Whenever we needed something, I would talk with her and she'd provide it from the fund. Most of the lamps and furniture were donated by friends and local people. I bought our living room carpet at a good price from an Afghan friend in New York who imports carpets from Pakistan; he came to visit when he was delivering to stores in Boston.

When we were in Pakistan, Mr. Baskin, the owner of the local hardware store, contributed to our fund by making keys for people's homes. He charged $1 per key, and must have made five hundred to help my family. He's a very kind man. Right now he's making five thousand keys to raise money for the YMCA building.

After I arrived in Eastham, it wasn't five or six days before I began working in Mr. Baskin's hardware store. It is the largest in the area, stocked from floor to ceiling with just about anything that people need for their homes. Customers come in from all around the central part of Cape Cod. We're usually quite busy.

I work five days a week, usually forty-seven and a half hours, with Wednesdays and Sundays off. I leave home at 8:30 A.M. and work until 5:30. All of us in the store help with whatever needs to be done: the cash register, maintaining stock, sales, making keys. The two most difficult things for me are to answer questions and to mix paint. People ask me questions about tools or products that I have never seen in my life.

For instance, there are twenty different types of pliers, each with a special use. And there are many types of electrical switches and adaptors. Sometimes customers ask questions that even Bill Baskin can't answer.

I earn around $250 a week after taxes, which comes to around $12,000 a year. It is a good job—steady work providing service for the community. I've learned to do anything that the job requires. But I am not very happy, because it's not my profession. I would rather be at a hospital or medical institute, where I could be learning new things while I wait to take my certification exam.

Sometimes I think that I am not going to be able to go back into medicine. I'm trying to save at least $10,000 so I can support my family while I take the medical refresher course I need before I take the certification exam.

I have some of the medical texts that I need to study, but I'm so exhausted when I get home from work that I don't have the energy. And I have responsibilities to my family. My kids have all kinds of questions about life here. My wife and I try to maintain communication with family and friends inside Afghanistan and scattered around the world. And we have to do the shopping. If the kids are sick, I am not legally allowed to write out a prescription, so we have to take them to another doctor. I always go, because my wife can't speak English.

And there are the memories of the tragic situation that we left behind. It wouldn't be so hard if we had left a homeland that was in peace.

There is no hope that we can go back to see our parents. The combined stress of all these things keeps our minds unsettled.

My oldest child, Roya, who is eight, even now, after being here more than a year, will once in a while tell me, "Father, I feel like I have left a very precious thing back home." I ask her, "What is it?" She says, "My homeland."

One day I came home from work; from the road I could hear somebody crying very loudly in my house. I thought, "Maybe the kids fought with each other. Maybe they've done something wrong and my wife has punished them."

When I walked into the house, I saw Roya crying very loudly. So was my wife and the other children. I asked my wife, "Why is everybody crying? Is there anything wrong?" My wife said, "We didn't have anything to do, so I opened our photo album. We looked at the pictures of our families and the old days, just to have fun for a while. When Roya saw the pictures of our relatives, she started crying. It reminded her of the bad days."

My wife and I come from large families where there are a lot of people in the house at all times, a lot of noise and activity going on. Now, with me working and the kids at school, it is very quiet and lonely for Aqela. Especially because our house is surrounded by a forest, without neighbors very close by. Her hardest transition to living in Cape Cod is a feeling of isolation.

Even though she was a high-school teacher in Kabul, here she is helpless, because she doesn't know the language. To regain a teaching certification, it will cost a lot of time and money to go back to school. In this part of the Cape, there are no adult English-language classes for foreigners.

My wife depends on me a lot because of her language problem. There is no one else who she can speak with to unburden her mind. She can understand a little of what people say, but she is too shy to try to express herself. She tells me that she is afraid that she will sound silly and people will laugh at her.

There is no public transportation in this area, so Aqela is usually trapped inside the house. It has been wonderful that, whenever we need to shop, my friends have taken us around. But we are not comfortable asking people for a ride, because we don't want to interrupt their family life. During the summer, all of our friends are busy with the tourist trade—it is the only time when many people can make money—so my wife and I don't like to impose.

I used to ride my bicycle to the hardware store. It takes around a half-hour. But for the past two months, my neighbor Mark has been very kind. Every morning he drops me off at my job. Sometimes he lets me practice driving. I recently took the written part of the driver's test and scored a hundred percent. On the 26th of November, I take the real test. It's really a great feeling to be getting a license. Right before the Thanksgiving holiday. With all the support the community has given, our life here has truly been blessed.

The best benefit is that the school system is good for the kids. At first they were unhappy, because, when we arrived in April 1986, they had to begin classes at the end of the school year. They didn't know any of the language. But watching television has helped them to learn English quickly. Their favorite show is "Sesame Street." They love it. On weekend mornings, they wake up very early to watch cartoons. Sometimes they skip their breakfast. My wife and I keep calling them and calling them to eat. But they won't come. They say, "Please wait a minute until we watch 'Sesame Street.'"

This semester, the school committee decided that, since they had been to only six weeks of the previous school year, and their knowledge of English wasn't sufficient to keep up, my oldest daughter had to repeat second grade, even though she was ahead of the other kids in math. But my second daughter was allowed to move up from kindergarten to first grade.

They are doing well now. Sometimes they have gotten the star of the week in their class. My oldest, Roya, now speaks English without a foreign accent. When she invites her classmates home to play, I am amazed at how well she speaks. Hopefully, by the end of this school year, they'll have no more language problems. That gives me a good feeling about their futures.

Still, they have their hard knocks. Sometimes my children wear clothing that was donated to us. They have come home from school crying. I ask them why. My daughter told me, "The girl who used to own this jacket teased me that I am wearing her jacket." They tell me that they won't go back to school, because they don't have new clothes like the other kids.

It's hard to rationalize our situation to the kids, especially little girls. I say, "It's a common thing in America for people to exchange their clothes. The reason people gave us these gifts is because they love you." But the kids understand our true situation. When we were in Afghanistan, we never wore anything old.

Making new friends takes time, to adjust to a very different culture and manner of acting. They tell me, "In Kabul we have very close friends. You wanted us to leave, so we left them behind. Then we lived in Pakistan and made new friends. You were the one who made us leave them. Now we are in the process of making new friends at school here. And you tell us that we are going to move again next year. We don't understand. We don't want to leave our friends."

To get back into my profession, I have to move closer to where the certification study programs are located. In Massachusetts there are only four or five centers, in Boston, Cambridge, Newton, Amherst, and Springfield. We will probably have to move to one of those places and rent another house.

Admission to the study programs is given twice a year, January 1 and July 1. I have to pay for the course, pay for the exam, and provide for my family during the six months of study. Classes are from morning until evening, and the time after dinner must be spent on intensive study. The toughest part is going to be the basic sciences—biochemistry, microbiology, anatomy, and physics. Those subjects are far from my mind, because I studied them fifteen years ago. Medical sciences are easier, because I have six or seven years' experience as a doctor.

If I pass the exam, I will be recognized as a doctor in this country. But finding residency is a difficult task. I must apply to many different institutions and hospitals. I really don't mind whatever state where we will have to go, but the constant moving is difficult for the children.

My daughters tell me, "Father, let's not move from this place. We like the school and we like the kids." It's especially nice that the school bus comes right to the front of the house.

This morning, because it's Sunday, the kids have a singing rehearsal. They are picked up by one of their friends' parents to go to the church, where they attend social programs. Even though we are Muslims, I let the kids go to church with their friends. It gives them the opportunity to be in touch with other kids and learn about American culture and beliefs.

People here have been more than kind to us. I don't know how I can ever repay their affection and the love that they have given us. But sometimes I still feel like I am here as a stranger, an alien. I am not ashamed of the work I am doing, but I would feel more at ease if I was back in my own profession. And I always remember what my American family told me: "There's no place like home." It's true. Even though we are safe and the kids are happy in school, my heart is still in Afghanistan.

In 1987, Daud began the medical certification study program in Amherst, Massachusetts. Respecting his daughters' wishes, Daud allowed his wife and children to stay in Eastham, while he rented a small room in Amherst. He comes home to see them on weekends. In mid-1988, at the time this book went into production he was preparing for his certification exam.

HONEY

Atlanta Ballet

Maniya Barredo
Born in Manila, Philippines
Ballerina
Atlanta, Georgia

I was born to be a dancer. I danced even before I walked." In the Philippines, Maniya "Honey" Barredo was the vivacious child star of her own musical television show. Today she is prima ballerina of one of America's foremost dance companies, the Atlanta Ballet. In an age when willowy porcelain-skinned ballerinas dominate the art, almond-eyed Maniya is an exception.

She is barely five feet tall and ninety pounds, but on stage she is larger than life. As the orchestra begins to play, her quicksilver pirouettes and graceful leaps transform Maniya into the half-bird, half-human Odette of Swan Lake; a soft and bewitching Juliet; the flirtatious coquette of Coppelia; and the lovable Sugar Plum Fairy. Like many foreign-born artists who have come to America to practice their art at the highest level, at thirty-five years of age Maniya has risen to the top of her profession.

On a mid-August afternoon in the old downtown section of Atlanta, the heat shimmers off the gray sidewalks. A few blocks from the towering air-conditioned skyscrapers of the New South, on the top floor of a converted two-story warehouse near the deserted intersection of Peachtree and Pine streets, sweat-soaked dancers are on their toes, learning their paces for a new ballet season.

In a compact gymlike rehearsal studio, empty except for a black baby-grand piano in the far corner and thin waist-high barres along the east and west walls, two dancers, a man and a woman, repeat the same dramatic movements again and again in dreamlike sequence. Maniya, in dark-blue leotard and transparent flowing chiffon skirt, fluidly arches her back and extends her petite arms and fingers in a perfect arabesque, then revolves effortlessly on her toes toward her well-built partner. In a single lyrical motion he lifts her above his shoulders, balancing her, doll-like, on his palms. He tenderly lowers her back onto her toes. They release their embrace, take a deep breath, and return to their original positions, absorbed in the choreographer's critique of each subtle movement. They then repeat the sequence with startling precision.

Maniya's uncanny ability to control her every gesture with poetic elegance, even after eight hours of grueling rehearsal, is a product of God-given talent and her fierce pursuit of perfection. She has toured internationally with Dame Margot Fonteyn's Stars of World Ballet. And she has collaborated with masters like Mikhail Baryshnikov, Alicia Alonso, Maya Plisetskaya, and Burton Taylor. Her recognitions include the prestigious Philippines Award for Best Classical Performer Abroad, as well as a listing in Who's Who in America. *After living ten years in Altanta, she is one of but a few Filipinos—1.5 million live in the United States—who speak with a lilting Southern drawl.*

Although Maniya has achieved phenomenal success, at the time when she first arrived at New York's fiercely competitive Joffrey School, she almost gave up on her dream.

I arrived in New York from Manila, alone but exhilarated. I was eighteen on my first big trip away from home. My uncle was to meet me at the airport, but I couldn't find him in the crowd.

I saw some people getting into a long black limousine, so I went up to the driver with a slip of paper that my parents had given me. I said, "I want to go to this address." I had no idea where it was. My parents told me that my uncle lived somewhere in Queens, not more than twenty minutes from the airport.

The driver dropped people off at different locations. After a long ride, I was the last person in the back seat of the car. All of a sudden, the driver parked in a dark, secluded place. I didn't have much life experience, but I had enough sense to know that I was in trouble.

I started crying uncontrollably. I said, "I just arrived in this country. Please, don't hurt me." It was horrible. Thank God, the man had some compassion. I was able to reason with him, and he took me to my uncle's home. That was my first day in America. It was June 1970.

The next day, I was supposed to audition at the American Ballet Center, on 8th Street and Avenue of the Americas in Manhattan. Well, my uncle put me on a subway in Queens and said to get off at West 4th Street. I had never ridden on public transportation in the Philippines. I always traveled by car. I didn't even know what riding in a bus was like. But there I was on the frantic New York subway. I was petrified. And I was too shy to ask anyone for directions. I missed my exit and went all the way to God knows where.

At the end of the line, I was the only person left on the train. I pulled my rosary out of my purse and began praying. Finally the train started back toward Manhattan. Eventually I found West 4th Street.

The American Ballet Center is the school of the Joffrey Ballet. It's one of the most recognized dance institutions anywhere. I auditioned for a scholarship, even though they didn't know me from Adam. It was humbling to watch the other young American dancers. I was a big star in Manila—I danced command performances for visiting presidents and in other big events. Now I not only had to learn a new dance vocabulary, but to learn to live all by myself in this culture. The only thing I had going for me was guts. I wanted it so badly. I walked in and did my best. And I received a partial scholarship.

In Manila, I started dance lessons when I was four and became a professional at eight. First of all, for the joy dancing gave me. But it was also a necessity. Even though my family was considered comfortable, all nine children were going to private schools. I practically paid for my entire education with my dance earnings, and also for some of my brothers' and sisters'. I had a difficult childhood. In a house full of problems, my dancing helped bring a little happiness to my family.

My father's great-grandparents were the pioneers of modern transportation in the Philippines. But Dad was a black sheep and squandered a lot of money. I think that's affected my opinion of most Filipino males: they go out and have fun while their wives stay home. . . . My mom had to take care of all the needs of her nine children while Dad enjoyed the pleasures of life. That's why at an early age I wanted to help my mom so badly.

I don't know how my parents managed to stay together. But to this day Mom is still with Dad. He's mellowed now, and he finally accepts responsibility. He has even apologized to the family for his shortcomings as a father.

I'm the fourth-born, right in the middle. Because of my painful growing up, dancing was heaven for me. My mom encouraged me to perform. She had a been a ballet dancer in Manila before she met Dad. Then came the war, the Japanese invasion. She got married at fifteen, and Dad was only seventeen. She stopped dancing and had one baby after another. My oldest brother was born during the country's liberation in 1944. Mom never really had a chance to experience life or travel, the way I have been able to through my dancing. I love her.

When I feel down, I think about what she went through to raise us kids. She was an absolute saint. I still call her at least twice a week to let her know everything I'm doing. That's her way of seeing the outside world. Now she's running the family trucking company. Dad decided to go on semi-retirement and left managing the business to her.

When I was born, in 1951, my parents gave me the nickname Honey, because I was completely honey-colored—my skin, hair, everything. By the time I was two years old, my hair began turning black, but the name Honey stuck with me. It became my stage name. To this day, people in the Philippines still know me as Maniya "Honey" Barredo.

Mom never questioned what I was going to be. She says that, when I was one year old, I was singing and dancing all over the place. I danced before I even walked. The only way I would stop crying was if there was music.

When I was three and four years old, I never liked playing with the kids. My eldest sister was dancing, and I wanted to be just like her. But my father believed in discipline, and he didn't want me to dance. He said it would be a waste of my time. But Mom was determined. She snuck me to and from ballet lessons.

My sister was a beautiful dancer. But after she got married at eighteen, she quit, while I kept on. To this day, we talk about that. Now she regrets her decision. I say, "You shouldn't complain. You have five beautiful kids. I haven't any. There's a trade-off for everything in life."

My first teacher was my aunt, Julie Borromeo. She had danced in the United States before coming back home to open a school. She gave me a scholarship. My next teacher, Totoy de Oteyza, trained in Europe. There's also a tradition of dance in the Philippines, though. The Bay-anihan group travels throughout the world. And there are also ballet companies.

I think that, among the peoples of Southeast Asia, Filipinos are the most musical. As we grow up, the first thing we are taught, even before we say "Mama" and "Papa," is how to sing. We have innate talent in movement and dance.

I don't consider Filipinos to be totally Oriental, because we're in fact Eurasians. We were occupied by Spain. We were occupied by the Japanese. Influenced by Chinese, by Americans. I feel that we are very lucky to have the best of East and West in us.

It is estimated that eighty-five percent of our fifty-five million people are Catholics. Sometimes I think that my strict Catholic upbringing is both a hindrance and the source of my strength. I went to a private school run by nuns, where I went to church every day. They thought that I was going to be a nun as well. But after I left the country, I saw a different world. Today my religious beliefs are very internalized. My strong spiritual feelings give me strength. I think that good performers usually have a sense of inner concentration and peace. The stage is my offering. It's the most sacred part of who I am.

I began dancing professionally when I was in the third grade. I had my own national TV show called "Lollipop Party," which I cohosted with an older lady named June Keithley. We had children celebrate their birthdays on the show, and I would sing and dance for them. I also was a guest on many other shows. I sang wearing big ribbons in my hair and did a little soft-shoe—I was quite a ham.

When I was nine or ten, my voice started to change. The first time it cracked I said, "That's it. No more singing. I'm just going to dance." And around that time I felt a responsibility to help support my family.

After high school, I had one semester of college. My mom thought that I was getting too serious with my boyfriend. She feared losing her little ballerina. So she said, "You have to go away—to the States." To this day I still ask her, "Mama, protective as you were of me, how could you send me to New York City?" She tells me, "I knew that you had to have a challenge to succeed. I couldn't watch you become a housewife and have babies right away."

New York was a rude awakening. At the Joffrey School, dancers, younger dancers, were much more polished than I. In my first class, the instructor called out, "First position." I looked around, and everybody was so pretty. I felt like an ugly duckling.

That evening, I came home and called Mama. I cried buckets and told her, "I'm coming home. I can't do this." And she said, "Are you a quitter?" I didn't want to let her down. So I said, "I won't quit."

In retrospect, it's all so funny now. I was eighteen, but still a child. Let me tell you, I grew up that first week. Dressing rooms in the Philippines were very proper. Dancers went into the bathroom and changed clothes privately. But in New York, even thirteen-year-olds weren't as inhibited. They would snicker at me, because I was so shy in my corner. They'd be talking about who they went to bed with the night before. I was absolutely mortified. I was innocent, ignorant—I didn't even understand when men were coming on to me. And I had never known what it was like to attend five classes a day, each one an hour and a half long.

In Manila I went to a regular academic school and then worked out at a dance studio from eight to ten o'clock in the evening. Here young kids were taking correspondence courses so that they could devote full time to dancing. There were no professional dance schools back home.

The New York dance scene was a fascinating world for me. In Manila we didn't learn much about the fine points of technique. We just copied all the tricks that we saw when foreign companies visited. In class, if our teacher said, "Jump in the air and turn," we'd jump in the air, turn, and land. We didn't know how to use our muscles correctly. In New York I would come home from class in pain. After a month, my mother asked, "Are you going to stay or come home?" I said, "I'll try another month."

One day a secretary at the school told me, "Mr. Joffrey said that you'll never become a real dancer. You should just be a secretary or a nurse." I became very depressed and began eating obsessively. I got fatter and fatter, up to 115 pounds. I'm five feet tall, and my usual weight is around eighty-six pounds. I was so unhappy. I missed my family. And I was all alone, because I moved from my uncle's home to a girls' dormitory on 13th Street. I phoned Mom and said, "I want to go home." So she flew to New York.

We rented a tiny studio on West 69th Street, where Broadway and Columbus Avenue branch off. No kitchen, just one tiny room. And we were short of money.

One day Mom was walking on Fifth Avenue. She was window shopping at Sak's department store, admiring their fabulous displays. She had never worked a regular job, because of all her children. But she walked right into Sak's and asked for a job. She didn't have a Social Security card or anything.

They asked, "Have you ever worked before?" And she said, "No, I raised nine kids." She's not very tall, only around five three. But she is impeccable, very old-school. And they hired her! So we had some money. And she helped me to get emotionally settled.

Even though some people at the school gave me a hard time, I stayed with it. My mentor, Mr. William Griffith, was the principal teacher at the school and of the Joffrey Company. He's a big guy, around six two, the bluest eyes you ever saw, and a low, low voice. He knew that I was eager to learn and understood what I was going through. From the start, he took to me like a daughter. He talked with me and tried to give me confidence. But after I gained so much weight, he began to call me Rice-a-roni, and said that I was "dancing like an elephant."

Mr. Griffith does have a temper. He's a perfectionist who uses every conceivable means to get a dancer to do things right. He even hit me with a stick. But if it weren't for Mr. Griffith, I would never have succeeded.

One day, after my mom went back to Manila, I came late for class. I hadn't been to school in a while. Mr. Griffith looked at me and screamed, calling me horrible names. I began crying and said, "I quit."

He stormed into the dressing room after me and carried me out to the teachers' lounge. He threw me onto the couch. Here was this big man in tears. He said, "Don't you realize, darling, what you are doing?" I was crying and said, "I don't want to dance any more. I want to go home. Nobody likes me. I'm different." And I told him how the secretary had insulted me.

Mr. Griffith said, "Are you going to listen to all that?" The sincere look in his eyes and his deep emotion shook me. He said, "Most dancers

would kill for the talent you have. You've got to stay with it and prove
to people what you've got. Stand up for what you believe is right and
just be yourself. People will like you."

I was smaller and darker than anyone else in the school. I didn't know
any other foreign students. The Asians that were around were American-
born. And I felt so far behind everybody. In my eagerness, I wasn't
giving myself a break. I took more classes than I should've, because I
felt so insecure. I wasn't prepared to have to grow up so fast.

The confrontation with Mr. Griffith knocked sense into me. When
I woke up the next day, even though I was fat, I felt very thin. I let go
of my insecurities and I worked my tush off to earn a full scholarship
at the school.

I still had no spending money, so I auditioned to dance at Radio City
Music Hall. I was too short and roly-poly to be in the Rockettes chorus
line, but I worked as a ballerina, four shows each night. It was good
money, which meant that Mom didn't have to send me anything. I
mean, Mr. Griffith got me *dancing*. I was a brand-new human being.

I auditioned for the Washington [D.C.] Ballet, a well-respected regional company, and received a contract offer. But instead I applied for
and received a grant from the Rockefeller Foundation. It was the first
fellowship they had ever given in ballet. It was an honor to be invited
to join the Washington Ballet, but I knew that once you're in a company
you don't have time to train. I told myself, "I need one more year of
catching up." That was the best decision I could have made. The next
year, in 1972, Mr. Joffrey offered me a contract to join his company.
That was a total surprise.

I was thrilled to perform with Joffrey Company II—the apprentice
company—and then Joffrey Company I. But deep inside I wasn't happy.
I didn't feel comfortable with the company's style of dance, so I left
after one season.

I needed a job, so I went to a dance festival in France for a month
with Larry Richardson's modern dance company. Before we left, I auditioned for Canada's Les Grands Ballets. Mr. Fernand Nault, the director, had taught at the Joffrey when I was in that company. I just
loved the man. After his class, I went up to him and said, "Mr. Nault,
if you have a place for me in your Canadian company, I would love to
come." While I was in Paris, the contract from Mr. Nault arrived. After
I finished the French tour in December, I went straight to Montreal to
dance in *The Nutcracker*.

After three years in the United States, I was beginning to feel more
at home. New York taught me a new culture and a whole new way of

dancing. But I was still unsure of who I was. I wasn't even twenty-one years old yet. Everything was still a dream. In Montreal I began to know myself as a dancer. But maturity as a woman was nowhere in sight.

I fell in love with a member of the company, a wonderful American dancer named Manny Rowe. He had just returned from playing the lead role in the rock opera *Tommy*. I was tired of being alone. Within six months, in the summer of 1974, we were married.

Manny and I had some real highs dancing together. Our visit to Manila as guest artists in 1975 was especially memorable. It was my first time home in five years. We danced *Romeo and Juliet*, which was beautifully received by Filipino audiences.

There are times when I perform when it feels like Honey, the person, is watching this creature, Maniya, moving on stage. It's like levitation. The dance becomes timeless and spaceless, like it isn't really me out there. Those moments don't happen very often. But when they do, it's worth all the years of hard work, tired muscles, and hurting feet. Nothing in this life comes close. It's like dying and going to heaven.

A particular thrill was being invited by my idol, the prima ballerina Alicia Alonso, to perform in the 1976 International Dance festival. Later that summer, Manny and I decided that we needed a change of scenery and new challenges. So we took a tour of the Southern United States, Manny's home area. We visited his former teacher Robert Barnett, a former soloist under George Balanchine at the New York City Ballet who had become artistic director of the Atlanta Ballet.

Mr. Barnett knew that Manny was thinking about quitting dance, so he offered both of us positions in his company. We told him that we would think it over, and went back to Montreal to begin the new season. Bobby flew up to see us dance. He offered Manny the directorship of the Atlanta Ballet's Chamber Ensemble, beginning in the 1977 season. And he offered me a contract as prima ballerina. That was a wonderful feeling.

Atlanta is where my life began to jell. Mr. Barnett and I clicked artistically. Sometimes I think that I'm closer to him and his wife, Ginger, than to my own family. Even though I've visited Manila on many occasions, it seems that they only remember me as I was before I left seventeen years ago.

The summer of 1985 was a sad revelation. I went home and they treated me as if I were still a kid. Mom and Dad wanted me to live by their rules. They didn't want me to drive, even though in Atlanta I drive by myself every day. It was as if I entered a world that I understand a little bit, but I didn't really know.

I realized that, if I hadn't left Manila, I would've matured very differently. There are strict social rules in the Philippines about how a woman should be—terribly subservient. In families, the man rules, even though the woman really runs the household and raises the family.

It's only in the past few years, since my mother returned from New York, that she has taken charge of her life. She realized her abilities and took charge of the family's trucking business. It's unheard of in the Philippines for a woman to have a corporate position—not to mention being voted "Trucker of the Year."

The Philippines now has a woman president, Cory Aquino. But that is very unusual in our culture. She is surrounded by aides, who are mostly men. Very few, if any, women were elected as senators or representatives.

I've become a permanent resident of the United States, and I'm applying for my citizenship. I feel very American, but with Filipino emotions. I can never forget my roots. That blood will always be in me. It's a very important part of who I am.

I have so many pent-up feelings about the Philippines. Especially when I see dancers here in America who don't appreciate what they have. They complain about not having a chance to succeed. But they should see students in Manila, who have to work out in hundred-degree heat without air conditioning. They don't even have a tenth of the facilities that dancers have here.

I am one of twenty to thirty-five Filipino dancers with major companies abroad. That's more than any other Asian nationality. Most left after I did and have also reached their goals. In Atlanta we have three other Filipino dancers: Nicolas Pacana, my partner, and two sisters, Mia and Maiqui Manosa, who I knew in Manila from the time they were babies. They, too, had a dream.

Because of my success in this country, I've become a role model for a lot of Filipino dancers, giving them hope and a sense of pride. When my mom asks me to come home, I tell her, "The day I come home will mean lost dreams for a lot of young kids. While I'm still dancing in America, it gives them hope."

I always teach classes when I visit Manila. It's an uplifting experience. Last summer I taught around seventy kids. They started out frightened little girls. But within a week they were just beautiful, absolutely confident and open like the wind.

They gave me a surprise farewell party. I'll never forget this. . . . I sat in the middle of a large circle. Each child took a turn standing up to tell me what she got out of the class. One little girl said, "You made me believe again." Another child could hardly speak. I told them, "The reason why I share what I know with you is because this is what love is all about. We all should share and reach for a goal."

Some dancers in the Philippines write to me and ask if I will come back to teach full-time. I enjoy visiting in the summers, but my home is Atlanta. Right now the company is preparing for our new performance season, which opens in October. I'm working my buns off to get ready. I had three months off during the summer. Now it's like, *boom*, I practically live in the company's rehearsal studio.

I get up at 7:30 in the morning and get to the studio by 9:00 to warm up for my 10:00 A.M. class. Rehearsals start at noon and go until 6:15. We have a one-hour break at 3:15—that's it. At 7:00 P.M. I go home, do laundry to wash the three different leotards I use for workouts, and do chores. Finally, I have my one meal of the day, and by 10:30 I'm in bed exhausted.

There really isn't time for a social life, except functions to raise funds for the ballet. For instance, tomorrow evening I'll go to a small reception for donors. After ten years in Atlanta, I've received enough media recognition that people are familiar with my name.

Atlanta is home for me. I feel a responsibility to help the community any way I can. I'm doing commercials for the Red Cross. I was a spokesperson for the Humane Society. I try to do the same for the public television station when they need to raise money, and for the Girl Scouts. I've even been "auctioned off" for a dinner or a picnic to raise donations for worthwhile causes.

I've grown here as a whole person and have developed as an artist without anyone pushing me—except myself. People who come to see me dance are very warm. On stage I want to give them the best I can offer, and more. They appreciate it, especially the kids. A special time is Christmas, when we do *The Nutcracker*. Some children who have been involved in the productions have gone on to perform professionally. It's a good feeling to have touched those kids so that they are inspired to go for something. Even if it's not ballet, they've been motivated to fulfill their dreams.

After I experienced so much pressure in New York and Canada, where I really had to fend for myself, I appreciate the way that people now care for me. The Barnetts have been like a second family. And although my first marriage didn't work out, I've recently become engaged to a wonderful man. His name is Lewis Patterson Thompson III, but I just call him Patterson. He owns a small video-and-photography shop. He had never been to a ballet until after he met me. But he understands my needs as an artist. And he's shown me a beautiful world outside of my dancing. We go on fishing and sailing trips. Even little things like bowling and working in the garden together are a real joy.

My only regret is being away from my parents. But, eight thousand miles from home, I've found a family here. I'm even developing a Southern accent. My speech is slowing, and I drawl my vowel sounds. Now on the phone my mom asks me, "What's happened to your English?"

When I reflect on how much this country has given me, I no longer feel like an outsider. Sure, I would've been a star in Manila. But I never would have reached my full potential as an artist or a human being.

SOLIDARITY

Jozef and Krystyna Patyna
Refugees from Trzebinia, Poland
Factory Workers
Providence, Rhode Island

Jozef Patyna is solidly six feet tall. His broad shoulders, naturally wavy brown hair, and clear blue eyes suggest a European soccer player or movie star. He has worked with his thick, powerful hands his entire life. Still youthful at thirty-nine, he and his wife, Krystyna, are machine operators in a small factory in Providence, Rhode Island. Less than five years earlier, they were deeply involved in a passionate struggle for democracy and human rights in their homeland.

Jozef was a coal miner in southern Poland in 1980 when a grassroots movement for workers' rights and national independence spread throughout the country. The nonviolent uprising led by farmers, students, and blue-collar workers gave birth to the Solidarity Union, led by a humble electrician named Lech Walesa. Solidarity, with ten million members—almost a third of Poland's total population—became the first independent labor union in Soviet-controlled Eastern Europe.

During Solidarity's first national congress, Jozef was elected to the union's executive committee. His task was to mediate disputes between workers and government officials. By December 1981, a growing crescendo of student demonstrations and labor strikes indicated the demand for true democracy in the upcoming national elections. In response, Soviet and East German troops massed along Poland's borders.

Solidarity's leaders called an emergency meeting in Gdańsk, a northern port city, to attempt peace talks with the government. In the predawn hours of Sunday, December 12, a group of Solidarity organizers informally gathered in Jozef's hotel room to discuss conciliatory promises by the government. They didn't realize that heavily armed militia were surrounding their building. Without warning, police stormed into Jozef's room. Within hours, secret jails throughout the country were filled with Solidarity activists. Hundreds of other people were killed or disappeared.

Jozef endured months of brutal incarceration before suffering a heart attack. Released to his hometown, he was under constant police surveillance. A government blacklist made him unemployable. He faced three choices: suicide, a return to prison, or fleeing with his wife and two children out of the country. In late 1983, following thousands of Polish patriots who had already fled, the Patyna family arrived in the United States.

The Patynas live in a two-story white house on a quiet tree-lined street in the urban valley of the Mount Pleasant neighborhood, one of Providence's seven hills.

Their living room is graced with a bright painting of Pope John Paul II, which is reflected in a large mirror above the fireplace. On the mantle is a glass beer mug, inscribed with the Virgin Mary of the Passion, the logo of the Silesian coal miners' guild. A single red candle is set on top of the television.

On a comfortable beige sofa, Jozef shows me a few of the precious items that he carried from Poland. Among them is a triangular banner from Solidarity's first National Congress, and handmade stamps that he and other union activists secretly crafted while they were incarcerated. He pauses to reflect on a telegram he received from his friend Lech Walesa after Walesa was awarded the Nobel Prize.

Krystyna, whose melancholy expression conceals a buoyant sense of humor, held a thick antique dictionary to help Jozef express himself in English. From early afternoon until long past midnight, we sat together, with plenty of good food and coffee, as Jozef and Krystyna shared the spirit of their survival.

JOZEF: I know a very beautiful place up the coast in Massachusetts. In the evenings during Christmas season, they turn on thousands of colorful lights. My wife and I go there every year with our children. And we remember our first Christmas in this country.

We arrived in Rhode Island from West Germany on December 21, 1983. It was a very cold Wednesday night, ten o'clock. We were four people, including my wife, Krystyna; our teen-age daughter, Magdalena; and our eleven-year-old son, Przemyslaw [Shem]. We were exhausted from the time change—it was 4:00 A.M. European time— and the long flight.

Our American sponsor, who met us at Providence Airport, was a stranger. She was a middle-aged woman who volunteered to sponsor us through a refugee-assistance agency. She didn't speak Polish and had no translator. We couldn't understand what she was talking about, because we couldn't speak English. We felt very awkward using sign language. [Laughs] We just gestured with our hands.

KRYSTYNA: Now we can laugh about it. But at the time we were very confused and frustrated.

JOZEF: She drove us to a building in Central Falls, just outside of Providence. We were in a second-floor apartment with three bedrooms. The heat was shut off. We couldn't make tea or hot coffee, because the gas was off in the stove. No electricity. She dropped us off in the dark and said, "Wait for me. I'll be back."

We waited . . . all day Thursday, all day Friday. Nobody came. We had no water for baths, no heat. In the combined kitchen—living room there was a table and three chairs for the four of us. No radio or television. We had to keep our coats on because of the cold.

Our sponsor returned on Saturday. That was an emotional time, because it was Christmas Eve, which is a big holiday in Poland. She gave us $50 for shopping.

I was very angry. I didn't care about myself—I had lived in worse conditions during jail in Poland. But I was worried about my wife and children. I tried to tell our sponsors, "We only want three things: Show us the school for our children. Help me look for a job. And find us a decent apartment." I said, "When I have a job and am earning money, I will pay you back for everything. I don't want to be on welfare or receiving financial aid."

The sponsoring agency found us the apartment and nothing more. After the New Year holiday, my wife and the kids and I walked to the school by ourselves. It was the middle of winter, and the sidewalks were covered with snow. We only knew how to say "Good morning," "Goodbye," and "Thank you." But the principal and teachers were very kind to us. They couldn't understand Polish, but they knew what our children needed. My daughter went to high school and my son was in middle school.

Krystyna and I were anxious to find work. After a month, a Polish man told us about a local factory. We walked to the office and filled out applications. Soon the factory called my wife to work. The next day they called me. We are still working there, making safety belts for cars, parachutes, and other uses.

At first, working at the factory was very difficult, because we didn't speak English. I operated a machine that made plastic thread. Watching that same machine all day was terribly boring. My mind would drift back to Poland. But I told myself, "Don't think about the Solidarity Union or Poland now. I have a family to provide for. I must work well and care about this job."

KRYSTYNA: Close to four hundred people work in the factory. The owner is an American Jewish man. The management are Americans. The bosses are Portuguese. Workers are Polish, Lithuanians, Portuguese, Cambodians, Indians, Puerto Ricans, and other Latins.

JOZEF: American workers in the factory see so many newcomers from Latin America, Asia, and Europe. Sometimes they ask me, "Why did you come here? Can't you live in your own country?" I say, "I can't, even though I would rather live in Poland than here." We came to the United States as a result of my involvement with the Solidarity Union. After I was released from jail, no factories in Poland would hire me. All jobs are controlled by the government.

The authorities forced my wife to leave her job as an accountant at the city hall. We had young children and worried about their futures. I was constantly being watched by the secret police. It was only a matter of time before they would arrest me again.

Our town, Trzebinia [pronounced "Trebeenya"] is in the south of Poland, between the industrial city of Katowice and Kraków, the country's traditional cultural center, where one of the oldest universities in Europe is located. The region is called Upper Silesia, famous for coal mines and steel mills. The Vistula River flows through small hills and valleys that lead into the Carpathian and Suvety mountain ranges. In the old times, our region was part of a small Polish kingdom that separated Germany from Russia.

KRYSTYNA: Trzebinia is not a very large town [population around thirty-five thousand]. The people are friendly, but it's not the best area to live, because all the factories burn coal for power, which creates a lot of smoke and pollution. The government doesn't permit environmental-protection efforts like in the United States. The climate in our region is much colder than here in Rhode Island. Winters are much longer, with a lot of snow. And summers are cooler, with a lot of rain.

JOZEF: Like many of my neighbors, I worked in a coal mine that became part of the Solidarity Union after 1980. The Solidarity movement was the first time that Polish people felt a sense of self-determination and hope since the Germans and Soviets agreed to invade and divide Poland between them in 1939. At the end of World War II, Stalin promised Churchill and Roosevelt that Poles would decide their own future through democratic vote. But America and Britain allowed the Russians to do what they wanted. There was no fair vote in Poland. Instead, the Communists killed off Poland's nationalist leaders. I was born in 1947, the year that Poland was officially declared a Communist country.

Poland was shut off from the Western world. But my father always listened to Western radio broadcasts. In my house, everyone talked about what was happening in Western Europe and discussed the changes in Poland.

Religion was very strong after the war, even though the Communists tried to drive people away from the church. When Catholic people applied for jobs, officials said, "Get out of here, go to church." And the secret police put pressure on them.

In my area, the public schools were mostly Catholic. We had religion lessons, and pictures of saints and crucifixes were hung on the walls. Like most small kids, I was never interested in politics. My problems began on the day the crucifix was removed from our classroom wall, when I was ten years old.

I went to a public elementary school located inside a church. One morning, when we arrived for class, the crucifix was missing. A friend and I went to a priest and asked, "Where is the crucifix?" He told us, "The crucifix is no longer allowed." We told him, "We want the crucifix. We are going to put one back on the wall."

The principal, a woman, came into the classroom and asked, "Who put this crucifix here?" Me and my friend stood up and said, "We did. We don't understand why a crucifix shouldn't be there." She got angry and beat us.

My friend and I came home from school and told our mothers what happened. It became a big incident in our town. The principal happened to live next door to my grandmother. Our mothers went to her house. The woman said that she was very sorry. It was the Communists' order that crucifixes not be allowed on the walls.

The crucifix in our class lasted one more week. Put in its place were pictures of Lenin, Stalin, and Polish Communist leaders. Some people in my town joined the Party—not because they believed in the ideology, but to have a decent job. All the newspapers and radio stations were controlled by the government. All we ever heard about was Poland's "love for the Soviet Union."

It was stupid, because throughout history the Russians have continually tried to dominate the Polish people. Personally, I don't like the Russian government, but I have empathy for Russian citizens. The Communist system has taken away their freedom, too.

No, there weren't any Party members in my family. [Laughs] My father worked in a huge factory that made electricity. In our area, the main industries are the big power plants and coal mines. People have small gardens near their homes, but there are no farms.

I was eighteen years old when I finished high school in 1965. Like most Polish youth, I continued to live with my parents. I took a job in a coal mine that was just 250 meters from my parents' house. The mine was deep underground, so it didn't take up a lot of space in the neighborhood. All fifty-five hundred people who worked in the mine lived in Trzebinia and the surrounding towns.

We worked with drills, picks, and shovels to break walls of coal, a quarter mile beneath the ground. I fixed machines that move coal up to the the earth's surface. Every week I worked a different shift. Underground workers had an overlapping three-shift system. First shift was 6:00 A.M. until 2:00 P.M., second shift from noon until 8:00 P.M., and third shift was 6:00 P.M. until 2:00 A.M. We worked four consecutive days, then one or two days off. This didn't give a husband enough time to see his family.

The government wanted the mines working around the clock every day of the week, because coal is a main export earner for Poland. Much of it goes to the Soviet Union. The Russians take all the resources they want from Poland and pay very little in rubles, which aren't worth much. That's one of the main reasons why Poland is bankrupt.

Before 1980, when Solidarity was formed, the government projected that Poland would produce 180 million tons of coal per year. For every one million tons, one miner died. An average of two hundred miners died every year. Sometimes underground walls of coal collapsed, crushing or smothering men. Sometimes large boulders fell onto people from the ceiling. Machines broke down and ran over miners. Thousands of smaller accidents happened, like broken fingers, arms, legs . . . traumatic amputation of limbs. Miners had large families with lots of children. If you were injured, you would have a hard time feeding your kids.

When you have good health, the government sees you as a useful asset. But when your health is bad, officials say, "Get out of here. We don't care about you." We have no Social Security or welfare like in the United States. Many of us worried about our futures, especially after we had families. I was twenty-one when I married Krystyna. She's from my town.

KRYSTYNA: I'm just one month younger than Jozef. We met at a party when I was finishing college. Our families didn't know each other because we lived in different parts of Trzebinia and worked at different places. We dated for a year and a half before we were married. While we were courting, in 1968, discotheques were popular, and we would go on dates to the cinema. When we decided that the time was right, our parents made all the plans for the wedding ceremony and party, similar to Catholic weddings here.

For newlyweds in Poland, the greatest difficulty is housing. We put our name on a waiting list for an apartment shortly after we were married. But it is usually a ten-to-fifteen year wait to finally be accepted. So we lived with my mother. My father died when I was very young, and I didn't have brothers or sisters.

After one year, our daughter, Magdalena, was born. My mother's apartment only had two rooms and a kitchen. After our son, Shem, was born, we managed the best we could in the small space. We were very lucky: after ten years we were in our own place. [Laughs] A new street was constructed over the site where my mother's apartment stood. When the government demolished the old building, we received a small apartment nearby, and my mother was given her own place.

Salaries are very low in Poland, and prices are usually rising, so husband and wife both must work. I was an accountant in an administrative building, similar to a city hall. After a few years, I was made manager of the financial department. Around twenty people worked in my section.

Polish women are not much different from American women. But in Poland women are always worrying and struggling to get even the most basic needs, like food, for their families. After work we have to stand in long lines to shop. To buy meat, I had to wait a half-day in line. During Christmas season, the wait might even be three days. Family members take turns every few hours standing in the lines.

JOZEF: Americans can't imagine that. [Laughs] Oh, my God! A coal miner must work all day to earn enough money for two pounds of ham.

KRYSTYNA: Sometimes the place where women work will let them leave an hour or two early to stand in line to shop. When we came to West Germany and Rhode Island, it was unbelievable to walk into a supermarket and see so much food. And no long lines!

JOZEF: My first shock about life in the West was when I attended a miners' conference in England in 1981. In the markets there were so many different types of oranges and fruits. So many kinds of meat! It sounds crazy, but I thought, "This can't really be meat," because there were no long lines or people rushing into the store to buy it.

When I returned to Poland, I told my family, "It's incredible. It's already been forty years since the end of the war, and Polish people still have nothing. Even though we have good farmland and very capable farmers." Poland is very rich in natural resources. We were a top exporter of food before the war. What's happened now? It's the same situation in the Soviet Union—the Ukraine has beautiful soil.

Polish people born after the war have never known freedom. Still, the idea of freedom and democracy is what the people have an instinctive need for. People listen to Western radio. They read underground newspapers and books, which are very popular. When people buy a book and finish reading it, they exchange it with a friend.

Before 1980, I had no contact with dissidents in Poland. I worked and raised my family. I was not involved in political activities. But in my coal mine we talked all the time about news on the Voice of America or Radio Free Europe, which many people listen to.

In the summer of 1980, people in my region heard about labor strikes occurring in Gdańsk, Jastrzebie [pronounced "Yastrembia"] and Szczecin [pronounced "Shetseen"]. We didn't hear anything from the Polish media, but we knew from the Western radio. The government newspapers never mentioned the new independent unions, and we had no contact with other areas of the country, because we lived in a small town, without cars.

We discussed the situation in our mine and in the community. We questioned why working and living conditions were deteriorating from poor to worse, and why prices at the stores were growing. My friends and co-workers asked each other, "What is happening in Gdańsk and Jastrzebie? What can we do?"

A small group of miners talked with a factory director. We said, "Give us a car so that we can drive to Jastrzebie, where there is a miners' strike. We want to find out what is happening."

Jastrzebie is located in a large coal-mining area, southwest of my town, toward Katowice and the Czechoslovakia border. Since none of us owned a vehicle, my friends and I asked a factory driver to take us, because we didn't know the way. The trip to Jastrzebie was seventy-five kilometers (fifty miles) on unpaved roads.

When we reached Jastrzebie, the miners' strike was already over. But they had reached an agreement with the government to be allowed to form a new independent trade union. This would be separate from the government-controlled unions, which didn't give the workers any benefits.

We asked the Jastrzebie miners what we could do. They answered, "You can form a new union." We said, "Okay." They gave us ideas, and we went back to Trzebinia and began to organize.

When we told the miners in Trzebinia about the plan for a new union, everybody was excited—except the officials at the mine. [Laughs] They were very angry. They thought that, because our area was isolated, they could keep out new ideas and preserve the Communist union. Around 150,000 people worked in the mines. And there were two large power plants, a huge steel mill, and many smaller factories. Some coal was used to fuel the factories, and the rest went for export.

Solidarity was recognized by the Polish government as an official union in September 1980. It was the first independent union ever in a Communist country. The government was unsure of what was in

Jozef Patyna addressing a Solidarity meeting in Poland

the minds of Polish citizens during the August strikes. So government officials said, "Okay, we'll sign this paper, the Solidarity Charter. Now, everyone go back to work. No more problems." But their plan didn't succeed.

Following the Solidarity certification, my friends and I formed a Solidarity chapter in our coal mine. Workers in the mines feel a strong affinity for Saint Barbara, the patron saint of miners. We prayed to her very much; it is a tradition. There was a portrait of Saint Barbara in the entrance to the underground pit. All three to four thousand miners, who work underground, and two thousand administrators, Communist or non-Communist, pass before this picture each day. They stop before it and quietly pray.

Once, in 1961, a Communist manager took the portrait out of the mine. On that same day, he broke his leg. The people told him, "See, you broke your leg because you took down the portrait of Saint Barbara. She must be in the mine." So the picture was brought back. The Communists never tried to take it down again.

As a Solidarity organizer in my area, the first thing that entered my mind was, "People want to pray to Saint Barbara right now." So, on the holiday of Saint Barbara, in October 1980, our new union organized a ceremony at our mine, attended by ten thousand people.

Everybody was well behaved. The Communists who were observing the ceremony told me, "This day has never been better. We have never seen this many people and the priests with the picture of Saint Barbara." It was a beautiful time for everyone.

The only security for the ten thousand people was the Solidarity organizers—myself and three other people. No problems at all. We only had to remind people, "Be quiet, please. It's Solidarity time, Saint Barbara time." Not only miners and their families attended the ceremony, but also neighbors and friends. The total population of our town was only thirty-five thousand, so almost a third of the local people showed up.

Not only the miners in our area or shipbuilders in Gdańsk, but all segments of Poland's population were in need. Retired seniors had very small pensions. They desperately needed more money to match the high inflation. Many people came to Solidarity. They told us, "I want to become a Solidarity member, too. You go to the government and tell them about my needs."

We demanded a standard five-day work week for miners, with weekends off. Mining work is very strenuous, and the workers need rest and time to maintain the machines. Of course, the government disagreed with the proposal. This was stupid because, when machines are properly maintained, there are fewer breakdowns. And when workers are rested, they work harder and are more productive.

I continued working in coal mines in my area until the Solidarity National Convention in Gdańsk in September 1981. Gdańsk, a northern port city on the Baltic Sea, was Solidarity headquarters.

Each region selected delegates to attend the Convention. I was one of 108 delegates representing Silesia. Nationwide, within one year Solidarity had grown to ten million members [out of Poland's thirty-seven million total population]. Members had to be workers. Farmers had a distinct union associated with Solidarity. Intellectuals from Warsaw, Kraków, and other big cities had related organizations like KOR [Committee for the Defense of Workers], who were invited to attend the Solidarity Convention. They weren't allowed to vote, but they performed an important role as our legal advisers. Solidarity members were mostly ordinary workers who had no political experience. Before each day of the Convention, we went to Mass.

Eleven people plus Lech Walesa were elected to Solidarity's National Commission executive committee. I was one of those elected. I was made the chief of the negotiation department. My job was to intervene in strikes and mediate between workers and government. I signed legal documents for Solidarity headquarters and observed the government's actions. Only when it was necessary for extra leverage would I intercede.

From October 1981, I worked out of Solidarity's headquarters in Gdańsk. It was a crazy, difficult time. When we tried to discuss with government officials various essential needs for people to live better in Poland, the officials disagreed with everything.

For instance, the government opposed Solidarity's proposal for citizens' control of food production. As part of the government's provocation to break the union, many food markets were closed down. Since they controlled the distribution of food, they could cut off any region. The response of the people was, "We need to eat. No food, no work." Strike. Many, many social brush fires broke out. Some people argued whether to take moderate or more forceful action. Lech Walesa and I acted as firemen for the union. We would drive together, going without sleep sometimes. Or we had to go in two separate cars to strike in different regions. When we arrived at the site of major incidents, not only did we have problems with government officials and the police, but there were conflicts within Solidarity itself.

In October and November 1981, there was a big problem in Zielona Góra, in the western part of the country. It was the biggest strike in Poland. The government fired a union activist, which set off a protest strike by 160,000 factory workers and farmers. When I arrived in Zielona Góra, I found that the local Solidarity chapter had much different ideas for dealing with the government than did the union headquarters. Too many workers were on strike, which shut down food and services in the entire region. The government was in no hurry to negotiate, because they didn't care about the people's suffering. And the authorities knew that internal conflicts would destabilize the union. They were hoping we would self-destruct. My role as a mediator was impossible sometimes. And, to make matters more complicated, some police agents infiltrated the union. So we had to be careful about who we trusted.

There were incidents where Solidarity members were roughed up by police. Some of us were arrested and jailed for short periods of time. I had to leave the strike in Zielona Góra to rush to a mine accident in Sosnowiec, in my home region. There was a gas explosion in a mine shaft, trapping many injured miners underground. It was an extremely dangerous situation, because all of the mine's airshafts were contaminated with the gas.

I was driving to the accident site when the police stopped me in

Katowice. They detained me for a few hours as a form of harassment. This type of incident made life even more difficult for my family and me.

KRYSTYNA: When Jozef became involved with union activities, I was supportive, because he was working twenty-four hours every day, either at his job or on union matters. After he moved to Gdańsk, I was like a widow. Our daughter was eleven or twelve years old at the time, and our son was only eight years old. Fortunately, they were in school, while I worked all day at the city hall.

JOZEF: We discussed my union activities. I told Krystyna, "You must forget our family life. It is time for Solidarity. After two years, I will come back. This time is not ours. It belongs to Solidarity."

Many of my friends and their wives talked about their relationship the same way. Our families were very supportive, because we all could feel something new in Poland. We thought, "Personally, we may lose everything. But we must preserve Solidarity."

KRYSTYNA: None of us were sorry about the sacrifices we had to make. If husbands were involved with the union, wives helped each other. I had a friend who lived a few blocks from our home whose husband was also involved in Solidarity. We did whatever we could for each other. Before this time, none of us had ever been involved in politics. We approached it as a very close-knit community.

JOZEF: Personal and community commitment made up for the union's lack of financial and material resources. At Solidarity headquarters in Gdańsk, the entire eleven-member executive committee worked in one room. It was the size of a modest living room in an American home. We had one long table that we all worked at. One telephone to share. One cabinet for our clothes. That was it.

All the while, the room was full of visitors, who came to see us from all over the country. For privacy from government investigators and surveillance devices, we held meetings in restaurants. We would travel by bus to areas of Gdańsk, far away from our headquarters, to avoid the secret police.

The government owns all buildings, so we had to make a formal request and then accept what they gave us as a headquarters office. You can imagine how difficult that was. And the government was able to rig the office with all types of surveillance equipment before we moved in.

Our second-biggest problem was finding apartments for the committee members. Living in a hotel was nearly impossible. Our rooms were constantly searched by the secret police. We never left anything in our rooms.

Besides moderating in regional crises, the union was trying to address basic needs like food distribution. Inflation was continually climbing, and wages were not comparable. And the balance of our country's exports favored the Soviets against the interest of the Polish people.

In mid-November 1981, the Solidarity leadership met in Warsaw for talks with the government about problems like food shortages and rising prices. After ten days, we decided that it was useless to continue the talks. Instead, we decided to campaign for free elections. Change could only come through a truly democratic process. And the February 1982 national elections were just a few months away.

The Communist Party's idea of elections or "democracy" is to give the people a list of candidates, all from the Party, whose ideas are indistinguishable. In contrast, Solidarity's idea was to pursue a true democratic campaign for parliament, city halls, and other local offices, like in the Western countries and Japan.

Opposition candidates would need access to the government-controlled media, so we asked the government for access to mass communication. We asked for press coverage and television and radio time to present our positions to the public.

The Solidarity leadership didn't think of the union as a political party. We wanted the elections to be open to any Polish citizen or political party. After forty years of Communist rule in Poland, we felt that we weren't asking for too much. In fact, the Soviets promised free elections in Poland to the Americans and British as part of the Yalta Agreement at the end of the Second World War. We were just asking the government to grant the Polish people the provisions for self-determination that were guaranteed in the Yalta Treaty.

The Communists were afraid of the ground swell for democratic elections. They knew that they would not only lose control of the people, but they would lose their system of government. And the Russians saw this as the beginning of a larger revolt in Eastern Europe, the Baltic countries, the Ukraine, and other conquered territories within the Soviet Union.

At the end of November, the Soviet general in charge of the Warsaw Pact forces visited the Polish government. Following the Soviet visit, Jaruzelski [Poland's Prime Minister] made a speech threatening "a state of war." We worried that Russian tanks would charge in. There are Russian soldiers stationed in Poland as part of the Warsaw Pact. And we knew that the Soviets were already taking precautionary meas-

ures—Polish soldiers were denied ammunition for their rifles, because
the Russians feared that they would defend Poland if an invasion
occurred. The Soviets feared a widespread national revolt that would
get out of their control. The approaching 1982 national election was
becoming a *de facto* referendum on whether Communism would survive
in Poland.

Those of us in Solidarity's leadership roles remembered very well
what happened in Hungary in 1956 and Czechoslovakia in 1968 when
the Russian army suppressed national movements for freedom. We
understood that we might be imprisoned or die. None of us had any
bodyguards or weapons to protect ourselves.

We were very conscious of the secret police following us and trying
to listen in on our conversations, but we didn't play any tricks on
them. We were very straightforward. We never joked with the government, but the government always tried to trick us.

On the weekend of December 11 and 12, 1981, the National
Commission of Solidarity met in Gdańsk to discuss the campaign for
democratic elections. We heard various opinions from Solidarity
branches around the country of the increasing tension with government officials. Strikes were still occurring intermittently.

We suspected that the government would take strong action against
the union, but we weren't sure what their tactics would be. We
expected some sort of martial law, but Solidarity leaders continued
to attempt discussions with government officials to foster better relations.

On Saturday afternoon, December 12, the governor of Gdańsk
sent a letter to Solidarity. He gave us information about a new headquarters for the union. Everyone was happy. We said, "Ah, yes. Very
good. Now everything will be better." We didn't know our "new
location" would be the police jail.

That night I couldn't sleep. In my hotel room, three friends and I
sat up talking about events at the National Commission conference.
Two of the people were friends from our Solidarity headquarters office
and a woman Solidarity delegate from Warsaw. At 3:00 A.M., we had
no idea that the government had declared a "state of war." Our hotel
was surrounded by police.

The police broke into my room and took us to the Gdańsk police
jail. After a few hours, in the early morning, they took us to Strzebielinek [Chebeeleeneck]. I was among forty prisoners from Solidarity
headquarters. We were surrounded by some two hundred police with

guns and dogs. We were confined in a prison fenced in by electric wires. One of the union members in our group said, "It is finished. Not only Solidarity, but our lives as well."

I can honestly tell you that many of us felt the same fear as this friend. But none of us cried or openly talked about it. It was like being in a school, reflecting on our lives—what we'd been doing and what we would do if we survived. It was not heroes' time. We were nervous. But happy at the same time. Do you know why? Because we were *together*.

The state of war was a big shock for all of Poland. The government demonstrated brute power. General Jaruzelski's forces killed coal miners in Katowice, and other people in the streets of many cities. For twenty-four hours, on December 13, telephones were shut off throughout all of Poland. Solidarity had organized many labor strikes during the year it was legalized. But Jaruzelski showed how to *really* make a strike.

The Russians were definitely involved. We had much information about Russian soldiers in Polish uniforms. During the previous year, we received information from textile workers who were making Polish army uniforms, which were being sent to the Soviet Union. And after the "state of war" was declared, the Polish government pasted Russian documents written in Polish on walls in the streets.

KRYSTYNA: After I received word that Jozef had been arrested in Gdańsk, I tried to find him. The government issued a statement: "If anyone wishes to find your husband, brother, or anyone from your family who has been arrested, you must go to the police station nearest to where you live."

I went to the police station at Katowice a few times, because it was the largest in our area. I joined many women who were looking for their husbands. We stood in front of the gate to the jail. It was snowing. That was a very cold winter, around ten to fifteen degrees below zero. We stood outside for hours, but the police didn't give us any information. They always said, "Come back in a few days. Maybe we will know something then. Your husband isn't here."

I was fired from my job at the city hall. I found another job as a clerk at a garbage-collection and street-sweeping plant, where they dumped all the garbage bags. Like everything else, it was owned by the government. I took a salary cut at that job. My children were only eight and twelve years old. It was hard to get food. Even to buy bread, I had to stand in long lines.

The police declared curfew between 8:00 P.M. and 6:00 in the morning. In the afternoon, as curfew time approached, the police went to the store lines and took women to work at their station all night. The women had to wash floors and windows in order to reclaim their place in line the following morning.

The police continually harassed me by taking me to the police station. They asked about my husband's activities. I had to leave my children alone at home to attend the interrogation sessions. I knew other wives who were actually jailed. I asked to visit my husband. Sometimes the police responded by yelling at me and giving more harassment.

I had no word from Jozef until the end of December, when I received a letter. I immediately wrote to the authorities in Gdańsk. A week later, I received a response with my husband's location. The next day, January 8, 1982, I got on a train and went to see him. It's a long trip from the southern part of the country to the far north, where Jozef was imprisoned. It took two days by train.

I arrived in the north during a very big snowstorm. The road to the prison was closed, because snowdrifts were more than six feet high. There was no communication—everything was closed. The local people told me, "You will have to stay in a hotel overnight. There is no way to get to that place."

I woke early the next morning, worried that I wouldn't find a way to get to the prison. I went into the street and met two men driving a snowplow truck. They were clearing the road that led to the prison. I told them where I was going, and they were kind enough to take me with them.

Strzebielinek Prison is located on a lake between Gdańsk and the Baltic Sea. It was even colder because of the closeness of the water. As we came near to the prison, the men told me, "We can't go with you to that place. You have to walk."

I got out of the truck and began walking through a forest on a narrow path. It was like a tunnel between two high walls of snow. I carried a basket of food for my husband. Oh, my God! I was freezing and the path was slippery.

On the trail I met a man, a stranger. He asked where I was going. I said, "To the prison." He knew about what was going on, and told me, "Last week they took some prisoners out from the prison and drove them someplace. Nobody knows where." I thought, "Could my husband be one of them?"

JOZEF: The previous week, the government took thirteen prisoners— who were my friends from Solidarity—out of Strzebielinek and moved them to a larger prison, near Warsaw. On the same day that my wife came to visit me, at around 2:00 P.M., some police took me and three friends to Katowice jail.

KRYSTYNA: We were very lucky. I was able to see Jozef for an hour that morning. We had no idea that the authorities would be moving him out of the prison a few hours later. I might have come all that way for nothing.

JOZEF: To see my wife was very special. A policeman told me, "Mr. Patyna, don't call me a Red. I am good to you and your Solidarity friends. I will allow you a half-hour longer to be with your wife." I said, "Okay, no problem. Thank you very much."

A few hours after my wife said goodbye, policemen took three friends and me to police headquarters in Gdańsk. We arrived before dark. Inside the jail we met another friend from Solidarity, Vacek Adamczak. It was an old jail. Oh! It smelled so terrible that we couldn't sleep. The following day we continued our journey.

We arrived in Katowice jail after dark. The police took us into a small room where we had to take off all of our clothes. We were naked and guarded by six policemen. My friend was called first for interrogation. I was a little nervous, because I didn't know what had happened to him. When I entered the interrogation room, my worst fears were confirmed.

Like all of the other prisoners, I was beaten by the police. They used their hands, feet, and a hard rubber baton. I tried to put up my hands to shield my head from their blows.

The police spoke to us using very hard language. They said, "You, Patyna. You don't like Communism. I will give you Communism now." And they proceeded to beat me.

After interrogation, we were put in a cell together. We were too afraid to talk. My entire body was bruised. Time became abstract, because we had no watches or clocks inside the jail. And we were afraid for our lives. My friends and I were all tortured. The police told us, "We will kill you."

Katowice police headquarters is like a fortress. Three levels of the building are underground and five floors aboveground. It is the biggest building in the region. While the building was being constructed, Solidarity asked the government to change it into a hospital and clinic. But the police moved in after the Bydgoszcz crisis in March 1981, which was the first major incident where police violently broke up a Solidarity meeting and badly beat up union members. In response, the country's workers went to the verge of a general strike. From that time, the Katowice police hated Solidarity members.

My friends and I were the first Solidarity members brought to this jail. But after we arrived, more union members were brought in and beaten. I prayed to Saint Barbara. She is not only the patron of coal miners, but also for prisoners, because she was imprisoned for her faith.

KRYSTYNA: It was very difficult to get permission from the authorities to visit Jozef in Katowice jail. I went with my daughter, Magdalena, who was eleven years old. The guards only allowed us ten minutes to talk with Jozef. And a woman officer wrote down everything we said. My daughter started to cry when she saw her father. The woman told her, "If you cry, I will stop this visit."

Jozef had noticeably lost weight. He was skinnier and had a beard. He looked very different with long hair.

JOZEF: I had a book with me in jail that I had bought the day before I was arrested. When my wife came to visit me in Katowice, I gave her the book. The police didn't know what was inside. I didn't even tell Krystyna.

The book was titled *Parasol*, which was the name of an underground resistance group in Warsaw during the Second World War. Inside the book, I put the Solidarity stamps that we made in each prison cell. And on the borders of the book's pages, I wrote a brief diary of what was happening in each prison. My friends from the union wrote their signatures in the book, too, and a little poetry.

KRYSTYNA: I was going back home in the train. I opened up the book and saw what was inside. I thought, "Oh, my God." If the police had caught me with this, I would've been put in jail. [Laughs] But it was important at that time to get the information out.

At home, we lived in a small city where everybody knows everyone else. The community is very close-knit. So, while Jozef was a political prisoner, the children's teachers did not act in a hostile manner toward them. However, children whose parents were involved in Solidarity will always have a government file. They will be discriminated against the rest of their lives.

JOZEF: In the community my name was well known because I was a union leader. So, when I was a political prisoner, many people tried to help my family, and the church was also very kind.

I was held in Katowice jail until February 15, when we were moved to Zaborzyce (Zobzha) jail. We were mixed in with criminals, who gave us a very rough time. It was part of the government's strategy to break us psychologically.

In Katowice, three prisoners lived in fifteen square feet. But in Zaborzyce, sixteen prisoners were fitted into a cell that size. We had no fresh air, no mattress. We slept on the floor in our clothes. The toilet was in the cell.

In March, I was hospitalized because of a problem with my heart. I was pretty ill. The authorities terminated my jail sentence in July 1982, but I remained in the hospital until August.

When I came home to Trzebinia, Solidarity was already underground, but we still had activities. I wasn't permitted to work by the government, because of my background, so I traveled around the country for the union, meeting with many people. The secret police were watching me all the time. Their reason for not stopping my travel was that they hoped to gain information by observing who I met with. I only met openly with friends who were already being watched by police. There was no way that I could meet anyone secretly.

After each meeting, the police would call my friends and me to their headquarters and ask, "Why did you meet this person?" We would say, "Because I like this person. He is my friend."

Was my wife upset about what I was doing? [Laughs] Krystyna worried but never complained. She knew that everything I did was for Solidarity. It was a very crazy time. The police continued to arrest some of our friends. But our personal safety was secondary to the concern we had for the Polish people. Sometimes I was afraid. After having been in prison and beaten by police, I knew that I wasn't immune to punishment. But there was work that had to be done.

During February and March 1983 were the third Solidarity Union elections. It was so different from the 1981 Convention, because we had to meet with delegates in their homes. We prepared documents that were sent to Pope John Paul II, the Polish Parliament, and the International Labor Organization at the United Nations headquarters in Geneva.

These acts were a very important statement by Solidarity and a great embarrassment to the government. Because, even though they followed and investigated us all the time, we were able to prepare the documents and get more than eight hundred signatures from around the entire country.

The documents had to be hand-carried from one friend to another, at a time when the government was keeping a tight rein on all of us. The authorities had to ask themselves, "How did they do that?"

Although some Solidarity leaders were still in jail under harsh sentences, Lech Walesa was freed and still the Solidarity leader. I met with him a few times during 1983. The first time was after New Year, in Gdańsk. The next times were during June, around the time of the Pope's visit to Poland. An important memory for me is the Pope's Mass at Częstochowa [Chestohova]. Around two million people attended the service, and there was a great outpouring of support for the Solidarity Union. I was there with my daughter.

The monastery in Częstochowa, where the shrine of the Black Madonna is located, is the center of Polish faith and history. She saved Poland from the invasion by the Vikings hundreds of years ago. The Pope's visit there in 1983 was an important and incredible experience for the Polish people.

Pilgrims from our town walked fifty kilometers to see the Pope in Kraków. We held a long banner that said, "God gave power for you and the Polish people." The police took the banner away from us. They were afraid that the sign looked like a Solidarity statement.

Underground newspapers printed everything about the Pope's visit that was censored in the government newspapers. Solidarity ran an underground paper in my region. Weekly editions were made with a small copy machine. The print was very light, but it kept people informed and hope alive.

I wanted to stay in Poland, but I was afraid for my family. The police broke down my friend's door and beat everyone . . . wife, kids. They asked no questions. They just beat the family up, then walked out.

Other men and their wives were arrested at their homes and taken away. The police left small children inside the home alone by themselves for a few days until the parents were released from jail. It was a difficult time. Nobody is sure how many people were killed—maybe sixty, maybe more.

I decided to leave the country toward the end of 1983. I came to that decision after traveling around the country for a few months and talking with friends who were living in the same circumstances as I. Though Lech Walesa was still influential, other friends and I knew that our time in Poland was over. We had so many police problems that we were no longer effective. And we risked endangering people by meeting with them, especially underground Solidarity members. So we decided to look after our children's futures.

My family and I needed official permission to leave Poland. The secret police control the issuing of passports. But we were fortunate that the American embassy in Warsaw agreed to accept us to the United States. The American government had a program that allowed Solidarity members to immigrate, and other governments, like France, Canada, West Germany, and Switzerland, made the same offer.

We left Poland on December 14, 1983. We were first flown to West Germany, where we stayed for only one week. The German government provided a special hotel for Solidarity refugees. All of us rested before flying to the United States.

I told American officials that we would like to live in a small city. We were afraid to live in a big place. Our greatest obstacle was that we didn't speak any English.

KRYSTYNA: We had never heard of Providence, Rhode Island. We knew a little about New England, but we had no idea where Rhode Island was. We felt completely disoriented when we arrived. It was a sad time for us. In Poland, Christmas eve is like American Thanksgiving. It was the first time in my life that I felt so far away. Alone in our apartment, we felt cut off from the world.

Without a car, we had to walk to the store. It didn't seem so far to get there. But, carrying shopping bags in the middle of winter, it seemed a lot longer walking back. [Laughs]

JOZEF: We survived. [Laughs]

KRYSTYNA: Besides needing food, we didn't have anything in the kitchen to eat with. We had to buy silverware, dishes, and cooking materials, too. Nobody took us to the market to show us how to compare food prices, and we couldn't read English or speak the language to ask questions in the stores. Our sponsor one time drove us to Star Market, which is more expensive than other stores. Fortunately, we had brought enough clothes from Poland.

JOZEF: To be honest with you, the first month here, we were hungry much of the time. Only $110 the four of us had to live on for three weeks! Our sponsor was unbelievable. We came from a culture in Poland, not a jungle. I can't imagine the problems with sponsors that refugees from non-Western societies have when they arrive here.

KRYSTYNA: In the factory where we work, there are many Cambodian people. They live very close together and help each other. I admire that. I didn't see the same type of relationship among Polish people here.

JOZEF: Last week, we saw a television program about Cambodian people in Providence. I felt very sorry for them. They've been settled in a bad neighborhood near downtown. It's very callous of relief agencies, a form of discrimination. Even though there are rules against discrimination in the American Constitution, it is there in everyday life. The newcomers always have to struggle, unless they come by their own choice with a lot of money.

We found out that the owner of our building was a Polish American. And there were some Polish people in the neighborhood. But nobody volunteered to help us. I did not want to ask anyone, "Hey, help me." To beg is no good.

In Poland, we were used to neighbors' and friends' volunteering to help each other. Especially during the Solidarity movement, people were very close. We came here and found that everyone only looks out for their own interests.

At the time, our feelings were hurt. But, looking back, my wife and I are very happy, because we helped ourselves. Everything we now have came from our own work.

KRYSTYNA: It took us two weeks to get situated in our apartment because of the holiday season. As soon as our children were in school we immediately began looking for a job.

JOZEF: The factory where we found work was just a five-minute walk from our apartment. For the first few months we couldn't speak English, so we couldn't really communicate with other workers. We used hand signals. And there wasn't time to speak. Everybody was busy on their machines.

After three months of working, we saved enough money to buy a secondhand car. I asked a friend to go with me to the used-car lot, because I had no experience with American cars. I paid cash. Krystyna and I didn't know anything about credit at the time—nobody told us. I went to the car lot while Krystyna was shopping with her friends. When she came home, she was so surprised to see the car sitting in front of our building. [Laughs] It's the same car we drive today. I've tried to keep it in good condition.

KRYSTYNA: Now I've learned to drive, too. Jozef's brother wrote us a letter after he heard that we bought a car after just a few months in the U.S. It seemed unbelievable to him. In Poland, very few people own cars. They usually live a short distance from where they work and travel by bus. But for Americans personal mobility is a very strong trait. The car is very symbolic of America. In Eastern Europe, if someone has a car, people say, "He is very rich."

JOZEF: An average Polish worker has a hard time owning a car, because gasoline is very expensive. It's ironic, because Poland has oil under the ground and they could transform the coal. But the Russians don't permit Poland to have it—they want Poland dependent on them.

At the factory, my wife and I started out working second shift. But last August, I changed to first shift, from 8:00 A.M. until 4:00 P.M. Krystyna still goes in at 3:00 P.M. and gets home around midnight. It was difficult when we both worked that shift, because we could only spend time with our children on weekends.

From the time we left Poland, we told the children, "You must study to have a chance in this country. There is no chance for us— we are too old to study. You must try hard in school for your own benefit."

Our daughter, Magdalena, started school here in the tenth grade. At first she was frustrated, because she didn't know English. Fortunately, the quality of education where we lived in Poland was equivalent to Providence.

Our son, Shem, finished fourth grade in Poland, so they started him in fifth grade here. But after just two months, he was promoted to sixth grade. People coming from Poland now are not stupid. The level of education in Polish schools is higher than in America. But it is nearly impossible for students to enter a university there. That is the greatest difference between the two societies.

Education is free in Poland, but there are still expenses. Parents must give university students money for food, rent, and books. With the standard of living so poor, these types of expenses are a great burden on most families. And though the level of high-school mathematics is very high, the young people have no opportunity to use that knowledge. Poland doesn't have much technology.

Our children began school here during the winter-spring semester of 1984. The following semester, in September 1984, Shem advanced to a junior high school. After two months, he passed a special test and was placed in advanced classes for gifted students. This year, he graduated from the gifted program. He passed another series of difficult tests that earned him entrance into Classical High School, which is considered the best in Rhode Island. It is very difficult for students to keep up with the study program there, but my son enjoys the challenge.

Shem likes his teachers and has made some very good friends. Kids who attend Classical come from all areas of Providence. There are Cambodian students, too. The kids from Asia are very smart. They live in poor and dangerous areas, but their parents encourage them to study, just like we do with our children.

Magdalena is now a freshman at Boston College. She receives a partial scholarship, and is studying nursing. But we also must pay $2,000 a year. That's a lot of money for us, but we are very proud of her.

KRYSTYNA: Our son is only fourteen years old, but he's very tall for his age. Jozef is six foot one, and Shem is already taller than him. In the past year, he's sprouted up from short and fat to tall and thin. I think that children in America eat better and take more vitamins than kids in Poland. But the greatest health improvement for us is the quality of air. It's so fresh here, living close to the ocean.

During our first year in Providence, we lived in three different apartments. The first neighborhood was like a slum. So we looked for a better place for our kids. Our first apartment was in such poor condition. As soon as we started working we put in new rugs, new wallpaper, painted the ceilings. We made the apartment look like new. The landlord never reimbursed us for the materials or the work, which is required by law. Instead, he raised our rent $40 more each month. That was a lot for us, because our combined wages were only $300 a week. So, after five months we decided to move into a building across the street.

JOZEF: Our second apartment building was like a temporary hotel, with rooms too small for us. But we had very nice Polish neighbors. Our landlord was an old man, more than seventy, and very kind. He charged very low rent. When I fixed up the apartment, he wouldn't accept our rent money for two months. I put in new wallpaper, painted everything, cleaned all the floors.

We stayed in that place through spring and summer. In August, a friend found a larger apartment for us in Providence. We had the upstairs of a large house owned by a very nice Polish-American family with three children. We paid only $180 a month. Small rooms like in Poland, but the kids had their own bedrooms. The only problem was that we didn't have central heating, and in the winter it was too cold. Krystyna and I wanted very much to buy our own house.

We settled into our jobs at the factory as a regular routine. We began attending English classes at the International Institute, located in a Methodist church. The first year, our teacher spoke very fast, and we didn't have enough time to practice our lessons. We had class from 9:00 A.M. until noon, five days a week. We'd come home and have a small lunch, then be at work by three o'clock, come home around midnight. We'd go to bed, then wake up by 7:00 A.M. and prepare for school. The only time we had with our kids was on the weekend.

Our second year of classes was much better. Our teacher was from India but was educated in a British school. She understood our problems. When students couldn't keep up with a lesson, she would repeat it so that everyone could understand. The students came from many different countries: Japan, Brazil, Portugal, Haiti, Latin America, and Eastern Europe. There were so many beginning students waiting to get into the school that, after our second year, the Institute cut our intermediate program.

KRYSTYNA: English is still awkward for us. When someone comes to visit our home, we use a Polish-English dictionary to find words. I always hope that people don't laugh at my speech.

JOZEF: We are thinking of applying at the International House for their English classes. It's at Brown University, which is just a short drive from our home. The classes are taught by Brown students and retired teachers and only cost $15 a month. Now I'm trying to learn on my own, by reading a book a few days each week.

KRYSTYNA: Our children became American in their attitude very quickly, because of their friends. When you hear them speak English, they have already lost their Polish accent. But in the house we talk Polish with them so they don't forget the language and Polish culture. That is very important to us.

JOZEF: We brought a big wooden crate of books from Poland, some literature and poetry. We have a large photo book of Kraków, a book of Polish paintings, books about Pope John Paul II . . . just souvenirs of our country. They will be good for our grandchildren to know where we came from.

Special to me is a book about Solidarity. Even now, though I am thousands of miles away from the coal mines, I still pray to Saint Barbara.

On our bedroom wall is a painting of the Black Madonna by a friend of ours in Poland. There is a painting of the Pope on our living-room wall, with a Polish eagle on his chair. The eagle is the symbol of Poland, just like the U.S.A. — Americans have the bald eagle, Poles have the white eagle.

For most Catholics here, the role of the church is secondary in their lives, a one-hour-a-week obligation. In Poland, the priests had an important role in our struggle for freedom. They served as intermediaries in the community, because they knew many people. Those of us in Solidarity knew that we could trust them. In Providence, we invited a priest to visit our house only one time, to bless our home after we first moved in.

We bought this house in February 1985. We decided it was better to pay off a mortgage for ourselves then rent to a landlord. I got into our car and drove around this neighborhood, looking at houses for sale. We liked this area, because it was near high school for Shem and Magdalena. We wanted a good place for the children to grow up. Magdalena only lived here for one year before going away to college, but it was a good year for her. She will have good memories about our family and a home that she can always return to.

When we decided on this house, my friend brought me to a lawyer's office and to the bank. In Poland there isn't lending from banks like here, where you can do so much on credit.

We didn't have to do much work on the house when we moved in. The wood floors are very nice. We only had to sand and refinish them. And I did a little painting.

KRYSTYNA: We changed the kitchen around. The cabinets are all new. We did that ourselves. We believe that the kitchen is the most important place in the house.

JOZEF: The next job will be the bathroom floors. We can find enough to keep us busy around here. [Laughs] The house was empty when we moved in.

KRYSTYNA: We didn't even have a bed to sleep on.

JOZEF: Right away, we bought some furniture from people on the next street. For $150 we bought two bedroom sets, a coffee table, end tables, a few lamps. When I brought the furniture home, we felt like very rich people.

In the living room we have a mantel and fireplace that we haven't used yet. During the winter, for heat we pay for oil. And now that we are working different shifts, we need to buy a second car.

KRYSTYNA: If we send a photo of our house back to Poland, people will think that we are very rich. And to own a car is special. They see us dressed nice. They think that we are in heaven and that it's very easy to get rich in America. They don't understand how hard we work, and how we sacrifice to save money.

The value of money is relative to the country you live in. In our factory, starting salary is now $4 an hour, or $32 a day. That would be an entire month's salary in Poland for an experienced worker. When Polish tourists come to America, they try to work during their vacation. They return to Poland rich. With one American dollar you can buy two pounds of ham. That's equivalent to eight hours of hard work in the coal mines.

JOZEF: We want to invite my brothers to come here. (Krystyna doesn't have any brothers or sisters. Her mother is sixty-two years old.) But we can't afford to sponsor anybody. We would have to send them money for airplane tickets, but we are just able to afford house payments and bills and our children are still in school. We have enough problems trying to provide for this family. But I cannot forget Solidarity Union. . . . It is my union always.

KRYSTYNA: In this country, it is very complicated to pay taxes. Last year, we tried to fill out the forms ourselves, but we didn't know how to deduct property-owner taxes and mortgage. We don't know how the new tax law will affect us, because our combined income is not very much—not even $40,000.

JOZEF: We cannot even afford to put aside money for a private retirement plan. Where we work, very little is given for retirement. Now, what money we can save is put aside for our children's education.

Magdalena comes home from Boston College on some weekends. But she can't come often, because she has to spend a lot of time studying. Nursing is very demanding. And she is helping herself by working part-time at a nursing home.

Shem says that he would like to go to Brown University. We'll see. He's just starting high school this year. Living in America, he is more independent than boys his age in Poland. But he spends a lot of time studying. For fun, he plays sports, like basketball, after school. And he's learning about responsibility by working in a neighbor's Italian restaurant a couple of days each week, washing dishes. That's a good start for him to learn about working.

KRYSTYNA: High-school students don't take jobs in Poland. Nobody will hire them, because there are few private businesses. You must be eighteen years old to find a job. Even if the parents manage a government clothing or food store, very seldom do their young children help them. In America this is much different. We don't mention that Shem is working when we write to our parents. They would think, "Oh, the poor child. He is much too young to go to work."

JOZEF: Out of the $30 to $40 Shem makes each week, he is learning to budget his own pocket money. He has a savings account. He only takes out a few dollars for bus tickets and small things he needs.

We've had a few hard knocks, but we like living in Providence very much. When our friend from Solidarity, Vacek Adamczak, visited us

from New York, he said, "I can't live here. There is nothing happening." It's quiet. That's good. We love it. Providence is a good place
to raise a family.

We aren't afraid about the next day or what will happen with the
police. But we have no close friends here. We miss our relatives and
our lifelong friends from our town. In Poland, you can visit friends
without having to telephone beforehand. American people really guard
their privacy.

In Poland, we spent many nights staying up and talking with our
friends. Especially during Solidarity time, we would prepare some
food and talk into the night. That was the best time. In the morning,
some people would go to work. And whoever didn't have to work
would go to bed. [Laughs]

KRYSTYNA: I think that it makes my husband very happy to have the
opportunity to talk with you. For the first time in a long while, he
has somebody who is interested in the subject of Solidarity. . . .

JOZEF: Driving around Providence, you will see a lot of people with
stickers on their car fenders. Spanish people like to put "I love Jesus."
I only have a "Solidarnosc" sticker. And now we have a Boston College
sticker.

KRYSTYNA: We are very proud that our daughter attends that school.

JOZEF: We bought the Solidarity sticker here. If people put such a sign
in their window in Poland, they would be in a lot of trouble. You
can be jailed for two years for such a sign.

It's kind of ironic that, after working so hard for a union in Poland,
the factory where we work here doesn't have a union. It's an entirely
different situation here.

I have attended Solidarity support meetings in the United States.
From what I have seen, people mean well, but they don't understand
what Solidarity needs. People who attend these meetings might spend
a combined $10,000 on travel. Is that helpful to Solidarity Union?
Solidarity's work has to be done inside of Poland, not outside.

For $200 I could buy the best typewriter and send it underground
to Solidarity members in Poland who need it. For $1,000 I could buy
a copy machine. When I talk about this, I get very frustrated. I can
do nothing for Poland now.

I cannot say that I am happy to have left Poland. The aspirations
of our people still persist. Even though Solidarity has been driven
underground, activity is still going on. It will continue for many years
to come.

KRYSTYNA: My husband fought very hard to have the government give the miners a five-day work week, with two days off. Now we work in the factory here without a union. But there is no comparison with the working conditions, wages, and standard of living in Poland. Food and clothing are much more accessible here. We own a car and a home; people only dream of these things in Poland. The opportunity for the children to have a good education and advance in society is tremendous.

JOZEF: I am loyal to both the United States and Poland. I don't see any problem with my double loyalty, because freedom in the United States affects freedom in Poland. And the situation in Poland affects freedom in Western Europe and the United States.

Before World War II, when Hitler and Stalin made the pact to invade Poland, many people in the West tried to pretend that it didn't matter. They said, "It won't affect us. That's their problem." The world is a small place. I feel depressed that the struggle is still going on in Poland and I am not there. But if I was there, I could not do much, because of the secret police. And I had no job to even help my own family.

Krystyna and I have decided that we will spend the rest of our lives in this country. This is our second homeland. Spring and autumn in New England are beautiful. We have gone for drives along the coast, up to Cape Cod. This past year, we took a trip to Plymouth Rock.

KYSTYNA: We are thinking that, after our children are on their own, we will sell this house and buy something smaller.

JOZEF: Our dream is that, when we retire, we'll buy a camper-trailer and travel around the United States.

TRADITION

Tesfai and Lem Lem Gebremariam
Refugees from Eritrea Province, Ethiopia
Medical Technician and Hotel Chambermaid
Hyattsville, Maryland

In the parking lot of a low-income apartment complex on the outskirts of Washington, D.C., children full of after-school energy are roller-skating and jumping rope. Although many of the children are black Americans, some have light caramel-colored skin and angular Caucasian features. They speak an ancient language, Tigrinya, which they brought from the Eritrean highlands of the Horn of Africa.

Their legends tell them that they are descendants of the biblical marriage of King Solomon and the Queen of Sheba. And they are survivors. Many of their kin are among millions of human skeletons slowly dying of thirst, starvation, and war in the infernal desert wastelands of Ethiopia.

Eritrea, the northernmost of Ethiopia's fourteen provinces, is among the territories most severely affected by drought. And for more than twenty-five years, the mountainous Mississippi-sized territory of four million people has endured Africa's longest-running war.

In 1962, landlocked Ethiopia forcefully annexed Eritrea for its 620-mile coast on the Red Sea, which straddles the oil-shipping lane between the Suez Canal and the Indian Ocean. Ethiopia's Emperor Haile Selassie abolished Eritrea's native languages and flag, and this sparked an armed revolt.

Fighting in Eritrea was sporadic until Ethiopian army officers overthrew the aging Emperor in 1974. A Marxist junta calling itself the Derge (which means "Committee" in the dominant Amharic language) initiated a brutal campaign to collectivize the empire's farms and businesses. Most Ethiopians, who are devout Coptic Christians or Moslems, attempted to maintain their traditions. The Derge responded with a massive bloodbath.

In 1977, an Ethiopian colonel, Mengistu Haile Mariam, shot his way to power. He then declared a "Red Terror" campaign. The Derge's forces slaughtered thousands, especially professionals educated in the West.

Resistance movements grew, not just in Eritrea but in many provinces—each separated by ethnicity and culture (some eighty languages are spoken in Ethiopia). By 1978, when Soviets and Cubans arrived to save the embattled Derge, Eritrea was controlled by two tenacious rebel forces. Their leaders had, ironically, been previously trained and assisted by the Soviet bloc when Ethiopia was allied to the West. In gratitude, the Derge gave the Soviets naval bases on the Eritrean coast.

In subsequent years, collectivization, military offensives, and natural disasters have decimated a once-prosperous land. A million people are estimated to have perished, and two million have fled. In late 1987, neighboring Sudan still housed seven hundred thousand refugees. With another cycle of drought and pestilence beginning in northern Ethiopia and Sudan seething with its own economic and social problems, refugees are caught in a damaging crossfire.

Prior to the 1974 coup, there were no Ethiopian communities in the United States. The few Ethiopians living here as students or diplomats or working in international organizations were given temporary asylum. Since 1977, the U.S. has resettled a small number of Ethiopian refugees each year directly from Africa, mostly from the educated elite (only five percent of the population have a high-school education). Approximately fifty thousand Ethiopians are scattered throughout the United States. The largest communities are in California, Washington, D.C., Texas, and New York.

Washington, D.C., has become a center for Ethiopian culture. The area's fifteen thousand Ethiopians, who are drawn from the empire's major tribes, have established close to twenty restaurants, a couple of social clubs, and at least five churches representing Coptic, Catholic, and Protestant sects.

Although they come from a rigid social system, the Ethiopians are adapting. Starting at the bottom of the job ladder—driving cabs, busing restaurant tables, cleaning hotels, and servicing retirement homes—they are gaining job experience as they improve their English and attend night classes.

In order to maintain traditions and a feeling of home, Ethiopian refugees have settled in clusters around the Washington area. In this U-shaped apartment complex in the Hyattsville suburb where Eritrean children play with black Americans and other refugee children, from Vietnam and Cambodia, I visited a number of Eritrean families.

Tesfai and his wife, Lem Lem Gebremariam, former guerrillas in the mountains of Eritrea, live in a one-bedroom ground-floor apartment. Lem Lem, age twenty-four, a tall and attractive woman with shoulder-length raven-black hair, is exhausted after a long day of work as a hotel chambermaid. She keeps a watchful mother's eye on her year-old Jerome, wobbly in a thick diaper, who is making his own music with teaspoons on the coffee table. Five-year-old Adiam, in a powder-blue dress and red tights, is sitting on the floor quietly drawing with colored pens.

Tesfai, age thirty-one, is a nurse's assistant at a psychiatric hospital, and he attends technical classes, hoping to graduate to a more promising career. On the wall above us, a woven straw African disk with a concentric red-and-white star decor hangs between two crossed ceremonial hunting spears. Across the room, a seductive album portrait of the rock singer Madonna is perched on a wooden shelf above the stereo system.

We watch a brilliant television documentary on the East African savanna. Herds of wildebeests and elegant giraffes gracefully stampede in billowing clouds of dust. In the cover of tall grass, lions stalk their prey. Tesfai remembers similar areas in Ethiopia *before the Derge and the drought. His words are filled with energy and emotion. When he pauses in the midst of a story, Lem Lem continues his train of thought.*

TESFAI: In my village, I can trace my family back almost twenty grand-fathers. They descended from the man who originally camped on the land. Their sons and grandsons all married and raised their families in the same village area.

As a boy, I helped my father on the farm. We had two oxen to pull the plow in our field. Our enemies were wild animals. If we left any livestock outside after dark, hyenas would attack them. Foxes liked to kill lambs and baby goats. I carried a big stick to chase the wild animals away.

To work the land is very hard. Since we were surrounded by mountains, the way we made fertilizer was to break stones and crush the rocks into powder. We mixed this with the wastes from cattle. This is how we grew most of our food.

Eritreans don't like to take assistance from society. It is no shame to be helped by your brothers or sisters, but to depend on outsiders is like being a beggar. Your family will be shamed.

We arrived in Washington, D.C., from the refugee camps in Sudan in August 1984. My wife was five months pregnant with our youngest child. Right away, we asked friends how to find work. We said, "If there is a job available, we will do it."

LEM LEM: The second week we were here, the Convention Center hired us. For six days, Tesfai and I worked together, busing tables. After that, I found a full-time job at the Ramada Inn. But, three months later, I had to stop working when the baby was born. The children were too young for me to be away from them.

TESFAI: At that time, we had to take public assistance for the family, because we couldn't afford to pay the $4,000 or $5,000 hospital bill. We didn't have insurance, and I was attending a medical-assistant training program without bringing home a paycheck. This caused great conflict. I told myself, "We need to take the money to pay the rent. But if we take it, I feel completely worthless."

Immediately after finishing my training, I found a job at Saint Elizabeth Psychiatric Hospital. My job has been to take care of the more than one hundred Cubans who came during the Mariel boatlift. They are kept in a separate part of the hospital, because they need a lot of help. Some are very tough guys, some are crazy. Many were criminals—some were thieves, others were into drugs. Some killed people.

It's ironic that in Eritrea, for many years, my wife and I were fighting for our freedom against Cuban soldiers. Now that we have freedom in this country, I am taking care of Cubans. And even though I didn't have time to take advanced English classes, I was sent to Spanish classes by the hospital.

Now, most days I attend medical-laboratory-technician classes in Washington from 8:00 A.M. until 2:20 in the afternoon. Then I get into my car and drive for a half-hour to Saint Elizabeth Hospital. I work until 11:30 P.M. By midnight I am home.

It's very difficult to live this way. But my wife and I don't have any second thoughts about our jobs. We have rent to pay and two young children. Our baby, Jerome, is fourteen months. And our daughter, Adiam, started kindergarten this year. She is very American. When we arrived here, she was only three years old, so she doesn't know much about Ethiopia. She plays with American children and speaks perfect English. When we go to the shopping center, we don't know some foods. Adiam tells us everything, because she sees them advertised on TV.

LEM LEM: Now that the baby is a little older, I'm back at the Ramada Inn doing housekeeping. And some evenings I work part-time at the Westin Hotel. Two jobs, twelve hours a day. It's very hard being on my feet all that time.

TESFAI: She is also trying to attend English classes and to complete her high-school equivalency. Lem Lem was just a young teen-ager when she had to flee her parents' home in Asmara to escape the Derge's soldiers. Even before she escaped, schools were closed, because the Derge were killing and arresting students.

Since the Derge took power, thousands of refugees have fled Eritrea. The United States accepts relatively few people from Ethiopia each year. But there are ten times that many Eritreans in Sudan who need to be resettled.

I know some people who were rejected by American immigration officers and killed themselves on the same day. They made up their minds that they had to live in America. They failed the immigration hearing because the [Eritrean resistance] Fronts had also fought against the previous Ethiopian regime, which the U.S. supported. So these rejected refugees went off and committed suicide. They didn't have any alternatives.

LEM LEM: Most Ethiopians accepted to the United States are from the cities and have some schooling. Many poor farmers from Eritrea can't flee to Sudan, because the Derge army blocks their escape. Even when some of these people do manage to reach Sudan, they refuse to leave Africa. They still feel very connected to their land and families they left behind. They say, "If we go to America, we are lost."

TESFAI: The people who come from cities like Asmara have European influence. The Italians dominated Eritrea from 1890 until World War II. Then we had self-rule as an autonomous province until 1962. And until 1977 the U.S. Navy had a base very near Asmara. The Americans were well liked. Some Eritreans worked on the base. And Americans came to bars in the city. A lot of the music we heard on the radio was disco music, like Aretha Franklin and James Brown.

LEM LEM: Many Eritreans who escaped to Sudan are Christians, who don't feel comfortable in a Moslem country. Refugee life is especially hard for women. In Asmara, we dressed similar to Americans. Countryside women wear traditional white dresses with embroidered designs. But in Sudan, all women must be covered head to toe like Moslems and wear shawls over their faces. Men are always shouting at them.

TESFAI: The independence movement in Eritrea began in 1962, when the Ethiopian Emperor Haile Selassie annexed Eritrea, because Ethiopia did not have a coastline, but Eritrea has six hundred miles of coast on the Red Sea. Haile Selassie tried to abolish our flag, language, and culture. During his reign, though, the fighting was not very great, because Selassie visited different areas and gave people some assistance to help solve their problems. But after the Communist Derge overthrew Selassie in 1974, the Ethiopian army entered the cities and began killing.

In the countryside, the Communists tried to change traditional property rules. Farmers did not accept the changes. They wanted to live by their own traditions. The farmers' rules had been good for generations. For example, if my father grew enough food for the family, he would sell the extra crops in the city. Everyone was fed.

The result of the Derge's policies, especially after 1981, was starvation. Part of the reason was a lack of rain. But the greater cause was that the dictator Mengistu's soldiers killed many farmers. The rest were afraid to work in their fields. The young fled or joined the resistance forces. Only the old people and children were left on the land.

If there had been no war or Communism in Eritrea, I would have finished high school. In my small village, only a few children were able to study. Most towns in Ethiopia only have an elementary school. If your family didn't need you to work on the farm and could afford books and board, a child could go to the province capital for high school. Out of Ethiopia's population of around thirty-five million, maybe ten thousand high-school students graduated each year. Only five hundred were allowed to enter the country's only respected university in Addis Ababa, the capital.

An added problem is that the Ethiopian government wants all young men to go into the Derge army. My cousin was taken by force from our village to join the Communist military. He died after two weeks. I don't know if they made him fight in Eritrea, in Tigre, or against Somalia.

Close to Christmas in 1974, the Derge army approached Asmara. We heard the sound of big guns in the surrounding countryside. People became frightened and said, "Maybe tomorrow they will capture Asmara."

I was studying for the university entrance exams on the night of January 1, 1975, when hundreds of Ethiopian soldiers opened fire in the streets of Asmara. They killed thousands, including women and children, for no reason. The soldiers threw the bodies into the river. That's when I went to the countryside to join the ELF [Eritrean Liberation Front]. I had to be very careful to sneak in the darkness through the Derge's patrols.

LEM LEM: I was only thirteen years old in 1975. If a girl was old enough, she was taken by the Derge soldiers to be made pregnant. If she resisted, they threatened to kill her. The family could do nothing.

In the highlands of Eritrea, where we lived, the people are Orthodox Christians. In the lowland area, the people are Moslems. In both traditions, it is a disgrace for an unmarried girl to have a baby. She will not be accepted to marry an Eritrean boy. Rape is a deliberate Derge strategy to eliminate future generations of our people.

Because of the danger, during Mengistu's "Red Terror" campaign in 1977, my parents agreed that I should flee Asmara. I was sixteen years old. Like many other girls, I joined the Front to fight against the Derge. Yes, I was afraid. I had never dreamed that I would be a fighter. I was taught to shoot a rifle at one of the Front's training camps. Then I was given an M-14 rifle and assigned to a company of guerrillas.

TESFAI: Although Lem Lem and I were neighbors when I was a student in Asmara, we never knew each other very well, because she was just a child when I joined the Front. And when she joined the ELF, I was fighting in a different part of the country. As a soldier in the Front, I was involved in guerrilla operations in coastal areas, in the desert, and in very rough mountains. Throughout Ethiopia, there are many different Fronts fighting against the Derge and their Russian and Cuban forces. In Eritrea there were two main Fronts, the ELF and the EPLF [the more Marxist Eritrean People's Liberation Front].

In the ELF we were mostly highlanders, predominantly Christians. We said that we were democratic, but the Front's politics could not be identified as any Western ideology. Our forces used small-scale guerrilla tactics and large-scale attacks. The Derge only controlled Asmara and the ports of Massawa and Assab. The Fronts controlled much of the countryside. Roads were usually affected by the fighting, cutting off the cities.

So there was hunger.

When Americans sent food aid to Ethiopia, the people didn't get much. Mengistu didn't have money to pay his soldiers, so he gave them the Western aid. I remember sometimes after a battle we captured sacks of this donated food from the Derge army. We distributed it to the local villagers, because they had nothing to eat.

LEM LEM: Our uniforms were usually just khaki shirts, short pants, and plastic sandals to protect our feet. Sometimes we went two to four days without food or water. Staying alive was our most immediate concern.

TEFAI: Our biggest problem was the jet fighter planes. The Communists used napalm fire bombs and cluster bombs that kill any persons or animals in a hundred-square-meter area. We only had machine guns to fight against them. Once we shot down an aircraft and captured two pilots.

In the lowlands, the Ethiopian army used tanks against us. Our tactic was to aim small hand-held rockets at the treads, to stop the tank from moving. Then our soldiers would jump onto it and fight with the crew, who, as the war progressed, sometimes were Russians, Cubans, or Yemenis. We were able to repair some of the tanks we captured and use them against the Derge.

We had drivers and other specialists who defected from the Ethiopian army. Among the prisoners we took were fellow Eritreans who had been drafted by the Derge. After we gave them some orientation, they joined our forces. They proved to be very valuable, because they knew how to use Russian equipment and weapons. We received very little outside aid, so we had to rely on captured weapons and supplies.

In the highlands, it was difficult for the Derge to use tanks against us. They couldn't move on the main roads, because we would ambush them and we had their garrisons surrounded. So they had to drop their supplies in by parachute from airplanes. Sometimes we could capture weapons and food when they missed.

At Barento, we had the Ethiopian army under siege inside the city from January to July 1977. Many soldiers died on each side. At least six times every day, the Ethiopian MiG jets would bomb us. We dug a system of underground tunnels to protect us from the high-explosive bombs and napalm.

During 1977–78, the Fronts controlled ninety percent of Eritrea. At this time, the Ethiopian army was also fighting Somalia in the Ogaden Desert, three hundred miles to the south. Then the Derge showed its true colors by switching Ethiopia's military alliance from the United States to the Russians, who previously supported Somalia.

In 1978, thousands of Soviet advisers and Cuban troops came in full force to save the Derge. In exchange, the Russians were given the important naval bases of Massawa and Assab, on Eritrea's coast. This gave Soviet warships the strategic advantage over the United States at the narrow mouth of the Red Sea. On land, Soviet advisers took charge of the Ethiopian and Cuban armies.

It was ironic, because when Ethiopia was allied with the U.S., members of the Fronts went to Cuba and Russia for military training. But the pact with Mengistu gained the Soviets their goal of occupying the Eritrean ports, directly across the Red Sea from Saudi Arabia. The Fronts became the Soviets' enemy. The Russians only care about those bases, not the people in Ethiopia. That's why eventually the West had to save the population from starving.

The Ethiopian army reinvaded Eritrea with 250,000 soldiers. During the heavy fighting, I was wounded and hospitalized. The good news I received during that time was a letter from Lem Lem. Even though we were not so close when we lived in Asmara, I was happy to hear from a friend. When I recovered, I was made a field medic. I went back to the front lines and gave first aid during terrible battles against the Derge and Soviets. The Front was heavily outmanned. We had to fight tanks with small arms, but throughout the fighting we held our ground.

During this time, by lucky coincidence, Lem Lem was also given medical training. In the Eritrean countryside, medical professionals were very scarce. Because of my battlefield experience as a medic, I was assigned for training at a field hospital.

The Front's hospitals are built underground, because of the threat from MiG aircraft. In some places, we were bombed every day. But no matter the conditions, in the field hospitals there were always some doctors and nurses on duty. There were surgical facilities, X-rays, laboratories. We worked with whatever medicines were donated by European or Arabic countries. We even had some volunteer foreign doctors from countries like Italy.

Toward the end of 1978, Lem Lem and I were assigned to the same medical team. We set up clinics in houses that were not destroyed by bombing, to help both wounded fighters and the local villagers. We served like doctors and nurses in some places. The most tragic were farm areas where the Derge and Soviets continually bombed and planted land mines. When farmers and their families tried to work the land, they were killed or maimed. We could give injections, blood transfusions, and stitch up minor wounds, but if someone was seriously injured, we couldn't do the surgical work.

TESFAI: There aren't many Ethiopian doctors. Every year, at most, fifteen graduate from the medical school in Addis Ababa. Before the Derge, our doctors graduated from medical schools in America, the Scandinavian countries, and Italy. They would come back to Ethiopia. Now, if a student is outside the country, he doesn't come back. And if anyone had studied in a Western country before, the Communists either persecute them or always suspect them. This is why many medical professionals had to escape.

LEM LEM: That's why my husband and I had to serve the people like doctors and nurses. We went into places where the Soviet MiGs dropped hundreds of bombs a day. We lost many friends. Villages and towns were reduced to piles of rocks. Much of the time, we didn't have food or water for three or four days.

TESFAI: Under those conditions, Lem Lem and I developed a strong bond of devotion and mutual respect. Before the war, when I was a student in Asmara, we were too young to have any feelings of love. Before the Derge, most marriages in Ethiopia were arranged by parents. The marriages bring the families closer together. It is surprising to Western people that most of these marriages are very successful. In Ethiopian and Eritrean cultures, divorce is very uncommon. We are loyal to each other. In American culture, people take marriage lightly and divorce easily. That's why people from my country have a problem marrying an American.

In Eritrea, weddings are the biggest time for celebration. All of the bride's friends give her presents, like dishes and other household needs. The wedding celebration lasts for a month or longer. During the first fifteen days, the new couple hardly ever leave the bedroom. Everybody comes by the house during that time to visit, eat, and play cards with the relatives. After the Derge took power, however, everything changed. There is only fighting, starvation, and despair. Since 1975, we have no culture.

LEM LEM: Sometimes in Asmara there may still be a large wedding, but not like before. Families are separated or have members in prison or killed. Others are fighting or have escaped to Sudan. Mothers don't want to celebrate when they are crying.

TESFAI: Lem Lem and I decided to get married in 1979. I was twenty-four years old and she was eighteen. The celebration was simple, but we were happy to be together.

We stayed in the field with the Front until after our daughter, Adiam, was born in September 1981. We made the decision to become refugees because, even though the ELF and the EPLF had successfully counterattacked the Derge and the Soviets, they began to fight each other as well. It was a struggle for power. A few people wanted to be the big leader.

The rivalry was tragic. Even though the Derge could not defeat us with their army, our own fratricide gave them success. Individual families had members in both Fronts. For instance, a father would be in the ELF and his son or brother in the EPLF. Our Front was defeated by the EPLF. We were not amateurs—the ELF had been fighting for twenty years. But the EPLF was joined by the TPLF, from Tigre Province. Together they forced our soldiers to become refugees.

In January 1982, our small family joined a small group of ELF survivors and fled to the Sudan coast. There were six or seven people in our escape group, including my cousin. At the border, Sudanese soldiers told us that if we gave up our guns there would be no problems. So we said, "If you give us no problems, that is good." And we gave our guns to the customs officials.

We walked for three days through the desert, until we reached the city of Kassala. My sister was already there. We had heard in Ethiopia that "Sudan is very good," but when we got to Kassala we found conditions for refugees were very bad. Even Asmara is more modernized than Sudan.

We chose to live in the city rather than a refugee camp. But we didn't have money or a resident ID. If police catch a refugee without one, they take him directly to prison. You have to pay them money for everything. So I took any job I could find.

Sudan has always been a poor country. When the Ethiopian refugees came, the merchants thought we all had money. The price of everything became very expensive. For example, they charged £10 [$20] rent for Sudanese people. They raised the price for everyone to £100 after we arrived, so the local people resented us being there. They charged us high rents for apartments with no bedroom, no kitchen—our whole group lived in just one room.

A building had five to ten rooms, all sharing one bathroom. Up to a hundred people would share one toilet and one shower. Some buildings didn't even have that: people walked outside to use a public bathroom.

LEM LEM: For Christians it is hard to obey Moslem customs. They called us foreigners, and we were kept on the fringe of society. We did meet some very nice Sudanese, who invited us to eat in their homes. But refugee life is especially rough on young girls, sixteen or seventeen years old, who have never been away from their homes before. They struggle to find jobs. Also for married women like myself, who have babies. We have to share a room full of people without privacy.

Many women found work in the houses of rich people. They cooked, cleaned, washed clothes—everything done by hand. The maid had to stay in the house the whole week, sleeping there, with only one day off to visit her husband. For a whole month's work she was paid £60 or £70. In comparison, rent is usually over £100.

TESFAI: As more and more refugees were coming into Kassala, we had a hopeless situation. So we traveled to the capital, Khartoum, where we stayed for two years. I found some construction work, but the pay was not enough to feed my family. So I decided to attempt an escape by boat to Saudi Arabia, across the Red Sea.

At Port Sudan it cost £100 to go to Saudi Arabia by small boat. But at the time I was about to leave, one boat fell apart at sea and twenty-five people died. I realized that this type of trip was too dangerous, and if the police caught me, that would mean jail. By chance, I heard that a job had opened up at the Port Sudan Medical Aid program. I was hired as a medical assistant in the vaccination clinic, which was funded by organizations under the United Nations.

I knew some English from high school, so I was assigned to work with British doctors. I also met Americans who worked for relief agencies. We all worked long hours, because a lot of Eritrean refugees were entering Sudan. Many were countryside people—some arrived with their cows and oxen. Inside Ethiopia, the Derge army was killing most of the livestock needed to cultivate the land. Without them, food could not be grown, so many people were starving. Added to the famine was the shipment of Ethiopian crops to the Soviet Union in exchange for the guns supplied to the Derge.

In the clinic, we mostly treated Ethiopians, although Sudanese came in, too. These people could not afford to see Sudanese doctors or private hospitals. I had the same duties as regular nurses, giving out medicines for common illnesses and vaccinations to prevent disease, especially to children.

In Eritrea, malaria is a big problem, particularly in the lowland area near Sudan. But the most common illness is diarrhea from amebic dysentery caused by impure water or contaminated food. Other diseases we saw were polio and diphtheria. Some kids died from measles. They get a very high fever and died from dehydration in the desertlike climate. In both Eritrea and Sudan, the biggest killers of children are diarrhea and measles.

My wife and I registered as refugees through the United Nations. UN officials introduced us to the American Joint Voluntary Agency office, where we were interviewed to see if we qualified for acceptance to America. After we passed the JVA interview, we were sent to the American immigration officers.

We knew that they looked unfavorably on former members of the Front. [Because some members had embraced Marxism and had been trained by the Soviet bloc during Haile Selassie's rule.] But I told them the truth, that I had been a fighter. I had done nothing to be ashamed of. Fortunately, we were accepted and began a four-month orientation program.

We had three hours of classes every day about life in America and the English language. For those of us who already knew English, we had classes on culture: how to ride a subway, how to use a shopping center, and many other necessary activities in this country. Those classes were very helpful, because in our country there are no large supermarkets and we don't have refrigerators to keep food fresh or frozen for long periods of time. We go to small shops and bargain over prices with the merchants. And in the countryside, we grow most of our food. We only need to buy little things, like coffee, sugar, or oil, which are not very expensive. A nickel's worth of salt can last you three or four months.

Besides attending classes, I continued working in the clinic until we departed for the States in August 1984. We were informed in Khartoum that we were going to Washington, D.C., and given the address of our sponsor, the International Rescue Committee.

As we flew into New York at night, we saw the harbor lights from the plane's window. The city lights reminded us of Asmara. The most difficult part of our arrival was that we didn't have relatives to greet us. It was after midnight when our connecting flight arrived in Washington. Only Mr. Canh, a Vietnamese representative of the IRC, was at the airport to welcome us. He drove us to a hotel in Washington. We were so exhausted from the long trip and the time change that we rested the entire first day.

On the second day, we went to the IRC office. We were so happy to meet some Eritrean friends there who we had known in Sudan. They were waiting to apply for jobs. Afterwards, they invited us to their apartments. We had lunch at one place and dinner at another friend's home. They told us how to get around the city, how to use the bus. I told them, "Our main concern is finding any kind of work."

LEM LEM: Even though we had the orientation about American life in Sudan, we still felt a little awkward in Washington. We spoke enough English to understand what people said, but it was difficult for Americans to understand us because of our accent. [Laughs]

We moved into this apartment complex in Hyattsville. We are just a short bus ride from Washington, and many of our friends were already living in this apartment complex. When we first moved in, they helped us to find furniture. They brought us a dining-room set, a king-size bed and a small bed for our daughter, a sofa for the living room, and enough cooking and kitchen materials. Since then, little by little, we've been buying what we need to decorate the apartment.

In the beginning, one friend or another would drive us to the store to buy whatever food we needed. In our culture, we like to have a lot of relatives or friends eating together. The way Eritreans eat, we cook a big bowl of spiced beans or chicken or lamb stew. We then cover a large round tray with a kind of soft, thin pancake called *enjira*. On the *enjira* we serve the main courses of food, with smaller pieces of *enjira* on the side. Everyone shares the meal, eating with their hands by using pieces of *enjira* to pick up the food, like a small sandwich.

TESFAI: I have come to like American food, but it took time, because the spices and texture of Ethiopian food are very different. After living here for two years, we have shifted our expectations and feel more comfortable being a part of this society. It's true that we went through many changes, trying to forget about life in our country before the war and adjusting to this life style. Living in a large apartment complex, my wife and I working different shifts, sharing responsibility for the children—this is a big change from how we lived before.

In Ethiopia, we don't feel good when little children, like my daughter, play outside without parents' being with them. But it is common for children in the apartment complex to play in the large parking lot by themselves. We have good communication with the neighbors, and we keep an eye on each other's kids.

LEM LEM: In our country, families usually have between five and ten children. In the cities, the wife stays home to take care of the children most of the time; maybe one percent of the women hold regular jobs. But in the countryside, wives cannot stay home; they have to work on the farms. When the husband cultivates the land with the oxen, the wife follows behind, planting the seeds, and women have to do all the housework and cleaning. Men never cook, only do the outdoor jobs. Inside the home, women have equal rights, but in public, men have the dominant role in our culture.

TESFAI: I came from a big family, nine brothers and sisters. My mother always helped my father grow food during the planting season and she helped cut the crops at harvest. They worked side by side.

LEM LEM: But in the city, my mother didn't have an outside job. The only women who work are nurses, teachers, and bankers. People in Asmara wouldn't understand if I told them that I was working in the hotels here doing housekeeping.

TESFAI: We have both worked hard for the two years we have lived here. The rent hasn't been too high, so we've been able to save a little money for each of the children's college education, little by little. Our son, Jerome, was born here, so he is automatically an American citizen. The rest of us must wait five years from the date we arrived to apply for American citizenship. For now we are mostly concerned with working and trying to save.

My wife and I leave for work or school at the same time in the morning. But with the shifts we work, we see each other for only a short time in the evening and early morning. When I get home from the hospital and Lem Lem gets home from her second job at night, we go right to sleep. We are so tired. The only time we get to talk is in the morning, when we are driving in the car.

LEM LEM: Sometimes the hotel work slows down, but the Ramada is usually busy. I try to put in a few extra hours at the Westin when I'm not in school. On Mondays, I attend GED class for my high-school diploma. And on Tuesday and Thursday, I have English as a Second Language classes.

TESFAI: Working in the hotels, she gets paid more than $7 an hour. She makes more money than I do. In hospitals, if you're not a registered nurse, the pay isn't much at all. But when I finish technical school, work will pay a lot better.

For more than one year, I've been a psychiatric aide for Cuban Marielitos. It was sad that, when ordinary people tried to escape from Cuba, Castro opened all of his jails and mixed in these prisoners. They have caused trouble. Some have killed people, some are on drugs, others are thieves. I always have to keep an eye on them. You never know if they are going to hit somebody.

Most of them had spent ten or fifteen years in prison, so it's hard to do anything with them. They were given a lot of drugs in the Cuban prisons. Even though they are criminals, when they tell me stories about their lives, I cry. I understand that they are dangerous, but they've had a very bad life in Cuba. I try to treat them like human beings who have a mother and brothers, so it is not too bad.

I am very grateful to the hospital for sending me to a private medical school. I chose the eighteen-month medical-laboratory-technician course. When I complete the program, I can get a job with doctors or hospitals anywhere. The only problem is finding time to study. Right after classes, I drive straight to my job. When the patients are quiet and sleeping, I am able to do some reading.

Right now it is a hectic and difficult life for my wife and me. But this is not uncommon for many Ethiopian refugees. When they first come, many are discouraged. They have difficulty finding a job commensurate with their educations. They see some crime; some people have things stolen. We don't like drugs in Eritrea, and I have heard a lot about drugs since we've been here. But I don't know any Eritreans who use them.

Ethiopians like to work. If we have to be home, off work, for two weeks or a month, we get upset. We like to spend money and appreciate that we have to earn it.

A new car costs at least $6,000, and we like to have a good car. It's kind of a competitive attitude.

Whenever new people from Ethiopia arrive in our apartment complex, we give them a party and try to make them feel welcome. We try to help by inviting them to come by if they have any questions. But after a while everybody is working and has their separate lives, so they drift apart.

LEM LEM: I know some people who have very troubled minds. They worry about paying the rent, they don't have a car, they cannot go to school, and they're very far away from their families.

Sometimes I have communicated with my younger brother and sister, who are still in Asmara. They are asking me to bring them to England or America. But how can I help them? They are in Eritrea studying Marxism-Leninism in high school now. They don't believe in that, but this is one way that the Communists are trying to erase our traditions, our culture. I am worried that the Derge will force them into the army. I have told my sister that, even though there are still many refugees, it is a big problem for a young woman to try to escape to Sudan now.

TESFAI: There are still Eritrean Fronts fighting against the Derge and the Soviets. In the countryside, the Ethiopian government continues to force farmers into collectives. Many people are still dying because of these policies, even though the world seems to have forgotten them.

Tonight a friend called on the telephone to tell us that her mother died in Ethiopia. We are going to her apartment this evening with three or four other families so she will not have to be alone. We will stay until late, then come home for a little rest before we go to work in the morning.

In Eritrea when somebody dies, a member of the family will notify all of the people in the surrounding area. Everybody takes time from what they are doing to come to the home. For two weeks, day and night, some friends help to cook and do the housework to make it easier on the family. In the evenings, other friends and relatives bring food from their homes for everyone to eat together. They make jokes and everybody laughs, even though they are very sad. Guests stay until around 1:00 A.M. so the family won't have to cry alone.

Now, in America, we try to do the same thing, but only for three or four days. In American culture, people are too busy.

No matter how long we live in America, we remain very concerned about our families back in Ethiopia. Our parents are always on our minds. If any friend's father or mother dies, we are all deeply touched. We cry and shout just like a baby, because it is like death twice over. First is the actual death. Second is the fact that we cannot be with them, even for the funeral. We are far away from home, but we always hope to be reunited with our families.

We would like our children to grow up in America. That is our decision. They have a chance to get a good education. And to live in any other country as a refugee we would have problems being accepted. Everybody says, "You are foreigners."

In America, we have the same rights as everyone. It's true that my wife and I have to work very hard, to be an American, you have to work hard. But nobody asks us, "Where are you from?" They can tell when they hear me speak that I was not born here. My accent is still very noticeable. But nobody makes a big deal out of it. This is our chance to live.

UPTOWN

Trong and Thanh Nguyen Family
Refugees from Vietnam
Social Worker and Restaurateur
Chicago, Illinois

Ten years ago, the most active businesspeople in the heart of Chicago's Uptown area were muggers, drug dealers, and street-corner prostitutes in vinyl miniskirts. A once-prosperous neighborhood known for elegant homes and grand Art Deco ballrooms, Uptown declined during the postwar suburban boom. It hit rock bottom during the Vietnam War years. Burned-out buildings and abandoned storefronts were taken over by gangs and addicts. Homeless drunks, reeking of cheap wine, lay spread-eagled on broken sidewalks, oblivious to the roar of elevated trains.

In the years after North Vietnamese tanks rolled into Saigon in 1975, waves of frightened and disoriented Vietnamese "boat people" began arriving in Chicago. Overwhelmed by the size and rhythm of the city, they had no relatives or ethnic community to welcome them. Their sponsors, relief agencies, were nearly as penniless as the refugees. The only affordable housing was Uptown. The refugees had left one war zone to enter another. Unable to speak English and defenseless, they became the neighborhood's easiest prey.

Parents like Trong Nguyen, the father of five young children, were still in shock from the loss of their homeland. The pathetic living conditions and malevolent streets of Uptown jolted them out of depression. Although they still had nightmares of war, their greatest concern was their children's future.

Today, Uptown is one of Chicago's up-and-coming neighborhoods. A dynamic rivalry between the refugees and a group of ambitious Chinese-American businessmen has transformed the once-abandoned Argyle Street business district into a flourishing Oriental market. On weekends, suburban tourists who used to lock their car doors if they had to drive through the neighborhood, now stand in line outside of popular Vietnamese restaurants to enjoy delicately spiced cuisine. Uptown has been rediscovered. The lure of "Little Saigon" has drawn a new generation of Chicagoans to visit and live and restore some of the neighborhood's former elegance.

When I began interviewing Vietnamese residents of Uptown, the name of Trong Nguyen was most often mentioned as that of a "hero" who organized the refugee community and coordinated efforts with community agencies to transform the neighborhood. Trong, age forty-seven, has the soulful eyes of a poet who leads by gentle persuasion. For ten years, he's operated out of a cramped second-floor office at Travelers and Immigrants Aid.

On weeknights and throughout the weekend, Trong manages his own struggling business, the Song Huong Restaurant, on the North Broadway border of Uptown and neighboring Edgewater. It's a typical "mom-and-pop" enterprise: his wife, Thanh, does all the cooking, and his son, Tran, age nineteen, a drummer in a New Wave rock band, and daughter, Thanh Tram, a precocious high-school freshman, serve customers.

TRONG: I have always believed that, if you just stay home and do nothing you are not a person whom others will respect. Since I came to Chicago in 1976, I've been involved in building the Vietnamese community. Of the twelve thousand Vietnamese who live in this city, more than half live in a fourteen-block area around the Argyle Street business strip, between Broadway and Sheridan roads.

Uptown is called the Ellis Island of Chicago. Some thirty languages are spoken in the area. Besides the Vietnamese, there are a thousand Cambodians, two hundred Laotians, and some Hmong. But most of the people are American blacks, Appalachian whites who came from the coal mines of Kentucky and West Virginia, Mexicans, and some American Indians.

In 1975, when the refugees first began arriving, the area was a dumping ground for derelicts, mental patients, and everyone else the city didn't want. Drug addicts, gangs, and prostitutes hung out in abandoned buildings owned by absentee landlords. Some refugee families with children live in transient hotels alongside winos. Large multistory housing projects like on the corner of Argyle and Sheridan were very dangerous. Refugees were constantly robbed and beaten.

The Argyle Street business strip had only a few struggling businesses, like small Chinese restaurants, a mom-and-pop bakery, and a tavern with naked dancers. Most storefronts were empty, with a lot of threatening people on the street.

When my wife and I came to Chicago, our major concern was to feed our five small children. We had Vietnamese pride and did not want to take public aid. We wanted the American community and authorities to respect us.

In Uptown, we felt like we were thrust from one war zone to another. Local community organizations strongly opposed the refugees. People talked about a "Yellow Horde invasion." They started a lawsuit campaign against the city for bringing Indochinese into their area. They said, "Because the refugees are moving in, rents are going higher."

The absentee landlords in the neighborhood were horrible. The [community] organizations had started a boycott against them before the refugees arrived. This created a lot of vacancies in some of the run-down buildings. The voluntary agencies who sponsored the refugees saw the cheap rents and placed refugee families in those apart- ments. That allowed slumlords to stay in business.

At the height of the tension, the city brought the community associations, some refugee leaders, and voluntary agency represen- tatives into a room to talk. Commander Howard Patinkin of the police department moderated the session, because it was getting to the point of violence. At the meeting, the community groups realized that the refugees were good people, and an agreement was made for the voluntary agencies to coordinate with local residents.

Just trying to begin a new life here, we had so many difficulties. When I worked as a janitor at Water Tower Place, a co-worker told me, "Trong, do you know that America is overpopulated? We have more than two hundred million people. We don't need you. Go back where you belong." I was shocked to hear people trying to chase us out. I thought, "Who is going to feed the children?" In America, a single income can never feed the family. Even though our youngest was just a baby, my wife had to find work.

THANH: When we first came to Chicago, I cried a lot. In the factory where I worked, there weren't many Americans. Most were Mexicans, some legal, but also many illegal aliens. They acted like, as Vietnamese say, "Old ghosts bully new ghosts." They cursed our people.

Some Mexicans said, "You come here and take our jobs. Go back wherever you came from." I was very upset and cried. They said so many things. Then one day some of them said, "You come here to make money, then go back home and live like kings." That was too much. I couldn't hold it in any more.

I told them in a very soft voice, "We are Vietnamese people. You don't have enough education to know where our country is. Vietnam is a small country, but we did not come to America to look for jobs. We're political refugees. We can't go back home." I didn't call them bad names or anything, but I said, "You are the ones who come here to make money to bring back to your country. We spend our money here." After that, they didn't bother us very much.

TRONG: In 1978, just before the boat-people crisis began, I found a job as a caseworker with Travelers and Immigrants Aid. My goal was to help those in need. After seven years in that job, when the Vietnamese community had become stabilized, I decided to open a restaurant. For my wife, working in a factory was such a heavy job. She tried so hard to stay with that type of work to help feed our family, but she was laid off on different occasions. When friends sometimes came to our home, they enjoyed my wife's cooking. They said, "Maybe one day open a restaurant, so we can eat your cooking more often."

They were joking, but it gave us the idea to open our own business. In June 1985, we opened this restaurant. We named it Song Huong, after the Perfume River in my home area of central Vietnam.

As a social worker, I've never made much money. I didn't qualify to borrow from the bank. To open the restaurant, we had to borrow from friends. To keep our operating expenses down, my son and two oldest daughters help out. I know that isn't professional in terms of building a reputation for a good restaurant, but we have no other choice.

My life here has been working for the community. I never thought about making a lot of money for my own use. Sometimes my wife says, "It seems that you care more about the community than your own family."

My children here are my nineteen-year-old son and my fifteen-, fourteen-, twelve-, and eleven-year-old daughters. Sometimes the children have expressed disappointment that I'm not home very often. I explain to them that when you have a bowl of rice, no matter how small, you have to think about those people who don't have any rice to eat.

In Vietnam, I was involved in social activity since I was sixteen years old. As a student in Saigon, I saw many war victims, especially children in orphanages, who were abandoned by society. So I organized a group of students to visit the orphans. The girls in our group gave the little ones a bath and took care of their clothes. The boys played with the kids and contributed our pocket money to buy them milk, candy, and toys. We wanted to give these kids at least a short period of happiness.

My father was a soldier from the time I was born, in 1940. He was recruited by the anti-Japanese resistance to go to England for military training. He was then sent to China on a secret mission. In Kunming, which was the headquarters of the Free Chinese fighting against the Japanese occupation, he met my future father-in-law, Vu Van Bach, who had been a revolutionary leader in northern Vietnam since the 1920s.

As a member of the non-Communist Vietnam Quoc Dan Dang [VNQDD] he was imprisoned by the French for taking part in the Yen Bay uprising in 1929. That event is known as the beginning of

Vietnam's modern struggle for independence. When he was released from prison, he went to China to work on the railroad. In Kunming in 1942, he learned that the Allied army was trying to recruit Vietnamese to go back home to fight the Japanese.

Bach saw an Asian soldier in a British uniform. Bach addressed him in Chinese. The soldier said, "I am Vietnamese, I don't speak Chinese," and they became like brothers. The man in uniform was my father. The Vietnamese group was moved by the British from China to Calcutta, India, for training. I believe it was funded by the American OSS. At the same time, the OSS also set up a secret zone in China to train Ho Chi Minh's Communist forces.

My father had had no idea that I was born. When he left Vietnam at the outset of the war, he and my mother were just married. She hadn't yet realized that she was pregnant. During the war, they lost contact. When I was two or three years old, my father parachuted into Laos as part of a twelve-man reconnaissance team to scout Japanese positions. The Vietnamese Liberation Forces working out of Calcutta were like the Special Forces. They did many secret missions for the Allies.

Somebody told my mother that my father was in Laos. She left me with my grandparents and went to search for her husband. Unfortunately, my father's mission was to march through Laos into Burma. He never found out about my mother's trip, and, in the chaos of the war, she disappeared.

In 1945, the Allies appointed Chinese General Lu Han to oversee the Japanese surrender in northern Vietnam, while the British went into southern Vietnam. While Ho Chi Minh took power in Hanoi, my father, Mr. Bach, and other non-Communist resistance leaders came back to Saigon. But the British dissolved the Liberation Army. And, the final blow, the British invited the French colonialists back.

In Hue, my home area, Emperor Bao Dai began to build an army. My father knew how Ho Chi Minh had betrayed and assassinated many nationalist leaders, so he accepted an invitation to join this new army. His idea was first to defeat the Communists and then drive out the French.

When my father came back to Hue, my mother was still missing. I was living like an orphan with my mother's parents in the countryside. It was an area where my father sometimes fought. But he did not know that I existed until I was nine years old. In November 1949, during an operation against the Communists, my father found me.

My father brought me to Hue, where I lived with his new wife and began going to school. And in 1950, when my father was transferred to Saigon, I went with him. We finally found my real mother in 1955. She had been living in Laos, remarried with a couple of children. I continued living with my stepmother and her parents in Saigon. I spent most of my time studying.

When the French prepared to leave Vietnam in 1954, my father, a lieutenant colonel, gave a lot of help to the emerging leader of South Vietnam, Ngo Dinh Diem. He helped to protect Diem from both the Communists and French loyalists. After Diem became chief of state, my father was loyal to him. In 1958, Diem's brother Ngo Dinh Canh wanted my father to join his party.

My father answered, "In this life I have God above me. And as a soldier, I am loyal only to my country. I don't want to join any political party." For this, he was discharged from the army and kidnapped by the police in Saigon. He spent a year and a half in the secret Chin Ham prison, located in a cave near Hue.

The political climate in South Vietnam was very unstable, with many rival personalities and factions competing for power. And in 1959, the Communists organized a Liberation Front. So, after my father was released from prison, he was called back into the army by Diem's most powerful brother, Nhu, to help form the Vietnamese Special Forces. When I graduated from high school in 1962, the Viet Cong had already stepped up military activities. Because of the growing war, I knew that sooner or later I would be drafted. So I decided to join the army.

I graduated from the Military Academy at Thu Duc in November 1963. My class was called Revolution 1–11. That was the date when President Diem was overthrown. I graduated second in the class, so I was allowed to choose my assignment. I spent a year working at a training center before I was accepted into the Special Forces. Our base area in Tay Ninh Province was pretty dangerous, because it was so near the North Vietnamese bases in Cambodia.

At the end of 1965, I was transferred to the 81st Airborne Ranger Battalion, based in Nha Trang. We were moved anywhere in the country where there was serious trouble. Our unit was the first to knock out a North Vietnamese tank in the A Shau Valley in 1966. The battle began at night. The hand to hand fighting was horrible. It was so dark that we couldn't see anything but the flashes from rifles. To know who was in front of us, we had to get down on our knees to touch the feet of oncoming soldiers. If he wasn't wearing boots, we knew he was North Vietnamese, and we'd shoot. The Northerners would touch the head—if a soldier wasn't wearing a Communist pith helmet, they would shoot. We fought through the night, with big losses on both sides.

We had been warned about NVA tanks, but we had never seen one. Fortunately, we carried portable antitank rockets. I always instructed my soldiers, "We only have one rocket per man. I want you to set up in teams of three. Always aim together and fire at the same target."

When we heard the roar of the tanks coming toward us, we were stunned. But we positioned ourselves as I had instructed. We fired and stopped the first tank. The men shouted, they were so happy! Then we stopped a second tank. When the battle ended, we had paralyzed the enemy offensive. Later, we took part in many other large battles, from the Khe Sanh area all the way down into the Mekong Delta.

Nineteen sixty-six was also the year that my wife, Thanh, and I were married. We had been good friends since childhood, like brother and sister, because our fathers were so close. When our parents decided that marriage would be a good thing for us, we obeyed. But immediately after the wedding, my Ranger battalion was again continually sent on missions anywhere the Allied Command decided was urgent. We worked closely with the American Special Forces' Delta Project, which did a lot of work in enemy areas. We rescued Delta teams that were trapped or surrounded. I was wounded a few times, but never seriously.

In late 1968, after attending Officer Leadership and Pathfinder training in the United States, I became very sick with an enlarged heart. I took a less physically demanding position as aide-de-camp to General Lam Son, the head of special forces. But my health got worse. In January 1970, I was medically discharged from the army. I returned to Nha Trang.

My wife was happy to have me home. But I felt torn, because I liked military life. Our two sons were three and four years old. To support the family, we opened a bakery at Cam Ranh Bay, near the sea.

Our business did well. I did the baking at night, and my wife ran the shop during the day. But I weakened from working long hours and continued to suffer from my illness. So my doctor advised me to stop. We had to close the bakery at the end of 1971.

A friend came to see me and said, "I understand you have a lot of time on your hands. There is a new military team called Special

Missions Advisory Group that is recruiting former Special Forces." I became the head translator for the Americans who trained the group. After the year of training, they were moved to Da Nang. I didn't want to be separated from my family, so I took a job with the province administration in Nha Trang.

I was made the community-development officer. My responsibility was to visit villages to study the needs of the people. Then I would make a report and suggest a budget to USAID to assist local self-help projects. After a year, I was promoted to the regional office. Then USAID hired me as a livestock specialist and in 1973–74 I became an agricultural-program manager. We introduced strong new strains of rice that were being developed in the Philippines and Thailand.

Our area in II Corps was pretty peaceful, and the agricultural pro-grams were very successful. For the first time, the people could grow two crops in a year, which made them more prosperous. This made them very happy.

In the spring of 1975, the North Vietnamese broke the Paris Peace Agreement and began a major offensive in the South. I stayed in Nha Trang until the Communist army was advancing on the city. On April 2, my family joined a crowd of two to three hundred people who planned to evacuate to Saigon. But at Nha Trang Airport, the planes were already taken by the air force.

We telephoned the American embassy in Saigon. They promised to send an aircraft for us. So we camped at the air terminal and waited until midnight. The plane didn't come. Most of the people were panicked, because they had all been American employees. At the last minute, the Americans were abandoning them and their families. So they began to chant anti-American slogans.

I stood before them and said, "Look, even if you are anti-American now, you cannot save your heads. The Communists will still punish you for working with the U.S. government."

They shouted, "How are we going to find a way out? We cannot take the road, we cannot fly."

I told them, "See that C 130 airplane unloading supplies? When it is empty and ready to return to Saigon, we'll rush onto it. Many trucks and cars have been left here without keys. I'll cross the ignition wires of one and start it up. We need someone to slowly drive the car behind a procession to the commander's headquarters at the radar station. Children and women walk in front, so the guards won't shoot at us."

When we approached the radar station, the guard shot into the air and shouted, "Stop." But the general agreed to transport us to Saigon. We all fit, but we had to leave our luggage behind.

In Saigon, the AID headquarters asked me to help with a feasibility study for planting vegetables and raising livestock around the city in case of a long siege. For several days, our group drove out to surrounding areas. But each day the team became smaller as members fled the country.

My wife and I didn't wish to leave Vietnam, especially if we had to leave our parents behind. We had five children with us. Our youngest daughter was just an infant. And my oldest son, who was nine, was separated from us: he was with my mother outside of the Saigon area. When I realized that the situation was hopeless, I reluctantly prepared evacuation documents. An American friend said, "Trong, your extended family is so large, sixteen people. How can you make it in America?"

On April 28, 1975, my extended family group was driven to Tan Son Nhut Air Base. There was a large crowd of maybe ten thousand people waiting at the terminal. The evacuation was planned for five the following morning. We kept the kids close to us and tried to get a little sleep on the ground.

Around midnight, the North Vietnamese bombed the airstrip. Everyone panicked. People were crying and some began running to escape. So I stood up and shouted, "Please, listen." I kept shouting and shouting. People looked at me like I was strange. When it became quiet, I said, "Panic kills people more than guns. We have to cooperate."

I called for young men to help keep order in the crowd. And I asked the people, "Please, throw away your luggage. The evacuation will be very fast, like lightning. We don't want people left behind because of suitcases."

Around 5:00 A.M., C 46 helicopters landed in front of us. U.S. Marines checked out the landing zone and took security positions. A man spoke Vietnamese through a loudspeaker in his hand. People hurried to the helicopters. My own family was divided onto three different aircraft.

We landed on the huge boat, the *Pioneer Contender*. I had mixed emotions. I felt that we were going to heaven—the United States. But I already missed my country. I realized that I would never see Vietnam again.

After a short period on the island of Guam, we were brought to a refugee camp in Fort Chaffee, Arkansas, near Little Rock. There were quite a few Vietnamese already there. Everybody was asking about "sponsors."

Many Americans visited the camp, just like a slave market. Many were rice farmers in Arkansas who wanted Vietnamese as cheap laborers. They would invite refugees into the coffee shop and talk with them. If these Americans thought, "Oh, this or that person is good," they went to the office to fill out sponsorship papers.

My former USAID boss wanted to sponsor my family to Washington. I said, "No, I don't want to bother a good friend. My family is too large." I was afraid that he would have to feed all sixteen of us.

To make resettlement easier, I divided the extended family into three groups: my wife and kids; my parents' group; and my in-laws' family. My sponsor was the pastor of a Methodist church in central Ohio. He owned sixteen hundred acres of land, with around a million pine trees that needed trimming. He also had chestnuts, blueberries, and grapevines.

I helped him draw a plan to improve his property. But that wasn't what he wanted—he expected me to be a simple laborer. And we had misunderstandings about religion. I am a Catholic, and my wife is a Buddhist. I told him, "In front of God we are equal. I believe in God the same as you. But I want to keep my own religion."

Every week his wife, Elizabeth, would drive us to the supermarket. My wife is a good cook, but she didn't know anything about American food, like ground beef. Thanh wanted to buy pork, but Elizabeth said, "No. You are limited to a twenty-five-dollar budget a week." And the sponsor wanted me to talk English with my children. I said, "No, they will learn bad speaking habits from me. It's better for them to learn correct American English at school."

We were lucky that the town's Catholic pastor, Father Ron, allowed us to live in his rectory. But, after two months, the sponsor wanted to send us back to Fort Chaffee. I was afraid to go back to the camp. If we returned, as many others had, it would look bad for the refugee program. So I asked the sponsor, "Sir, please wait one more month. I will look for another sponsor."

Father Ron didn't want to create a problem with the Methodists, so he took me to his native town, a short drive away. The church agreed to sponsor my family. Our first day in Lancaster, Ohio, I found a job as a donut baker. I worked twelve hours a day, six days a week. The shop owner trained me and paid $100 a week. My kids enrolled in school, and my wife stayed home with the baby.

I was still coming out of shock from leaving our homeland. My emotions were very unstable. I was constantly dreaming of Vietnam. I had a lot of nightmares. My boss had very much sympathy for me. But I felt too much stress.

After nine months of working in the shop, one day in mid-1976, I made ten dozen donuts that didn't rise enough. One of my co-workers yelled at me. She said, "If you don't want to work, get out. We don't want you here." I said, "I'm sorry. I quit tomorrow."

I drove to Chicago, where my in-laws were living. The second day, I found a job as a janitor at Water Tower Place, the most luxurious shopping mall. My wife and children came to join me a week later.

The majority of the janitors at the mall were Vietnamese. The company liked to hire us, because we did the job well. But sometimes the superintendent of the building came to my supervisor and said, "We want these gooks out of here tomorrow." So some Vietnamese went to the Department of Labor, who ruled that the superintendent's prejudice was illegal.

Uptown was the area where many Vietnamese refugees were sent by the voluntary agencies. My wife and I found a place to live in the Albany Park neighborhood, which had a lot of Koreans and other Asians. We found that my income was not enough to meet the family's needs. So although Thanh's English was not good, she found a second-shift job at a factory making plastic cups. We rotated responsibility for the children.

My son, Tran, was nine years old, and my daughters were five, four, three, and one. My two oldest children had a lot of problems with their classmates in Chicago. The school in Albany Park was a mixture of white, black, Asian, everything. Tran was beaten sometimes, and his teacher wasn't patient with him, because he didn't know English. I went to the school and told the principal that I thought the teacher was being unfair. The principal was sympathetic and said, "I understand." After that there was no more problem.

After one year at the mall, I was appointed supervisor. My responsibility was the Continental Bank. But the next year, in 1978, I realized that there were a few thousand Vietnamese refugees in Chicago who needed assistance. When I heard that Travelers and Immigrants Aid was looking to hire a caseworker, I took the job.

I found an apartment large enough for all of my children in Uptown, on Argyle and Sheridan, right in the center of the Vietnamese refugee community. Robberies and crime throughout the neighborhood were severe. My cousin, who lived one floor below me, was robbed twice.

Thieves came into his apartment, tied up his family, and robbed them.

Every day, after finishing at my office, I would go on the street and ask people about their needs. To improve the area, the first thing we had to deal with were the community associations, who wanted the refugees to leave. So we worked with the church, the police, and local officials. As a caseworker, I served as a mediator between the refugees and the authorities. Many problems occurred at the medical center and in the schools. Small issues were magnified by language and cultural differences.

For instance, in Vietnam, when both parents work, their older children take care of the babies. But in America, that creates problems. The schools would call the homes to ask why students weren't attending class. In many cases, neither the parents nor the children could speak English. Since I was the one who registered the kids in school, the authorities would call me to help.

I would visit the families at night to explain the law to them. They would respond, "But I need them to watch the little children." I'd emphasize, "If you don't obey the law, they'll take away your children." There were no day-care centers. That put extra pressure on families working in low-paying jobs who were trying to be self-supportive and stay off welfare.

The older kids attend Senn High School, which is considered the most ethnically diverse in America. Some seventy-eight languages are spoken there. There weren't many problems with the white American kids, but other ethnic groups really gave the Vietnamese children a hard time. Especially the blacks, Mexicans, and Chinese.

Chinese kids from Hong Kong chased the refugee children: "Go home. Go back where you came from." Usually the refugee children kept quiet. They listened to their parents: "Go to school to learn and study—not to fight." But the children couldn't be patient any more.

A fight began between a Vietnamese-Chinese and a Hong Kong Chinese boy. It quickly expanded to four, six, twelve kids, then became a big battle. Some of the Hong Kong kids were hospitalized. The first response was a lot of prejudice toward the refugees. In the newspaper, an authority said, "Because Vietnamese kids grew up in wartime, what they know is killing, nothing else." It became a hot issue in the community. And the parents of the Chinese kids tried to sue the refugee parents. So I called a lawyer. I told him, "I need your help. I don't have money to pay the fee for the children. And most of their parents are on welfare." The lawyer said, "Okay, I'll see what I can do." We had a long conversation about refugee life here and our culture. The lawyer adapted well. He used all the facts I gave him and won the case.

That was a small victory compared to other problems in the community. Crime threatened everyone's daily life. Muggers robbed refugees on the street, in the lobby of apartment buildings, in the elevators, in the stairwells, everywhere. In Vietnam, people seldom had locks on their doors. We had to teach them to bolt the door or hook the chain on the lock.

Whenever an incident happened, the refugees would call my office. One day there were more than thirty robberies. We needed to develop a strategy to deal with all the crime. So I called the police, the church (which has Vietnamese priests), the voluntary agencies, and community leaders.

We decided to organize what Chicago police call "beat representatives." These are citizens' groups that watch the neighborhood and call police if there's trouble. And among the refugees, we developed an "ambush" strategy.

Refugee men organized committees to catch robbers. One notorious building was a twenty-four-floor high-rise on West Lakeside. Muggers very badly tormented the refugees who lived there. And there were a few other large buildings where crimes occurred every day.

Our strategy was to set up ambushes from the high-rise buildings. Refugees opened their windows to look onto the street. One person acted as bait and walked alone. When a robber started to follow her, the watchers from one building would signal the other buildings, just like a military operation. When the robber grabbed her neck and took her purse, which had phony money inside, the citizens' patrols began to follow. They converged on him from all directions until he was surrounded. The refugees kept him cornered until the police arrived to take him away.

The police were very supportive and stopped many robberies. When word went out around the neighborhood that the police were active and the refugees were organized and defending themselves, much of the crime stopped.

During 1980, at the height of the Vietnamese boat-people crisis, my wife quit her job at the cup factory to work for the Intergovernmental Committee for Migration to greet refugees at O'Hare Airport. She helped transfer them to connecting flights. Her job was very tough, because the refugees were arriving at all hours of day or night. It was dangerous for her to come home alone after dark. There were still problems in the neighborhood—a lot of rapes—and I was afraid that, if we stayed, the children would grow up with a bad influence. So I decided to move.

I looked for a home close to the neighborhood, but no landlords wanted a family our size. Sometimes I thought, "Is having a lot of children a crime in America?" Finally, a friend in Des Plaines, on the North Side, close to the airport, was selling a home for $50,000 with a very low down payment. I didn't have enough savings, so I borrowed money from friends. I just closed my eyes and bought it.

I continued working in Uptown every day at my Travelers Aid job. We were resettling a lot of refugees into the area, and I worried about their future. Uptown was still a disaster, and the Vietnamese boat people, the Cambodians who survived the holocaust, and the Laotians and Hmong were less educated than the Indochinese who arrived in 1975. Many refugees came from rural areas, unprepared for city life. They didn't have a higher education or any skills except farming. I couldn't move them into apartments considered good, or even livable. The families were usually large.

I felt hurt, because I did not want my family to live in that neighborhood, so how could I tell other people to live there? I was determined to improve the neighborhood, but how to do that was the big question.

The business strip on Argyle Street was a disaster area. Around sixty percent of the buildings were owned by a Chinese association, Hip Sing, which had a vision in the late 1960s of turning the area into a new Chinatown. But they had little success, because of crime and the depressed environment. Still, the Vietnamese thought that maybe it could be a good place to start our business area.

We asked the Hip Sing to rent us some abandoned storefronts. They said, "No, you're not Chinese. This is the New Chinatown." But I began to work closely with a Chinese manager of one of the buildings. I said, "If you can help us, we can all benefit. There aren't that many Chinese living in the area. If you let the Vietnamese rent spaces, this area can be developed. And I can place new refugees in apartment buildings that the Hip Sing owns, that have a low occupancy rate. They will shop here on Argyle and the area will grow and develop." He agreed.

I didn't know anything about business in America; I could only advise refugees on social issues. But we were able to provide a translation service so they could obtain business permits. The neighborhood began to grow.

Nearly all the businesses owned by refugees were started by families pooling their money together or borrowing from friends. The first places were restaurants and small supermarkets. As more refugees moved into the neighborhood and new businesses were springing up, the gangs, the drug addicts, and the winos had fewer and fewer abandoned buildings to hang out in. And as the neighborhood began to come back to life, the police sent more security. But in the alleys and side streets it was still something else.

Argyle Street became a kind of a beachhead where people could have a semblance of ordinary life. From my Travelers Aid office I began sending a newsletter to teach the refugees about American life and personal safety. But the refugees needed a community center staffed by their own people. There is more pride in a community when an ethnic group can take care of their own. It takes pressure off the welfare system when successful members of an ethnic community help others to find jobs. People can adapt to their new society without having to be ashamed of their own culture.

In 1980, I heard that the U. S. Department of Health and Human Services planned to contribute grants for Mutual Assistance Associations. I gathered friends, and we wrote a proposal that was awarded a federal grant to develop a Vietnamese Community Service Center through the Vietnamese Association of Illinois. We found office space on Broadway, a few blocks from Argyle. We searched for a good director, and we trained a small staff.

The Center opened in the winter of 1980 with only two donated desks and a dozen folding chairs. A group of volunteers built plywood tables and benches to furnish classrooms. Sometimes the heater broke down and the staff had to work in many sweaters, scarves, and gloves.

Despite conditions in the office, the Center grew very quickly. After a year, the Center was awarded a state grant, so there was enough money to continue services as the Vietnamese population blossomed. Now the Vietnamese Association has expanded the center to twenty staff members. The director is a very talented young woman, Ngoan Le, who has great initiative. And Mr. Zung Dao, who owns a successful restaurant business in the neighboring Edgewater area, runs the Center's Community Economic Development Project. That is the only program in our area to teach refugees how to do business in America. And we are helping other refugees, like the Ethiopians who just opened a restaurant on Argyle Street.

Argyle has become an international area. There are more than fifty Vietnamese family-owned businesses on the strip. There are also stores owned by Khmer, Lao, Chinese, Ethiopians, a Jewish kosher butcher, two Hispanic grocers, a black record shop, and an American bar. There are Japanese, Thai, Indian, and Mexican restaurants in the area. And a McDonald's.

I remember in 1978–79, when I worked with American sponsors from the suburbs, if I said, "Why don't you come to Uptown to work with the refugees?," they would say, "No way, it's too dangerous." Now people from many areas like to come to Argyle Street to shop, and enjoy coming to community activities like the annual Argyle Street Festival or Lunar New Year Celebration.

The Vietnamese restaurants do a lot of their business from tourists on weekends. Many don't earn a lot, but they survive by family manpower. For example, Mr. and Mrs. Phan, who own the Nha Tang Restaurant, had a simple dream. They came here as boat people in 1979, worked in a factory to save enough to make a $700 lease payment on a small storefront to open a twelve-table restaurant. His wife is a very good cook, and they charge low prices. Since they opened in 1981, they stay open seven days a week from 9:00 A.M. until 10:00 P.M. They earn enough to keep the family well fed and have a little profit left over for saving.

The most famous place in the neighborhood is the Mekong Restaurant, on the corner of Argyle and Broadway, which attracts many people from the suburbs and other states. The owner, Mr. Lam Ton, worked with the U.S. State Department in Vietnam.

The first year his restaurant opened, in 1983, Lam Ton lost money. The neighborhood's reputation was still very rough. But, all of a sudden, his business turned around after some Chicago newspaper people wrote very favorably about the restaurant. The Mekong brought Uptown into the limelight, especially in 1985, when a lot of media attention was given to the tenth anniversary of the fall of Saigon.

Newspeople saw a lot of new stores with posterboards written in Vietnamese. They wrote stories emphasizing how the refugees revitalized Uptown and turned the slum area into a more beautiful place. They began calling Argyle Street "Little Saigon."

But as the neighborhood's good reputation began to grow, that created a problem. The Chinese Hip Sing organization, who dreamed that the area would become the "New Chinatown," started to feel like second-class citizens.

The Hip Sing office building is right next to the el train station on Argyle, and they still own a lot of property that the Vietnamese lease. So they consider themselves the ones who control the area.

"Little Saigon"—Chicago's Uptown district

On one occasion, the Vietnamese organized a big Mid-Autumn Festival for the children, and we had a Lion Dance on Argyle Street. One Chinese man came out of the Hip Sing building and said, "Did you ask our permission to dance on this street?" I said to him, "Why do I have to ask your permission? This is a public street, and all of our businesses are here. This is America. The streets are built by the taxpayers, not you guys."

He said, "I don't want to see you people, because the Lion Dance is for Chinese." I said, "The kids enjoy it, even if they don't do the dance properly. Their joy is our goal."

The Hip Sing, under Jimmy Wong and Charley Soo, did work hard to develop the area. Improvements like the sidewalk renovation by the city were made thanks to their lobbying. But they never had enough population for a New Chinatown. It was the Southeast Asian refugees who decided that, even if we were put into a slum, we would improve the neighborhood. And we had enough people to support new businesses on Argyle.

The small family-owned businesses can only employ a limited number of people. So refugees travel to jobs on the South Side of Chicago or in the suburbs. Many are unskilled factory workers, like machine operators. Other refugees work as painters or mechanics. During the past couple years, Chicago has turned into a service-based city. In a lot of new hotels, refugees work in housekeeping or maintenance jobs. And many of the earlier, better-educated refugees went to school to become electronics technicians at places like GTE or AT&T.

At first, some Vietnamese refuse to work at menial jobs because they don't want a lower social standing than they had in Vietnam. Others take welfare because they are lazy or don't have the right encouragement to study English. I try to motivate them. But sometimes I'm told, "Forget about being a social worker. Who are you to tell me what to do? You are Vietnamese, just like us. You have no right to push me."

The Vietnamese Community Center has been instrumental in changing people's attitudes from being so negative. The Center now has five programs: Employment, Social Adjustment, Youth, Women, and Economic Development. Within a few years, the Vietnamese welfare dependency rate declined from eighty-seven percent to fifty-five percent, and now only around twenty-five percent are unemployed or on public assistance.

After I saw the neighborhood begin to turn around and living conditions for the refugees improve, I thought, "How about their moral and cultural life?" There are family conflicts, because the children are learning so quickly in school to adopt American culture. The parents might learn a little English at work, but it is a very slow process. They have to rely a lot on the children. The kids watch television and forget about the Vietnamese cultural values. The parents are shocked. They feel they have lost authority. There are arguments. The children want to move out or run away.

To deal with the generation gap, we started counseling sessions for the parents and children at the school, to keep them from drifting apart. There are boys who have both parents working or who escaped from Vietnam alone. They have a lot of unsupervised time and begin to get into trouble. I try to work very closely with the schools to follow the progress of students and develop strategies for teachers to work better with the children.

The principals and teachers are very cooperative, because the refugee children have made a positive impact on the schools, regardless of the language problems. And we've developed an effective bilingual program. Still, there are always some kids who sneak out and hang around the streets. Usually, if a Vietnamese kid is picked up, the police call the voluntary agencies. We talk with the kids and their parents to find out why they are in trouble. Is it their way of crying out for help?

Only two days ago, at 4:45 P.M., as I was leaving the office, I received an urgent message. A black Amer-Asian boy had been stabbed very badly. I rushed to the hospital emergency room. He was stabbed in the chest. I asked him, "What is the matter with you?" He said, "Uncle, I don't know. I was just walking home from school with my friend. Suddenly a black American came and hit me on the shoulder and then stabbed me."

Other Amer-Asian children have had trouble because they are abused, both mentally and physically, by both American and Asian kids. There have been two suicides, one in Uptown, the other in a suburb. The kids, both boys around nineteen, jumped out of windows. They'd been in America for two years and felt rejected by their parents and by society.

At the Community Center we try to create activities for kids. There are three main youth clubs: Boy Scouts, the Buddhist Family Club, and Catholic Youth. Sometimes we organize sports. And to reduce the generation gap with their parents, we have Vietnamese language classes for the kids while their parents study English at a nearby public agency.

My own children like the new fashions, the New Wave. I've tried to stay with the Asian Confucian tradition. As a father, I have to be strict. But in this society, you can't force children to do what you say. They have their own lives.

THANH: Our children were very young when we came here. So we have adjusted and let them have some freedom. We realize that we can't live the way we did in Vietnam. But we try to teach them to respect family life. I tell my children, "The U.S. is liberal. You have the right to drive a car. But when you see a 'One Way' sign, you can't ignore it and say, 'This is a free country, nobody can tell me what to do.' That will lead to a bad accident where you can get hurt. You must also think that way in terms of family rules."

TRONG: Our oldest daughter is fifteen. I wouldn't be happy if a boy asked her to a dance at school or for a date, but it would be okay to go to a party at school, because it would be under supervision. Sometimes we compromise and allow her to go to a party at a friend's house if we know the parents.

Vietnamese tradition is not as strict with boys. I gave my son more freedom when he was in high school, but I had to know where he was going and who he was associating with. I told him, "I give you freedom, but you have to be home by 10:00 P.M., or midnight." If he didn't come home at the time limit—"Sorry," the next time he asks. But sometimes, when he was having a lot of fun and wanted to stay out a little longer, if he called me to ask permission, that was fine.

Last year, after Tran graduated from high school, he moved out on his own. That was a great shock for me. We didn't have enough money to send him to college, so he started working full-time to save for tuition. His high-school grades were average, but he is very artistic, a good drummer. In his free times, he practices a lot with his band. During days he works at a company downtown, and in the evenings he comes into our restaurant to help.

This first year of the restaurant business was miserable. Little by little, our customers have been building up. Our location, on the border of the Uptown and Edgewater neighborhood, is not the greatest. Promotion and advertising cost money that we don't have. My son and two oldest daughters help to keep our costs down. Another reason I have the girls working here is to learn how to communicate with people. If they can handle serving customers, it will help them to handle a lot of other situations in the future. My oldest daughter is very shy, but she's becoming more relaxed and talks with the customers a little more. My second daughter, Thanh Tram, is more outgoing and enjoys dealing with customers.

THAHN TRAM: When most Americans first meet me, they think that I'm seventeen or eighteen and was born here. When they find out that I'm only fourteen and was born in Vietnam, they are surprised.

I don't work at the restaurant on weekdays during the school year. But if I don't have any homework, I'll call the restaurant and see if my mom and dad need me. I come in all day on weekends and during the summer.

The best thing about working here is that I've gotten better at speaking Vietnamese. Where I go to school in Des Plaines, there aren't Vietnamese to talk with. I only talk Vietnamese if I talk on the phone with friends in Uptown. But by working here, I've learned how to talk and write better.

I became a citizen with my parents two years ago. The whole family took the oath of citizenship together. Now most of my friends at school say that, because I have my citizenship, I am American, no longer Vietnamese. I always tell them, "I'm still Vietnamese, no matter what. I'm never going to be all American. I always have to stick to my country."

I cried one time in school when they were talking about Vietnam in class . . . the war and everything. Some kids saw me crying and said, "Why are you crying?" I said, "No, my eyes are tearing." They said, "If you want to cry, why don't you go outside, like a little baby?" I said to them, "If you lost your country, wouldn't you cry?" They said, "No. Not if you can't even go back." I told them, "I wish that I was over there rather than here." They said, "Do you want to die?" I said, "Even though I like it here, I also want to be in my own country." So a boy shrugged his shoulders and said, "Whatever you say."

Most of the kids call me "stuck up." I don't mean to get them upset. I just can't express my feelings. No one at my school thinks about what it's like to be a refugee. No one ever cares, unless I have a real close friend who tries to help me through these problems. Otherwise I never tell anyone about my feelings.

I was very young when I came here. But I still remember what my house in Vietnam looked like, and the beach. One time in Des Plaines, I was sitting by the small lake near my home. It was getting dark; the sun was orange. I sat down on a bench and closed my eyes. I saw myself on the beach in Vietnam. I started crying. I opened my eyes and saw the sun setting over the lake. I cried even more and began talking to myself.

My sister and her American friends came up to me and asked what was wrong. I didn't want to tell them. When I told my sister, she said I was stupid. She asked, "Why are you still thinking of that?" Her attitude is that we're American now; we shouldn't think of the past.

This year, I started ninth grade. It's not worse than junior high, except the homework is a little harder. The only thing I don't like this year is that my parents won't let me play the sports that I like. They say the volleyball will ruin my hands, but that's a sport I'm good at. They don't want me playing basketball, because it's too rough, but I played in seventh and eighth grade. They say, "Why don't you play tennis?" But I don't even know how to play. And I don't want to do swimming because sometimes I have trouble holding my breath.

My sisters and I do volunteer work at school. And I like my counselor a lot. At first I was shy and wouldn't tell her anything. But once I got to know her, I've seen her as a real close friend and I tell her

everything about my life. I know what I want to be when I grow up:
I want to be a doctor, like a specialist in the laboratory.

Now that I'm in high school, I can take more classes like science
and labs. I'm just starting to learn computers. I'm not that good on
them yet. I'm looking forward to starting biology classes.

TRONG: Thanh Tram has a very nice dream to become a doctor. I only
hope that I will be able to support her education. To become a doctor
takes a long time and a lot of money. She gets mostly A's in school
and graduated from middle school in the Honor Society.

She is very mature for a fourteen-year-old. But I worry a lot about
my son, Tran. I want him to go further in his education. His high-
school grades were kind of average—B's. He's still deciding what he
wants to do.

TRAN: I didn't know what I wanted after I finished high school last year.
My dad wanted me to go to college, but first I wanted to support
myself. I moved out on my own because I wanted to have more life
experience. Now I live in this neighborhood, on the street next to
the restaurant. A guy from my band rooms with me.

I don't expect playing the drums will be my profession. I just love
music. It's a way for me to forget about my problems. When I get
home from work at night, I listen to mostly Vietnamese music, because
you can concentrate on the lyrics and feel the music better. But when
I get up in the morning or go to parties, I like New Wave. For a
while in high school, I only listened to heavy metal. That drove my
parents crazy.

The band I'm with plays all different kinds. Some Vietnamese music,
some rock songs like "Jump" by Van Halen. But we play mostly New
Wave, because at parties that's what a lot of kids expect. We play
only on weekends, because most of the guys in the band work or go
to school.

I work downtown at a hearing-aid company, doing shipping and
receiving from nine to five. Then I take a bus to Uptown and work
in the restaurant until eleven o'clock. I would like to start school this
winter semester, so I have to work full-time. But I don't take any
money for helping my parents. I do it because I have a responsibility
as their son.

There has been some conflict in my family because I want to
establish myself on my own. But my loyalty to them hasn't changed.
When I lived at home, I argued with my parents a lot. I had an attitude
just like American kids. But once I left, I realized how much I respect
them.

Before I moved back to the Uptown area, I practically forgot the Vietnamese language. I was eight or nine years old when we left Vietnam. When we came to America, I had to concentrate on learning the new language. In high school there were only two Vietnamese kids, so I hung out with American kids. There were a lot of different groups that kids hung around in. There were the jocks, the wimps, who always studied, the burnouts, who partied all the time. Each group never associated with the others. I like to hang around with all groups. I don't care if they're the wimps or the Melvins. But some kids' attitudes were, "You be with my group only, or we don't want you around." So I said, "Forget it. I don't need no one."

For all four years of high school, what I mostly did was go to school and come straight home. I'd listen to music, study, and play my drums. At that time, I really hated the Vietnamese—I don't know why. I played with only American kids, even though I didn't have many friends. Now that I'm back in Uptown, I like the Vietnamese better. Friendships with people here are a lot easier, even though the neighborhood is rough.

There is a problem with drugs in Uptown. Whether you like it or not, some people are going to press you: "Hey, do you want to try some good weed?" I don't do it, because I think it's really stupid. You just ruin your health.

Some Vietnamese kids adopt a punk style of dressing and wearing their hair. The way they dress is called New Wave. When I go to work, I dress normal. But when I go out, I dress that way, too. There are two groups in Chicago that are called New Wave. One group causes trouble and the other doesn't. Most kids that dress New Wave are decent, they just go with the style. But a few kids in Uptown, mostly without parents here, really cause trouble. They harass and beat people up, anything to get into trouble.

I can't stand some of the punks around here. Not only the Vietnamese—there are a lot of American punks. On the subway, they harass people and steal their money. The other day, on my way home from work, I saw three black kids beating up this one old guy in downtown Chicago.

I think, "Maybe I can do something about it. Fight them, get rid of them." But what's that going to do? You can't take the law into your own hands. Ever since I was a little kid, I never started any fights. I don't like violence at all.

I can remember some things about the war, when we left Vietnam. It was hard . . . terrible. Men were fighting, pushing children and women to the ground, so they could get a place on the plane. People were panicking to get out of the country, because the Communist army was coming. There was shooting. My parents said, "Follow us; we have to go." I didn't realize that we were going to a new country.

Among refugees in the U.S., each age group has their own point of view. From what I see in Uptown, I wouldn't say that everyone is keeping a positive attitude. Some people don't care about their old culture any more.

I'm almost twenty years old. I don't have enough money saved yet, so I'll start at a community college in the neighborhood, Truman College. When I have enough money, I'll transfer to a better school.

I don't like seeing kids my age who are messing around real bad. They're hurting people and hurting our reputation. I want to do something about it. So I decided to study law enforcement in college for two years and then join the police academy.

TRONG: I was very upset when my son went out on his own. I was worried about his well-being. In the Vietnamese community, I saved a lot of families from the generation gap, but when the problem came to my own family, I couldn't solve it.

My children were very young when they came here, so their values have become much more American. I try to behave as an American too, but in my heart I am always Vietnamese. I dream that one day I can get back to Vietnam. I was born there, grew up there. . . . I still remember that, in the past, my father and father-in-law worked for our people's freedom. What I am doing now is very different from what they did. We have freedom here, and sixty million people in Vietnam still do not have that. I still dream of somehow helping them to win their freedom.

INDIANTOWN

FATHER FRANK

Father Frank O'Loughlin
Born in County Clare, Ireland
Pastor, Holy Cross Church
Indiantown, Florida

BLUE CAMP

Francisco and Isabela Jacinto
    Ramírez
Refugees from Huehuetenango
    Province, Guatemala
Migrant Farm Workers
Indiantown, Florida

FATHER FRANK

Ten miles east of Lake Okeechobee, on the edge of the humid Everglades marshlands near Florida's largest citrus grove, a sleepy one-stoplight town was built on the campsite of a Seminole Indian hunting ground. The main street is a two-lane highway that traverses sandy clusters of pine trees and fanlike palmetto bushes on either side of the Saint Lucie Canal.

Every year, from November until spring, while tourists visit nearby Palm Beach resorts, Indiantown's three-thousand-resident population is doubled by migrant farm laborers who stream in to pick thousands of acres of oranges and limes and fields of winter vegetables. Legal and illegal Mexicans, Haitians, Jamaicans, Puerto Ricans, and hard-luck black and white Americans sleep in old cars and ramshackles trailers or crowd into stuffy cinderblock houses, matchbox wooden shacks, and huge barrackslike apartment complexes called "camps."

Beginning in 1982, entire families of small brown people with Asiatic eyes began straggling into Indiantown, speaking an incomprehensible language. They are descendants of the ancient Mayan civilization, displaced by civil war and poverty in the mountains of Guatemala. Unfamiliar with electricity and indoor plumbing, and unable to read or write in their obscure Kanjobal dialect, most of the Indians had never heard of the United States before they fled massacres in their remote villages. Many had bellies bloated from malnutrition, and swollen feet and legs from the long journey through Mexico.

Today, close to a thousand Kanjobal men, women, and children are trying to make a home in Indiantown. One attraction is the availability of low-paying, back-breaking agricultural jobs. But, more important, fearing that immigration officials will deport them back to the killing grounds of their homeland, they've found a safe haven where a small Catholic church led by an Irish priest is defending them.

Father Frank O'Loughlin, pastor of Holy Cross Church, has fought for twenty years to bring hope and dignity to migrant farm workers. Tall and thin with blue eyes, reddish-brown hair receding high on his forehead, and a warm baritone brogue, he has comforted the rural poor and challenged labor bosses and government authorities. Although Father Frank has adopted some unconventional tactics to remedy the wretched *living conditions of parishioners, he maintains the traditional black shirt and jacket outfit of an old-school Catholic priest.*

I'm off the boat myself. Twenty years ago, I arrived from Ireland, newly ordained at the West Palm Beach parish. I became involved with migrant farm workers almost immediately.

The first time I ever had a knock on my door in the middle of the night to anoint the sick, was a call to the shack of a migrant Mexican family. No electricity, no water; a large bed filled the only room. I had to climb on this bed to reach the woman who was dying. There were five or six kids sleeping with her as she died. I couldn't get over this.

I started going back to that desolate part of town, into those shacks. There was a wonderful kind of Mother Teresa, a nun called Sister Aquinas, a gritty, tiny woman who was the only one paying attention to these people. She went around browbeating parishioners for money and food to feed the migrants. I'd go around with her.

I had a hell of a time when I went into the houses or shacks. The interiors were so grimy that I'd stick to the chair where I sat. I could hardly breathe from the smell of urine. I'd be afraid for my life that they would offer me something to eat.

Very often, what passes for a house is a hovel that is open for two or three months of the year, while the farm labor is needed. It's rat-infested, roach-infested. Just a place for workers to lay down between long days of picking fruit or vegetables.

In the famous book about migrant farm workers in the Lake Okeechobee area, *Uprooted Children*, Robert Coles says, "Even animals have a place where they belong. But these people don't." I used to read that passage over and over again, and choke on it. That's one of the reasons why, after I became pastor in Indiantown, we started a housing office. And we started a sewing co-op, directed by Sister Teresa Auad. I wanted people to have a place.

I made a deal with the first nuns that came to work in Indiantown that they would stay to work for a long time. I told them, "The point is to become a landmark, so no matter how much the migrants travel, when they finally swing back this way you'll be here. Something will be stable in their lives." That's how the Holy Cross Service Center started.

Why did I become a priest? Oh, God, I can't even remember at this stage of my life. I went into the seminary right after high school.

I was born in September 1941 in a little tiny place called Lahinch, in County Clare. It's in the west of Ireland. I attended a fancy high school called Rockwell College. A gorgeous place: two thousand acres, a golf course, lakes for rowing. There were kids from all over the world. It was a remnant of British institutions where well-known firms would guarantee to employ students because of school ties. They would put you through university. I was going to study accounting. [Laughs] But I changed my mind.

The seminary I went to is called All Hallows. It was founded in the nineteenth century to send priests on boats with Irish immigrants, wherever they had to go. During the famine years, when there was a huge immigration from Ireland, some priests actually lived on the boats. They were called "coffin ships," because sometimes two-thirds of the passengers would die on board. This was during the mid-nineteenth century, when more than two million people left the country, most of them to America.

I was ordained in 1965. I came directly to the United States, assigned to the Diocese of South Florida. When people ask me what I'm doing here, I tell them, "The first Irish priests in Florida were here in 1785. I'm just keeping up the tradition." [Laughs]

In 1976, I became the pastor of Holy Cross Church. The original settlers in the Indiantown area were the Seminole Indians. The Clements family were the first white settlers in the area. Charlie Clements, who was born and raised here, was the priest at Indiantown before I took over. He ran a parish for the Anglos in the area. Nobody likes to mention it, but many of them were once part of the migrant flow. Some of the wealthiest were literally cowboys on cattle and dairy ranches.

In the respectable houses near the church, with nice yards, are people with year-round jobs in the citrus groves. They do maintenance, irrigation, whatever. Across the railroad tracks is called the Booker Park area of Indiantown, where American blacks and Haitian, Jamaican, Mexican, Puerto Rican, and Guatemalan migrants live. Their homes are cinderblock shacks, matchbox wooden huts, and a very basic apartment complex called Blue Camp.

When I arrived here, I started having Mass for the Hispanic farm workers, who more than double the town's normal population of three thousand during the growing and harvesting seasons. Immigrants are traditionally the most upwardly mobile people in the U.S. They're the highest achievers. But the opposite is true when people work in migrant agriculture. It puts them in the reverse direction.

When I first came to Indiantown, I had posters on the doors of the church promising a free college education to any migrant kid who finished high school. The posters stayed up for years. It became apparent that no farm-worker kids were going to finish high school. The parents need them out in the fields. They begin work as young as eleven or twelve years old. Kids a little younger stay home to look after the babies.

One year after I arrived in Indiantown, I was assigned two nuns, Sisters Joan Gannon and Carole Putnam. They were able to give a hand to whatever seemed to be needed. Within twelve months, Joan set up Holy Cross Service Center, and Carole organized a day-care program. The county gave us what used to be the school building for black children. People always think of migrant farm workers as Mexicans. But in Florida there are still black Americans who migrate to farms in the Carolinas during the summer.

Joan and Carole wanted to live in Blue Camp. I wouldn't agree, because in that kind of overcrowded ghetto they would never get a night's rest. Babies crying, drunks, arguments, radios blasting—life is constant turmoil. I didn't want them beaten down by the living conditions.

So the women moved into a house in Booker Park. The sheriff and leaders of the black community raised hell about it. Their chances of being molested by a drug addict were enormous. There were eighty-year-old women being raped. Black leaders said, "If you live on this side of the tracks, everyone will suffer, because it happened to the two white nuns."

But Carole and Joan insisted on living there. And because they did such good work in the community, they were taken to heart by the people. We tried to approach community service from every angle: housing, emergency and crisis intervention, day care, and the service center. At the same time, we began helping undocumented people— illegal aliens—to adapt by having classes in language, culture, driver's aid, anything people needed.

We built a little hall on church grounds and decided to open our own little school. Not that we could afford it. But we decided that for the migrant children it was an absolute necessity. Hope Rural School opened in 1979. It was four rooms: a kindergarten, a kitchen with dining space, a first grade, and a second grade. Just enough to teach basic reading, writing, and 'rithmetic.

I remember that, even before I came to Indiantown, Variety Children's Hospital in Miami brought in a random busload of migrant kids from Emocholee. They found thirty-nine diseases among the thirty kids.

Indiantown only has seven percent of the county's population, but we have twenty to a hundred percent of the various intestinal diseases. That's because of the squalor. I got phone calls at the church from farm workers beginning to break out in blisters across their necks and chests because they'd been exposed to pesticides. Their kids got into the bathtub and got the rash, too. They were beginning to have respiratory problems and starting to panic.

We went running over to them. Nobody knew what to do. We say, "Let's go to the emergency room." And they say, "We've got a bill at the emergency room, so we can't go there." I can talk to the ambulance crew. I say, "There's a poison control center at Good Samaritan Hospital. Let's go to Good Sam." The drivers say, "Good Sam is C.O.D.—Cash or Die."

The growth of the agricultural industry in Florida skyrocketed with the formula for orange-juice concentrate. Self-made Florida farming entrepreneurs made vast fortunes from scratch. They made it on the backs of farm workers. The picking rates paid to workers when I came to Indiantown were 55¢ for a ninety-five-pound bag of oranges.

To pick a bag of oranges, you have to climb up and down a thirty-foot ladder. On a very good day, where the condition of the fruit on the trees and the weather are just right, the average person can hope to pick around $40 worth.

If you go into the groves and meet some of the black farm workers, they are some of the finest athletes you'll ever see. These men are big and strong, with huge hands. They are the fathers of professional athletes. Tremendous physical ability. But who do the growers want to hire? The little five-foot-tall Mexicans or Guatemalans, who can hardly maneuver up a thirty-foot ladder with a ninety-five-pound sack of oranges hanging around their necks. Yet they are the most desired employees, simply because they are vulnerable to every kind of exploitation.

Until the early 1980s, the majority of the migrants were Mexican. When the Guatemalans began to arrive, they were illegal and worked cheaper than the Mexicans, so they got the jobs. Mexicans who had legal papers and wanted a little-higher wage were displaced. They shifted up to Fort Pierce.

Farming in the area is largely corporate. Among the big employers are Coca-Cola and Minute Maid Orange Juice. Concerns like Mutual of New York and Metropolitan Life are major shareholders in these big farms. They hire farm managers who are fairly enlightened Joe College types. They like to separate themselves from the Old Boy generation. The fact is, they don't effectively run different operations.

In one of the corporate groves, I helped file a lawsuit by John Robinson, who is the only black ever to become a foreman. It was made clear to him every day that his promotion was a token gesture. One morning his crew boss told him, "John, climb over the transformers and fix that thing." John said, "If I climb over the transformer, I'll be electrocuted." He refused.

We filed a civil-rights suit in his behalf. A whole lot of workers signed on, including a crowd of women. The females, mostly Hispanic, had tractor-driving jobs. They'd be sent out to some remote part of the grove. A boss would follow and sexually molest them. They'd say to the guy, "How long is this going to continue?" And he'd say, "How long do you want to keep your job?"

These women finally got brave enough to go home and tell their husbands. The worst boss named in the suit was asked, "Is it true that in the presence of workers you refer to people as niggers?" He said, "I don't seem to offend nobody except the niggers."

I've spent many years fighting against crew bosses. The owners of huge farms say, "I have no employees, only a few office staff." Who picks their thousands of acres of citrus? They say, "I have no idea. I simply hire a labor contractor." The crew boss. He's the one who directly controls the lives of workers. I've had weddings where guests were in the church but the bride didn't show up, because the crew boss wouldn't let her off to attend her own wedding.

Those guys can be as vicious as they like. One boss of a whole bunch of people broke a man's back with a shovel. Mexicans and Guatemalans work for this guy, who is himself a Hispanic. If anyone stands up to him, he calls the Border Patrol to take the worker off his hands.

Over the years, I've seen this same boss go after one girl after another, fourteen or fifteen years old, and get away with it. One time I got fed up. I confronted him: "If you get to this kid, I'm going to nail you. This time you're going to jail." And the guy literally weeps, pleading and carrying on that he was in love. It was the most amazing thing. He couldn't understand that I knew what he was doing.

He finally did get the girl—and got away with it. First the daughter, then the mother, the next daughter, the next daughter. Bang, bang, bang.

The whole migrant-labor system replicates conditions in the Third World. The poverty, the social stratification with big growers, foremen, and classes of serfs. I remember one of the big sugar barons complaining about the setting up of a day-care center. She said, "Where are we going to find our ignorant workers?"

I started an organization for the defense of undocumented workers around the state of Florida. Although in the 1970s there were a few steps forward legislatively to benefit farm workers, the growers got around the law. They switched from using American farm workers to looking for people "south of the valley," meaning undocumented Mexicans, who couldn't claim any of these new benefits. Today, the heart of the agriculatural industry in Florida is the undocumented workers.

For many years, the Border Patrol, as I knew it, showed up at the end of the growing season to hustle workers to wherever the industry needed them. Especially after the vagrancy laws were declared unconstitutional—sheriffs could no longer fill up jails with local poor people, then carry them out to the fields as labor gangs for the growers.

Suddenly, in the early 1980s, there was an uproar over the aliens. The Border Patrol would arrive with a couple of buses. They'd grab undocumented people off the street for deportation. They raided the market where all the workers stop in the morning on the way to the fields, and on their way home in the evening. Then the patrolmen started kicking in people's doors.

At 5:30 or 6:00 A.M., local people were frantically pounding on my door, asking, "What are we going to do with these children? Their parents have been taken by the Border Patrol."

These poor Mexicans were put on buses and taken to Brownsville, Teaxs, to be sent across the border. There was hysteria in all the farmworker communities. I called some people across the state and said, "Let's have a meeting to figure out what to do."

They said, "You've got to be kidding. People are afraid to go out of their homes, even to go to the bathroom. The Border Patrol is camped in the middle of town. Everybody is laying low, hoping their door won't be kicked in."

I started training people around the state to catalogue Border Patrol abuses. We did a drill to practice writing down what happens and the officers' names. I gave out small prayer cards or holy pictures with a picture of Our Lady of Guadalupe, revered by all Mexicans. On the back was a psalm: "Lord, defend us from our enemies and let Your justice reign." The bottom said in Spanish, "If you meet the Border Patrol, remember, don't say anything or sign anything." And three telephone numbers were listed where they could call us.

After every Sunday Mass that I performed, we'd simulate a mock raid at the church. We'd role-play what happens when the Border Patrol picks you up. Without rehearsing, if the real thing happened, people would go into shock.

These Mexicans were all *campesinos*, rural peasant people. They talk to you the way that peasant people do everywhere. They'd sit in the chair and go through the whole simulated arrest very patiently. Then they would ask, "What do I say the fifth time he hits me over the head?" Because, in their cultural experience, they are very cynical that anything can be done for protection against the powers that be. But we kept drilling them, hoping that in an emergency they wouldn't feel so intimidated.

As we were going through all these activities, a local crew boss went to a Texas border town. He used a woman to make a radio commercial in Spanish: "Come to Indiantown. There're jobs and a priest who will defend you against the Border Patrol." Using that ad, he conned a heck of a crowd of people. They waited in Indiantown for weeks with no work. We had to fight with him about that. I wasn't aware of the radio stunt until Border Patrol guys came to me complaining.

Among that crowd, in late 1982, were the very first of the Kanjobal Mayan Indians from Guatemala. Most don't speak or read in English or Spanish, although one man, Alonzo, carried a Bible. At first I didn't recognize that they were different from the Mexicans. A number of the people who come from Mexico are Indians with no experience in the modern world.

The Guatemalans didn't have a place to stay. So they slept in the church for a couple of nights. Later they found rooms in the Yellow Camp building, better known as the Roach Palace. They worked in the fields.

In early 1983, the Border Patrol grabbed six Guatemalan men and a woman off the street. Their children ran and disappeared. The last thing the adults were heard to say as they were loaded into the van was the little chant that I was teaching in the drills. They were taken to Krome Detention Center, outside of Miami.

For six weeks, they wouldn't speak a word to anyone. The Border Patrol tried everything possible to figure out who they were. They even brought in an anthropologist. We didn't want to ask the INS [Immigration and Naturalization Service] for "the Guatemalans," because we didn't know the consequences. Finally, a secretary said that the mystery detainees were listed as John Doe numbers one through six and Jane Doe.

We worked with civil-rights lawyers from the American Friends Service Committee and Florida Rural Legal Services. We said, "We want to represent the Does."

The legal ordeal lasted two months. We went to court with the Does and requested that they be released in care of the parish. We promised that we'd bring them back when the court was ready to rule on their applications for asylum as refugees. Crimes against the Indians in Guatemala were internationally notorious. The INS was aware of this.

In a *Wall Street Journal* article, a Guatemalan army commander said the Indians are "a sea in which the guerrillas move. We must dry up that sea to kill the fish." Indian villages in Quiché and Huehuetenango provinces were annihilated. Before 1981, there were around a hundred thousand Kanjobal in Guatemala. Around five thousand have been killed, mostly in 1981–82. An estimated four thousand are in the U.S., primarily in Los Angeles. And around forty thousand have taken refuge in Mexico. The killing of Indians in northern Guatemala had such an impact on the INS judges that they granted that the Kanjobal stay under our care until an asylum trial could be arranged.

It was amazing that they were released. Not even the crimes in Haiti had that kind of impact on the INS. In Miami, we had the experience with the Haitians where it took colossal court cases to get anyone released. Part of the reason was the millions of potential Haitian asylum seekers, compared to a relatively few Guatemalans. For the past three years, whenever Guatemalan Indians are picked up by INS, we simply send a letter from the parish saying that we'll be responsible.

The Kanjobal community in Indiantown grew rapidly through word of mouth. Though most don't read or write, they send cassette tapes to their relatives. Some Kanjobal came to Indiantown in the regular migrant stream. The local crew bosses pay a Mexican coyote [a professional alien smuggler] $1,000 per worker. The worker, in turn, is in debt peonage to the crew boss to pay back the debt. It is a form of slavery.

The Border Patrol have found some Kanjobal have taken a circuitous route. Even though they were promised to be delivered to Florida, labor contractors had them working in Arizona and Colorado. All the time this is going on, the crew boss is ripping them off: the workers are charged a larger debt to work off based on the distance that they travel.

In Indiantown, the crew bosses try to take advantage of the Guatemalans. They designate certain Kanjobal to be their lieutenants. They become truck drivers and foremen in the groves and fields. Then the bosses corrupt them and want them to fiddle with people's wages. And pay them in beer or wine instead of cash.

The Kanjobal people resisted. They set trucks and houses on fire. We didn't know what the hell was going on. The Kanjobal found ways to bring people to heel who tried to assume authority imposed by outsiders.

The police didn't get involved, because we never called them. There are two sides to the railroad tracks in Indiantown. There're always problems in the migrant community—drinking and fighting. Although not as much after whole Guatemalan families came. There was a lot more when there were only young Mexican men. In any migrant community, there's always bad bars where people are killed every weekend. The cops seldom cross the tracks to investigate.

Before the Guatemalans came to town, the most recently arrived group were the Haitians. I used to have meetings with them every other week. The Haitians' first summer in Indiantown, the only work available was picking lemons. That is the nastiest citrus work. You get all cut up, because of long thorns on the branches. And you don't make much money, maybe $10 or $15 a day.

It was remarkable to see the Haitians' solidarity and their sense of community. They were very much the desired men. A lot of black American women were anxious to have them.

When they first went up the migrant stream, they refused to be paid with wine. Crew bosses hated them. Incidents occurred where groups of Haitians got out of bed in the middle of the night; they'd go into the barns of farmers who hadn't paid them fairly; they took the crop that they had harvested and spread it back on the fields; and they'd be gone in the morning.

All that spirit gradually eroded after a few years in the migrant stream. It gradually breaks people down. Some Haitians discovered that, if you have your own wheels, you're not as vulnerable to the whims of crew bosses. But once they got the cars and independence, the community began to unravel.

I've seen the same process happen with the Guatemalans. Young guys come to town after being in California, Colorado, and a few other places in the migrant stream. They're rough as hell, quite unlike the first groups we saw. The community breakdown comes in the lack of fidelity to their women and the roughness in the home life. Drinking takes place, and there's a fair amount of wife and child abuse.

Every ethnic migrant group has a problem retaining their traditional social structure. When the children are the only members of the family who speak English, roles of dependency get reversed. Parents have to rely on the child to communicate with outsiders, to use the phone and identify what is inside packages in the stores. In any migrant-labor town, in ghettos like Blue Camp or White Camp, there is always a problem with alcohol and prostitution. Dealers come around to sell drugs.

We have two Guatemalan translators, Antonio Silvestre and Jerónimo Camposeco. They were granted U.S. political asylum, because they were targeted by death squads for their community organizing in poor Indian communities in the mountains. When they arrived at the Service Center, I told them, "Our job is to discover the values that sustain the people at home in Guatemala. We'll encourage them to reclaim those values here in this culture."

That's what we try to do in sermons in church, or when talking with parents at PTA meetings at the school. The Service Center has an English class and other educational programs. But it's absolutely awful trying to get people to attend classes during the growing season. From day to day, they are never sure if they have work.

Growing vast amounts of fresh fruits and vegetables is a speculative business. It's a racket of hitting particular markets on the right days. A grower can make millions on a strawberry crop. Or he might have to plow it under because it wouldn't pay to harvest. He might need five hundred workers today, and none a few days from now. A huge migrant-labor pool is available. Workers never know from day to day if the boss will toot the horn for them to be bused to the fields.

Every morning, the women get up at 3:00 A.M. and prepare tortillas for breakfast. The men get up at 5:00, prepare for work, and wait. If by 7:00 A.M. they heard the boss's horn, they climb aboard. The bus takes them to the fields; then the crew boss may say, "We're not picking today." If they work, nobody ever knows exactly what time they'll be home in the evening. It's inconceivable to have as little control over your life as these people have.

Despite these problems, the people's responsiveness to our programs has been fantastic. One night, I was driving back to the church and I saw an uproar in the neighborhood. A car had run up on the front yard of a house. Cops were at the scene. The fellow who owned the house was screaming. If the car hadn't got caught in a hole, it would've run right through the wall.

The driver of the car was Guatemalan. All of the passengers were fellow migrants who had been to the English class at our church. They were thrilled to see me. The driver asked me to explain to the police that what he was doing was actually good. [Laughs] He told me that there were a lot of people in the Blue Camp who didn't have a way to class that night. So he, who had never driven a car before in his life, had been kind enough to drive them.

The man who owned the house, an American, was really upset. He was waving a baby around. He said that the baby had been asleep just inside the wall of the house that the car almost crashed through.

The question has been raised whether rural Guatemalan Indians can function in Florida. Can people come off the side of a mountain where they lived very primordially and survive in this consumer environment? Having only known a barter society, can they adapt to a cash economy?

They were startled to earn $125 a week, which is more than they could earn in a year at home. But they must pay for rent, electricity, laundry, food at the grocery store, and private or public transportation.

In any migrant town, housing and food costs are terribly inflated. To beat that, they cram ten people into a room that should accommodate four. They don't have beds sometimes. They sleep on mattresses on the floor.

In Guatemala, they washed clothes in the river. And they never had a flush toilet, a bathtub, or a shower. At the Service Center, generous volunteers like Claire Siefker try to teach them basic hygiene. For instance, in Indiantown you can't leave food sitting on the table. If you open a package of cereal, five minutes later it's going to be full of roaches. So we teach them to put food in cans.

The people faithfully attend the hygiene classes. Everyone is issued a scrub brush for their nails and a toothbrush. The problem is that some people ignore the advice from our nutritionist and go down to the market on the side of the road to buy expensive junk food. They like the sweet tastes.

We explain to them about parasites in the dirt surrounding their shacks. There are all kinds of bloody bugs. During the summertime, children play in the dirt or the shallow water in the drainage ditches, where they pick up all kinds of diseases. They come down with infections and are covered with scabs.

The Kanjobal come from a cool climate high up in the mountains. Their bodies are not conditioned to the humid, tropical Florida weather. So the children come down with all types of diseases. They are the first in town to get measles and chicken pox. We take some to the hospital. Many have never seen a doctor in Guatemala. The people of Indiantown have shown a beautiful generosity. Doctors have donated their services.

When the Kanjobal kids first showed up at Hope Rural School, we had no idea who they were or what they had been through. They couldn't speak English or Spanish, and they were frightened. These little kids would sit in a corner against the wall very quietly with very sad eyes. But they loved to go outside and climb to the top of trees. There was no way to go up after them to bring them down, so we just let them be. Eventually the other children began to communicate with them.

Sister Esperanza, the school's principal, recalls the day that a TV news team from Miami came to the school in a helicopter. That was the first time we had an idea of what these kids had been through. They ran to hide under the table and were crying. A volunteer teaching assistant asked, "What's wrong?" The children said, "They're going to kill us."

When the pilot of the helicopter heard this, we walked into the building and spoke to the children one by one. He said to them, "There are good helicopters and bad ones. This is a good helicopter. Would you like to see it?" One boy, Santiago, who was seven years old, went with the pilot. It was very touching the way that the child went inside the helicopter and began exploring.

In 1984, I asked a respected psychologist, Neil Boothby, who had previously done studies of children from war zones in Asia and Africa, to work with our Guatemalan children. They were all in kindergarten. he sat with them in the classroom for three months. A technique he used to let them "paint their fears."

At first the kids only drew black shapes. They could use any color, but they only chose black. Neil asked them, "Why do you only draw shapes? Didn't you see something? Don't you remember?" They said, "Yes." And they began to draw airplanes with bullets shooting at little houses. And men with red blood color. Through this therapy, we saw the rage inside of them, which we'd never realized because they are so outwardly gentle. This was part of the process of them coming to peace within themselves.

Then Neil asked them to remember what was positive about their country. The children drew mountains and houses. He told us that they were going to be all right. But those memories never die.

The teachers on our staff try to reinforce the kids' values. The Kanjobal kids call our gardener and maintenance man Uncle Tommy. He knew that the kids love the earth. So he let them plant in the garden and watch the seeds grow. For instance, the other day he asked the kids to pull radishes and bring them to Heidey, the cook, for the school lunch.

The Kanjobal children are very reflective. Sister Esperanza saw two kids sitting on the lawn by themselves, very quietly. She asked them what they were doing. They said, "Waiting for the grass to move." Which was beautiful.

Over the years, I've observed a tragedy that happens in many farmworker families that doesn't show in early childhood. It begins as the restrictions in the kids' world become insurmountable—whether at school or whenever they show any ambition in the community. Like if a boy wants to play little-league baseball, and the coach isn't into "little greasers." With each rejection, the kids make a self-destructive, self-hating judgment about themselves. When are the Guatemalan kids going to encounter these refusals?

Around the time of the Statue of Liberty celebration in 1986, I went to court in the farm-worker community in Fort Pierce, near Indiantown. There, nine kids are on death row. They were arrested as teen-agers. None of the Guatemalan kids have gotten into serious trouble yet. Their family ties are still pretty tight. And they're still distanced from the mainstream culture. But there're beginning to be TV sets in the homes. The changes are going to come.

If tomorrow all the Kanjobal were taken back to Guatemala, I'd be delighted—if I thought that they'd recover all that they left behind. But if they return to the San Miguel area, those who fled through 1983 may eventually be killed. These people will not be tolerated. Though the atrocities committed by the army seem to have stopped since 1983, the land that the refugees owned now belongs to others—possibly a rival neighbor or a colonel. He's not going to have them coming around.

And the guerrillas are still a brutal threat.

If you go to San Miguel and ask about the people who fled, the military's standard line is "They're in the hills with the guerrillas." That justifies the confiscation of their property and continued persecution.

The new immigration law in this country gives amnesty to people who arrived up to 1982, which rules out most Kanjobal. But a provision includes those who have done farm work since 1983. Under that provision, many Kanjobal will be covered. But it is difficult to gather documentation to meet the rules.

Often migrants do not receive the wage stubs from checks that farmers are obligated to pay their workers. The crew bosses deduct taxes and Social Security from the wages, but, instead of paying it to the government, they pocket it.

It's an enormous task for us to try to get accurate information from the migrants about who they worked for. Often they say something like "I worked for Juan." Nobody knows Juan's full name or what company he represents. This is because most Kanjobal don't speak English, and not even much Spanish. All they know is that they pick oranges or peppers. They might know the name of the guy who drives the bus to the fields. They might know the name of the contractor, who they call the *padrone*. And during the summer months, some of the Kanjobal travel to farms in the migrant stream, to Colorado, Georgia, Virginia, Michigan, or New York.

One way the Immigration Service deters asylum cases is to deny migrants work authorization, so they can't apply for a Social Security card. So they're forced to get false cards in order to work. This puts them even deeper under the control of the labor contractor. He can turn them over to the police any time.

Fortunately, under the new immigration law, farm workers are allowed to show false documents that they had used before the law went into effect as proof of previous employment. But we have to hope that five people didn't use the same name on false Social Security cards.

We've had a problem trying to convince the Kanjobal to come forward. They're not used to dealing with a system of laws, because of the lawlessness in their homeland. These people don't have a ghost of a chance for security in Guatemala, and they have no security that they will be allowed to remain in Florida.

If the business of an immigrant is to learn to function in a new society, the business of these people is to worry. When you talk with them, they are very stoic. Like rural people I knew in Ireland, they never express their best hopes or their worst fears. When we look at an American child, we say, "What a beautiful little girl." They would never say a thing like that. They wouldn't want to burden a kid with their hopes. And they never express their fear. It's a trait of people whose whole lives are at the mercy of nature, which is very fickle and unpredictable.

There are around nine hundred Kanjobal in Indiantown now, including children. With a new wave of young single men, there could be a thousand at the height of the growing season. In June 1986, the INS was ready to begin hearing the asylum cases. Kanjobal, by and large, are not people with a political opinion. But the 250 asylum applicants who fled during the terror have a well-founded fear of persecution.

Petrona, a young woman who works in the sewing co-op, witnessed the massacre of her entire family. At her asylum hearing, she recited the whole story of the skinning alive of her father and brother. The judge turned to the defense attorneys and said, "You guys don't think this is a case, do you?"

All of our efforts at the Service Center, the church, the school, and the housing program are supposed to make another statement to these people. What we call Gospel. Even if a man has to travel in the migrant stream, the wife can stay put with a few of the kids, who can finish their education. If they find a shack of their own, they can put some work into it, and it becomes a home.

BLUE CAMP

Blue Camp, a two-story concrete ghetto that covers a sandy lot the length of a football field, was built as a crash pad for Mexican men who dominated the farm-labor force in Indiantown in the 1960s and 1970s. Today, Blue Camp is a Kanjobal village. Scrawny black chickens scamper in and out of open doors on the ground floor. Packs of mangy dogs lie in the shade of gas-guzzling secondhand cars and station wagons the migrants buy "cheap" from local hustlers. Children quietly play on a cement walkway that links second-floor apartments. Cries of babies echo from one end of the building to the other.

Francisco Ramírez, age fifty-one, and his wife, Isabela, forty-one, were shepherds in the mountains of Guatemala. Compared with the adobe-and-thatch hut where Isabela cooked on a wood fire in the middle of the room, the soiled, cramped quarters of Blue Camp are deluxe. Their ten-member family, including three children, share two small rooms. In the front room, a bare mattress and narrow army-style cot form a right angle around the kitchen table. One bare light bulb hung mid-ceiling casts a pale glow on dank blue walls covered with decades of smudges and yellowish grime. Large brown cockroaches flitter in and out of cabinets above the rusty kitchen sink, where Isabela is washing dishes. Her sleeping three-month-old grandson is slung on her back, Indian-style, in a soft wraparound blanket. They have no telephone or television. In place of a real stove, the women cook on two 12-inch electric hot plates.

The room fills with family and neighbors, who listen quietly, except for a two-year-old child in diapers who sits on the cement floor with a squeaky rubber toy, as Francisco and Isabela tell their story in the Kanjobal language. Our translator, Antonio Silvestre, an associate of Father Frank, fled Guatemala after death squads targeted his efforts to form farming cooperatives in impoverished Indian villages.

FRANCISCO: As we prepared to leave Guatemala, we saw army helicopters patrolling the mountains along the border. I knelt down and prayed to the Lord, "Please, dear God, my wife and children and I have never done any bad things. Send us Your blessings. Help us to find a place to go to work. We need to live and find a better situation to survive as a family."

We got up off our knees and continued walking toward the Mexican countryside. At that time, we didn't know anything about the United States or Indiantown. But when we reached Baja California, in June 1985, people said, "There is a place called Florida where you can find jobs."

We have lived in Blue Camp for almost one year and three months. To pay rent and buy food, we accept almost any kind of work. My wife would like to have a job picking fruit. She is a good worker and very honest. But she doesn't have legal immigration papers. Employers are being very careful now, because they don't want to pay fines for hiring illegal workers.

My wife's name is Isabela. Living with us in our apartment is our daughter, Micaela, who is seventeen, and her husband Pedro, twenty-four, and their three-month-old son, Benjamin; my son Jiménez Francisco, twenty; my youngest son, Domingo Francisco Jacinto, six, my nephew, José Pascual, twenty-seven, with his wife Margarita, twenty, and their son, Roberto.

The apartment is one bedroom, a kitchen–dining room, and a bathroom. We have electricity and running water. We work to have enough money for food. In Guatemala, we didn't have work, we had poor land, and we didn't have money. Still, sometimes when we dream at night it is about our village and working the land there.

We lived in *aldea* [village] Chemalito, a community of fifty houses and around three hundred people, high in the mountains. For Kanjobal people this is considered a large village. Most, like San Sebastián, have only a few houses. We had no electric lights, no stores or clinics, no McDonald's. Where we grew up, there was no school. We didn't speak Spanish, only our Kanjobal language.

ISABELA: I remember, on the rare occasions when a strange white person from the city came into our village, we would run to our houses and hide.

FRANCISCO: We were very afraid of outsiders, because in the past the Indian people have always had trouble with abuses by *ladino* [Spanish-speaking] people.

Chemalito is near the Mexican border, around a four-hour walk to San Miguel Acatán town, where we went to church and to buy some food in the market. In the village, we build our houses with wooden sticks or adobe mud walls. The roofs are woven from tall grass.

When it is time to build a house, the family invites the whole community, who are relatives and friends. With fifty people working together, we can build a house in two days. The adobe is poured by hand from pails into the wooden frame.

When families are poor, they use dry leaves as thatch, even for the walls of the house. It is very dangerous. One family we know lost their home, because thatch burns very easily. Their baby was playing with the cooking fire and burned the whole house down.

Houses only have one large room. All family activity takes place there—cooking, sleeping. Part of the room is used for storing grain and seeds for the next season's planting. In a corner is a large earthen pot that holds water from the river. Sometimes we build raised platforms for sleeping; otherwise people sleep on mats on the ground.

ISABELA: Our lives in Guatemala seem funny to us now. Thinking about a fireplace made from three rocks. Grinding dried corn by hand for tortillas. Here, we can buy everything already made at the market. If we could go back to our village in Guatemala, we would like to bring the stove from this apartment.

FRANCISCO: In the mountains, it's hard to find wood for cooking fires. We have to walk a long way carrying a big load of firewood on our backs. We use little twigs of pine to start the fires, because they are very combustible. But during the rainy season, it's terrible cooking in the house. The smoke from wet wood fills the house and sticks to our clothes for a long time afterward. [Laughs]

ISABELA: People live very poorly in the villages in Guatemala. Sometimes they eat just three tortillas a day, that's all.

FRANCISCO: We had a very small plot of land near Chemalito that we tried to farm, but we couldn't grow much in the rocky soil. The summer is very dry, without rain. There is no grass around our village for our sheep to eat. We had to walk through the mountains to find pasture. So we bought another small piece of land near San Sebastián, where we would live for three months of the year. It was a very isolated place, very far from the nearest town.

ISABELA: We were very afraid, because bandits were killing other farmers. We felt very isolated up in the mountains by ourselves. We had to bring all the children. And we had sixty to seventy sheep. It would take us two days walking. We carried our tools, food, and extra clothing in baskets or nets on our backs.

The sheep would bleat like babies, moving slowly and eating grass along the side of mountain trails. And we had an old horse who moved as slowly as the sheep. [Laughs] Sometimes we put the children on his back.

Those mountains are very steep and rocky. We traveled on very narrow paths, not wide enough for a motorcycle. On some peaks, both sides of the trail are sheer cliffs. They are very dangerous, especially for the children.

February, March, and April are summer in Guatemala. There is no rain at that time. We must wait until after Good Friday and Easter for the rain to begin. That is a very special time for everyone. In the evening in the village, we all discuss the patterns of the clouds and the wind to determine when we should plant the first seeds of corn in the ground.

FRANCISCO: Sometimes when the corn grows to around a foot high, a hail- or sleet storm destroys the crop, or we have problems with insects, like snails, that destroy the seedlings. If our crops are destroyed, we have no choice but to travel to the big plantations in the south to earn enough money to survive.

These huge farms are on the Pacific Coast in the lowlands. Whole Indian families from the mountains have to crowd into large trucks owned by plantation labor contractors. Sometimes sixty to sixty-five people are crowded in, squeezing each other during the long journey. The truck is covered by a large canvas. You can imagine how stuffy . . . and the odor, as we bump up and down the unpaved roads. People get motion sickness, because they are not used to riding in a vehicle.

Traveling over the high roads, along the peaks of the Cuchumatanes Mountains, it is terribly cold. When the truck stops to let us out to relieve ourselves, it is too cold for our bodies to function.

When we reach the lowlands on the coast, we suffer from the other climate extreme: it is too hot for us. We work hard, cutting sugar cane or picking cotton or coffee. We sweat a lot and come down with illnesses.

Before 1980, a *campesino* working in the lowland plantations would earn around $1 a day. Many people from my home area travel to the southern farms to earn survival income, but I went only three times in my life. I had other skills. I made jackets from the wool of my sheep. We also made wool ropes, and nets that served as carrying packs from hemp plants. We sold these in the market in San Miguel and other towns.

The people of San Mateo Ixtalán really appreciated our jackets, because it gets very cold in the high mountains. In places where the climate is a little warmer, we sold rope. No matter how much people appreciated our craftsmanship, we didn't make enough money, compared with the amount of work that went into making our products.

We sold a boy's jacket for 3 quetzals—around $1.25. It takes a whole day to make a jacket like that. This doesn't include the time to raise the sheep and shear off the wool. When I was strong, I could carry ten or twelve jackets in a net on my back to sell from town to town.

One day, when we were traveling to a northern town, some border police stopped us. They said, "What are you carrying?" We spread our jackets on the ground. They asked, "What do you have inside them?"

ISABELA: We carried some tortillas in a small cloth bag. The policeman tore open the tortillas to check them, for I don't know what.

FRANCISCO: Sometimes Kanjobal people would go to Mexico to bring back medicines, liquor, and tobacco to sell in Guatemala. Prices in Mexico are much cheaper. Sometimes the border police allowed them to carry the items, if the trader paid them a little money or they took a little for themselves. I learned to speak a little Spanish in my travels, so I could understand what they said.

ISABELA: When I was a girl, I had to take care of the sheep. The nearest school was in San Miguel town, very far from my village. So I never learned to read or write in Kanjobal or Spanish.

My husband and I met when I was a teen-ager. We were both shepherds in the mountains. It was very romantic. Our relationship developed over the years. We began living together and had children. This is the Kanjobal tradition. In our area, boys and girls would be at least sixteen when they were married. But I was twenty years old and my husband was thirty.

FRANCISCO: I got married very old. [Laughs] After Isabela and I had children, Father James Colton, a Maryknoll missionary, convinced us to get married the Christian way. He was the first missionary in our area. We went to San Miguel to get married in the church.

ISABELA: After the ceremony, we traveled back to our village and made some traditional food for our relatives and friends to celebrate with us. We were too poor to afford to pay for a marimba or musicians. Twenty-five to thirty years ago, nobody in my village was Catholic. We had our traditional Mayan religion.

FRANCISCO: The Mayans don't believe in one God. They believe in a big spirit in the mountains. They go to the sacred places to pray that he blesses the village and the families.

Chemalito has a traditional spiritual leader, an *alcalexah* [pronounced "alcacha"], who leads prayers and knows how to interpret the Mayan calendar. It is based on the moon and determines when to celebrate New Year and other festivals. The *alcalexah* lead the ceremonial prayers for planting corn and at the harvest. Farmers ask them to come to their homes to pray for the families' health. Sometimes they go to the sacred places in the mountains to pray. Our family also believes in Jesus Christ.

ISABELA: Many Kanjobal people believe in both the Catholic and Mayan ways. And, recently, the Protestant Church. Only lately has the Kanjobal language been put into a written script—the Bible, the New Testament. But most people, like myself, don't read or write.

The Mayan leaders don't ask for money from the people, but they collect beans and corn from each family so they can live. After Catholic teachers came to Chemalito, my family stopped giving food to the Mayan leaders. They became angry at the Catholic Church, because of the competition. But the greatest problem began in 1980 or '81. *Ladino* and Indian guerrillas came into our area with guns. They threatened or killed people who didn't support them.

The government's army suspected that the Indians in the mountains were collaborating with the guerrillas. Some people did, but many of us were Christians and only wanted to live peacefully. But the army said, "We have to teach you how to respect the government." They went into villages with lists of suspected guerrillas. They didn't waste time looking for the people on the list: they just killed whoever they saw in the town.

My nephew, José, who lives with us now, was the first of our relatives to leave Guatemala. Soldiers came into his village, Suntelaj, which is four miles from Chemalito, and killed ten people.

FRANCISCO: We didn't have anyone killed in Chemalito. But in 1981, soldiers came into La Cholaj, a neighboring village. They told the people, "You are Indians and you are guerrillas." They pushed forty people—men, women and two children—into a house that they used as a prison. One old lady came to the soldiers and begged, "Please, let go of my son—he is innocent." The soldiers said, "You, too. Go inside." Then they poured gasoline on the house and set it on fire. Hours later, only ashes remained of the people.

After the massacre in La Cholaj, we became very afraid. Our whole family decided to walk to Mexico and stay on the other side of the border. We love our home country, but we fled because we love our lives more. Our group was thirty-four people, including some relatives and friends. We had a meeting and decided to flee together.

We knelt down and prayed before climbing down the mountain slope into Mexico. We were very, very lucky. No helicopters or army patrols saw us. And in Mexico we met a farmer who was a Mayan

Indian like us. He said, "I know that in your country you have a problem. You are welcome to work on my farm. It is a peaceful place. If you want to go to the church to say the rosary or attend a Mass, you can take my horse."

We worked on this man's large coffee plantation for one year, cutting grass with a machete. Isabela stayed in the house taking care of our children. Domingo was just one year old. The farmer gave us a chicken and a rooster so that we could have baby chicks, and he gave us a couple of pigs. We took good care of them. After a few months, we had many animals around the house, and some meat to eat.

We were very happy in that place. But in 1982, after one year, we started hearing about Guatemalan military helicopters and army patrols in the border area looking for people fleeing to Mexico. The farmer warned us, "It is dangerous here. Maybe the Guatemalan army will come and drop bombs."

ISABELA: The farmer offered us another house, in Ocosingo, his home area. He said, "I am Mexican. I am safe. But you, please, go to my other house." We went to Ocosingo for just one night. After a long discussion, we decided to go farther along the coast, to the Baja peninsula.

FRANCISCO: We left by bus to Baja with the money we had saved. For the next three years, we worked on a huge farm in Baja, picking tomatoes. We lived with many other migrant families in a big house with many rooms. Every day the foreman would take the workers to the farm by bus or truck. Around five thousand people worked at that place, many Guatemalans and many Mexicans.

We could see the ocean from our house. It was very dry land, like a desert. So the hundreds of acres of tomatoes were watered with a generator-powered irrigation system. The water came from a source maybe twenty miles away. Tomatoes were grown all year round. We worked from 7:00 A.M. to 4:00 P.M. every day. There was no school for the children. My son Jiménez was a teen-ager; he worked alongside me in the fields. My daughter, Micaela, had just entered her teens; she worked with us. My wife stayed home to take care of our little son, Domingo.

ISABELA: The problem with that place was, we didn't have water. Every morning at 4:00 A.M., we had to carry water for two kilometers in two pails balanced on a pole on our shoulders. Oh, it was so painful! And that place had cold weather at night.

FRANCISCO: A Guatemalan friend came to visit me. He said, "On the other side of the border, in the North, you can find a better job. You can find a better house. There are problems down here. Why don't you cross the border?"

ISABELA: We liked what we heard about the United States. But we hadn't saved enough money in Baja, and we were concerned about having problems with American immigration police. We heard that they checked people's papers. Some of my relatives were caught trying to enter the United States. They were afraid that, if they were sent back to Guatemala, they would face serious danger. So they used a trick and said, "We're Mexicans."

FRANCISCO: It was very dangerous to return to Guatemala. The army looked for people who had been out of the country. We would be suspected as guerrillas. We met a group of Kanjobal who fled after us. They said, "Please, don't go back to San Miguel. The war and violence are still going on. The army is still killing people. Go forward." We left Mexico for the United States in June 1985.

We began walking north from the farm in Baja along the big road. We bought some Spanish bread and a can of orange juice. Our group was very small, just my wife, the three children, and I. We were concerned about how we would live in the United States. We had no idea what to expect. And we had saved only enough money to make the trip.

Many Guatemalans use Mexican "coyotes" to guide them across the border, but many times these men take advantage of the people. They ask, "Give me two hundred dollars, or five hundred." The Guatemalans say "Okay," because they are afraid. They have no idea what to do once they reach the border. Sometimes there are robberies, murders. We decided to cross the border without a "coyote." We didn't give our money to anybody.

When we were close to the border, we rested alongside the road in the bushes. When we saw the Border Patrol, we got down and hid. The officers didn't see us. The problem was that we ran out of food and water, and we were so exhausted from walking all night. We did not want to cross at the main point, near San Diego. So we kept moving east, parallel to the border.

Early in the next morning, we saw the border police capture a group of people as they tried to cross. Two or three trucks were patrolling back and forth. The area was very dry. There was no fence, no grass, only scrub bushes and very small trees.

At 10:00 A.M., we were still hiding. It was bright daylight, but we were so hungry and thirsty in the hot sun that we decided to take a chance. We huddled close together and moved as quickly as possible, though it seemed like forever. We looked around and didn't see any border police, so we kept moving through the brush, off the side of the road. We were very tired and had no idea where we were.

We didn't have any bread or water. We looked horrible and felt like we were dying, especially the children. It was an act of God that we met an American man. He talked to us in English. We couldn't understand his language, but he looked like a good man. It sounded like he was saying, "Where do you come from? Who are you?" We couldn't answer, but we tried talking in our language.

He said, "Ahh. I understand. You are very poor people. I can help you." He gave us some water and green lime fruit from a bag that he carried. He gave our small boy, Domingo, some candies.

After the man left, we prayed and thanked God. This man saved our lives. Then we continued walking. A few hours later, we approached the city of San Isidro. A car pulled up to us, driven by a Mexican. We didn't have any American money, but the man offered to drive us near the town. Once there, we met another Mexican who drove us two hundred miles or more to Los Angeles. We had never seen a big city before. It was eleven o'clock at night when we arrived. All the lights were on, like a million stars. I said, "Thank God we are in Los Angeles."

We had the address of my brother. We were so happy to see him. But we were so tired that we slept soundly until morning. My brother had come to the North while I was working in Mexico. We discussed our plans with him. He agreed to loan us enough money so that we could fly to Miami. He knew enough English to take us to the airport and buy our tickets. I felt sad to say goodbye to him again.

When I was working in Baja, I met a man who gave me a piece of paper with the word "Indiantown" written on it. He told us that we could find work there. He instructed us to take an airplane to Miami. From there he said to just show the piece of paper to any taxi driver. He didn't mention that Indiantown is a two-and-a-half-hour drive from Miami, and how expensive the trip would be.

In Miami, we showed the paper to a black taxi driver. The paper had no address, no name of a friend, only the word "Indiantown." The driver motioned to us to get into the car and he began to drive. It was a Sunday morning.

ISABELA: The ride cost $100. That almost finished our savings.

FRANCISCO: The driver dropped us off right here at Blue Camp, where many Kanjobal live. A man from our home area in Guatemala saw us arrive. He ran to the church, where our cousin Andreas was attending

Mass. The man was very excited. He told Andreas, "People from our area, your relatives, are at Blue Camp with their luggage. You must go see them right now."

ISABELA: We didn't know that we had any friends or relatives in Florida. I was so surprised to see the faces of two men that we knew from San Miguel. We felt very happy to be with other Kanjobal, who knew us and spoke our language. If we didn't have our people here, maybe we would have traveled somewhere else—I don't know where.

FRANCISCO: Because it was summer, the off season for agriculture in Florida, we had to look very hard to find work. In the beginning of the second week, I was hired by a large farm to lay long strips of plastic across a field used for planting peppers and tomatoes; plastic protects young plants from bugs and weeds. At the end of the week, I was paid $75. That was a lot of money to us, compared with not more than a few dollars a day in Mexico. During that week, we moved into this apartment in Blue Camp where we still live.

ISABELA: We were thrilled to receive the first paycheck, which seemed like so much money. But we quickly learned how hard it is to save. Whatever we earn is usually spent on rent, food, and clothing. Sometimes we spend $100 on the family's food. Because Indiantown is a migrant farm-worker area, prices are very high. If we can find transportation to a residential city like Stuart, prices are much better and there are more markets to choose from. But we don't have a car. And our household has grown to seven adults, two small boys, and Micaela's baby.

FRANCISCO: Micaela met her husband, Pedro, here in Indiantown. They started living together, in the Kanjobal tradition. They didn't have a party or wedding ceremony. Their baby, Benjamin, is three months old now. Then my nephew, José, and his wife and small son joined us in March 1986.

Where do we all sleep with only one bedroom and this small kitchen–living room? We have two cots in the living room, one cot in the bedroom for Isabela and me, and the children sleep on mattresses on the floor. We don't have a telephone or a television. For entertainment we have a guitar to sing Christian songs together, and a cassette player with tapes of marimba music from Guatemala. José bought an old sewing machine that the women are learning on.

ISABELA: And we have a small washing machine—we don't have to go to the river. [Laughs] We take the wet clothes to a dryer in the laundromat around the corner.

FRANCISCO: The importance of living here is that we've found a relatively peaceful place, where the army isn't looking for us. In Indiantown, we haven't any problems with the police. We are Christians. We go to church on Saturday, Sunday. We ask the strength of God to be better people every day. We only hope to work so that we can buy some food and clothes.

ISABELA: It's better here, because we are alive. Nobody is trying to kill us.

FRANCISCO: In late 1985, I found work picking oranges in the huge groves up the road. But now I am working in a nursery near Stuart. We grow ornamental plants, small palm trees, some flower bushes, and small fir trees. I care for the plants, do some weeding, and transfer plants from the soil into boxes for shipping. I don't understand enough English to communicate with the owners, but our crew leader is a lady who speaks English—she translates into Spanish for us.

I usually work full-time, five days a week. Unfortunately, I've had to miss the past couple of days because of an infection in my eye, but I will be back at the nursery tomorrow. I leave the apartment at seven every morning. A Guatemalan friend with a van takes me every day. Usually I bring home around $130 a week, after taxes are taken out.

People make more money in the short term by picking oranges. But for a man my age, it is much better to work in the nursery. Picking oranges, you not only get very dirty and exhausted, but you have to be big and strong enough to handle a thirty-foot ladder and maneuver it from tree to tree. Pickers wear a big bag around their neck to hold the oranges. When it is full, it weighs more than ninety pounds. It is dangerous to wear that when you are high on top of the ladder and off balance, stretching to pick an orange more than an arm's length away. And there are long thorns on some trees, especially lime, that cut you very painfully. Even when we wear long-sleeve shirts, we still get cuts up and down our arms. The ladder can be unsteady and swings around. If it tips over, it will not only hurt you, but anyone who might be underneath. There is no workers' compensation or insurance to provide for your family. Picking oranges or lemons, people can only work part of the year. But in the nursery I work year-round. The workplace is very quiet, and I get along well with the boss and crew leader.

I have seen some Kanjobal come to the nursery for only one or two weeks; then they are fired. But I have worked there for five or six months now. My pay has remained the same, $3.50 an hour. I accept that, because they have to budget how much money they can spend on workers. So I don't complain. We appreciate our lives here.

My son Domingo is going to school—we like that. After only one year, the children can speak some words in English. And at school, Domingo is eating some American food at lunch. Domingo, what kind of American food do you like?

DOMINGO: Hamburger. [Big grin]

FRANCISCO: Wow, I'm surprised to hear that. It's big progress for him.

ISABELA: English is the biggest problem for us. When we need to go to the hospital, people talk with us and we don't understand what they say. At the clinic, we can't communicate with the doctors. At the school my son attends, his teacher would like to meet with us. And we would like to look for better jobs, but we can't, because of our language problem.

FRANCISCO: We would like to learn English, but after eight hours of work, I am too tired to attend classes and study at night. The children are happy to be in school. They learn the new ways faster than us. Older people have hard heads.

The children must learn English, how to read and write, to find a good job. We don't want Domingo to spend his life working in the fields like us.

ISABELA: Our son likes his school very much. We are very happy and proud that he has the chance to get an education. In Guatemala, it would've been impossible.

DOMINGO: [Very shy] I like to learn English. I am in first grade. My teacher, Mrs. Merton, is teaching us reading and how to write. And arithmetic.

MRS. YVONNE MERTON
ESOL TEACHER
WARFIELD ELEMENTARY SCHOOL, INDIANTOWN

I was curious to find out how Domingo and other Kanjobal children who had never experienced school or a written language were adjusting to American education. I was equally interested to see how the local public school was adapting to these children's special needs.

At Warfield Elementary School, migrant children are a small percentage of the student body. Foreign students are required to attend a special English-language program until they are integrated into regular classes. The ESOL (English for Speakers of

Other Languages) classroom has a vibrant atmosphere. On the morning I visited, the walls were decorated with colorful figures of Snow White and the Seven Dwarfs and other Disney characters. Santa Claus and cut-out paper Christmas trees hung by strings from the ceiling.

Children, clustered around tables, were drawing pictures and practicing handwriting. Another group of mostly Kanjobal children recited the alphabet in unison as a Mexican-American woman pointed to letters on a chart. With unbridled enthusiasm, though a little off key, they sang, "Hap-py, hap-py we will be, when we know our A-B-Cs."

Little Domingo Ramírez, his jet-black hair parted neatly down the middle, was doing arithmetic exercises on a portable green chalkboard. The teacher, Yvonne Merton, who looks well under thirty, with short, curly blond hair, expressed enthusiasm about the children's willingness to learn.

YVONNE: I have twenty-four Kanjobal children out of thirty students. I teach basic reading, writing, and arithmetic to children between four and ten years old. Their attendance fluctuates with the migrant farm-worker flow. The top kids exit into the school's regular second-grade class. It's their first step into the mainstream.

I try to instill in the kids that there is nothing wrong with being a migrant worker. I tell them, "You have nothing to be ashamed of. In life you can be anything you want. You don't have to be a farm worker when you are older."

My aide, who is a Mexican woman, gives the newest students the basics in English. I begin to work with them around the time they can recite the alphabet. But when we had the migration of Kanjobal, who did not speak Spanish, the usual process was not possible.

All of a sudden last year, a large group of forty to fifty Guatemalan children showed up the first week of classes. They were shy, because they couldn't communicate, and we didn't know their language at all. So, right from the start, we immersed them in English.

We started by using a lot of pictures. We used objects that they could touch and learn from. It was slow at first, but they are bright children and inquisitive. And they are young—once their light is turned on, they learn like crazy.

We also use holidays as teaching tools to understand American culture. This past Thanksgiving, we spent a lot of time talking about the Pilgrims, and how the Indians helped them to survive during their first year in America. We showed a film and pictures. Then we had a Thanksgiving feast in the classroom. We put all the guests at one long table. The children made place mats.

Domingo Ramírez at the Warfield School

I thought that, although their families are poor, each child could bring a carrot or an onion, or some other vegetable. We got everything together at eight-thirty in the morning. My aide and I brought three crock pots and made vegetable soup right in the classroom. With carrots, onions, cabbage, corn, and beans—every vegetable you can imagine.

The soup cooked all morning, while we had our reading lesson. Then for lunch we had our feast: soup, cornbread, fruit punch, and pumpkin pie. Everyone really enjoyed themselves. It was lots of fun.

The Kanjobal children are no discipline problem. They are excited about learning. The students in their second year are almost ready to start a regular second-grade reader. They're passing tests in the ninety-five-percent level. This time last year, they couldn't speak ten words of English.

Domingo Ramírez is in his first year in our class. He had no previous schooling. When he started, he couldn't do much of anything. He had very little language comprehension. When you put anyone in a strange environment, they will stumble for a while, but the twinkle in his eyes is always there. After just a few months in class, his light is ready to flip on. He's learning the ABCs and basic math. We have him talk about things at home, things at school. We play rhyming games. Anything that involves vocabulary in a meaningful context.

Every nine weeks, we have parent conferences, when the report cards come out. Every time I've had hundred-percent participation by the

Kanjobal parents. Antonio Silvestre from the Holy Cross Service Center comes in to translate. Even though they are not educated themselves, they care so much about their children.

The first part of this school year, we had an open house. There was a brief assembly where our principal spoke; then all the parents went into the classroom. I had the kids sing along in English with a few songs on the record player that we learned for the open house. One song was "The Pawpaw Patch," about the Kentucky mountains. The kids love to sing. I told them that the pawpaw patch is like a garden, and used pictures to show them. The kids also sang "He's Got the Whole World in His Hands" and "Old MacDonald."

The parents were thrilled, and the kids were just beaming. Mr. Ramírez stood up. He held everyone spellbound while he spoke in Kanjobal to the children. I could only pick out a phrase here and there, when he used Spanish. Like *"escuela es muy importante"*—"school is very important." He spoke for five or six minutes, using gestures like pounding his fist into his hand. The kids sat motionless. They were very respectful.

He said, "It is very important to listen to your teacher and be happy here in school." He interjected the word "English" throughout his speech: "How important it is for you to learn English." After he finished, he walked over to me and shook my hand very graciously.

That speech stayed with me. I thought it was truly remarkable. I told a lot of people about it. Although he is uneducated and very new in this country, Mr. Ramírez realizes the value of an education.

In their Blue Camp apartment, Francisco and Isabela reflected hopefully on Domingo's future:

ISABELA: It is our dream that our son can grow up in this country, where he has some opportunity. Domingo must be very sharp and intelligent, because he is learning English very quickly.

FRANCISCO: We are encouraging him to plan to attend high school. He has to take advantage of learning and the educational system. If he went back to Guatemala, there are no teachers in our town. And survival is so difficult—even children have to work. And in our village there is no doctor or clinic. Most Indian families have six or seven children, and maybe two or three of them die because of malnutrition and lack of medicine. Most of the towns have this same problem. If someone is seriously ill they must walk for hours to a clinic in a big town. Even then there is not much medicine, maybe just aspirins.

ISABELA: In the villages, Guatemalan homes don't have bathrooms. People have to dig outdoor latrines. This is very unhealthy, because children pick up parasites that swell their stomachs. Here in Indiantown, we are very happy to have a bathroom inside the apartment. It is a very big change for us. We never imagined that it would be possible.

FRANCISCO: The United States is a very nice country. Americans are lucky to have flat land with rich soil, not rocky mountains like where we lived in Guatemala. In Guatemala, we have to carry our firewood, even after a long day of field work, or if we are sick or tired. Here, when we come home from work, we have earned money and can buy anything we need to eat. We have an electric hot plate to cook. The refrigerator . . . ours doesn't work, but it is a wonderful invention.

ISABELA: Here we can eat chicken very often. But in our village it was only on special occasions. We could only buy a small piece of meat a few times a month.

Life is safer here in Indiantown. But there are many social problems in Blue Camp. Some nights, even at 2:00 A.M., we cannot sleep because many things are happening outside, people drinking a lot and fighting. The police come sometimes and take them away.

FRANCISCO: I have seen American people drinking, but not fighting. The Indians have to learn how to drink alcohol. Some of the drunks were also heavy drinkers in Guatemala; they continue the same way here, only worse. They make problems and have to go to jail and pay fines. Their social problems affect the whole community. When we hear trouble outside, we close our door. We don't go out to look. We don't want any problems with anybody.

ISABELA: The other night, there was a fight behind the building, between two women, about some man. Maybe this is not a good place to live. Some black people and Mexicans come here to sell bad things. And it is easy to buy beer any time at the grocery store. Last Friday, a Kanjobal man was killed. Somebody cut his throat near a *cantina*, only one block from Blue Camp.

FRANCISCO: God says, "If you go by the good road, you can find happiness. If you go by the bad road, you find punishment." Since we have been in America, our family has stayed very close. In the evenings, we play the guitar together and sing songs that we have learned at church. We have a lot of faith.

Last week, in church, the priest said, "When some people need to come to Mass, they don't like to come. But if there is a *cantina* open, they spend all their time drinking and fighting."

ISABELA: We are very concerned about the social problems among the

Kanjobal. It makes us very sad and very worried. Especially because the white community says, "All of you Kanjobal are the same." It's not true, because there are many very good people. It's only a small group that makes trouble.

There are some people in the community who are always at church. We try to attend Mass on Thursday, sometimes on Saturday, and also every Sunday. We thank God for everything we have in this country, but we worry that somebody may tell us that we will have to go back to Guatemala.

FRANCISCO: We think of our country—we are Kanjobals. Maybe some day, if we save money, we can go back to build a house and live the last years of our life in the town where we were born. But we cannot go back now, because conditions in Guatemala remain unstable and dangerous.

If the American government accepts us, I would like to stay here and become a citizen. We prayed to the power of God, and He helped us to get here.

Officially, we are classified by the Immigration Service as illegal aliens. But I hope we can apply under the new immigration law because between 1985 and 1986 I worked picking citrus and planting tomatoes and peppers.

At the nursery where I now work, we have the W-4 tax form that proves that I have been working. I haven't tried to ask the bosses at the big farms for my pay records. It is a very strange legal system for us. We always need someone to translate. But so far we haven't had any problems with Immigration. In the future, if we have any diffi-culties, we will call Antonio or Father Frank at Holy Cross.

As soon as I qualify under the new law, my wife will be able to obtain her papers for work. If we can take care of ourselves, we will have a good life here. I am happy that my son is doing well in school. It would be wonderful if he can get a college education. But we cannot imagine that. We are poor people.

ISABELA: It is an impossible dream. But we would like to send Domingo to a university if he is intelligent enough.

THE PEDDLER

Hugh Patrick Brown

Cha Ok Kim
Born near Kwangju, South Korea
Import-Export Businessman
New York City

Orphaned during the Korean War, Cha Ok Kim kept from starving by selling cigarettes in the streets of Kwangju. In 1971, fresh out of graduate school and newly married, he landed in New York with the dream of becoming an international statesman.

Three years later, Kim and his wife were living in a transient hotel with three hungry babies. He invested his savings in a bag of ladies' wigs and began peddling door to door in Harlem.

Today, a few blocks south of the Empire State Building, among the warehouses, wholesalers, jewelers, and trading shops of midtown Manhattan, Kim's import-export company is doing $4–5 million of transactions annually. In his own words, he is "a self-made man."

Many well-educated Korean immigrants, limited only by language, have demonstrated extraordinary savvy in adapting to American business. In fact, almost ten thousand Korean-owned small-to-middle-sized markets, services, and merchandise shops have helped revitalize New York City's economy. From Coney Island to Flushing, Koreans have changed the face of the city.

Many Koreans in this city work "twenty-five hours" in a day. We set up small businesses in run-down areas where other people are afraid to go. In New York, Koreans have opened gas stations, grocery stores, liquor stores, cleaning shops, warehouses, and import-export businesses like my own. They have helped restore areas like Harlem. That's why Mayor Koch has said that Koreans are number one. We have gone into parts of the city where people had given up.

Sometimes, in these places, American people want to fight with us. They ask, "How come, after being in this country only two or three years, you Korean people have your own store? You make money. Maybe the Korean government or American government gives you special assistance." This was never true for my generation of immigrants. We came with very little money. Some people, like me, started as peddlers.

I put ladies' wigs in a bag that I slung over my shoulder and walked the streets in Harlem and Brooklyn. I would go into bars where many black people drink. Sometimes men had guns, axes, knives, and tried to rob me. One of their tricks was to have a lady call from an upstairs window, "Hey, I need a wig." I would enter the building. On the stairway, a man would be waiting with an ax. He'd say, "Give me your money."

I was a peddler for seven years before I established my import-export store in the midtown Broadway business district. Between West 26th Street and West 34th on Broadway, there are many wholesale and import-export warehouses—more than sixty percent are owned by Koreans. There are two large Korean banks. The area is very alive, with a lot of traffic and delivery trucks always in the street.

Our store is open from seven A.M. until sometimes 8:30 to 9:00 P.M. We sell more than three hundred items wholesale. My wife has a good sense of the types of products that people like to buy: hats, gloves, sunglasses, scarves, costume jewelry, many styles of belts and toys. All day long, small retail-shop owners come in to resupply. We usually need ten people in the store to deal with customers. My wife, her father, my two brothers-in-law and their wives, and myself all work together as a family. While we are at the store, my mother-in-law watches our children.

Originally, the businesses in this district were owned by Jewish people who came from Europe. They worked hard and made enough money to move out of the city. Their children told them, "You've worked very hard at your business to support us. We appreciate that. But I want to be a doctor, or a lawyer, or an investment banker."

As empty spaces opened up during the past ten years, Koreans moved in. We keep the neighborhood alive, and by paying taxes and generating income, we help the city.

When I first opened my store, I bought merchandise from a wholesale store owned by a Jewish mother and father. They were very kind to my wife and me. They helped with whatever we needed. As they became older, their son took over. He complained right away: "I don't like this business. I've got an education that's better than this." He eventually sold the business to a Korean.

The older shopowners made enough money to be comfortable. Now they open later and close early. They go on vacation. But we Korean people are just starting. We don't have bank credit. We borrow from credit unions, our family, or friends. That's peanuts. After a number of months, when the business becomes established, we can begin to borrow from the banks to expand a little larger. We try to make enough money to give our children the chance to attend university and plan their future.

I have three children. My oldest, John, is a high-school freshman. My two girls, Julie and Joon, are thirteen and twelve years old. John told my wife, "Lawyers and doctors make money. I am thinking about that."

My wife, Min Cha, and I have been here for fifteen years. But my first thirty-five years I lived in Korea, so of course I'm still Korean. I can't change. But my children are very American. They speak Korean pretty well. I had them attend Korean-language school in New York, but at home they speak in English.

I try to get them to speak Korean with me. I saw that my son learned to speak Spanish in school. I told him, "It's very good that you can speak Spanish so well. How about studying Korean?" He told me, "Spanish is easier than Korean."

In the Korean language, tonality or vocal pitch gives words different meanings. And there are four or five different dialects. Because of radio and television, there is now a standard language taught in Korea's high schools and universities, but different regions still have their own accents.

I come from the region of South Chŏlla, the South. I was born in 1935 in Hwa Soon, a small town in the countryside near the city of Kwangju. My family was very poor. My mother and father never learned to read and write. Korea was suffering under Japanese control. The people in my area had to struggle, farming on the side of mountains and working in coal mines.

During the middle of World War II, when I was eight years old, my mother died. And when I was fourteen, just before the Korean War, my father passed away. To survive, I became a peddler in the streets. I worked for my big brother, who is twenty years older than me. He sold his merchandise, like gloves, scarves, and cigarettes, from a small wooden pushcart. I would shout, "Cigarettes!"

Because of the invasion by North Korea and my job, I had no time to go to school. But I still wanted to study. I knew a young man who had gone away to study in Japan for a few years. When he came back to Korea, he was very important because of his education.

I kept my mind active by reading magazines, novels, anything I could find. But during the war, from 1950 to 1952, there was nothing to eat. Sometimes people had to steal food from the army because they were so hungry.

In my area, in the far south, we were away from the main line of battle, but our town was bombed many times. Many buildings were damaged or destroyed. My house was very small, so we were lucky that it wasn't hit.

North Korean Communist guerrillas stayed up in the mountains. During the day we had the army to protect us. But at night the guerrillas would come into the towns and attack. We were very afraid of the Communists. Many people died.

More than anything else, I wanted to study so that I could achieve something in life. My older brother didn't understand. He told me, "To do business is better than studying." So I continued to work with him in the streets, peddling cigarettes. We made enough money to live, but I had no time to prepare for the exams to enter middle school. I took the test two straight years. Both times I failed.

During the war, when I was sixteen years old, I traveled to Kwangju with my brother. To earn a living, we caught fish in the harbor in Yosu and traded them in markets in small towns. Sometimes boys I knew who were students came by my fish stand in the market. I would hide from them, because I was so embarrassed. I wanted to go to middle school with them, but there was no way I could stop working.

Within a year, business had gotten a little better. I made a bag from cloth that I strapped over my shoulders like a backpack to carry fish from market to market. At the time, there was a lot of fighting going on and many soldiers. I could sell at the train station, to the crowds. In the evening I would return to Kwangju, where I found a job in a bakery making bread.

We woke up at one o'clock in the morning to prepare bread. Each day I worked eighteen hours, with only six hours' sleep. During this whole time, I never surrendered my dream of going to middle school.

During that summer, some university students came into town. The oldest one commanded me, "You study English with us, and mathematics. If you succeed, you can go to high school." They came into the bakery and taught me while I worked. Even though I never attended middle school, I learned enough from them to qualify for high school.

In 1953, when I was eighteen or nineteen years old, the Korean War was coming to an end. The country was devastated. My only hope was to earn a high-school diploma. I was almost twenty-one by the time I started high-school classes. In my generation, most Koreans had their lives disrupted by the war. It was not uncommon for a person to be so far behind in life.

To support myself during high school, I delivered newspapers and continued working in the bakery. And for two months, during summer vacation, I traveled to the coal mines. I dug coal underground with a pick and shovel.

Every morning at three, I would begin my shift at the mine. It was pitch-dark underground, so we worked by gaslight lanterns. The law stated that you could not work underground if you were more than twenty years old. I was over twenty-one, but the owner said, "You look very young. Since you are under twenty years, you can work down there." Nobody in the mine knew that I was a student.

It was very dangerous underground. We filled bags with coal and carried them out on our backs, in continuous eight-hour shifts. Sometimes I worked double shifts, because the amount we were paid for one shift was barely enough to pay for rice. The second-shift money I saved for my school tuition. One morning, as I prepared to enter the mine, two or three men were killed when the walls caved in on them. One of my co-workers warned me and was afraid to go down the mineshaft. I thought to myself, "I know that there is a chance that I will die. But I need the money to study."

In my off-duty hours, I would try to attend some private classes at an institute, in English, math, and geometry, to make up for the years of schooling that I missed. In 1957, I finished high school. To my surprise, I was offered the opportunity to go to college in the capital, Seoul.

From my home district, Seoul was thirteen hours by train. There were very few cars, and no highways through the mountains.

In Seoul, I took evening classes at Chung Ang University and worked days. As my studies progressed, I was able to support myself by doing private tutoring. I was able to switch to day classes. My goal was to become a professor of international relations.

When I tutored high-school students, sometimes I was paid; other times I helped students free of charge so that they could qualify for high school or college. As when I worked in the bakery, a lot of people were very poor and couldn't afford to pay me. But without the extra help they would not have been able to achieve a higher education. Like myself, many youths lost their family or were separated during the war. They came to Seoul looking for work. To help these youths, for many years I tutored at night, and I organized a student association at the college.

I graduated with a degree in international relations in 1961, when I was twenty-seven years old. I was always interested in political science and how different countries in the world get along together. I never thought of becoming a businessman.

Following graduation, I joined the army. I received six months of training, then for the next thirty months I was assigned to KATUSA, the Korean army's liaison group with the American military. When I was discharged from the service, I took a job in the Defense Ministry while I studied in a graduate-degree program. It was very difficult to get into graduate school at that time, because there were only a few universities in Korea.

At the Defense Department I continued working with Americans, as a clerk in the Safety Section. Our responsibilities were diverse, from traffic control to making sure that soldiers knew how to carry their weapons safely. I sometimes acted as a translator for the American advisers. The GIs I met were impressive people. I became good friends with some of them.

In 1967, I received my master's degree in international relations. Some of my American friends and people in the Korean government suggested that I go to the United States to continue my studies. My dream was to become a university professor.

Around that time, on a visit to my family, my brother-in-law introduced me to a young woman who was a pharmacist in Yosu. Her name was Min Cha, and I liked her very much. In the Korean tradition, on the first date the man must visit the girl or woman's home to introduce himself to her family. After that, we began to spend our free time together. I would travel from Seoul whenever I had the chance. Because my parents were gone, my sister and her husband acted as intermediaries to arrange the wedding with Min Cha's parents. Even before we married in 1970, we both thought that going to the United States was a good idea.

Though we didn't have much money, American Immigration looked favorably on our request because of my wife's occupation. She fit under a profession that the U.S. government wanted at that time. A hospital in Philadelphia gave her an invitation. We took some extra English classes and made preparations to travel.

Before we left Korea, I participated in the political campaign of a friend who successfully ran for Congress. I gained good experience. After his election I told him, "My idea is to go to the United States to study more about democratic political science. I will earn a doctorate degree, then come back to Korea to help you." I thought it would be easy.

We arrived in the United States in September 1971. Our first home was in Camden, New Jersey, outside of Philadelphia. My wife had a good friend there. Before we left Korea, I looked at a map and thought,

"Camden is a good location. Not far from both New York and Philadelphia. I can work during the days and at night go to New York to
attend university classes." In reality, Camden is two hours by train from
New York.

I began looking for work the first day we arrived in the United States.
The next day I found a job at the Amalgamated Textile factory in
Philadelphia. Everyone there was stronger and much bigger than I. My
legs were too short to work the machines. But after a while I built up
big muscles in my legs.

Min Cha had no idea that she was pregnant when we left Korea.
Because of this, she was unable to take the job at the hospital pharmacy.
She tried working in a factory. Eight hours on her feet . . . she would
have to take a half-hour break in the ladies' room during the middle
stages of her pregnancy. In Korea, she had never worked at a hard
physical job. Before the baby was born, she had to stop working.

My pay was $2 an hour. I only brought home between $65 and $70
a week. In April 1972, my son, John, was born. After six months of
working, I had only saved $300. I realized that, after taxes and carfare,
I was only earning $1.50 an hour. There was no way that I would be
able to take care of my family and save for my graduate studies, which
cost at least $700 a semester. I thought, "We have to go to New York,
it's better there."

In March 1973, after my second child, Julie, was born, we moved to
New York City. We lived on West 95th Street, in a residential hotel.
The neighborhood was not great, but rent was only $100 a month.

I was able to find another job in an Amalgamated Textile factory in
midtown Manhattan, making men's clothing. The pay was a little higher—
$3 an hour. But living expenses were also higher, so there was no change
in our financial situation.

In December 1974, my wife gave birth to our third child, Joon. It
was a very difficult period for us, living in one room in the hotel with
three small children. The baby was crying. My wife and I only got five
hours of sleep each night.

I inquired about my education and found that it was very hard to get
accepted into graduate school. First I had to pass the English-language
test. Though my English was proficient enough in Korea, here people
couldn't understand my accent and I needed a larger vocabulary. So,
while I worked days at the cutting machine at the factory, I studied an
English dictionary that I kept beside me.

My supervisor would yell at me when he saw me studying, "You are being paid to work." So I kept the dictionary hidden under the machine table. When the supervisor wasn't looking in my direction, I would peek at it to try to learn a new word while I kept the textile machine running. I wouldn't recommend this as the best way to study. But I had to spend eight to ten hours a day on the job, so I had no other choice.

I developed a study system. At night I would study part of the dictionary at home. I wrote down definitions of words on a piece of paper. In the morning I folded the paper and put it in my shirt pocket. Then, while I ran the cutting machine all day, I would sneak looks at the paper to memorize new words.

Around thirty Korean families lived in the Monteri Hotel. Most of them had decent educations in Korea. Now some less educated Koreans are allowed into the United States for family reunification. But fifteen years ago, only higher-educated and professional people were allowed to immigrate. All of the men at the hotel had finished college, as had my wife. There were medical doctors, pharmacists, engineers. But here we were starting from the bottom, looking for any kind of work to support ourselves. We would get together to try to determine how we could study and take care of our families at the same time. Because of our language problems, we couldn't find good jobs in offices or banks.

Tuition is very high for foreign students at New York University, which was where I wanted to study. I determined that going into my own business would be better than factory work. At the time, ladies' wigs were very popular. My idea was to get ladies' wigs and take them around to make money. This is where my childhood experience as a peddler was very helpful.

My wife went to various wholesale stores during the days, while I worked at the factory. We were able to buy wigs for $3 apiece in bulk orders. On weekends I would go into the streets and sell them. I started out peddling in Harlem.

I put fifty wigs in a cloth bag that I carried over my shoulder. I would walk into any place—restaurants, bars, hospitals, and door to door. I learned to stand in a visible place on the sidewalk. I'd pull a wig out of the bag and start combing it. Ladies would come up and ask what I was doing. I would pull a few wigs out of the bag to show them the different styles. I'd say, "Do you like red? Okay, here's red." That wasn't so dangerous, because I dealt with ladies only. But sometimes men followed me, looking for a chance to rob me.

In one day of selling wigs I could make as much money as one week in the factory. So I left the textile job and expanded my selling trips to

Newark and Philadelphia. Then I found out where the black neighbor-hoods, where people appreciated our low-cost merchandise, were in Boston, Cleveland, and Detroit.

I saved enough money to begin graduate school in NYU in September 1974. On weekends and during vacations, I went on the road with friends, selling wigs throughout the Eastern United States. We would take a bus to Buffalo, Detroit, Miami. Sometimes five of us would pile into a friend's car and go together. We'd carry an almanac with us. I'd study the demographics of each neighborhood of the city we were approaching. I'd say, "This neighborhood is dangerous; we have to be careful. This area is more high-class, middle-class." After we visited an area, we had established customers, who would recognize us or be waiting for us to come back again.

We'd go to Albany, Syracuse, and Buffalo. Then we'd swing across to Cleveland, Toledo, then Indiana and Detroit. We would just follow the road maps and the almanac. I had a Korean friend who was a professor in Miami. He lived there for fifteen years. But after one or two short peddling trips, I knew Miami better than him.

I would walk down a street and see someone having a party in their backyard. They'd say, "We don't want to buy any wigs." I'd say, "Okay. I'll just rest here for a minute." I'd look around and choose the most beautiful lady. I'd go up to her and start to talk: "Whether you want to buy one or not, I'd like for you to try this new style one time." I'd take out a wig that was very beautiful. She'd shout, "Oh! That's beautiful." And all the people would come around and buy. [Laughs]

Sometimes men would buy for their wife or mother. Older people saw us working all day, came to us, and said, "Why don't you come to my home and marry my daughter?" [Laughs] They saw how hard we worked and thought we'd make good husbands.

In the mornings I would go from store to store, from 9:00 A.M. until mid-afternoon, collecting wholesale orders from merchants. I would telephone my wife in New York and tell her where to ship the orders. Then, around 4:00 P.M., I would peddle on the streets. I'd look for a good spot to sit and display my wigs. I'd earn $50 to $100. After sundown, my friends and I got into our car and drove to the next city.

Around 1:00 A.M., we'd stop at a roadside rest area to get a few hours' sleep. We'd try to be in the next town by 9:00 A.M. Fridays, Saturdays, and Sundays were our best days. We'd be so busy that we couldn't talk or take time to eat. We saved a lot of money this way.

On a weekday, we might be on the highway between Toledo and Columbus. I'd look in the almanac and see that we were approaching a big cigar factory. We'd pull into the factory parking lot at 5:00 P.M., when people were getting out of work, stand outside with our bags, and sell. Black ladies liked the wigs, because they don't have long straight hair. Most couldn't afford to buy a $300 or $400 human-hair wig. My wigs looked like human hair but only cost $10. They were made from a nylon material. The colors were black, red, all shades of brown. And older women liked mixed gray. Some women bought a few different colors to match their dresses.

In Indianapolis, we'd stand in front of a big hospital. Sometimes we'd go right into the lobby and sell. A nurse would come by and say, "Okay, I want to buy a wig." They would go get their money and forget about their patients. Police would come by and check us. They said, "You can't work here. The nurses will get distracted, and their patients will all die."

One time we were standing on a sidewalk and people came by in a long black car, going to a funeral. They stopped at a red light and came over to buy wigs.

When a policeman would check me out, I would show my New York sales license. Sometimes that would be legal. But other times I had to purchase a permit at the local city hall. The prices varied from $3 to $60.

Sometimes we tried our luck in restricted areas. The police would come by to warn us. The next time, angry, he'd say, "One more time and I'll send you all to jail." I'd say, "Officer, I'm a student. I don't have tuition. That's why I sell here." He'd look at me and say quietly, "Well, then, that's okay. You're a student. You can stay here except from ten until twelve." Sometimes the police helped us like that.

For us, time was money. And we had orders to fill. I would send the money we earned to my wife with new order forms. She purchased the requested number and sent me two to three hundred wigs by UPS to a city where we were going to be in a few days. We asked her for as much merchandise as we could carry in our peddling bags. All the money we made, we reinvested to keep our business growing.

After a few months on the road, my business was established. A group of Korean graduate students came to me in New York and asked me to teach them how to do business. They said, "You purchase the wigs wholesale, and we will buy from you for ourselves to sell." That's business, right? I named my company Dong Jin, "Going East," because I imported from Asia.

The students branched out to different cities. They'd go their separate ways all over the United States. Each was responsible for their own

peddling business. My wife and I only supplied them with merchandise.
I was like the organizer of a group of businessmen. Now some are
professors back in Korea, some are presidents of large companies, others
work in the Korean government. And some are American citizens and
doing quite well.

At first, my wife and I used our apartment as our warehouse and office.
When we began to import wigs, business was brisk. Within four months,
I found a small office at 1261 Broadway, in the midtown business district.
I would go out on the road selling while my wife ran the warehouse.

Min Cha had to bring our three small children with her to the warehouse. We didn't have anyone to babysit, but it was important to keep
the business going. She would walk up and down Broadway comparing
prices in different import and wholesale shops to find the best deal. We
knew some Korean importers and factories in the area. We could buy
a wig for 50¢ and sell it at a fair price for our friends to peddle.

Our children were only one, two, and three years old. Oh! my wife
had to take them everywhere with her! [Laughs] The babies would go
into the stores and play with everything.

Once we got our business going, we moved to Flushing, in Queens,
in 1976. Shortly after we moved, my wife's parents arrived from Korea.
Now, there are almost forty thousand Koreans living in Queens. Back
then the neighborhood was mostly Jewish. We found a nice apartment
with enough room for the kids, who were becoming pretty active. When
my wife's parents moved in with us, her mother helped with the kids.
That made things a lot easier.

Our home in Flushing was very near the subway to Manhattan. I read
newspapers and studied while riding to school. We didn't buy a car until
1979. So, on wig-selling trips to different cities, I continued to use the
Greyhound bus, the Amtrak, or my friend's car. I had a lot of interesting
experiences while peddling. One time I was able to learn a lot about
politics in this country.

Worcester, Massachusetts, was the home of Senator Edward Brooke,
who was the only black U.S. senator since the post–Civil War period.
He was on the Foreign Relations Committee. I went to his election
campaign headquarters to ask questions about U.S.-Korea relations and
to see how they ran a campaign. About twenty or thirty women who
worked there told me that they wanted to buy wigs. I said, "No, I came
to see Senator Brooke." I spoke with some of the Senator's aides about
political situations. They liked me and said, "While you're doing your
wig selling, why don't you campaign for Brooke?" I said, "Okay." And

went house to house for Brooke. Thirty or forty people bought my wigs. [Laughs]

I asked Brooke's aides many questions about how they handled the Senator's re-election. Twenty or thirty campaigners for Brooke went into a neighborhood to shake hands with people. I told the lady campaigners, "How about wearing a red wig? You'll look very beautiful." The staff bought wigs so they would look nice. And they taught me how to do a political campaign.

In some cities I would walk into the neighborhood bar. There would be many people drinking, many ladies. I'd say, "Hello, ladies. Wigs for sale. I am a student trying to pay for my schooling." The owners of the bars were always black people. Sometimes people would say to me, "You go back to your own country." I said to them, "You go to your country. This is my country." They'd say, "You're Chinese. Why do you say this is your country?" I'd say, "Because I am an Indian. You're from Africa. This is my country. I'm not Chinese, I am American Indian." [Laughs]

I make a joke. But it's true that some American Indians came from Manchuria and Korea centuries ago. They came across the Bering Strait into Alaska, then down the Canadian mountains into the United States. Look at Indian facial structures. They are very Oriental. Same eyes, same bone structure. Eskimos in Alaska, and Apache Indians and Koreans have some similar customs.

Once I met a man and said hello to him in Korean. He didn't understand. I said to him, "You are not Korean?" He said, "No." I said, "Are you Chinese?" "No." "Japanese?" "No." "What are you?" He said, "American Indian."

One time I was in Detroit. My friend went into a bar to sell, and I went into an apartment building. A man called, "Hey, Chinese." And he started going toward my friend with a gun. I saw him and said, "I know you want to rob my friend. We know kung fu. The Oriental custom is not to report to the police. If you try to rob us one more time, I will attack you."

In the Korean army we learned self-defense called "tae kwan do." One or two robbers we could fight off. But if there were more than three with an ax or gun, no way. I was robbed many times—seven or eight times. In New York Harlem, dangerous areas of Detroit, Cleveland, Toledo, Richmond, Atlanta—people would come up to me with a gun and pull off my bag.

One time the robbers jumped into a car. It wouldn't start up for them.

I asked local residents if I could use their phone to call the police. The police wouldn't come. They were afraid of that neighborhood.

My first ten years in the United States, I never rested. I worked seven days a week and studied, too. My teachers assigned us to read three to five hundred pages every week. It was very hard to keep up with my studies.

I finished graduate school at New York University in 1977. I was forty-two years old and had no money saved: I spent everything on my education and taking care of my children. My wife was still developing the wholesale wig business, which was just successful enough to support my education. Because she put so much time into the business and caring for the children, she never re-entered her pharmacist profession.

I was very sad. Even though I finished my second master's degree, after six years in the United States I still didn't have any money. I said, "All right, a master's degree is enough for me. Now I will establish myself." So I picked up the bag full of wigs and again began going door to door. In one or two days I made $200 or $300. My plan was for my wife and me to help ourselves by expanding our business. We could create very good jobs for students by peddling in their spare time.

I began to teach the students: "When you come into our wholesale shop, we'll give you enough credit to sell for the week." Twenty or thirty students asked us, "Mr. Kim, if you import the products from Korea, we will buy at wholesale prices from you."

The plan began to work, and we were able to save and expand. In 1979, we moved our Dong Jin Trading Company into our current business building, on the corner of Broadway and West 29th Street. I didn't have the $10,000 necessary to put down on my store, so a friend cosigned for a bank loan. The space is a thousand square feet. With a twenty-foot ceiling, we were able to build a loft to use as our business office. And we have five hundred square feet in the basement for storage. There were four of us on our staff—my wife, her father, one employee, and me.

We would open in the mornings, at 8:00 A.M. At 7:00 P.M., we would close the doors and begin packing the out-of-town orders until 1:00 A.M. or 3:00 A.M. We slept right in the store. Woke up at 6:00 A.M. and got back to work. After six months, we were making enough money to hire two more employees, including my wife's brother, who arrived from Korea.

We set up a small machine to make ladies' belts for wholesale. There was a customer demand, and when we ordered belts from the factory, sometimes they couldn't deliver. So I said to my wife's father and brother, "Let's try to make our own belts downstairs. We can cut the cloth with scissors and sew on metal buckles."

The two of them worked all day long, producing around three dozen belts each. We made around $1 on each belt. My brother-in-law became frustrated. He told me: "Working like this, we'll never make any money. I'm going to buy a cutting machine. This way we can produce ten dozen belts per person each day."

When we earned back the money we spent on the machine, we bought another. Soon we had three, four, five machines. The next step was to rent another small space, in a building on West 31st Street, a few blocks from our store, to be our factory. I went to the bank at least twenty times trying to get a loan to improve the business. But they always refused. I said, "Okay, I must work harder."

Other Korean friends had the same experience with the banks, so we decided to form our own credit union or investment corporation. We each put $500 into one account, creating a seed fund of $8,000. Each month we contributed to the fund. The account can be used to help finance projects of our membership or to make small loans to other people who would like to start their own business. As they continually paid back the fund, the account continued to grow.

Enough Korean businesses were established that we developed associations to help each other and introduce newcomers to the American system. For example, I had two managers who worked at my shop for four years. They were very faithful to me. I cosigned a bank loan so that they could each have their own store. I've also helped four or five other people find empty stores to buy in Brooklyn, Harlem, or the Bronx. I enjoyed helping these people to become independent.

Rent is a serious problem for any businesses in Manhattan. In Korea, rents go up at most ten percent in a year. But in New York City, a store owner can lose his business because of skyrocketing increasing. Some rents in this area have jumped from $1,000 a month to more than $10,000 in just five years.

Around sixty-five percent of Koreans in New York work in Korean-owned small or middle-size businesses, either as the owner or employees. On both sides of Broadway, between 25th and 34th Streets, more than half the stores are owned by Koreans.

In the building where our store is housed, we are still renting. But some friends and I pooled our money and bought another building in this neighborhood. One of my friends manages that building, where five or six companies rent offices. Step by step, I've learned to invest our money and still have enough to manage the import-export business efficiently.

The products we sell come in large quantity from Korea, Taiwan, China, Japan. Large shipments come into the warehouse every week. We use a small computer to make our orders and determine how much we need. My wife handles most of the day-to-day management.

In the factory we have stacks and stacks of materials that we cut into belts: cloth, leather, plastics. We use different machines in an assembly line: cutting, stamping holes, inserting buckles. We've hired a dozen people now to make belts and do the stock work. Some are Vietnamese, some are Chinese. They work only one shift, from 8:00 A.M. until 4:00 P.M. My father manages the factory and watches over the warehouse. We have ten thousand square feet full of merchandise. You can see three hundred different types of items piled to the ceiling. Long boxes from Japan contain scarves. Stacks of square boxes are full of gloves from Taipei. Hats from Korea . . . We need to expand into a larger warehouse.

I go on business trips throughout Asia to establish contacts with the trade agencies who ship products to my store. My customers tell me the types of items and volumes they need; then I place the orders. Many of my customers have small retail shops in poor neighborhoods, so we make sure the items we import can be sold inexpensively. Rhinestone costume jewelry we carry can be sold retail for $2 or $3. Sunglasses, gloves, baseball caps are all under $5 or $10. During Christmas, we sell a lot of small toys.

We ship orders to many states. I have good contacts throughout the East Coast and Midwest from when I was a peddler in all those cities. And some of our orders go to South America, Canada, even to Africa. We ship mostly by airplane, but you'd be surprised—people come in from as far away as Canada to buy in large quantities.

During the course of a year, we are doing around $4–5 million worth of transactions. We make a five- to six-percent net profit on that amount. We have to pay the overhead on our store, taxes, salaries for our workers, and other expenses.

A number of our clients in Manhattan are West Indian merchants and Africans who peddle on the streets, as well as Korean shopowners. We have to open early, because some clients like to come in before they open their shops. Others like to come in after they close shop. So we seldom leave the store before 7:00 or 8:00 P.M., and we still get up for work at 5:30 A.M.

In 1982, we moved to Paramus, New Jersey, a suburban area. After ten years of always working, studying, and taking care of the family, my business had become more successful. I thought that I could finally start to get a little more rest on weekends. At that time, my son, John, was in the fifth grade. He wanted to take a job delivering newspapers to save money for his education. I said, "Okay, good idea." Then he said to me, "Sunday is a very big day for newspapers. Father, you must help me by driving the car." [Laughs]

I've come full circle. When I was in middle school in Korea, I began delivering papers. And thirty-five years later, I am delivering newspapers again [laughs] with my boy.

For three or four years, John has kept the paper route and has saved a lot of money. He is very stingy; he never spends it. He appreciates that it is hard to make money. He has around $2,500 saved in the bank under his name. Sometimes, when he has too much homework, he subcontracts his paper route to another boy. He says, "I am the newspaper delivery president." His own business.

At first the family bankbook was only in my name. But one day John walked right into the bank and asked for his own account. [Laughs] And they gave him a bank book.

He came home and showed the bank book to me. He said, "Father, it's not your money. I told the bank I wanted my account under 'John Kim' only." Some Korean kids aren't like my son. He's a real individualist, a real American. [Laughs]

In the Oriental tradition, the father works and provides money to the other members of the family, and children believe that their parents' house is their house. But my son says that he is just living in my house, and eventually one day he will buy his own.

When I have gone back to Korea to teach at the university, I explain to my students about American customs. I say, "Some American customs are good, and some Korean customs are good. American individualism is very good—the frontier spirit has made this country great. But there are good things in Korean culture, like Confucianism. Respect for old men and respect for the family are very important. In America, young men are worshipped. But in Korea, old men are respected for their experience in life. And when parents get old in my country, they are not forgotten or abandoned."

In the first ten years I lived in the United States, I never went back to Korea. I couldn't afford the airplane fare, and I was too busy working and studying. In 1982, I took my first trip back, to establish my import-export firm. Now I go back two or three times a year on business, and

I am spending more time with educators, talking with both professors and students.

When I left Korea fifteen years ago, the per capita income was $300 per person. Thirty years ago, when I was in high school, after the war, it was $60. Now the per capita is $2,500. The country has gone through dramatic improvement in industry and the overall economy. Seoul is as big as New York, ten million people. Many buildings are new; some are sixty stories tall.

I've seen many positive changes in the society, too. The new generation of Koreans are becoming more open—they appreciate the idea of democracy. This is due in large part to our relationship with the United States and the experience people have had traveling to this country.

I have found great satisfaction visiting my home area. I visit elementary schools, middle schools, high schools, to talk with students. I tell them, "You must always be ambitious. I was born here. During and after the war I was more poor than any of you. But I am proof that you can go very far in life if you have an education."

I visit former classmates of mine. One is a lawyer, one is a dean, one is an elementary-school teacher, one is a general in the army.

I was invited to teach at Chung Ang University during the spring semester in 1986. The dean knew that I am now the president of the Far Eastern Research Center in New York. There are twenty members. Some are Ph.D.s and others are graduate students in political science. Every month we meet to discuss current issues. We also have seminars and invite newspaper reporters, so that they can better understand the Korean community.

I try to keep up with trends in international relations. In the evenings, when I come home from work, I study for a few hours about current developments.

I told some doctors and professors in Korea, "Your job is learning and teaching. I don't have as much time for that. But by studying every evening I build up my knowledge."

I taught a class in comparative government at Chung Ang University. And, privately, I spent time with students from fourteen to eighteen years old who, for reasons of poverty, were not able to attend middle school. I got forty or fifty of them together and borrowed a high-school classroom. Some of my friends donated books for each course. I've never forgotten the way that the university students helped me when I worked in the bakery in Kwangju. In my class at the university, I gave comparisons between American-style democracy and how the South Korean government is run. In some lectures I criticized the Korean government. Students had questions about some unfair government policies.

I've been concerned that some younger students in Korea blame the United States for all of their problems. They were born after the Korean War and don't understand what socialism or Communism is. They see some things in South Korean society that aren't right, and they hear the Communists' propaganda: "Everyone is equal in North Korea. . . . Workers have rights. . . . Housing is cheap." They start to believe the utopian dream that the Communists talk about.

Older Koreans understand what happened to our countrymen in the North and the sacrifices American soldiers made to save our country. Around fifty thousand GIs died in Korea. In recent years, the United States has helped to develop South Korea's economy with financial and trade support, and Koreans who have come to the United States have very friendly relations with Americans.

South Korea is going through the growing pains of turning from an underdeveloped country to a developed country. It's happening very quickly. There is some parallel with Japan. In Tokyo ten years ago, there were many student demonstrations against the government, and they were influenced by socialism. Now, as the income level has gone up, there are fewer demonstrations. If the Korean economy can continue to grow, it will create political stability.

Many capable young people from my country have come to the United States to study and work. Many Korean newspapermen and congressmen improved their skills by what they learned here. Their experiences have had a great influence on the political process in Korea. Congressional elections are scheduled for 1989. A new generation of politicians are emerging. I have a friend who is from a poor family, like me. He came to the United States and became a successful businessman. Now he would like to apply what he learned to help his home country. We would like South Korea to become a showcase of democracy.

Around thirty thousand Koreans immigrate to the United States every year. Many come to study or for better educational opportunities for their children. Many professionals, like engineers, come to learn new techniques. Even with economic improvements in Korea, people still enjoy a better standard of living here.

I said to my students: "Anything you want in this life, you must work for. Whatever field you wish to enter—professor, journalist, lawyer, judge—you must study and work to make your dreams come true."

Just compare nations. In this century, at one time Britain and France were on top. Now the Americans are at the top, but they have become comfortable and are starting to slide down. Countries like Korea and Japan are up and coming. They work hard to make money and expand trade. It comes down to a simple fact: there is no substitute for hard work. If you are lazy, you will lose what you have. The history of the world has always demonstrated this way.

I've learned a lot in the United States. All of my experiences—peddling, finishing my graduate studies, starting a business, raising a family—have helped me greatly to understand the world. People ask too much from governments. I have learned to be a self-made man. Still, I try to be generous and help others, because I realize that I came into this world bare-handed, and I will leave bare-handed. It is very important for peace of mind.

Around seven or eight years ago, when I finished my degree and established my company, I thought, "Who am I?" I remembered when I didn't have any money—the banks wouldn't lend to me. Now I am doing well, but I know from my Buddhist studies that all of this is related to perceptions of reality.

There is a famous Buddhist monk who I visit in Korea. I go to a temple in the mountains and sleep over night. In the morning I talk with the monk. I've come to realize that, even if I lost everything and was back to my bare hands, it would be no trouble, because a person's sense of well-being is ultimately in his mind.

There are two or three Korean Buddhist temples in the New York City area. Sometimes I visit the monks, but I have never been to services at the temples. I keep the Buddha in my mind.

I like to work for society. In the New York Korean Association, we have community activities like donating blood. Because we live in the United States, we want to give back something in return. Korean merchants try to have better relations with the people where their stores are located. They make donations to community projects and local churches.

I have been president of the Korean Businessmen Association. At some point, I might want to be a political candidate in Korea, to work for my country and maintain good relations with the United States. Would my wife like to go back to Korea? She is an American citizen, but she could accept living in Korea or the United States. Her two brothers and their families all want to stay in the U.S. They could run our store if Min Cha and I went back to Korea.

I am a Permanent Resident of the United States, but I haven't become a U.S. citizen. Some day, if I want to be a candidate for Congress in

Korea, I don't want people criticizing me, "You are a U.S. citizen. Why do you come back?" [Laughs]

I took my three children with me to Korea last year. They told me that they are not sure if they would like to live in Korea. They enjoy living in the United States; they are Americans, born here.

John, Julie, and Joon are all in Catholic schools, because in our area those schools have the best discipline and education. The children's grades are good. They have a chance to study and dream. They shouldn't have to continually work seven days a week, all the time, like me.

First-generation immigrants take any kind of jobs. But the second generation has higher expectations. Recently, I asked John, "What will you become in the future, son?" He said, "I think a doctor or lawyer— they make good money." He is very smart in English and mathematics. His high-school examination grades were ninety-eight percent, in the top two percent of students nationally. At the same time, he's learned, by watching my wife and me, how hard it is to work and save money. This is part of the Americanization process that happens to immigrants from generation to generation. It's happening to Koreans now, too.

THE AVIATOR

Oleg Jankovic
Displaced Person of Russian Origin
U.S. Naval Flight Officer
Arlington, Virginia

On May 1, 1987, in an outdoor ceremony at the U.S. Naval Academy in Annapolis, Maryland, forty-one-year-old James Webb was sworn in as the youngest Secretary of the Navy since Theodore Roosevelt. It was a proud moment for Webb's friend and loyal associate Oleg Jankovic, a navy commander, who sat in the audience with his teen-age son and daughter. Oleg had known Jim since they were seventeen, sharing affordable meals of popcorn and pomegranate-jelly sandwiches in a California college dorm.

Webb went on to the Naval Academy and became a highly decorated marine officer in Vietnam. Jankovic graduated on an ROTC scholarship, earned his flight wings, and flew dangerous reconnaissance missions over the Ho Chi Minh Trail. Although Jankovic stayed on active duty after the war, combat injuries forced Webb to leave the service. He entered law school, became an acclaimed author, and in 1984, at the ripe age of thirty-nine, was appointed Assistant Secretary of Defense. Among the first staff members Webb requested was his stoic former roommate, Jankovic, who had spent what felt like an eternity aboard aircraft carriers, flying reconnaissance missions near the coast of Iran.

Their enduring friendship stems from a tenacious and highly principled dedication to defending their country. Both come from families with proud military traditions, whose destinies were forged in the fires of revolution and civil war, one in America and the other in Russia. And although they both were born in 1945, they grew up in different worlds.

Webb's childhood was shaped by his father's proud return from World War II service. Jankovic's father and stepfather perished during the convulsive conclusion of that war. He was born in the chaos of European refugee camps, in a churning sea of displaced humanity. Thousands of refugee families, forcibly returned to the Soviet Union from camps in Western Europe, were put in gulags. Oleg was spared death or certain enslavement through courageous acts of his mother. He was seven years old, able to speak only Russian, when he arrived in a tough industrial town in western Massachusetts.

How does a boy without a father grow up to be a man? There are things that a mother can't teach him. You've heard the song "A Boy

Named Sue"? Oleg works just as well in a racially mixed lower-class neighborhood in Springfield, Massachusetts, where being different is a good reason to be jumped on. I learned the hard way.

My parents were both from Kiev, in the Ukraine. Although I have never been there, I've been told that I speak Russian with a Kiev accent. They fled Russia during the chaos of World War II, as the German army fell back in the face of the Soviet counteroffensive. Mom and Dad were part of the tremendous waves of refugees, both Russian and Eastern European, who fled both Stalin and Hitler. They lived in Czechoslovakia and then Italy as the Allied armies were advancing.

Early in 1945, when my mother was pregnant with me, my father disappeared, a casualty of the war. He was spying for someone. It is difficult to say at whose hands he met his end. I have heard the Germans, or partisans, or bandits, from various people. My mother was only twenty-three years old—very young to be alone and pregnant in a strange country during a war. Her name is Eugenia. American friends call her Jeanie. She kept my father's identity concealed from me until two years ago. Even then she would not tell me much. The events surrounding his disappearance have always been confusing to her.

My first memories are of a "displaced-persons" camp near Salzburg, Austria. I remember being in a crib in a stark room with a lot of people. In the camps, the only clothes and necessities people had were what came in relief packages or what they were able to carry. I also remember the alpine beauty of green meadows, steep mountains, and dark forests, in contrast to the rows of shoddy barracks where we stayed in the DP camps. There was some sickness in the camps, but at my young age, the more imposing images were the soldiers without legs, without arms.

When my mother was pregnant with me in Udine, Italy, through an agreement with the Allies the Soviets began sending teams into the camps to invite refugees to return to Russia. There were posters in Russian on signboards. The program seemed fairly benign. My mother signed up and was ready to begin moving into the repatriation center. She wanted to give birth in her homeland, near her family.

At this time, through a twist of fate, a man named Mikhail entered my mother's life. Mikhail was a Russian guerrilla leader with [British] Field Marshal Alexander's partisan forces in northern Italy. Mikhail was a dynamic individual, six feet tall, who had a reputation as being fearless in combat. Early in the war, he had been a Soviet bomber pilot. He was shot down by the Germans but evaded capture and returned to the Russian lines.

Unfortunately, Stalin was paranoid of possible turncoats working for the Germans, so the Soviet military did not trust prisoners of war who escaped from captivity and returned under any circumstances. Mikhail was put in a Red Army penal battalion, which was really an eventual death sentence. They were always sent where the fighting was the heaviest, to be used as cannon fodder. However, the Soviets needed pilots badly, so they pulled Mikhail out of the battalion and sent him back into flying.

The Germans shot Mikhail down again. This time he escaped from a Nazi prison and went west, to Italy and Allied lines. He volunteered to join a partisan guerrilla unit under Field Marshal Alexander for hit-and-run attacks against the Nazi army.

Immediately after the war, Mikhail went into a repatriation camp, where Russian officials processed voluntary returnees to the Soviet Union. At the first camp, they gave the refugees all kinds of promises. But when they were transferred to the next camp inside the Soviet zone of control, it was all barbed wire. Soviet officials lined them up and said, "You're all guilty. Your sentences haven't been determined, but you leave to-morrow." These shocked people were loaded onto railroad cars and shipped off. This began the Great Repatriations, which concluded in 1947.

Through agreements between Stalin and the Western Allies formalized at Yalta, between three and six million Russian and Eastern European refugees and prisoners of war were at first coerced and later forcibly sent back to the Soviet Union. Most were sentenced to Gulag labor camps. Some men were outright shot, because they were considered a threat to the Communists. Others, including women and kids, com-mitted suicide as British soldiers pushed them into railroad cars. For those who reached the Gulag work camps, the chance for survival was slim.

Mikhail, an instinctive survivor, immediately saw the play of this program. He managed to escape from the Soviet guards and returned to Italy. He heard through the refugee grapevine that a good Russian woman was in a desperate situation. So he traveled to Udine to find this woman, who was my mother. He talked her out of her plans for repatriation. He promised her that, if her baby was a boy, he would make a toy bear out of the warm fleece lining of an air-force flight jacket. I've still got that bear. I gave it to my own daughter.

My mother wanted to name me Gleb, after my father. But Mikhail convinced her that a more common Russian name, Oleg, would be better. When I was only two months old, we moved out from British-controlled northern Italy to the refugee–displaced-persons camps in the

American sector of Austria, because the British were much more aggressive in forcing people to repatriate.

The camps were in an alpine valley, near the river that goes through Salzburg. There were two camps, Glasenbach and Parsch. We were in both, at one time or another, for seven years. People of many nationalities lived in the camps: Slovaks, Croatians, Latvians, Lithuanians, a few Poles, as well as Russians. Most Eastern European languages, like Croatian, are similar to Russian, and most people spoke more than one language, so communication wasn't difficult.

My mother was able to bring some clothes, so we weren't dressed in rags. But there was just enough food to survive, not much more. Some was donated, and there was always the black market. Mikhail was good at that. He'd go to Italy, where there were a lot more goods. He would use whatever money he and my mother had to buy what we needed.

I grew up thinking that Mikhail was my father. He made quite an impression on me. I remember when I was four or five years old, wandering around the camp, old friends of his would stop me in the street. These were great men once, but they had become broken, either in body from battle or in their minds from drink. In me, Mikhail's son, they would see him and celebrate their own pasts. They told me great stories about his courage. Partly as remembrance for themselves, partly as guideposts for me.

I was not Mikhail's real son. But neither they nor I knew that. He had loved me, treated me as his own. Mikhail was the only father I ever knew.

My mother kept my actual father, Gleb, concealed from me. He came from a family of Russian aristocracy, very highly placed. When I saw pictures of him in Mother's photo albums, before I knew who he was, I did not like what I saw of him. He looked as if he were out of a contemporary issue of *Gentlemen's Quarterly*—the perfect continental gentleman. I thought it unseemly that a man should look so well put together in the middle of a war. By comparison, in most photos of Mikhail, he was in military uniform.

The camp was run by some of the Russian émigrés. These were people who had fled from Russia during the 1917 Revolution and subsequent civil war. They had settled in eastern and central Europe before being displaced during the war. These émigré camp administrators were overseen by American civil and military authorities. But the émigrés maintained a "better than thou" attitude toward the new arrivals. Mikhail didn't have a whole lot of regard for them. Being outspoken, he let it be known.

Mikhail was one of those men who find their place in war. In peacetime he might have been a doctor or an engineer like his mother and father, and lived an unremarkable life. But he was exceptionally fearless and confident in his abilities.

He fathered my sister, Tanya, who was born in Salzburg in 1946. In later years, my mother always cried when she saw *The Sound of Music*. In the panorama of Salzburg shown during the movie's titles, the hospital where Tanya was born is clearly visible.

Austria at the end of the war was under English, American, and Russian control, similar to the partition of Germany. By 1947, the largest part of the refugee repatriations, known as Operation Keelhaul—the code name was indicative—was largely over. But the Russians were still trying to take people who had served with the Germans. Many Soviet commissions came through the camps, looking through all the Russian refugees.

Unlike the British, the Americans weren't forcing many refugees or former prisoners of the Nazis to go. Mikhail stood before a couple of these Soviet commissions, but he had decorations and papers proving service with Field Marshal Alexander against the Germans.

At the close of this program, a Soviet delegation came to our camp. It was just a public-relations job, looking for voluntary returnees. After the Soviet team did their song and dance, Mikhail stood up. He said, "Do you mind if I say a few words?" The Soviet official said, "No," a little bit surprised, "go ahead." Mikhail said, "This is bullshit." He asked them some very pointed questions about the first Soviet zone repatriation camp that he had scouted.

The Soviet colonel told Mikhail, "I'm not going to forget your impertinence."

Not long after the confrontation, while my mother was cooking dinner on the wood-burning stove, American MPs came and arrested Mikhail. They put him in prison, to prepare for repatriation.

My mother went to visit Mikhail a few times. They had him in chains, because his skill as an escape artist was well known. He told my mother that he would indeed make a break at the first opportunity.

She took me to see him in the jail. I grabbed him around the leg and said, "Papa, come home. Come home." I was only two years old, going on three. That was a rough month for my mother. They had Mikhail in leg irons, and it seemed like the Soviets had him drugged after he was transferred to their zone. We had one telephone call from him. He wasn't talking clearly. The Soviets had coerced him, either through physical force or through drugs, to ask my mother to join him.

We never heard from him again. Apparently he was executed. When Mother tried to get an accounting for Mikhail from the American authorities, she was threatened with a very thorough review of her past. That would have revealed that she was a Russian. To escape repatriation, we were using a Czech passport for documentation, and some legal papers that she and Gleb had been issued when they lived in Czechoslovakia. This is what saved my mother, my sister, and me from repatriation. The Soviets asked for my sister and me to be handed over to them, as children of a Russian father—Mikhail. It was only because my mother pretended to be a Czech citizen that we were kept from them. Out of these circumstances grew a fiction that my mother maintained, even to her children, until near the end of her life. Mother used "Jankovic," my real father's family name, as her legal maiden name. Although my father was Russian, "Jankovic" is also a common Czech or Croatian surname. In the face of threatened repatriation, my mother committed herself to our survival.

There is still speculation as to why the American authorities handed Mikhail to the Soviets. Some people in the camp believed that he was set up by the émigré administrators. My feeling is that he may have been one of the people traded for American internees being held in the Soviet Union. Some American pilots who made emergency landings in Soviet territory during wartime missions were very slowly returned by the Soviets—even some of General Billy Mitchell's people who flew missions over Japan. The Soviets didn't hold them as prisoners of war, but they held on to them, possibly to exchange in return for favors from the U.S. government while the Soviets broke all of their promises on freedom for Eastern Europe in the postwar period.

My mother was alone with two small children. To provide for our needs in the camps, she started doing odd jobs, but progressed to running a warehouse for the U.S. administrators. There was an incident early on when my mother was doing laundry and ironing uniforms for American GIs. She left the iron on a pile of uniforms and burned a hole straight through. She was frightened. She had no money to replace the damages. When the American came, he said something to the effect, "That's all right." He paid for them anyway, and left without incident. Mother said that, if he had been a Russian or a German, she would've had hell to pay.

Those kinds of impressions of Americans stayed with us. Soldiers would come by in trucks and flip comic books to us. That was really big-time for us kids.

Throughout our seven years in the camps, I always had this sense of

The Jankovic family at the time of their internment, 1950

bobbing around in a cauldron of uncertainty. Tens of thousands of people went through those camps through the early 1950s. Those with illnesses had problems being accepted for resettlement. My family fit into that category because of my sister Tanya's health. When she was three years old, she contracted a tubercular infection and was labeled a handicapped child.

My mother was given an impossible choice. She could accept resettlement for herself and me and leave Tanya in an Austrian orphanage. Or she could keep the family together in a rootless existence in the camps.

Unknown to us, a minister in a small church in western Massachusetts told his parishioners about refugees in Europe who needed homes and sponsors. There was a publication printed by the United Nations that had a picture and a little story about my mother, my sister, and me, as well as many other refugee families. Mr. and Mrs. Curtis, who lived on a small New England Yankee farm, saw our picture and said, "We want this family here."

Mrs. Curtis made up her mind that she was going to sponsor us. Authorities kept offering her other families, without health problems, but she would not have them. Just like my mother, Mrs. Curtis is a woman who knows her own mind.

We were fortunate to get Tanya some treatment, and she took the cure. I was six years old when we arrived in the States in 1952. I spoke Russian and German, but no English. I thought that I would look really neat in my uniform. I thought everybody in America wore a uniform, because the only Americans I had ever seen were soldiers. But when I got here, it was a culture shock. People wore regular clothes.

We lived in the Curtis farmhouse, in Chesterfield, Massachusetts. It was awkward for all of us. We couldn't speak English, and they weren't quite sure what to do with these Europeans.

The Curtis family had a bunch of kids: Nancy, Naomi, John, and two older daughters. I think fondly of them always. John is my age. He's farming now in upstate New York. The kids really tried to be helpful. We shared toys, and they showed me around the countryside. I started school and kind of tumbled my way through first grade.

We heard that there was a Russian community in Springfield. So, eventually, we moved into the city. Most of the Russians in Springfield were new immigrants. Some came from the same camps we had been in. By that time I was speaking English okay, but not great.

My new school gave me an IQ test to see how dumb I really was. I'll never forget one question. The woman asked me, "Give me the name of three months of the year." I understood her to say, "There are three months in the year. Tell me their names." I thought it was a trick question, so I wouldn't answer.

Actually, there weren't more than a hundred Russian families in Springfield, out of around 180,000 total population. So there wasn't any absorption problem. The Russian kids who had been in the U.S. for a couple years were speaking English like natives.

We lived in a third-floor walk-up apartment, with hot water but no bath. We stayed there for a while before moving to Greenwood Street, a transitional neighborhood. Mostly Eastern European, Italian, and black. It had seen better days and was going downhill. Our neighbors were mostly lower-middle-class folks who worked in factories.

My mother found a job working at a precision chain factory. They made timing chains for cars, airplanes and bicycle chains on single-operator machines. That's what my mother did for about thirty years, until she retired. Eventually, she worked her way up to the most senior supervisory position available to a woman.

Mother worked long hours. An old woman, who we called Grandmother, watched over my sister and me while my mother worked. During the summer, Mom took a second job. It was not easy. But rather than feel deprived, we accepted it as something that needed to be done.

I didn't have any close adult male influence. I didn't have any uncles in America. Mother never remarried—she had already lost two husbands. So she buckled herself down into raising and providing for her two children.

In our neighborhood there weren't many one-parent families, which made Tanya and me unique. But many people said that my mother did better on her own than a lot of two-parent families. She devoted her whole life to getting us grown and educated, so that when we went off on our own we would be able to do better.

I always remembered my stepfather, Mikhail. In many ways I tried to emulate the example he set for me. My first friend in America was a black kid named Tony. We both loved airplanes and the air force.

Kids are very clannish. They always test a newcomer, especially if you are a foreigner. If you couldn't speak English, and had a name like "Oleg," you were in trouble. Everybody hit on me to see if I could handle myself. I had to fight because of my name. They'd tease, "Oleg, Oleg." I learned how to handle myself because of that. Sometimes I stood and fought. Sometimes I ran. I remember peeking around corners to see if they were waiting for me. Sometimes I took on seven or eight guys.

There's a poem by Lawrence Ferlinghetti that goes something like:

> In woods where many rivers run among the unbent hills and
>   fields of streets of our childhood
> where ricks and rainbows mix memories.
> When every living thing casts its shadows in eternity.
> And all day long . . . the sharp shadows
> shadowing a paradise I hardly dreamed of.

My fields were streets, too. I remember getting up real early on weekend mornings, around 6:00 A.M., and going out walking on my own. I remember those sharp shadows. When you stood in the shade, it was cold. And if you went into the sunlight, it was warm, bright. Walking downtown, looking around, just amazed at the modern world. I was only seven or eight years old.

In 1955, we moved to Lowell Street, to a house owned by a friend of my mother. It was a nice neighborhood, a step up the social ladder. Greenwood Street had brick sidewalks, and the grass was gone. Lowell Street was quite green, a lot of grass. A playground where we played baseball was right next to the river. And there was a big public swimming pool. During the summer, I'd hang around the pool all day. This area was called Goatsville. At one time, immigrants who originally lived there all had goats. There were no goats when we moved in, and we were the only new immigrants.

In our home, we spoke mostly Russian. I didn't really learn the nuances of the American language until we got a television. I was around ten years old. I needed the extra exposure to the spoken word. I had trouble with my school grades until then.

Saturday mornings, I liked to watch "Space Patrol," "Fury," "Sky King," and all the old kids' shows. But I could never understand the craze about Elvis Presley . . . all those women swooning.

When Khrushchev, the Soviet leader, was on television, I could easily understand what he was saying. I would always get ticked off when English translators would start talking and they would drown out the Russian. That was the heavy Cold War period, when Khrushchev told the Americans "We will bury you" and all that.

The common thought among the kids that I hung around with was that the Russians wanted to go to war with us. The Korean War, the Berlin Wall, the invasion of Hungary were all very frightening. My position was that Russians and Communists are not the same thing, but kids don't understand. They would say, "The Russians want to fight a war." And I would say, "No, no, no. You've got it all wrong. It's the Communist government over there that is the problem." Both my mother and Mikhail loved being Russian but hated the Soviet system. That's not an uncommon combination of feelings for Russians.

In Springfield there was an "old" Russian church and a "new" Russian church. There was yet another Russian church across the river. I was an altar boy. Our traditions set us apart from mainstream Americans. My sense of faith reminds me of a scene from the movie *The Jazz Singer* where the father says, "We pray this way because of the people who came before us. They died so that we can pray this way." The Russian Church has a thousand-year tradition. It hasn't changed.

The Russians in Springfield weren't a very tight community. I've talked about this with Russian Americans from other places, and the same is true for them. Maybe it's because Russia is such a big country and immigrants come from all different parts. But it's also true that, if three Russians get together, they will have four political parties. There is always squabbling. It's one of the few things I regret about the Russian immigrant experience. There wasn't a closeness in the community. It's very different from Soviet Jewish refugees, who congregate together. They make an effort to help newcomers settle in.

Every so often as I was growing up, I'd meet someone from the Austrian camps. When I was around fifteen, I remember walking home from church with my mother. An older man came from the opposite direction. We didn't know him, but as we passed, he stopped and addressed us in Russian. He asked my mother if she was the wife of "the Aviator." That is how she was still known.

In junior high, I settled in and did a lot better. My mother still wasn't making much money working in the factory, so I had no plans to go to college. When I was in eighth grade, out of the blue my mother said to me, "You'd better go to college." She came from the kind of family where that was expected. She didn't want me working in a factory.

I remember thinking, "Where are we going to get the money for college?" My grades weren't good enough for a scholarship.

I had worked a paper route before, but it wasn't regular. So, the summer after eighth grade, I got a job at the YMCA camp, and I caddied at the golf course. My first steady job was during high school, as a stock boy in a supermarket.

I started taking college-preparatory curriculum in ninth grade. By then my mother's words were self-fulfilling: "You're going to do it." I still had no idea of where I was going or what I was doing. But I always had my mother's love and effort in front of me as a challenge.

In high school I also did sports. Wrestling was my favorite. I weighed 168 pounds, but I wrestled heavyweight. I went up against people who had up to a hundred-pound advantage on me, and I'd pin them. I learned that it's not how fast you get to the top and stay there that counts: it's how you come off the bottom that really tells what you're made of.

I was only beaten one time—the first time I wrestled heavyweight. I found out about it only forty-five minutes before the match. Our regular heavyweight was sick. So the coach sent me up against this kid who weighed 210 and was about six feet tall. He was the best in our league, and his team was Cathedral, our big rival. I was nervous, and more than a little intimidated by his size. He beat me 6–3.

At the end of the season, there was a city tournament. The heavyweight championship, the last match of the tournament, had me against the kid from Cathedral. I figured he would try to get me in a fireman's carry. I went into the match ready for him to try. He made his move, and I spun him onto his back right away. He got frustrated and clawed at my face. I let him spin out on me and get to a half-standing position. As I went to take him back down, I sprained my ankle. The pain was intense. Because of the sprain, he got a couple more escapes to narrow my lead. But I stayed with it, and pinned him.

I graduated close to the top ten percent of my class, and even though

my economic situation hadn't greatly improved, I had an assistant principal who took an interest in me. He was in the naval reserves and
pushed for me to receive an ROTC scholarship. Needless to say, I was
very excited. I decided to see how far away I could go, and how expensive
a tuition I could get. I picked the University of Southern California. I
started college in 1963, the dawn of the Beach Boys surfing craze. The
California car-and-beach culture was a shock. And USC is a suitcase
school for rich kids of the Southland. I was still coming to terms with
America as seen in a New England industrial city.

I wanted to be an aerospace engineer. I didn't exactly know what that
was, but because of my love of aviation it seemed right. I carried nineteen
hours of engineering out of thirty hours of classes in the first year. An
overload. I was spending all of my time studying mathematics.

I tried talking with people at parties, and I always liked political
science and history, but I was so wrapped up in numbers that I wasn't
able to articulate my ideas. I knew guys with whom I was on par in
terms of intellect, but they were able to express themselves and I couldn't.
That really bothered me. So, after a year and a half, I got out of
engineering. The navy, who was covering my scholarship, wasn't too
enthusiastic about that. They were putting a lot of pressure on us to
finish school soon. The war in Vietnam was heating up, and they wanted
their officers.

I spent four and a half years at Southern Cal on the scholarship. I
paid for the last semester myself. The education was superb, because
I learned how to think. And that's not all. There was a time when I
pumped gas all night, spent my days on the beach, yet managed to
hold a 3.0 grade average. That, too, was part of my education. I ended
up with a bachelor's degree in international relations, specializing in the
Far East and the Soviet Union.

When I graduated, in January 1968, I received my commission as a
naval officer. My mother took great pride in my achievement. My naval
uniform gave her a sense of having made it in our new country and, on
a deeper level, a continuity with her family and cultural experience. In
Russia, the military always had a prominent role in the society. Being
an officer has always been well looked upon. And it was something that
men in my family in Russia normally did.

I didn't plan to make a career of the navy, but I felt a responsibility
to serve my country. I owed something in return for what was given to
my family. I originally requested to be assigned to naval intelligence,
but it was quite a lengthy process to get a security clearance. So they
sent me to my second choice: flight school. That was fine by me. I had

a strong desire to become an aviator, to follow the path of Mikhail. He had always been the only standard by which I judged myself. I didn't have 20/20 vision, so I became a naval flight officer, which is a copilot/navigator.

The navy sent me to Norfolk, Virginia, for a few months before flight school in Pensacola, Florida. At a dance at the Norfolk Officers' Club, I met a schoolteacher named Susan. It was practically love at first sight. We were married in April, during the early part of my flight training.

Our marriage was an improbable match. Susan's family roots went back to the first English colonists on Virginia's eastern shore, in 1629. One ancestor was an early member of the House of Burgesses. Another ancestor was a member of the second U.S. Congress. Her grandfather had been an admiral; he played a key role in the design and construction of the battleship *Arizona*, and the first aircraft carriers named *Lexington* and *Enterprise*.

Our backgrounds and traditions were very different. But there was a similarity, one which carried with it a great sense of loss. Where my family was a product of the Russian Revolution, Susan's family experienced the American Civil War from the Southern perspective.

Susan's father was a quiet, gentle man. Occasionally he would talk over a bourbon. He remembered his grandfather vividly: he had been a Phi Beta Kappa scholar in the mid-nineteenth century and by profession a schoolteacher. When the Civil War came, he enlisted in Robert E. Lee's cavalry. He died in 1929 at age ninety-four. Below his name, on his gravestone the inscription reads "CSA"—Confederate States of America. I learned a lot about the American experience from Susan's father.

In October 1968, I received my wings after jet-navigation training. Shortly thereafter, Susan and I were blessed with the birth of our first child. We named her Tanya, after my sister.

After Pensacola, I was sent to the West Coast for training in the "A-3 Skywarrior" jet bomber. Two squadrons were configured for reconnaissance. Any other specialties were unavailable or would have taken a lot more schooling. And I wanted to get to Vietnam.

I had mixed feelings about the war in Vietnam. My own family's experience with Communism taught me that it was the right thing to do. I also knew the intellectual arguments against being there. But the overriding factor was a very strong sense of patriotic obligation.

From August 1969 until June 1971, I was assigned to Heavy Photographic Squadron 61. We worked the entire Pacific rim, flying off of aircraft carriers. We'd go down to Australia, on up to New Guinea,

Korea, Japan. I saw Palau, Saipan, and Tinian—practically every major island. We worked out of Guam.

I spent a total of six months in Vietnam. We were based on the beach, at Da Nang Air Base. We flew over the Ho Chi Minh Trail at night, using infrared sensors to pick up enemy convoys and troop movements. When President Johnson announced that he had proof of the North Vietnamese abusing the cease-fire, he was talking about footage taken by my squadron.

The A-3 Skywarrior is a three-seater. We'd shoot a red flare when we spotted the enemy. Around ten miles behind us and five thousand feet above were F-4 or A-4 attack aircraft. When they saw our flares, they rolled in on the convoy.

The type of aircraft and missions we flew had taken some heavy losses. We had to fly low enough to see what was on the ground. Flying at five hundred feet above the ground, doing 360 knots—six miles a minute—down a mountain valley in the dark. My job was to keep us from crashing into mountains by using radar to stay clear of terrain that was higher than we were. People on the ground would try to shoot us down, but usually by the time they heard us and fired, we were past them.

I logged about 40 combat missions. I felt confident when I was flying those missions. But being in the air is a bit detached. It's not like being on the ground, where you are exchanging fire nose to nose. And the danger of our work was tempered by getting assignments to places like Bangkok or Australia.

In July 1971, I started a three-and-a-half-year intelligence assignment at Fort Meade, Maryland, near Washington. It was an exciting time. Susan was near her parents, and we were expecting our second child. Bobby was born in January 1972. Tanya began kindergarten. And I entered a master's-degree program in finance at George Washington University.

During the summers, we went up to Massachusetts to spend time with my mother. She took great pleasure in her grandchildren. Those were happy times for all of us. But, like many people of great strength, my mother had weaknesses. She suppressed them while we were growing up, but once my sister and I left the house for college, a dam burst. Mother had always been a heavy smoker, but she also began to drink. It was not evident for a long time, because she was strong and hid it. Now I could tell when she had been drinking. But I had no idea how serious it was. One of the most insidious things about alcoholism—its real effects are so easily hidden.

She had two circles of friends in Massachusetts: the Russians, which became smaller as people moved away or died, and the Americans, our neighbors and people she knew at work. She was still at the factory, where she was promoted as high up as you could go as a woman. She was a floor lady, a job supervisor. But she knew the technical aspects of her work better than the company engineers. If there was a problem, they would come to her. Yet, although some men knew less than her, because they were men they got paid more. Mother was my role model in all the things it takes to make it in this world. Consequently, I have few prejudices about what women can and can't do.

During my three years in naval intelligence at Fort Meade, I followed Soviet naval operations. I thought about the possibility of fighting a war against the Soviets. This is where my sense of being an American is most profound. Even though I am proud of my Russian heritage, I put everything I had into learning how the Soviets did things, so that if it came to a conflict, we'd win. My motivation comes from considering what my fate would have been under the Soviet system in comparison to the generosity this country extended to my family. If it weren't for this country's generosity, my fate as a child would've been certain annihilation.

In Russia today, although there've been some changes in the system, I don't see much difference from what had gone on under the czars. Today the Communist Party's top echelon behaves and lives like the czars' aristocracy. Only the titles have changed. Authority comes down from the top. People owe their allegiance to those above them. It's a kind of class distinction between authority and subordinates.

I had some of that attitude about authority in me when I was first commissioned as a naval officer. The dawning light happened early in my career, when I sat on a screening board for a sailor who wanted to enter the ROTC program. The qualification form we used on this ROTC board was designed so that any lawyer, doctor, or judge in small-town America would be comfortable with it. People of some stability in the community are often asked to rate potential candidates. I said to myself, "Many of these judges may not have served in the military. What do they know about an aircraft carrier, or what it takes to fly a low-level penetration flight into enemy territory, air-to-air fighter tactics, or anything like that?" My question was answered by a single entry on the form.

The issue of aptitude for service as an officer was handled in a very simple and straightforward manner, something you could have given to anybody's mother: "Would you feel comfortable putting the welfare of others in this applicant's hands?"

When I thought about that, I was impressed with the priorities in the American system for selecting officers. It's very appropriate for a democracy. Understanding this, I've always made my first priorty "Take care of your men." If my child has to go to war, I sure want the officers to have the welfare of their sailors or troops in mind.

In the late 1960s and through the 1970s, I really didn't understand America's attitude toward our military people. The My Lai stigma troubled me. My understanding of American servicemen and how they behaved toward foreign people was based on my own experience as a child in Europe. And I knew that, in Vietnam, incidents like My Lai were the exception, not the rule.

It was a frustrating experience for any American serviceman to go into and return from an environment like Vietnam. When my country went to war, I didn't question it. I didn't understand all the implications. But the people at the top—the politicians and the senior military staff—had a responsibility to me and the other young men and women they sent. And they didn't carry it out. That was a failure of leadership that we're still paying highly for.

I remember my cruise of the Indian Ocean during the Iranian crisis in 1979. That was probably the toughest duty I've ever done. The cruise lasted for 210 days, two hundred at sea. We were deployed down to the mouth of the Persian Gulf when the hostages were released from Iran. It felt like being dropped over a precipice at the end of the earth. From the time we mailed a letter, it took a month to get a reply from the States. By the time I received a response from my family, I forgot what I had originally written.

Back home, the nation was still in a negative post-Vietnam funk. Yet there we were, sitting in the Persian Gulf, very isolated. We knew if something happened to those hostages, we were the ones who were going to have to respond. We were ready to fight but I certainly had no desire to lose my life. I was flying in EA-6B electronic countermeasures aircraft, which negates enemy radar and anti-aircraft missiles. With the Soviet Union on the border, we couldn't rule out a conflict expanding to something more hideous or dangerous.

I remember the first day I got back to my home, near Seattle, following that cruise. I picked up a newspaper. The headline was: "Bishop Hunthausen Claims Submarine Base at Bangor an American Auschwitz." I had to put the paper down for a minute or two. Having just undergone a strenuous experience, and having witnessed the sacrifices of all those who were out there in the Gulf with me, to assure the safety of the people of this country—that headline was extremely insulting.

Through August 1984, I spent ten years coming and going from Naval Air Station Whidbey Island near Seattle. It was difficult for my family, because there was never a break. The entire U.S. Navy was cut in half during the mid- to late seventies, while the Soviet Navy was rapidly expanding and acquiring new bases all over the world. So those of us on active duty were constantly on call. My squadron was either getting ready to leave or away from home.

Following the Iran cruise, we were sent to the Mediterranean for nearly as long. The separation put a lot of tension on my marriage, sure. It was tough. During those ten years, visits to see our parents were few. I am a poor letter-writer, so I tried to spend time on the phone with my mother.

Susan and the kids stayed on the West Coast while I was gone. Bobby and Tanya grew up in Oak Harbor, on Whidbey Island. A very beautiful place to bring up a family. The problem was that I was never there. I can't blame the navy for my marriage falling apart, but it didn't help Susan's and my relationship any.

Following Whidbey, I got a pleasant surprise. I was assigned to work in the office of the Secretary of Defense at the Pentagon under my old college roommate, Jim Webb. My responsibility was to work on international issues involving mobilizing our reserves in case of a crisis in Europe. And later, in 1987, when Webb became Secretary of the Navy, I went with him as his Assistant for Policy.

My kids enjoyed living in the Seattle area and were reluctant to leave, but I hoped that the new job would give me more time with the family and save my marriage. And I knew that my mother's health was deteriorating.

When I went up to Massachusetts to visit, the change in Mother shocked me. It was as if all the pain and sacrifice she had made for my sister and me had manifested itself in her appearance. But I did not realize how close to death she was. My marriage was coming apart, and I was trying hard to save it. I couldn't give Mother the help she needed. We talked about it. She told me to put my energy into my marriage.

Even though our relationship was failing, our children reminded Susan and me of our success. We couldn't ask for better kids. Tanya, who is now a freshman at Mary Washington College, has the strength and Slavic beauty of her grandmother. When my aunt visited us from Europe, she said that looking at Tanya transported her back to her youth, so much was she reminded of my mother. And Bobby is now a tenth-grader. He plays baseball, soccer, does well at math, and plays a fair baritone horn. Bobby is studying the Russian language now. He's very much aware that he's half Russian.

I didn't bring my kids up with much of a sense of Russian tradition. It didn't make sense in our circumstances, and I felt it would have been a burden. There is an emotional price for what I went through . . . my memories of the camps. I have talked about it with the kids, but I don't want it to be a part of their lives.

My aunt visited us from Germany after we returned to the East Coast. I learned from her for the first time that my mother was also born in Russia, rather than Czechoslovakia, which our immigration papers had stated. What led to this discussion was the stark contrast with my wife, who is a tenth-generation American.

When Susan's father died, a couple years earlier, she found a family genealogy while going through his papers. I showed it to my aunt and said, "This is kind of neat. They have documented all these generations of their family. Look at us—we don't even know where we're from."

My aunt looked at me funny and said, "Look, I'm not going to tell you, because you have to get this from your mother. But our family was very substantial."

I asked my mother about this. She broke down and told me the true story. It was very painful for her. The events surrounding my father's disappearance were still very confused.

When I found out about Gleb, my real father, I began seeing myself differently. Things in me that I could not find in Mikhail's legacy, fit Gleb's well. The two men in my mother's life, while very dissimilar, were both unique. I gained much from my dual paternity. Gleb gave me life. Knowing that he is my father has given me insights into strengths that I had never realized. And Mikhail, who took Gleb's place, watched me birthed and nourished me when I would have otherwise perished. His imprint will always be with me.

What I haven't been able to reconcile is their deaths. Gleb took the cold gray path of espionage, in which there is rarely public acknowledgment. So no one knows of him and his lonely effort. Not even I, his son, can recount it accurately. Such is the fate of spies in war.

Mikhail's situation was very different. He was thrown into one of the most severe crucibles of the war, survived, and emerged a hero. Some of his deeds have been recounted in the Russian-émigré press. Any other nation would've made him a hero. The Soviet state destroyed him. The common thread in both men's lives that led to their common fate was that they loved Russia but hated the Soviet regime.

In my navy experience, I haven't met many other foreign-born career officers—only one pilot, who had fled Hungary after the 1956 revolt against the Soviets. The navy tends to be more mainline American. But my beginnings have never been a hindrance. In the fleet, they called me "the Mad Russian." I'm proud of that because I earned the nickname by working hard.

Working in the Defense Department, I've had to get special security clearances. Because I came of Russian parents and am foreign born, they probably checked up a little more on me than on other people. When I found out about my real father, I went in and talked with my superiors. I was worried. I was thirty-eight years old, a commander in the navy. In the full sense, I've been an American citizen since 1960. But I had this piece of my past that I had to explain. I had the sinking feeling that they might cancel my security clearance. Or my mother might be in trouble because she hadn't told them the truth about who she was. People had been deported for similar reasons.

I went into the office. I sat down and told the truth. The man said, "We don't get many of these types of cases any more. Fill out the forms." Which I did. And that ended the matter.

For almost twenty years, the navy had been both a brother and a father to me. It's a very good feeling to have come from outside this country and not only to become a naval officer but to work on the staff of the Secretary of Defense. The trust that has been shown toward me is a reflection on how this country works.

I didn't realize at the time how ill my mother was. Lung cancer. Within a year she was gone. The end came quickly. Doctors tried hard to save her. I rushed to Springfield when I got the news from my sister. Mother stabilized, and for a while it looked as if she was going to get better. I left for a few days to tie up loose ends at work, but was back at midweek.

I came to the hospital in my uniform, because I knew it would please her. Although I had spent hours traveling in my summer whites, there wasn't a wrinkle on me. By the time I arrived, she was unconscious. The priest came in and said the last rites. That was important to her, and I hoped that she had been aware enough to know it.

I stood vigil the whole night. She had only hours left, so I stayed with her. Mostly, I held her hand. Hers had guided me, protected me.

Through hard labor, she had fed and clothed me. It was fitting, as the end came, in her helplessness, that I hold her.

I stroked her forehead and temples, occasionally kissing her, and talking to her. Always in Russian, because it was our language, which no one else in the room understood. I told her that I loved her, and asked forgiveness for my shortcomings over the years. I recited poetry we had shared in my youth: two of Lermontov's poems. One was about a sail, the other a Cossack cradle song. When I was very young, she recited the cradle song so often that I grew to hate it. Years later, when I read it as an adult, I realized that it held much truth—I, the warrior, in harm's way; she, the mother, ceaselessly praying for my safety.

In the early morning, I left to clean up and change clothes. As I returned to my mother's bed, I called out, "Mama! Mama!" half expecting a response. None came. The intern who was working on my mother's case was surprised and looked up. She had never before heard that vocal intonation from me. In fact, I had not heard it myself in years. It was out of my childhood, the voice I had used to call my mother when I was in need, the voice she had always responded to. But not this time.

I took my place beside her again and held her hand. Before, its warmth had meant security, sustenance, all that was right in the world. Now it meant farewell. Her breathing slowed, came somewhat brokenly. Then a last breath and she was gone. I said my final goodbye.

Last December, I visited Salzburg. The city and the countryside are now prosperous but have lost none of their alpine beauty. The refugee camps are gone, replaced by bright, clean houses. No reminder is left of the tens of thousands of souls, set adrift by the war, who sheltered there. No marker stands in memory of lives and dreams broken and put together again as they, like me, drifted off to make new beginnings in the far corners of the world.

I reflected on the kindness of the Curtis family, who didn't owe anybody anything, but took my family in. The profound gift that they gave us was the *chance*. The meaning of that chance was very profound.

I saw them just after my mother died. They told me, "We wish that we could have done more to help you folks when you first came." I said to Mrs. Curtis, "What more could you have done? You gave us everything there was to be given. You gave us a chance."

HOUSE OF
DONUTS

Celia Vann Noup
Refugee from Cambodia
Donut Shop Proprietress
Lawndale, California

Celia Noup's claim to the American dream is a four-table donut shop near a busy freeway entrance on a wide boulevard that links Los Angeles International Airport to an infinity of gas stations, pizza shops, hair and nail salons, video rentals, one-hour photo marts, and clusters of boxlike tract homes.

A quick right turn onto Manhattan Beach Boulevard leads to ocean-front condominiums. A left turn traverses the Latin barrios and black ghettos of Compton and Watts. Mrs. Noup's little piece of Hawthorne Boulevard, in the Lawndale community, is part of L.A.'s urban sprawl that grew with the post–World War II highway boom. A place where newlywed returning GIs could afford their first homes with pleasant green lawns in "Ozzie and Harriet" neighborhoods.

In recent years, faces on the street reflect the jambalaya of peoples who have migrated to southern California from every conceivable spot on the globe. Celia Noup, age fifty, and her daughters are among the fifty thousand Cambodians who have settled in the freeway-linked Los Angeles and Orange County areas. They are survivors of a holocaust that has consumed nearly one-third of Cambodia's population.

In 1975, after the black pajama-clad Khmer Rouge marched into Phnom Penh, Cambodia's capital, a stream of zombielike fugitives began straggling into Thailand with tales of unbelievable slaughter and massive slave-labor camps. At the time Indochina fell, around a hundred Cambodians were living in the United States. Most were diplomats or college students. In the next few years, they were joined by around two thousand refugees related to government and military officials.

In 1979, Vietnam invaded Cambodia, pushing more than a half-million emaciated refugees into barbed-wire-enclosed camps along the Thailand frontier. The United States responded with a resettlement program primarily for those who had suffered because of previous association with Americans, and their surviving family members.

The first group of refugees, who were well educated, adapted their professional talents. But new arrivals, less familiar with Western society and overwhelmed by American language and culture, have floundered. Many were placed in the worst slums of New York, Providence, Boston, Chicago, Philadelphia, and other large cities. Finding few job opportunities and living in constant fear of robbery or beatings, they began migrating to the Pacific Coast's more promising job market and social-welfare programs.

With family members arriving from overseas refugee camps, California has become home for half of the 150,000 Cambodians in America.

Although they have found a sympathetic environment, most Cambodians—especially adults plagued with language problems—are limited to unskilled jobs that pay less than public assistance. The welfare system has discouraged parents of young children from starting jobs at base pay by revoking medical benefits from families of the working poor. Having suffered the loss of their country and witnessed relatives perish during four bloody years of the Khmer Rouge, and then experienced the subsequent hardships of living in refugee camps and being thrust into an alien new world, many Cambodians have given up on life.

Unlike other Asians, who have aggressively entered the American marketplace, Cambodians have never possessed exceptional business skills. Theirs was largely a village-based farming society; the small educated elite worked in government, administrative, or military professions. Most commerce was conducted by ethnic Chinese merchants and some Vietnamese traders. To survive in America, however, a growing number of Cambodians are learning to open small businesses.

Celia Noup, a high-school teacher in Phnom Penh, was widowed by the Khmer Rouge during the years of terror. She arrived in America on July 4, 1979, determined to hold her family together without taking assistance from outsiders. When she speaks of her husband, her eyes involuntarily fill with tears. But she has never asked anyone for pity.

Six or seven days a week, from before the morning rush begins on the Santa Monica Freeway until after the second shift has left the local aircraft factories, Celia works behind the counter of her shop. She moves slowly on aching legs, which cause her to see a doctor once a week for an injection to numb the pain. With a resigned lilt in her voice, she described her American dream.

I started this business from almost nothing at all. I named it House of Donuts, my own franchise. I spend most of my time in this shop, seven days a week. Why did a woman my age choose this kind of business? I know it's crazy. My children were already living in southern California. And my second daughter, Monie, was getting married here. That's why I moved from Washington, D.C., in 1983.

I get to the shop at 5:00 in the morning to open for breakfast, and I usually leave around 7:00 P.M. I work behind the counter, serving customers, and do the cleaning and sweeping. I work by myself most of the time. My youngest daughter, Parika, just began college, but she comes with me at 5:00 A.M. to help. At 10:00 A.M., she goes home to study, before she attends afternoon and evening classes at El Camino

College. She works another part-time job, at May Company, in the children's department. She wants to buy a car.

At first I didn't want to come to California. When my daughters and I came to the United States in 1979, we were brought to Virginia, just outside of Washington, by my sister-in-law. But my first daughter, Mealy [pronounced "May Lee"], who was twenty-three years old, had a friend in southern California. She phoned our house and said, "Mealy, if you cannot find a job in Virginia, why don't you come here? I'll help you find a job."

So Mealy came to me and said, "Mom, the work situation here is very bad. It's very frustrating for me. Even during the bad times in Cambodia under the Khmer Rouge, I worked with my muscles to earn a bowl of rice. Why can't I find a job here? Let me go. I don't want to be on public assistance."

We never wanted to take money from the social services. I cried the day they interviewed me. And I also cried when they asked, "Are you married? Single? Widow?" I said, "I'm married." I cannot say that I'm a widow. My husband's death was never confirmed. That's why my American citizenship papers say that I am married.

I am pursuing the American dream—to have a house of my own, for my family. I try to make my children understand: "You have to help me in the shop, so that I can save and buy a small house." But they have their own lives, their own families, other jobs. The money they earn is not that much. So they still need me as much as I need them.

When I became an American citizen a few months ago, it was very emotional for me. I was happy that I could be part of my new country. I do feel loyalty to the United States. I think of myself as both Cambodian and an American citizen. I cannot forget where I came from.

My maiden name was Thann Meng Vann. When I became an American citizen, I took an American name, Celia, and my husband's family name, Noup, because I hope that he will some day return. I lost contact with him as our country was falling in April 1975. The outpost he commanded was surrounded by the Khmer Rouge. I have never found out what happened to him after he was captured. Sometimes I have seen him in my dreams, but he never talks to me.

The first time I dreamed about my husband was in a hut where the Khmer Rouge ordered my family to stay after our city, Phnom Penh, was evacuated. In the dream, I saw him in our bedroom in Phnom Penh. He looked very sad. I woke up in the middle of the night. I shouted. I cried out loud.

The next day, the Communists sent an old person to talk with me, to tell me that they heard me in the night. They warned me not to do that any more. For four years they tried to kill me. They tried every trick in the book to catch me breaking their rules.

Now, in my dreams at night, people speak in the Cambodian language. But I never dream about Cambodia. No more. My dreams always take place in a house with my daughters that is unknown to me. It is always the same house, on a streetcorner, three stories high.

On weekdays, I live in the house that my daughter Mealy and her husband rent; it is only five minutes from my shop. On weekends, I live with my daughter Monie and her husband, in Torrance. I share the cost of food for the households. Sometimes I buy groceries. And I pay some rent for both Parika and me. I try to help my children as much as I can. I can't take it all with me. [Laughs]

I have four grandchildren, all babies—two years, one year, and a few months. The only time I have for them is on weekends, when my daughters are working at my shop. I babysit the kids while I do bookkeeping. I enjoy their company.

We've been here seven years now. My children still think like Cambodians, but their way of acting is American. At work or school they have become more aggressive. They will talk back to people when something is wrong. But not to their mother. They are still my daughters. We have been very supportive of each other through some very difficult times.

Mealy is married to an American who works with his brother for a trucking company. He's trying to build a savings account so that he can start his own business. They have two children. Mealy was crying the day of her birthday. She said, "Mom, I'm thirty now. I'm old." I told her, "I felt the same way when I turned thirty. I told your father, 'I feel so old.' " [Laughs] That was an eternity ago. Now I am fifty.

Monie is twenty-six. She's married to a Cambodian who works for the big Toyota office that imports all the cars. They also have two children. My third daughter, Romani, has a Computer Learning Center degree and works at a watch company in Inglewood. She's twenty-two and not married yet.

I came from a family of educated people. After the Communists took over Cambodia, none of my children had the chance to finish school. My husband and I protected Monie and Romani by sending them to France to attend high school just before our country fell. But Parika, my youngest, is my only daughter who is able to pursue a college degree. She doesn't know what field she wants to major in yet. This is only her first week of classes at El Camino College. She helps me in the donut shop, too. Parika has been at my side through all the changes during her eighteen years.

I know that American families have as much trouble as I do making ends meet. I hear that all the time from my customers. Most are white Americans who work at the aircraft factories and small businesses along Hawthorne Boulevard. Mexicans and Filipinos who live in this area are my customers, too.

A lot of Cambodians around here have donut shops. We told each other that in this type of business we can make a living, especially those people who don't speak English well. In Cambodia, we starved, but we endured. Here, we have to work very hard to survive. Rent is high, life and health insurance, car registration and insurance, and telephone bills are expensive, too.

In Cambodia, I was a schoolteacher for twenty years, but I could depend on my husband. It was my choice if I wanted to work or not. Here, I have to make my own living.

When I was growing up in Phnom Penh, my father was the principal of a primary school. My grandfather worked in the Royal Palace; he was chief cook for the King. And my father's sister was one of King Monivong's concubines.

I fulfilled my father's dreams of a college education at the Cambodia Institute of Faculty. I also studied in the United States for six months, in Michigan. I went back to Phnom Penh to finish my degree. Then, for twenty-two years, I taught at the Khmera-Anglais High School. It was the only high school in Cambodia that taught English as a second language.

My husband, Noup Paramoun, was a soldier since 1954, when Cambodia gained its independence from France. We were married in 1955 and lived in Phnom Penh.

Cambodia became directly involved in the [Indochina] War after Prince Sihanouk was overthrown in March 1970. The North Vietnamese started pushing deeper into Cambodia, toward Phnom Penh, from the border sanctuaries that Sihanouk had given them earlier. In September 1970, my husband was still a major when he was made commander of Battalion 24 and sent to Svay Rieng Province. That was the first time we left Phnom Penh.

Svay Rieng was a dangerous area on the South Vietnam border, only fifty miles from Phnom Penh. Its capital, Svay Rieng city, is just a few miles from the "Parrot's Beak" area of Cambodia, which juts into Vietnam. The Vietnamese Communists launched attacks into Saigon from these bases.

My husband never liked to talk much about his work, but he told me about one battle at a bridge that his men had to defend for three nights and days. They didn't eat anything during that whole time. After that, he was ordered to another hot area, in Kompong Cham Province.

During the third year of the war, in 1973, the American army left Vietnam. The Cambodian government told my husband, "You've been fighting for three years. Let's find a better place for your people, Battalion 24." So the battalion cut some lumber from the forest and built a base camp outside of Phnom Penh, near Pochentong Airport. Needless to say, I was overjoyed to have my husband home again.

They had hardly settled in when Svay Rieng almost fell to the Communists. All that remained was a small five-kilometer area. Battalion 24 had to be airlifted to rescue the city from the Khmer Rouge and Vietnamese Communists.

When the battle was finished, my husband came back to Phnom Penh to visit army headquarters. After the meeting, he came home very upset. He said, "Honey, they asked me to be governor of Svay Rieng." I said, "What will you do there? You have no education to be a politician. You have been a soldier all your life. You are a tough fighter, but not a governor." He said, "I have to give General Sak Sutsakhan an answer this afternoon."

General Sak told Paramoun, "Svay Rieng is your native area. Your father was a teacher there. I cannot find anybody more qualified to save the province at this moment. I promise, if I can find someone who wants the job, I will relieve you."

Nobody wanted the job, because it was too dangerous. All of the politicians fled the area. Because of its location, the area was continually under siege by the North Vietnamese and Khmer Rouge. Only the army was left to take care of the people. A few courageous officials stayed to help.

My husband tried to refuse, but General Sak said, "That's an order." My husband said, "I cannot refuse your command, but only for three months." Three months became two years. People in Svay Rieng loved him. He was tough, he was rude, but he governed very well.

I stayed in Phnom Penh with our daughters. My husband was so proud of the four girls. When he was promoted to general, our garden was full of guests. He introduced the girls to all of them. He said, "Here're my girls: Mealy, Monie, Romani, and the youngest is Parika."

In the spring of 1975, as the country was falling, Paramoun came into the city only for brief meetings and to lobby at army headquarters for ammunition. As soon as he finished his business, he went right back to his command. We didn't have a family life.

On April 14, 1975, the Khmer Rouge were tightening their siege around Phnom Penh. That day, Cambodia's president, Lon Nol, fled the country. For the first time ever, I decided to telephone my husband in Svay Rieng. Previously, I would ask my brother or other officers who worked in the Liaison Bureau to tell him that I was coming to visit. On the phone, I told Paramoun, "High officials are leaving Phnom Penh. Can I come with the kids to Svay Rieng to be with you?"

A few days earlier, my husband had been in the city for a meeting. I had also asked him if I could move to Svay Rieng. It was the first time that I had ever requested this. He had said, "Fine. Pack your clothes." I told him, "It will take time to get the kids ready. Can we go on the next trip when you come back?" He said, "Yes."

That was the first time I walked out of our home and followed his jeep. I watched it the length of our street until he turned the corner and was out of sight.

But on the 14th, his attitude had changed. On the telephone he told me, "You should leave the country with the kids and your parents. I cannot go with you. The soldiers here have asked me to fight with them until the end."

Those were the last words I ever heard from him. He said, "I would like to live, too. But I have to fight. I cannot leave my men. You and the kids should go now."

We had already sent our second and third daughters, Monie and Romani, to live with my sister in Paris a few months earlier. But I couldn't find anybody to take my married daughter, Mealy, her baby son, and my youngest daughter. On the 15th, I received no word from Svay Rieng. I went to see General Sak. I said, "Please, send a helicopter to get my husband. He's been fighting for years under your command. He's never failed. Please send somebody to bring him here." Sak said, "Don't worry."

The next day, on the 16th, the army Liaison Bureau said that Paramoun was still okay. After that, I heard no more.

The Khmer Rouge were rocketing and bombarding Phnom Penh. Where I lived there was no damage. My father came to my home and begged me, "Please, I know that you are a strong-willed person. But in this last moment, I believe your decision to stay here is wrong." Still I refused to leave my house, because my husband had told me to stay until we found a way to escape. Against my objections, Paramoun left some soldiers to guard our home. But my father pleaded, "Leave this house. You cannot be here when the Communists come."

I dismissed all of the guards. I said, "Go to your wives and children." I gathered my two daughters and grandchild, then went to my sister's house.

On the morning of the 17th, the Khmer Rouge marched into the city, dressed in black. People were clapping their hands and waving white flags, shouting, "Peace, peace."

One of my relatives went outside and passed out cigarettes to Khmer Rouge soldiers. They said politely, "Thank you, only one cigarette is enough. Not the whole pack."

Young Khmer Rouge soldiers, eight or ten years old, were dragging their rifles, which were taller than them. I remember thinking, "They are so young. And we surrendered to *them?*" I didn't see a tank or jeep, just people in black.

That morning, one of my husband's friends, a doctor, told me, "Please, don't go home." I asked, "Why?" He said, "Because when the Khmer Rouge came down our street, they asked me, 'Where is Paramoun's house?' They carried a small piece of paper with the address written on it."

I later found out that some Khmer Rouge commanders told soldiers that, when Phnom Penh was liberated, they would have the houses of generals to live in. When they marched into the city, the soldiers were very excited. But they never had a chance to live in these houses. The forced evacuation of the city started almost immediately.

The whole city, more than two million people, was forced out of their homes into the streets. My family walked with our neighbors until we reached Mao Tse-tung Boulevard, the main boulevard in Phnom Penh. All the population of the city was gathered there. The Khmer Rouge were telling everyone to leave the city.

Although my two middle children were safe in France, my oldest and youngest daughters were close beside me. Parika was only seven. Mealy, who was nineteen, carried her infant son. I kept my children huddled together. As soon as a parent let go, a child would be lost in the huge crowd. My relatives said that we would stick together, but the crowd was too thick. Everybody was pushing. And the Khmer Rouge kept ordering everybody, "You must go forward." They shot their guns in the air. Even during the middle of the night, the procession was endless. The Khmer Rouge kept shooting and we kept moving forward.

We came upon an orphanage full of babies. The nurses had fled to find their families in the panic and confusion of the crowd. Mats were thrown on the orphanage courtyard, loaded with cookies. All the children were crawling around it. Hundreds of babies—eight months, two months, one month old. None of them old enough to walk.

Holding on to my own two children, I ran to these babies. I washed some of them and put them back in rooms inside the building. They were all wet. I had to throw away their diapers. . . . There weren't any clean diapers. So I wrapped them in clean sheets and put them back in the cribs. But I could not stay with them. I heard the Khmer Rouge gunshots outside. Some women Khmer Rouge soldiers walked into the orphanage. They said, "You are very heartless people. Why do you leave them here?" What could we do? I had to leave them behind. Some were already dead. Others were crying in their cribs. They had not eaten for three or four days. Some were handicapped and couldn't move. Some women who had no children came in and grabbed an infant to carry out of the city.

Recently I saw the movie *Doctor Zhivago*, about the Russian Revolution. If you compare that to what happened in Phnom Penh, the movie is only on a very small scale. Even *Killing Fields* only gives you part of the idea of what happened in Cambodia. The reality was much more incredible.

During the first week, the Communists had us travel as far as we could go. They kept ordering, "Go forward." We'd say, "Where?" They'd respond, "To the Angkar." We'd say, "Where's the Angkar?" They'd respond, "You'll see the Angkar in front of you."

We didn't understand. We'd ask everybody, "Where's the Angkar?" We thought it was a big building or something. We looked for some direction where we should go. We were exhausted, hungry. People died, day by day.

During the long procession, as we went through the outskirts of Phnom Penh, we passed a jeep with two Khmer Rouge in it. They were looking through albums and watching people as we passed by. There were pictures of Cambodian officials in their books. They immediately arrested anyone who had anything military on their bodies—tied their hands behind their backs and took them away.

My brother-in-law planned to escape with us to Vietnam. Once we got outside of Phnom Penh, my mom said, "Go this way." Toward Vietnam, which is around seventy-five miles from Phnom Penh.

I said, "No. Many Khmer Rouge on National Highway 1 would know of my husband." The highway went right through Svay Rieng to Vietnam. That would've made us easy targets. So we tried an alternate road to Katum, in the Vietnamese highlands. But many other people had that same idea, and the road was too crowded.

We finally stopped at a marketplace at Ta Khmau. We cooked there. That night my aunt went to talk with the Khmer Rouge. She asked them to open the road that went toward Vietnam. They said, "Okay, your family can go."

When other people in the market saw us begin to pack, they did the same. We suddenly became fifty families. The Khmer Rouge said, "No, you cannot go. You must take the south road, to Takeo."

My brother's youngest boy had leukemia, so he told the Khmer Rouge, "We cannot go further. My son is sick." They allowed us to stay in that village. After we built a hut, my brother-in-law said, "I cannot stay. I must try to reach Vietnam, and then fly to France." So he left with his brother and son to Kampot, a port city, twenty-five miles from Vietnam.

When they reached Kampot, it was April 30. They heard the news: Vietnam had fallen, too. So they came back to see my mother and the rest of the family. When he reached us, his foot was bleeding. I was busy tying dried palm leaves together to make a roof for our hut. He came to me and said, "Impossible to escape now." But he heard in the marketplace that a few outstanding officials had been called back to Phnom Penh. He didn't realize that this was a trick. He told me, "I'm going to tell the Khmer Rouge the truth. Sooner or later I will be able to escape to France." I said, "Well, it's up to you."

A few nights later, two Khmer Rouge came with guns. They said that my brother-in-law, my brother, and my son-in-law had to go to Phnom Penh to help rebuild the government. My brother-in-law said, "Strange that they call at this hour. It's totally bizarre." I called my son-in-law. My brother was with his wife and children in another hut.

My mother was suspicious. She asked the Khmer Rouge, "How many people did you call tonight to go?" They said, "Oh, there's a truckful on the main street." She asked them, "Do my children need to bring some rice provisions to use while they work in Phnom Penh?" They told her, "The Angkar—the Communist organization—will take care of everything."

Still, my mom put rice, dried fish, and other provisions in a bag for them. They took off, my brother driving the car, one Khmer Rouge with a gun in the front, in the back seat a Khmer Rouge between my brother-in-law and my son-in-law. The boy was married to my daughter Mealy, who was only nineteen years old. Before he departed he told me, "Please, take care of my wife." He suspected that something bad was going to happen.

The Khmer Rouge brought them to a former professional school, as soon as they got on the road. This is where the local Angkar [Khmer Rouge officials] had their headquarters. The woman who told me this now lives in Long Beach. She was very close to the Khmer Rouge. She told me that the men fought back. My brother was a police officer; he knew judo and karate. My brother-in-law, too. But they were killed.

The man who killed them was the Khmer Rouge head man in the village. When he got home, he just banged his head on the wall. He regretted having to kill my family. He was angry. He said, "What kind of government is this? What kind of Angkar? Just ordering us to kill people."

The Khmer Rouge always carried out their executions very secretly. If the people witnessed them killing the doctors, intellectuals, the monks, we would have fought back. But the Angkar's politics and methods of control were very smooth.

At night, when the Khmer Rouge would call people's names and take them away, we knew that they were dead. But we did not want to accept that as reality. Even though we had fear, if we had seen it with our own eyes, we would have responded differently. We just couldn't accept it as being real.

My father died in July 1975 from dehydration caused by dysentery. We survived thanks to my mom. She was a really great philosopher and psychologist. She knew that Khmer Rouge spies hid under our hut.

Each night, when we came back to the village from working in the fields, Mom would say, "Children, let's all go to sleep." She would quietly warn me that the wood had eyes and ears. She'd say, "It's nine o'clock now. Go to sleep. Don't talk. Save your strength to work for the Angkar. You are all girls. There is nothing else to do but work. All the men are gone in our family."

Mom was actually saying for the Khmer Rouge spies to hear, "They are only girls. Don't kill them. We are the only members left of the family." The Khmer Rouge knew this very well. They had watched us all the way. They knew that we were lying to them about our identity. It was a horrible game.

If you hid your identity, that meant you wanted your past forgotten. We had changed from people who were intellectual, who used to think independently, into part of the Angkar's "populace." You became humiliated, allowed to live only as a slave.

We stayed in that village for three months. Then the Angkar ordered everyone, "Go to your hometown." Among my family, we discussed where we would go. My idea always was to escape. But the Khmer

Rouge sent us all to the countryside in Battambang Province, near Thailand, to work in the fields.

There were thousands of people in our work group. The Angkar didn't separate men and women, but young adults were sent forward, and children from seven years old were kept in a separate camp.

My daughter Mealy came back to see me every three or four months. She brought whatever she could catch on the way from the fields—lizards, crabs, worms, and wild leaves that were edible. She caught a little animal or insect and kept it in her hands until she reached my hut. Then she shared it with all of us.

My youngest, Parika, who was only eight years old, was sent to a camp where children were forced to work like adults, but with less rice to eat. They had their own children's community with their own Angkar leader, who was as young as fourteen years old.

Parika became very sick. She would sneak out of the children's camp to see me every night. She would crawl past the Khmer Rouge guards, then walk through the flooded fields with water up to her neck, then run to my hut in the village, hiding from the soldiers who stood watch.

I would save half of my rice ration so she would have something to eat. Parika would be exhausted from the three-kilometer trip, and she had to sneak back to her camp before dawn. She was sick with malaria. But there was no medicine at all.

One night Parika told me, "Mommy, I'm not going back. If I die, I want to be with you until the last second." I said, "How can we both eat? Your ration is in the children's camp." But my mom said, "Let her stay."

My grandson, who Mealy had left with us, was also dying. Luckily, three days before the infant passed away, the Khmer Rouge sent Mealy home to us. The Angkar said, "Go home, Comrade Mom, your son is dying."

All of us were staying in the same hut. While Parika and Mealy and I worked in the fields, my mom stayed home with the baby. For dinner the four of us shared three bowls of rice and a little salt every night, and some wild vegetables that I picked in the fields. If the commune's kitchen gave us some soup, it had only a little vegetables and some salt. There would seldom be more than one shrimp in the entire pot. Someone would grab it right away.

Shortly after Mealy arrived, my grandson's little body began to swell from diarrhea. He always knew that, when we heard the village bell, it was time to get our small ration. He couldn't talk, but he made a sign that told me to get it. In the morning, when I went to work, I would put some bran in a bowl for him. We just ate bran—the husks of rice. We would get sick to our stomachs, because the bran was too rough to digest, but people were so hungry they would trade a diamond ring for two cups of bran.

The morning my grandson died, it was just before breakfast. We heard the cowbell and he signaled for me to get the bran. When I came back to the hut, he was too weak to eat. Mealy came to the hut and cried when she saw him. After he died, Mealy was sent to work in fields far away. But she still found ways to visit.

My mom's death especially hurt Mealy. They were very close. Mealy was the person who dug the hole and buried Mom. She only asked people to carry Mom's body to the grave. Then she told them, "Thank you. Go back home. I'll take care of her."

At that time, Mealy told me, "I am going to keep moving forward. I'm not coming back to this village. My grandmom is dead." And she disappeared.

Six months later, she came back, bringing a bowl of rice for me. She said, "Mommy, I'm sorry. But I was so upset that Grandmom died."

Most of the Khmer Rouge soldiers were very young. But the chiefs of my village were very old. They were mountain people who had always been very poor. They never saw a marketplace. If you tried to tell them about civilization, you could be killed for revealing that you were educated.

I knew the danger, but I did tell the chief about these things. It began when someone told me that I could send a message to Phnom Penh. I knew this could be a mistake, but I did not care any more if I was alive or dead. I wrote a letter to my old friend Madame Yun Yat. She was the Khmer Rouge Minister of Education, Culture, and Information, and the wife of the army chief, Son Sen.

She and I were high-school and college classmates. And, even more ironic, Madame Ieng Thirith—the wife of Ieng Sary, the Khmer Rouge number-two leader—was the principal when I taught at the Khmera-Anglais High School. When Thirith was a principal, she never behaved in a cruel manner. Her sister, Pol Pot's wife, acted the same way. Thirith had also been my teacher in high school. She was very nice. We called her "Soft."

Before my friend Yun Yat joined the Khmer Rouge in the jungle, her husband was already with the guerrillas. When she was in Phnom Penh, I always visited her apartment. I knew that she was a Communist, and had married Son Sen because of their ideology. She would tell me, "My husband disappeared. Maybe the government put him in jail. His clothes are still here, his eyeglasses. He can't see a thing without his glasses. He must have been forced to leave."

I said, "I'm sorry. I didn't hear anything." That was around 1960. It seemed that she and I were already on different sides. She later joined her husband in the maquis, and left her children behind with their grandmother. The old woman cried. She told me, "What happened to my children? Why are they Communists?"

From my work camp in Battambang I wrote, "Dear Madame Yun Yat: I'm here in this village working for the Angkar." I praised the Khmer Rouge government for liberating the country. Then I said: "But, please, look to the hearts of the population. So many people are dying. A government without a population is a ghost government. I don't mind being hungry. But being sick is something else. You have to do something to help the people."

The village Angkar caught the letter. At that time, my hand was swollen from a shot that they had given me for malaria—not quinine, just some type of liquid that they put in a 7-Up bottle. They filled a syringe and stuck the needle into my arm. The tricep of my left arm became swollen like a grapefruit. I made a sling out of my scarf, to keep my arm immobilized. This was when my mom was deathly sick. I had to lift her in and out of bed.

After I took care of Mom in the morning, I would work in the fields. I was assigned to chase the birds, so they wouldn't eat the crops. One day, while I was doing that, the Khmer Rouge chief of the village came. He called to me, "Come here! On the ditch." I was afraid. He was a mountain person, very tall, dark complexion, around seventy years old. I asked, "You need to talk with me?" He said, "Did you write a letter?" I thought, "The time has come for me now." I said, "Yes, Father.'" I called him *puok*, which is how Cambodians address their father and mother. He said, "Why did you write the letter?" So I told him that I know Son Sen and his wife, and Ieng Sary and his wife, too. I told him that, if the letter reached Phnom Penh, they would send for me, because I had taken care of their children when they were hiding and fighting in the jungle.

I knew that the chief had never been to a city. He asked me, "What does Phnom Penh look like? Tell me about the big city. What do you eat there?" So I told him about the houses, cars, running water, electricity, refrigerator, telephone, TV. He had never heard about many of these things before. He said, "If what you have told me is true, then what are we fighting for? The Angkar told us that we are fighting for something that is good."

I told him, "In Phnom Penh we already have 'magic eyes'—television. Magic rice-cooker—electricity. We don't need a cooking fire. Why do you need to fight?" He was so surprised, this was magic to him.

I told him, "One night, when the sky is clear and the moon is not so bright, you will see one star that doesn't stay still. That is the magic star. It's called a satellite. People invented that. They built it and sent it up there. If they want to see you through it, they see you. If they want to see me, they see me." I lied a little bit to him.

The chiefs were so astounded that men could make stars. I said, "You believe that stars are made by gods or something magic. Now people can make that. Why do we Cambodians try to start a new society on an idea that is nonsense? Why did you destroy everything? You say that you have started to build the country from 'Year Zero' with your bare hands. What can you do with your bare hands only? When people use their heads, they create all of the things that you hear me talk about and believe are magic. Why do you do this to our country?"

The old chief listened to me for the whole afternoon. Then I said, "Now, will you send my letter to Phnom Penh?" He said, "I would like to, but it's not possible. I should kill you. No connection is possible between Phnom Penh and you. You are the population; you have no right to address the leaders. Don't do it again. I like you very much."

I said to him, "Why don't you go to Phnom Penh with me? You will see all that I told you. You will be very surprised." He said, "No."

That night, at the Angkar study session, the old chief said, "Nothing is worth as much as rice. People who live everywhere need rice. Those who ride airplanes, who go to the moon, still need rice. So let's cultivate rice."

That is the only thing we did—three crops a year, for four years. But we were never allowed enough for ourselves to eat. When harvest came, we had plenty for one month, but they would not let us dry the rice or save anything—they feared that we would save provisions for escape. Trucks would come to pick up all the rice we harvested. After that, we went back to the small bowl every day.

The Khmer Rouge used much of the rice to pay back their debt to China. On the surface, the Khmer Rouge talked about their "New Society" and "Year Zero." But on a larger scale, we were little more than a slave-labor force to help feed China.

My two daughters and I remained alive. But we became skinnier every year—only skin and bones. I believe that, if we had surrendered to fatigue and stayed home, we would have died, because lack of physical activity made one's health even worse. People who refused to work died very soon. Work kept our blood moving just enough to keep our bodies alive.

At mealtime, the Khmer Rouge would consider who worked. They gave you just a little bit—a spoonful—more rice. And in the fields we could try to catch crabs and pick wild vegetables along the paddy ditch. That filled our stomachs a little bit.

During the first week of January 1979, I began to see people from other places coming through our village. I asked them, "Where are you going?" They said, "We don't know. The Khmer Rouge just keep telling us to go forward." I asked where they came from. They said, "The outskirts of Phnom Penh."

A few days later, the same faces came back. I asked, "Didn't I talk with you a few days ago?" They said, "Yes. We went to Pailin, a district near the Thailand border. Now the Khmer Rouge tell us to come back here."

Then, one afternoon, the whole village was turned upside down. People ran to the barn to get rice, and put it in baskets that they carried on top of their heads. People called me from my hut, "Please help. We are leaving the village." I asked what was happening. They said, "We don't know. The Angkar told us to leave the village."

I immediately thought about my children. Parika was in the children's work camp. Mealy was in the Angkar community, not far away. I put my clothes in a small bundle and went to the road-crossing point to wait. I saw Parika coming. Then Mealy, with a whole bundle of white rice on her head. I asked her where she got it. She said, "They told us to take whatever we wanted." I told her, "We have two chickens, but I couldn't catch them." She said, "Mom, just walk with the village group, but don't go too fast. I will catch up with you."

Mealy waited until dark. She went back into the village and caught the chickens. She searched for Parika and me until we were together again. We kept moving forward to the mountains. I was very weak and couldn't keep up with the group. The Angkar came to me and said, "Walk faster and join us." I said, "I am sick. I cannot walk that fast. Comrade, do you have something for me to eat?"

All the way to the Cardamom Mountains, we planted rice and kept moving. One night, three male soldiers were walking quickly around our camp, stepping over our bodies. They were scared.

We asked them what was happening. They shouted, "Don't ask questions! Just get up and follow!" I couldn't follow anybody. I told my daughters, "Stay here." It was pitch-dark.

We slept until morning in a field of planted rice. It was almost noon when we suddenly saw three Vietnamese tanks. We were in an open area, cut off from the Khmer Rouge. We began to walk as fast as we could to find the National Highway. We came upon a small town, where we stayed for ten days. There I learned that my sister-in-law and her five children were all dead. Starvation.

My daughters and I had no food or valuables to trade. Mealy decided to go to a Khmer Rouge sanctuary to get some rice. But the sanctuary was booby-trapped with explosives and mines. Mealy went with some people who knew how to remove the mines. She took as much rice as she could carry and began to search for Parika and me along the National Highway to Battambang.

When we reunited, we made a hole in the ground and began to pound the rice to make it edible. She went back to the sanctuary to get more. In Battambang, a little marketplace was beginning to flourish. We exchanged some of our rice for a large cloth sack, which we used to carry the rest on our heads to market. There we traded uncooked rice for some cooked food.

Battambang had been a deserted city. When people re-entered it after four years, many camped in the ground floors of buildings or on the sidewalks. They built huts, using sheets of metal for roofs and pieces of cloth as walls.

There was no money. Gold came from what people had hidden or what they found buried under deserted houses. Some people traded silverware or gold jewelry for food, clothes, and other basic survival needs.

We stayed in Battambang for only twelve days. The Vietnamese soldiers with loudspeakers in the streets said, "The city is out of rice. The population must go back to the fields in communal farms and plant rice." We said, "Not good. Communism is Communism. We've already been through this for four years. Let's go somewhere where we can breathe the air of freedom." We went to the countryside, but in the direction of Thailand. I told my daughters, "If we have the chance, we will run away. We will escape." After four years of living under the Communists, losing many members of our family, and being close to death, we didn't care about losing our lives any more. We only cared about freedom, no matter the risk. There was still heavy fighting in some places. People were afraid of both the Khmer Rouge and the Vietnamese army.

Before we left Battambang, I was surprised to meet a cousin in a hospital. She was with two children. We made plans to escape: three doctors' wives, myself, and our children. Seventeen in our group.

We went to the outskirts of Battambang to wait for any kind of transportation. It was already dark. A truck pulled up with two Vietnamese soldiers. My cousin speaks Vietnamese. She asked them to give us a ride near the border. The driver said, "You must pay something." So all of us gave him some gold.

Halfway to the border, a Vietnamese soldier guarding the road shot his rifle into the air. The truck stopped and all of us got out. A Vietnamese officer asked if any of us spoke Vietnamese. They took my cousin away.

The soldiers questioned her: "What did you give the driver to ride in the truck?" She continued to lie until they almost killed her. Then she told them the truth. It was pitch-dark when she came back to us.

The Vietnamese were arresting many people in the Battambang area. Not only Khmer Rouge, but many innocent, non-Communist peasants and educated people who had survived the Khmer Rouge terror. The Vietnamese feared that these people would understand that the Vietnamese fight against the Khmer Rouge was only an excuse to invade and occupy our country.

Fortunately, the soldiers released us. We spent the night in a barn. In the morning, we came upon some people selling noodles and cakes. We ate everything—two big baskets. The children were so hungry. Then we continued to walk on the National Highway toward Thailand.

Vietnamese soldiers were keeping people under constant watch. During the night, soldiers shot at any suspicious movement. My daughters and I had a conference. We discussed whether we should try to return to Phnom Penh or go westward to Thailand. My daughter Mealy said, "Mother, don't go back home. Grandma and Grandpa are dead. And we don't know about Father. If he is alive, he isn't in Cambodia. Let's go westward, all of us together. Maybe we can make it."

Each day, little by little, our group moved closer to the Thai border. We knew that people were being robbed and killed by bandits when they tried to cross the border, and by the Vietnamese or Khmer Rouge. The day before our escape, we found shelter under a house in a small border village. We didn't know what to expect. We just rested and made something to eat. It was raining, pouring hard.

The next morning, as we were crossing the jungle, I looked down and saw a Lux soap wrapper on the ground. I told myself, "Thank God, we are back in civilization."

Being allowed into Thailand wasn't very difficult, because thousands of refugees were pouring across the border. The Thai were surprised by the Vietnamese invasion and the incredible sight of so many Cambodians close to death from hunger and disease.

The refugee camp we were taken to was hundreds of tents in a large muddy field filled with starving Cambodians. We were starving, too. We only had one spoon and a small kettle for boiling medicinal herbs. Our clothes you wouldn't believe—just rags, all torn and full of holes.

The Thai camps were very unsafe, especially at night. Thai guards would rob and do anything they pleased to the refugees. During the daytime, we could go outside the camp to bathe in the field. But if we stayed out too long, past a certain hour, the Thai guards would line us up outside the barbed wire. For punishment they made us sit in the hot sun for hours until we were dehydrated. At night, heavily armed guards would go from tent to tent looking for gold.

During three weeks in that border camp, I saw Cambodians buying clothes, shoes, food, and try to begin a new life. But I heard on the Thai radio that the refugees were going to be pushed back into Cambodia.

My children and I discussed if we should prepare to go back into Cambodia. I said, "Since we are here and have something to eat, let's be thankful. Whatever happens will happen. If we are pushed back we will die."

Then news on the radio about a push back became more intense. Thousands of refugees continued to arrive in the border camps. My legs were swollen from an injury during our escape, so I tried to find a doctor. At that time, a United Nations officer, an American man, was in the camp. Because I could speak some English, I talked with this man. He was very upset. He told me, "There is nothing that I can do. Refugees are being taken from my hands by the Thai."

Later that day, the United Nations officer came to my tent and warned us, "No matter how affordable the transportation may seem, don't go with anyone unless I am here. If my men are present, we will try to help you." A few days went by. I didn't know when he would be back or how to find him.

All of a sudden, a Thai major appeared at my tent. He said, "Call your daughters and put your things together. Leave behind anything you can't carry." I said, "Major, where are we going?" He said, "I'm going to take you and your children to Bangkok."

I said, "Are you sure we're going to Bangkok? Are you going to hand me over to the Khmer Rouge and send me back? The radio reports that the refugees are going to be pushed back." He said, "I'm going to take you to Bangkok."

I said, "Major, are you only taking my children and me?" He said, "Yes, and a few more people." He had a list. I told him about my companions. I said, "Even if they hand me back to the Khmer Rouge or the Vietnamese, I won't abandon my companions. We are four widows with small children. We came together in a group."

I wrote their names down and gave the list to the major. He walked away. I didn't know what would happen.

At 11:30 A.M., he returned to my tent. He called all the names I had given him. We were the first group to get into the back of a very old pickup truck. A family who lived in my tent said, "Don't you remember what the United Nations officer told you? Not to go unless he was present." I said, "I remember. But the major sounds sincere." It was June 8, 1979.

We got into the truck. The motor started, and we began moving. I just sat there praying. I really didn't know where they were taking us. We didn't turn left toward Bangkok or right toward Cambodia. I became terrified.

My trust in the major saved us. We were among just three truckloads of refugees taken from the camps to safety. During a four-day period, around forty-five thousand Cambodians were forced down a mountainside into a minefield. Many people died, and others were captured by the Vietnamese.

The old truck took us to Suan Thmei, a camp near Aranyaprathet town. Cambodians had lived there even before the Cambodian exodus began. They built markets and workshops. Some Cambodian artisans gave the camp a Cambodian appearance. When we got off the truck, people greeted us. They were happy that we escaped the pushback.

I asked them, "What are you all doing here?" They said, "We are waiting for sponsors so that we can go to the United States." Some had fled the Khmer Rouge takeover in 1975. They had been waiting all that time on the border for acceptance to a Western country.

My daughters received some pots and pans and a tent. We spent two nights in that camp. On the third day, the UNHCR [United Nations High Commission for Refugees] officers called my two daughters and me to get on a bus, without explanation.

The rest of the women and kids in our original group weren't called. They began to cry, fearing the worst for us. Reluctantly, we got on the bus.

Instead of going to Cambodia, the bus took us to Bangkok. It was the first time in four years that I ate ice cream. [Laughs] I later learned what happened to everyone else at Suan Thmei. At 6:30 A.M. the next day, the camp was emptied by Thai soldiers. Everyone was forced into vehicles and taken north to Preah Vihear. They were pushed down the mountain into Cambodia.

I was still in rags when we got to Bangkok. The only new piece of clothing I had bought in the camp was a sarong for Mealy—that's all that I could afford. In Bangkok, I met an old Cambodian friend of my husband, General Dien Del, who had returned to Thailand from Europe to organize a resistance movement. He took us to a clothing store. But we had a hard time finding anything that fit, because we were so skinny. We looked everywhere for clothes for my youngest daughter, Parika, who was twelve. She had a big stomach, swollen from malnutrition, and the rest of her was skinny. Thai people stared at us in the stores. We were barefoot, right in the business district of Bangkok. But we didn't care. We had escaped death. We were proud to have survived hell. So we weren't self-conscious about looking so terrible. And General Dien Del wasn't ashamed to walk with us.

A man from the French embassy brought us apples and other food. I was very grateful to him. The building we stayed in was near Lumpini Park, in the center of Bangkok, near the business district.

The Thai officials gave us a hard time about leaving the building unless we cleaned the bathroom and did other jobs. But, with requests from Dien Del, we got to go outside for just the one day. Our building was a holding center, kind of like a jail. We all slept crowded close to each other. For the first two weeks, there was no room for me to sleep. I waited until everyone was in bed, after vegetables were delivered to the kitchen. Then I spread a blanket on the driveway and slept there. Each night, as immigration people came to bring people to the airport, I kept having to get up. Back and forth all night for two weeks. It stayed crowded, because, as people departed, new refugees came in.

We were accepted to the United States thanks to my husband's military service. We were sponsored by my sister-in-law in the suburbs of Washington, D.C.

My daughters and I flew to the United States on July 4, 1979. We landed in Seattle, just for a transfer flight. As we landed, I thought, "This is real freedom."

Two months before, when I found the soap wrapper in the jungle, I thought, "This is civilization." But once we put our feet on the ground in Seattle, I told my daughters, "At last we are free." We were so happy. They began to cry. They said, "I wish Grandma was here."

Our first challenge in America was to find the connecting flight to Washington, D.C. In that huge Seattle airport, we kind of got lost. I spoke English a little bit, so I asked people where we should go. But we got to the gate too late. An airline official said we had to take the next flight.

There was a man with us who came from a remote village in Cambodia. He didn't speak any English. We all found a room in the airport where we slept on the sofas. We were so exhausted that we slept too long. The plane left without us again. Finally, we got on the next flight.

When we got to the Washington airport, the Cambodian man stuck with us. He said, "Please, I don't speak English." And his dialect of Cambodian was hard to understand, too. [Laughs] Years later, I met him in an adult-education center in Arlington, Virginia. He was studying English. He told me, "Teacher, I cannot learn anything." Four years in this country and he hadn't learned a word. But he had two boys who learned English well. They graduated from high school with my daughter Parika.

My sister-in-law, our sponsor, helped to get us settled. Our first apartment was in Herndon, Virginia, a suburb of Washington. Since we arrived in July, we had a few months before Parika started school.

I received a lot of phone calls from Cambodians living in many parts of the United States. Some were my former students at the Khmera-Anglais High School. Some came to visit me. They said, "I don't believe that you are alive." They were excited and phoned other friends: "Mrs. Paramoun is alive!" I was happy to see them, too. They were just like my own children.

My middle daughters, Monie and Romani, joined us from France. It was wonderful to be together again. But it was very tough at first, trying to care for the girls, go to school myself, and find a job. I didn't bring any money from Thailand, so for the first year I had to swallow my pride and take public assistance. I tried to survive with food stamps, but my older girls wanted to earn a decent living. So Mealy left for California to find work, and Monie followed soon afterward.

Romani began high school. And Parika began junior high without knowing a word of English. She had to attend two schools, one for English and one for regular classes. After about three months, she learned to speak and read pretty well.

I began taking secretarial courses, and we moved to Arlington. Even though I spoke English before, I had a difficult time speaking with Americans. I wondered, "Why don't they understand me?" Even after seven years in this country, I cannot express myself fully. I encouraged my children to learn the language fluently, like any American.

Mealy, who was twenty-three, left for California in October 1979.

Cambodian classical dancers at the opening ceremony of a Buddhist temple in Silver Spring, Maryland, 1986

A few months later, during Christmas vacation, Monie, who was twenty, joined her. In California, Monie found a job as a secretary at the Imperial Bank. Mealy already was a bookkeeper at another bank.

I missed my daughters, even though I was happy that they could work and start a new life in California. During our first two years, my youngest daughters and I put all of our energy into studying and trying to learn about our new country. I came to know a lot of Cambodians in the Washington area, and I did some organizing for the community. We made Cambodian food and clothing for American people.

I finished my secretarial course within a year. I found a job right away as a counselor in the Indochina Community Center in Washington. I was thrilled to get away from public assistance. I've found that America is a country where people have come from all over the world. You do your job, you get paid like anybody else, and you're accepted. But Cambodians I know in France, like my sister, feel differently. People are not accepted if they are not French. But in America, you're part of the melting pot.

I worked in the community center for three years while my youngest daughters continued to study. I was also very active in the Cambodian women's organization. When refugees had problems, they phoned me at my office or at home. I spent most of my time working for fellow refugees.

I enjoyed my work in Virginia very much, but keeping my family together was more important. In 1983, I came to Los Angeles for my daughter Monie's wedding. I decided to stay. There are around thirty thousand Cambodians in southern California. Long Beach has the largest concentration of Cambodians in the country. I called the community center in Long Beach. They said that they had no job openings. So I decided to get involved in running a store.

I talked with my sister-in-law in Virginia. She and her husband decided to come to California, too. She said, "Let's find a store. We'll do business together."

We saw that Cambodian restaurants are not very successful. But donut shops are very American. That's what many Cambodians do. We found a small donut shop in Gardena that we purchased from a Cambodian. We were too inexperienced to know that it was impossible to do business at that location. The woman who sold us the store told people that she felt like she had won a lottery when we bought it from her. My sister and I worked that donut shop for two and a half years, earning just enough to live on.

Fortunately, we didn't lose money, because I sold the shop to a Thai couple. And, at the same time, I found this shop in Lawndale. For a while my sister-in-law worked this shop while I worked the shop in Gardena.

My sister-in-law never adjusted to this kind of work. She had been a teacher's aide in Virginia and didn't know how to manage a store. And the hours in a donut shop are impossible—from 5:00 A.M. until 7:00 at night. She and her husband and two kids went back to Virginia last summer. Now, for most of the day, I work alone. I hired a young Cambodian man from Long Beach to do the night baking for me. He goes to school during the day. He's married, with one small son. I knew him in Cambodia, but lost touch with his family after the country fell. I do my own bookkeeping on weekends, when I have some time off, when my kids are at the shop. I'm clearing just enough profit to keep the shop open. To be truthful, it's not worth my hours.

My kids say, "Mom, you have to hire somebody." I tell them, "If I hire someone, then what do we have? Just enough to cover all the bills. That's no reason to work. For all of my effort, I'd like to have something, too."

I begin to regret that I came to California to go into debt. I would rather have come here with my husband. I still have hope in my heart that my husband is alive somewhere. . . . After twelve years, I still hope. I only have one photograph of him. It was taken at Mealy's wedding in Cambodia. At the ceremony, he was standing behind my daughter. That is the only photograph I have. My daughter brought it from France.

The idea of remarrying has never entered my mind. Even though I have to work very hard, I don't think I will ever remarry. I will sacrifice my time and my life for the children now. It's better that way.

All that refugees have is our work, our dreams. Do I still hurt from what happened in the past? When I opened my mouth to tell you my story, I don't know where my tears came from. It has happened before. I've cried and cried when former students have come to visit. The first time my sister phoned from Paris, I could hardly retain my composure. Everything is so different. I never dreamed that things could be this way for us.

My daughters don't like to talk about the past in Cambodia. They want to forget and think about their future. They ask me why I would talk about the past with anybody. I said, "The past cannot be erased from my memory. You are young. Maybe you can forget. Not me. The country is as important as my life. I never give up hoping to some day go back to Cambodia." But the war, the suffering there, never ends.

For young and old refugees in this country, life is tough. If you don't earn money, you cannot live. The more we work, the more we earn, and life gets better. That's why I don't mind putting so many hours into my store. Other Cambodians feel the same way. We appreciate that we do get something in return. Not like under the Communists—we worked for nothing. We couldn't even satisfy our hunger.

Another reason that I work and try to save money is to be able to sponsor my cousin and her family from Cambodia. She is just like my sister. We were raised together by my mom. Until someone told my cousin that I was here, she thought that my daughters and I were killed on our way to Thailand. She's living with her husband and seven children in my mom's house in Phnom Penh. We try to write to each other. But I don't have much time, because I'm always working. Sometimes I send her small packages. They are so happy to receive them.

I would like for them to be here with us. But now the American program for Cambodian refugees is being closed. Even people who escape to the border camps in Thailand are no longer allowed to come to the United States. But they don't understand. They say, "Sister, we are waiting for you. Hurry. Bring us out."

I know that things are getting more and more difficult in Cambodia under the Communists. I wrote them, "It's your risk. You are not a small family. Nine people cannot pass through the forest to Thailand unnoticed. It's very dangerous. But if you want to take your risk . . ."

I would sponsor them here as immigrants from the refugee camp. I would tell the American government that I have some income ready for them. They have a place to work in my shop. They don't have to go on public assistance.

That's one of the main reasons I want to have this donut shop and try to keep it open. There're three reasons: for my children, for my cousin's family, and for the little house that I dream of.

Whenever I can, I drive around and look at "For Sale" signs on houses. When I see a beautiful house on sale, almost new, I write down the phone number. I call up and say, "How much do you want?" They say, "It costs this much. Is this your first house? How much money do you have?" Of course, it's always too much. I don't have the money now. But the dream is always there.

I want the house not only for myself—for everybody to live in. My daughters, my relatives from Phnom Penh—they could live in the garage if we fix it up nice. We wouldn't have to pay rent and be bothered all the time. It's my American dream to have that little house.

"SMILE"

Hugh Patrick Brown

Mark and Irene Grottel
Soviet Jewish Refugees
Physicist and Computer Programmer
Brooklyn, New York

The most lively hub of Russian culture outside the Soviet Union is an hour ride on the "D" train from midtown Manhattan. Brooklyn's Shorefront peninsula, which includes the Coney Island amusement park, the sparkling sand of Brighton Beach, and the fishermen's haven at Sheepshead Bay, has become home for more than thirty thousand Soviet Jews.

A short stroll from the Atlantic shore, beneath a metallic canopy of elevated-train tracks, Soviet émigrés have created a mile-long market of family-owned butcher shops and bakeries, delicatessens displaying bright bins of red and black caviar, folk-art shops, even the Black Sea Book Store, with hundreds of titles in Slavic script. A potpourri of restaurants and nightclubs with colorful bandstands specialize in hearty Ukrainian and Georgian dishes. Known as "Little Odessa by the Sea," the neighborhood provides familiar smells and nostalgic colors of home, but with an important new dimension. Like the waves of Jews who fled persecution in Russia and Eastern Europe at the turn of the century, these newcomers now enjoy the freedom to worship without fear in the area's many synagogues and temples.

The Soviet Union's two million Jews constitute the world's third-largest Jewish population. By comparison, six million Jews reside in the United States, and over three million are in Israel. Through twenty centuries of global wandering following the loss of their ancient homeland, Jews on every continent have maintained a common identity through Hebrew, the language of the Bible. The Soviet policy of suppressing Jewish culture has severed people from their sacred roots. Most synagogues and all Jewish schools have been closed. Hebrew teachers have been sent to prisons and Siberian Gulags. Those who persist in practicing their religion face discrimination in education and employment.

In the late 1960s, after Israel defeated Soviet-backed Arab armies in the Six-Day War, a virulent anti-Semitic campaign in the Soviet Union stimulated thousands of Jews to request migration to Israel. Detente in the early 1970s set the stage for Jewish migration to the United States.

In subsequent years, before the Soviet door swung shut in the early eighties, close to half of the 110,000 émigrés accepted to America settled in the New York City area. They are a mixture of blue-collar workers who have taken to driving taxis and starting small businesses, and well-educated engineers, doctors, artists, and teachers who are

trying to reclaim their professions. Some are devout and others more casual about their
religious beliefs.

Mark Grottel, age sixty-two, a physics professor in Leningrad, and his wife, Irene,
age fifty, arrived in Brooklyn with their teen-age daughter and Mark's brother and
ninety-year old mother in 1979. They live in a multistory apartment building in
Sheepshead Bay, one quick train stop from Little Odessa. Irene, businesslike in stylish
short red hair and round eyeglasses, was retrained as a computer programmer. She
works for a corporate banking firm in the Wall Street area.

Mark has been unable to find a teaching job. The week before we met, he was
suddenly laid off after six years with a nuclear-engineering firm. His eyes are puffy
from nights without sleep, spent worrying whether prospective employers will consider
him too old.

MARK: I have to tell you my favorite story about America. It was maybe
one month after I began working at my first job in New York, at an
engineering firm. Every day I sat at my desk, concentrating very hard.
I was very serious. The problem was that I couldn't speak English and
I was trying to learn new skills. My co-workers would pass back and
forth in front of my desk. But I was concentrating so heavily that I
didn't pay attention to them.

One day a group of people came to the office. They just stood
there looking at me. I didn't pay attention to them. One of these
guys cried out very loud, "SMILE."

At first I didn't realize that he was talking to me. I looked up and
saw everybody looking at me. He repeated, "SMILE."

My supervisor said to him, "Sir, this man just came from Russia.
He has a problem with English." The man said, "Okay. He cannot
talk. But, still, he can smile."

I understood what they were saying. So I started to smile. And
everybody started to smile. When the group of men left the office,
I was told that the man was a vice-president of our company.

I always think about this incident and laugh. Because in Russia, if
you smile during working hours, your boss will say, "You are not
working. You are just wasting time." When a supervisor comes into
the work area, suddenly everybody becomes very serious. Here it is
just the opposite. The vice-president couldn't understand why I was
so serious. He was trying to cheer me up.

For the first time, I understood that in this country everybody has
to smile.

I have a Ph.D. in physics and was a professor in Leningrad. In
1978, during the high point of Jewish emigration, my wife, Irene,

and I decided to leave Russia. It was very difficult to make a decision about where we wanted to go—the United States or Israel? We had friends in New York who wrote letters saying, "Come here. It is more interesting and better for you."

IRENE: We received letters from Israel, where people had a hard time finding jobs. My sister had already emigrated to Israel and was not excited about her situation. We knew that there would be better opportunity in America.

MARK: There were five people in our family group who made the trip from Leningrad. Our daughter, Anya, was fifteen years old. And my mother, whose name is Raisa, and my brother came with us. The only possessions we brought were our clothes and furniture from our apartment that we are still using.

When we arrived in New York, we found it very different from what we had dreamed. We looked around, I was shocked. My previous impressions were from books where the buildings and skyline always looked magnificent and bright. I never suspected that the city would be so dirty or that living here would be so hard. In the United States, especially a high-pressure place like New York, it takes people with real initiative and drive to succeed.

IRENE: In Leningrad, I was a manager in a state patent office. In Russia, everyone works for one corporation—the state. Your job can be secure for your whole life. If you don't cause problems, you don't have to worry. But in New York, for the first time, we experienced fear that we can be fired. It doesn't depend on your skill or education. It's all in what the marketplace needs. Last month, Mark was told by his boss on a Monday that the following Friday would be his last day of work. They didn't have projects. That's it. Now he has to start looking for a job all over again.

The same week my husband lost his job, my doctor had me go immediately into the hospital for a major operation. Everything happened all at once.

MARK: I was worried about finding a job, but my wife's health was more important. Now that Irene is getting back to good health, we can't think of anything else but how to change my profession.

From the time we arrived in New York, I worked almost eight years in the engineering consulting firm. Our specialty was nuclear power plants. But the industry reached a low point following the Chernobyl accident. Everybody who specializes in this industry in the West is in very bad shape now.

After I was laid off, I went through a period of terrible depression and became physically ill. I had all the symptoms of a heart attack, just like before we left Russia. My doctor said it was because of stress. He advised me to rest and relax before I begin searching.

At my age, it's almost impossible to find a new job. This year I am sixty-two years old. I'm not sure what type of work I can find. I don't want to be on welfare and let the government take care of me. I've given some thought to trying to get back into teaching, but I am not sure who I should ask for advice or where to submit applications.

IRENE: I will return to my job at Banker's Trust in the Wall Street area next Monday. I've worked there for a number of years. I can never say that my job is secure, but at least in my profession as a computer programmer I can always find work.

It's true that we are desperate for my husband to find a job. In this society there is discrimination about age. They don't like to hire older people. Employers look for young, aggressive people who can move up. But we don't fall apart, because we know that, in this type of job market, if we change our skill a little bit and show ability, we can find some type of work. It just takes patience and energy to fill out application after application.

MARK: For some Russians who have come here, the openness and mobility of American society has been difficult to adapt to. Freedom is a very high responsibility. In Russia, we were never aware of it. The state decides everything for you: what kind of education you have, the job you get, your vacations, the apartment you live in. Medical care is provided, enough food to survive, and there is law and order in the streets.

When Russian émigrés arrive here, all of a sudden we are given the freedom to choose and make all of our own decisions. Some people are unable to go out on their own and make a life for themselves. They only see troubles—dirty subways, crime in the streets. Everything is very strange to them—the language and the pace people move at, especially in New York City. They get lost and want to run back to where life is familiar.

There was a highly publicized group of fifty Soviet Jews from the New York area who returned to the Soviet Union. There are others who have only seen the worst things in this country, or they are very lonely here and miss their relatives and friends. Many people cannot speak English, so they can't find a proper job. They prefer to return to Russia.

IRENE: It is extremely lonely being an immigrant. When we first arrive, we want to be part of America. We want so badly for society to accept us. We find jobs, study the language, and try to understand the culture. We try to make friends among Americans. It takes such effort. Sometimes we feel, "We can't go on." But that's life. If you want to live, you must have enough courage and intellect to realize we must do all those things . . . in order to belong.

Some people are overwhelmed by all the frustrations. They see all of the terrible things, like crime, the dirty subways. I have these insecure feelings, too.

Yesterday the subway train I was riding stalled on the Manhattan Bridge for forty-five minutes. I was trying to get to an appointment in Manhattan. Of course, I missed the appointment. [Laughs] I can't understand why New York doesn't have a clean and decent subway system.

MARK: In Leningrad, every subway station is very beautifully constructed. A train arrives every two or three minutes. The schedule is very precise. For fifteen years, in my memory, there was only one emergency situation where the train didn't come on time.

Leningrad has a very rich tradition. The Communist Revolution of 1917 took place in Leningrad. The city was Lenin's revolutionary headquarters. But the center of the city, formerly known as Saint Petersburg, is like a beautiful museum constructed during the reign of Peter the Great, in the eighteenth century. The architecture is in the style of Italian Renaissance and French baroque. All of the buildings are painted pastel colors: light green, beige, and gold.

The oldest part of Leningrad is built on hills in the junction of the Neva River. The Imperial City area covers two miles along the riverbank. On either side of the Winter Palace are mansions and palaces that are now used as official offices and apartments. The only architectural deviation is a huge blockhouse building with all kinds of antennas, known as the Bolshoi Dom [Great House], the local KGB headquarters.

Leningrad is famous for its many academic institutions and universities. Moscow has the same number, but it is a much larger city. It's much like the difference between Boston and New York. Boston is smaller, not as fast and aggressive, and is known for its universities and for its Early American tradition and history. People from Moscow always consider Leningrad too boring. And people from Leningrad consider Moscow too crazy, too fast.

IRENE: For career success, to climb the ladder for important positions in the bureaucracy, you must go to Moscow. Muscovites are the same as yuppies. They aggressively try to make careers. But they don't make a lot of money, because that is very difficult to do in Russia. You can't compare Moscow to what I've seen in New York, on Wall Street.

In Leningrad, everyone lives in apartment buildings. When I was a child, we shared a communal apartment with five other families. We all used the same kitchen and bathroom—three children and my parents—all sharing one room in a former mansion on the riverbank. Under our apartment there lived an old general who had his own large apartment. He was a very elite man in the bureaucracy.

Our building once belonged to an aristocrat who fled to England during the revolution. The building was very old, with very high ceilings, beautifully sculptured walls, redwood stairs, and gorgeous marble decor. The Soviet government made very small and simple apartments within the very large rooms. The five of us lived in a single space the size of my living room here in Brooklyn. Somehow we managed.

Today fewer people live in the communal apartments. There are more and more small, modern apartments—basically one or two very small rooms, a kitchen, a toilet in a small closet, and a bathtub in another small room.

When my sister and I were married, we went to live with our husbands. And my parents moved to an apartment building in a new neighborhood built during the postwar reconstruction period during the 1950s and '60s. Parts of the city were severely damaged by German shelling during World War II. There are still special signs that are kept in the streets for historical sake. They read, "This side of the street is more dangerous—because of the direction of German artillery."

I was born in 1937 and was very young during the war. My father was a soldier, an officer in the Red Army. My mother, my sister, and I were sent to Kirgizia, a rural area in the southern U.S.S.R. because the German army was moving very fast toward Leningrad and Moscow.

The Nazis had already seized the main food-production area in the Ukraine and some of the major industrial areas in the western U.S.S.R. So the Soviet government evacuated at least a million workers and their families to the southern and eastern regions, to construct a new war industry beyond the reach of the Nazis and produce food. The place where we stayed was just farmland with some shepherds.

Before the war, under the Communists' collective system, people had no incentive to work hard. And under government policy, millions of farmers were murdered or starved. But after the Germans invaded, people worked very hard. Even I worked in the fields, with other children. We picked grapes and wheat.

MARK: When the siege of Leningrad began in 1942, I was finishing high school. Nobody was prepared for such a disaster. My mother was teaching music at the Conservatory. When she was younger, she had been a performer in the Opera Company of the Maryinsky Theatre. It is on the same level as the Bolshoi. As the German army approached Leningrad, the Conservatory was moved to Uzbekistan, in the southern U.S.S.R. My brother and I went with my mother. In that region, we spent half of our time in school and the rest of the time working on farms or doing construction. We built homes and a large canal.

My father, who was a doctor, chose to stay in Leningrad. He worked in a large clinic, within an important educational medical institute. The chief of the clinic was a very famous Russian physician. He departed. But when my father was asked to evacuate, he refused to leave his patients. He took charge of the clinic throughout the siege, which lasted for nine hundred days.

At first, the authorities made the big mistake of concentrating all of the city's food supplies in one place. When the Germans bombed this place, all the food was immediately destroyed. During the next three winters, the people were rationed only one slice of bread per day. The people were starving and bombed daily. Their only link to the outside was Lake Lagoda. They named this the "Way of Life."

During the long brutal winters, there was no heat and no water. People burned anything available for fuel, including furniture, in small wood-burning stoves. And they had to chop holes in the ice to draw water from the river. Some people were so weak that they fell in and froze to death. There were corpses everywhere in the city. My father was in a little better situation in the clinic. There was some food for the patients . . . only a small amount, but at least they had a little warmth.

IRENE: My father was seriously wounded during the fighting. He recovered, but it was a long time before our family was reunited. I remember the day that the war ended as if it were yesterday. There was such a joy. All of the people in our area of Kirgizia gathered in a huge square, laughing and screaming. Everybody was kissing, not even bothering to know who it was they kissed and hugged. Tears were coming down their faces. It was a magnificent moment.

When we came back to Leningrad, a lot of the city was damaged by the bombing. Even though the people had shown a lot of courage, it was very painful. There was no transportation. Food was difficult to find. No new clothing . . . nothing.

My family shared one room with my aunt's family, because we didn't have anywhere else. We were so happy when my father found the one-room apartment in the mansion near the river. It was crowded, but at least we had our own place.

I had already begun elementary school in Kirgizia when I was six. In our school in Leningrad, we had no heat, but we still managed to study.

MARK: Our house had been bombed, but luckily the bomb didn't explode. Because of the siege, a lot of people had nervous breakdowns and psychological problems. And after the war, high blood pressure was a very typical illness among survivors, even for young people. This caused an epidemic of strokes and similar deaths. My father investigated this disease. He wrote articles and a book about it. But he was a victim, too. He died from a stroke in 1950. At that time, I was finishing my higher education. In college, I specialized in the physics of motion, which can be applied to aviation or ships moving in the water. Later I changed my specialty to strength of materials.

IRENE: We all went to state schools. There was no such thing as being Jewish, or having a Jewish education. Immediately after the war, we didn't feel anti-Semitism. All the Soviet people had to work together to recover from the war. I believed that I was a Russian.

The first time that I was made to feel Jewish was in the early 1950s. Anti-Semitism has always existed in Russia since the pogroms in the nineteenth century. When the rulers have trouble, the Jewish people are always the scapegoats. There was a famous trial during the czars' time when people claimed that for Jewish matzoh it's necessary to use Christian blood, and Jews drank Christian blood.

In 1953, the worst postwar period for Soviet Jewish people began. Stalin had killed several government officials through the KGB. He put the blame on Jewish doctors, accusing them of poisoning these officials. Stalin put them through a public show trial, which initiated a campaign of anti-Semitism. Stalin wanted to send all Soviet Jews to the Birobidzhan region, near the Manchurian border, four thousand miles east of Moscow.

I think that the Communists especially targeted Jewish people because the percentage of scientists, musicians, and the intellectual professions was substantial. But Jews never threatened Russian society. In fact, some Jews, like Trotsky, played important roles or supported the Communist Revolution. The Communists wanted to eliminate religious faith. They wanted everyone to become "New Soviet men and women." And they knew that the way to destroy Jewish identity was to make it impossible for Jews to understand their religion.

When I was a child, I was never aware of the Jewish population in Leningrad. It's not like in the United States, where there are Jewish community groups and organizations. My father told me stories about Jewish holidays, but we never celebrated any. We were completely assimilated into Soviet society. I belonged to the Young Pioneers and the Komsomol Communist youth organizations. I believed in all of the Communist propaganda. My father, who had been a soldier, was aware that this was all false. But my parents never made an issue of being Jewish. Occasionally they spoke Yiddish, but only when they didn't want the children to know what they were talking about. [Laughs] I always spoke Russian.

The assimilation of Jews in the Soviet Union was quite successful, because the state had shut down the whole culture—Hebrew schools, magazines, books, and the Yiddish Theatre. The first step was denying people a knowledge of their language. There was no Yiddish literature available. The history of how Jewish people came to Russia in the middle centuries, the traditions and rituals, were all being erased. So as a child I never thought about these things.

During the Doctors' Trial in 1953, there was a lot of anti-Semitic propaganda in the newspapers. That year, my sister applied for entrance in a university. They told her, "You are Jewish," and she was denied admission. We were afraid there was going to be another pogrom.

I was only sixteen or seventeen years old at the time. I felt a tremendous fear. There were all these rumors that the government were going to send us somewhere because we were Jewish. Sometimes we even heard ordinary people express anti-Semitic comments in the streets.

I began to realize the danger of being Jewish. But there was no place to study about what being Jewish meant. I was not very interested in religion. I was just aware that I was different from everybody else. I was not very sure why, but I knew that I was different.

My father was not in the bureaucracy, but he was in the intelligentsia. He was the chief of the supply department at a secret institute. So we had some benefits. The Soviet Union is a "classless society"— but with classes. At the very top are the bureaucrats. The elite have the best apartments, the best entrance to cultural events, and they don't worry about food. Everything is provided for them in special stores. Their life is almost like in the capitalistic world.

I remember standing in long lines for food. We waited hours to buy these "blue" chickens, which don't have any meat, only bones and skin. Everything you need, every moment of your life, is a struggle in Russia. The Soviet government always says, "You have to suffer now, you have to go through all these obstacles and sacrifices, because we want to prevent war." People conform, because there was tremendous suffering during the war. But sometimes I just wanted to drop dead and forget about the propaganda.

Ordinary people don't see the secret police all of the time, but we can feel their presence. If a person is fed up with standing in line all the time and complains too loudly, someone will visit her and tell her to behave. We are taught not to open our mouths or express our feelings. It's enough to struggle with everyday life.

When I worked in a chemical institute, a man in the institute decided to pronounce his ideas on how to improve Soviet society. He formed a small group. All of those people were sent to prison.

I worked in a patent office in a chemical institute from the time I graduated from college. In the Soviet Union, the word "institute" is used to define either a college or a state-owned company. Universities are considered very elite, at a higher level than colleges or institutes. Jewish people must have good connections to get into a university. I was allowed into the Technological Institute in Leningrad, which is not considered first-class.

At the chemical "institute" or company where I worked, I never felt obvious discrimination from my co-workers, even though there were periodic anti-Semitic campaigns by the Soviet government— especially slandering Jews who wished to emigrate. Russian people are usually very friendly, but to be promoted at your job is where nationality counts. Ethnic Russians always have priority. Even Ukrainians are not looked upon as unfavorably as Jews.

Mark and I were married in 1962. Even though my family was secularized, they would have been against me marrying a non-Jewish man, mostly because of tradition. Mark and I lived in his family's apartment. His father had been a high-ranking doctor, so we had some advantages. We had a telephone, which is quite a luxury. Most people wait on a list for ten or fifteen years to get a phone.

MARK: My job as a college professor was pretty respectable. Irene was working. And because of my father's status we were in a pretty good position. When we came to America, it wasn't because I needed to find work.

It is very difficult to explain life in the Soviet Union to Americans, who have never known that type of system. You cannot really see it as a tourist. The biggest difference that I've found working in America is that people here get paid a lot better. There is no question about this. In Russia, my "good" position paid 250 rubles a month. That is what I make in two days in New York. You can only live on such a salary in Russia if you don't buy anything extra. A pair of shoes costs 50 to 100 rubles, which takes you way out of the family budget.

And the everyday shortages . . . When you enter a long line in front of a store, if people think you're trying to get in front of the line, I feel sorry for you. They will practically jump on you. The same with transportation, like getting on a bus. There are always quarrels, always insults.

Material difficulties are only part of the problem. The best way to live in Russia is not to be an individual. In every job there are a lot of politics, even for teachers of physics or math. In weekly political meetings, authorities always demand that you make gratuitous political statements: "I hate American imperialism. I love socialism." I am not kidding about this.

At the college, our director was like a small version of the Communist Party's General Secretary. He could do anything he wanted. He'd say, "We have democracy." This means that, when you attend a meeting, everybody has the right to speak for five minutes. The director has a stopwatch and tells people, "Your time is up." Then he speaks for one hour. [Laughs] That is his democracy.

At the college, every week, teachers had to give their students a special political class for one hour. We had to tell the student about political matters which I didn't believe in. In these lectures I had to tell them the party-approved viewpoint. Year after year, it became so difficult. I felt as if somebody had grabbed my throat.

There were incidents where I felt that I might have said too much and was in some type of trouble. Everybody has this fear in the back of their mind. You don't know if people are your friend or the police's friend. Sometimes we found that people at work were reporting our conversations to the police. If you go about your life quietly and keep your mouth shut, the government will let you live. But if you raise your voice a little higher than others, immediately you feel the weight of the system. If you have awards or citations, the authorities can take these away from you. And you may receive a reprimand in your "work book," which the authorities keep on every person. If this happens, when you are laid off you will only find work at a very low level. Or they can make sure that you never find a job, then put you in prison for being unemployed.

IRENE: What finally made us decide to come to the West was when I came to accept that I am Jewish. I didn't belong to Soviet society. I could no longer lie to myself or my child.

My daughter, Anya, like all Soviet children, would get one set of ideas from the state at school. And when she came home, she would get the opposite view from my husband and me. For example, at school she would hear, "The Americans are bad and want war. The Soviet Union is trying to prevent war." The government drums false ideas into the kids' heads every day: "The best, the most justified society in the world is Soviet society. The most unjustified society is American society." Anya would come home and ask me if this was true. I kept telling her, "It's not true. They are lying to you." Then the child becomes confused and doesn't know what the truth is, and who is right and who is wrong.

In my youth, when I was a member of the Young Pioneers and the Komsomol, it wasn't confusing, because we didn't know anything about the outside world, so we believed whatever the government told us. After Stalin died in 1953, we started learning about other ideas from underground writers like Solzhenitsyn, who tried to open our eyes. We started to become aware that there was another life on this planet: other people, with different ideas and free societies where you could say whatever you want, and be whatever you want. It was a very attractive revelation.

My husband and I applied to leave in 1978, during the time when the heaviest Soviet Jewish emigration was going on. We were lucky that we didn't have any problems with the authorities. The Soviet government was trying to move out as many Jewish people who wanted to leave as they possibly could. It was like a trade with the United States. In exchange, the Russians wanted to obtain Western technology, bank loans, and other economic advantages.

We had an invitation from Israel, where my sister and father were already living. But Mark and I decided that the United States would have better opportunities. I had studied a little English in college, and I took some private classes for my own pleasure. Mark knew a little English from a few classes in college, but he couldn't speak very well.

MARK: It was very traumatic to leave Russia. We had no money and did not know exactly where we were going or what type of work we were going to do. In fact, we had to borrow from my mother to meet some of our expenses. Even though Irene and I were professionals, like most Russians, we never made enough salary to save.

Right before we were scheduled to leave, I became ill with stress symptoms similar to a heart attack. A doctor told me to postpone our travel so that I could rest before leaving the country. I took his advice, because I didn't want my health problems to become serious.

When we left Leningrad in February 1979, my mother and only brother were in our family group. Mother, who was eighty-one years old, wasn't concerned if we went to Israel or the United States; she just wanted to be with her children.

In Vienna, Austria, we were interviewed by Israeli authorities, which was the standard procedure for all Soviet Jews. We told them that we preferred the United States. We were sent to the office of HIAS [Hebrew Immigrant Action Society], which is responsible for sponsoring Soviet Jews to the United States. We were very grateful for the support we received from the people at HIAS and the JOINT [Joint Distribution Committee] refugee assistance organization. My wife and I were excited about starting a new life, but we also felt very disoriented. Our daughter, Anya, who was fifteen, had the most difficult time adjusting. She felt very lonely away from her friends.

We spent three weeks in Vienna waiting to be sent to Rome, Italy, where we would be interviewed by the American Immigration Service. In Vienna we stayed in a special apartment complex provided for people just out of the Soviet Union. But in Italy we were placed in an apartment complex in the outskirts of Rome. We couldn't speak Italian, but refugees from Russia all shopped in a special market that had the cheapest prices. We learned the words for buying food, asking directions, and the names of products. Some people picked up the language very quickly.

When we arrived in New York on May 23, 1979, some friends from Russia and representatives from the NYANA organization [New York Association for New Americans] greeted us at the airport. The people at NYANA helped to settle us in our first apartment in Brooklyn. Our area is called Shorefront. Local Jewish organizations gave us a lot of help.

IRENE: Throughout the United States, there are very strong Jewish community organizations like NYANA that help new people to assimilate. Throughout Jewish history, in all the periods of exile and displacement, going back to the captivity in Egypt during the time of Moses,

Jewish people had to survive. The only possibility was to support each other, be responsible for ourselves, keep working, and get educated. In ancient times, Jewish people were among the only cultures that could read and write. And over thousands of years, our traditions were taken anywhere in the world that we've been dispersed to.

It is written in the Bible, in the Torah, that our greatest responsibility is to be able to take care of ourselves. That's the attitude of the Jewish people—to be strong enough to take care of our own. In Brooklyn, Project ARI [Action for Russian Immigrants] gave us big help to find a school for my daughter. At the ARI office, Pauline Bilus, who is an American, pointed us in the right direction.

MARK: At first we needed good advice, because in this country, to survive, you have to know many more things than in Russia. We needed to learn about personal finance, real estate, bank credit. In Russia, nobody has a bank account. I never thought about owning a home. Investments? There's no stock market. I never dreamed about credit cards. It makes a big difference to have a community or support organization that speaks your native language and can introduce newcomers to this society. If it weren't for their help, it would've been very difficult for us.

IRENE: Immigration is a terrible thing, whether you are successful or not. At our age, we felt dislodged from the earth we were used to. All of our roots are there. That creates a lot of stress. At times it's like we are lost.

My daughter, Anya, is not an outgoing person. She's very shy. In her high school, all of the Russian children from our neighborhood were from different Soviet cities, like Odessa and Kiev. Anya couldn't find very much in common with them. She had a difficult time making friends. That is typical for many Russian kids. They are very lonely here.

MARK: My first priority was to find a job. During four or five months, I filled out at least a hundred applications. In October 1979, I was finally hired by an engineering-and-design company in Manhattan. It specialized in nuclear power plants. I went through a very big transition to restructure my profession, even though it was not very difficult technically. Mechanics and the strength of materials are the same in Russia as in the United States.

At first my co-workers laughed when I brought my Russian technical books into the office. They said, "We don't believe the Russians." I said, "Do you think we have different formulas from your books? Look, they are the same."

Russians are very good in the engineering field. After a while, my co-workers came to believe me. They would ask, "Do you have your Russian book? Can we look at it?"

My own expectations were that people who work in America would be special. Everything would be automated with machines, and people would be working hard, day and night. But I found just the opposite. Some professional people were not knowledgeable at all. I was shocked. I thought, "How could this society achieve such a high level of technology and science with these kinds of people?"

I'll give you an example. Drafting blueprints is done much more precisely in Russia than here. Russian supervisors demand that the difference between two adjoining surfaces must be not more than 0.0001 millimeter. If it doesn't meet these specifications, it is considered a disaster. But here, I ask about the same type of equation; they say, "Okay, make sure it is within a quarter-inch or something like that." [Laughs] This lackadaisical attitude was so funny to me. I couldn't understand how they could be so imprecise.

Sometimes my New York firm did very high-level design. When I was sent to Texas, I worked with a very strong, disciplined construction team. We worked so hard that we didn't have time to go to the bathroom. But each contract was very different.

I was sent to a construction site in Tennessee where a power plant was being modified to meet state regulations. My task was to intervene if any problems occurred and give advice. But the job was poorly organized and people didn't work at all. Some workers just sat around talking all day long. I was very upset, because I don't like to sit around or pretend to read technical books. I like to work.

It's possible that American quality has gone down in recent years because there hasn't been enough emphasis on precision or discipline in education. I don't believe that this is good. The American system is flexible, but not so strong. In Russia, there are many intelligent and educated people, but the society lags behind the United States in technology because of the difference in the two countries' characters.

I felt such a relief when I started working in America, because there were no political meetings at my job. Nobody asked me to say, "I love my President. I love the Republican or Democratic Party." In fact, it is just the opposite. [Laughs] Everybody likes to criticize the government. People can think and say what they please. It's very nice. American character is very independent.

IRENE: It seems that, in America, education has lost its status. What do people need college for? They can go to a technical school for three months and make much more money than a college graduate.

Recently my daughter graduated from college with a very good grade-point average. Her degree is in Japanese culture. She found a job in Manhattan at a nonprofit organization that brings together scientists and researchers from the United States, Korea, and Japan. She likes the job because of the interesting people, and she comes across a lot of valuable information in her field. But her salary is very small.

On the other hand, I met a Russian guy who isn't educated at all. He can't write in English properly. He doesn't know anything about American or Russian history and literature. But he makes $50,000 a year. He took a three-month computer-programming course.

Where is the value of education? What happens to society if people are only geared to performing a specialized technical job and they don't have any sense of culture or anything else in the world?

When I worked at Chase Manhattan Bank, my boss was a very nice guy. I can't say anything bad about him. But he boasted that he never read a book in his life, only what was necessary for him to earn his certificate. I asked him why. He said, "What do I need it for? Sometimes I read technical manuals, that's all." He is a boss, making good money. He has five or six people working under him. But in many ways he is like a newborn child, because he doesn't know anything about the world.

I am concerned about this, because we live in a democracy, which is precious, especially to those of us who have come from countries without freedom. If the public expects to have a role in voting and the decisionmaking of government, they need to better understand the world around them. If not, democracy is just a public-relations exercise and isn't worth anything. From what I've seen, many people in this country aren't interested in anything which doesn't help them to make money. Money is power, but it has nothing to do with education or knowledge.

The Americans I work with usually don't pay attention to your income or how fancy you dress. In America, you can be rich and dress very simple. In the Wall Street area, near the World Trade Center, where I work, there are people from so many different places that I honestly feel very comfortable. There is always a chance to fit in. People judge you by how you apply yourself, how you help your company. And your attitude toward people: you have to be very friendly, you have to smile all the time.

In Russia, it's very much the opposite. If you are sad, you show it. You complain to people about your mood. The whole day can be spent complaining and talking about your state of mind.

The people who I work with in Manhattan live in many parts of the New York area. Everyone is pleasant at the office, but after work we all go our separate ways. Maybe if we lived in a smaller town, the people at work would be closer socially. Still, I have been fortunate to have made a couple of good American friends. And, regardless of my family's struggles, I am very grateful to be in this country. On two different occasions, the medical system here has saved my life.

MARK: Our family qualified to become American citizens in 1984. That was a very proud time for us. When my mother, who is now eighty-nine years old, was going to her citizenship class, she was the only person in her age group who could write something in English. She wrote, "I love America." She passed her citizenship test. And she is now an American, too.

Mother lives a ten-minute walk from our apartment. We always try to be with her. My brother and I take turns sleeping at her apartment to keep her company. Her mind is still very alert and active. When we first arrived here, she went to English classes. But most Americans speak too fast for her to understand. She speaks Russian with Russian friends, and with Americans she speaks Yiddish, and she can also speak French.

In this neighborhood, there is a very large Russian community. Without knowing English, one can communicate with people. But most Russian shopping is done in the Brighton Beach area, which is just a short distance from us. At my mother's age, she has difficulty walking and traveling alone, so she feels isolated.

In Leningrad, she was much more social with many relatives and friends, and she was still teaching music. A lot of young people came for singing lessons at her home. But now, at her age, it's hard to start teaching again.

IRENE: I have no immediate relatives in this country. When we left Russia, my father and sister were already in Israel, and my mother had passed away earlier. My only brother, Zinovy Ostrovsky, is one of the thousands of Soviet Jews called "refuseniks." He's been denied permission to leave the Soviet Union.

In letters I receive from my brother, he is becoming more desperate. He first applied to leave Russia in 1979, right after my family left the country. He is forty years old now. The only family he has in Russia is his wife and seven-year-old daughter. Since he left his job as an engineer, he has not been able to find a job equal to his education. For eight years now, he works as a laborer in a state-owned restaurant.

Zinovy always writes about being reunited with my father. They were very close. That is the only hope that keeps him going. My sister and I haven't had the heart to tell him that father died last year.

In the letters I have received lately, Zinovy sounds more and more desperate. This is one that I received last year:

Hello my dears,
    It has been a long time since I've heard anything from you. I understand that you haven't received my letter. There's nothing new, we've heard nothing really tangible from the authorities. What's going to happen is unclear.

Masha is going to be six years old in a week and will start school soon. Who could have told me six years ago that our lives would be so uncertain? All hope lies with you, Father, and Eva. Only your efforts can lead to something. Mine is a dead end. The horror of the situation is the total absence of all prospects. How long do I have to wait?

With friends I pretend that nothing is wrong, that sooner or later I will see my family. But there are constant doubts inside me. Not long ago I dreamed that you came to visit. Other times I am sitting and all of a sudden remember Mother, you . . . I am even afraid to listen to the old tape you sent me. Right away there is a lump in my throat, and tears.

I understand that you are writing long petitions to different governments. But it all leads to nothing, only more troubles. I am most worried about Masha. Myself, I am finished. That's clear. But what will happen to her?

I am submitting the exit application again . . . and again. But there is no point in it. Because they said clearly: If we need you, we'll call you.

How long do I have to wait! That's the horror. I miss you all terribly.

                                        Love,
                                        Zinovy

My friend Pauline Bilus at Project ARI has been very kind to my family. Though she was born in Brooklyn, she is very active in trying to help gain the release of Soviet Jews. She was honored by the United Jewish Appeal, and brought me to the luncheon. I was introduced publicly to the group of 150 women, some of whom were members of other organizations. The UJA decided to adopt my brother. They've written letters to all the Soviet and American officials asking for his release. But there has been no response from the Soviet government.

Right after my recent operation, Pauline worked with the Student Struggle for Soviet Jewry to organize a press conference at New York University Medical Center, where I was hospitalized. I was a featured speaker, with several other families who have relatives who are also "refuseniks." I don't know how much good our efforts have accomplished.

I didn't want Zinovy to know about my operation. But last week, late one night, I received a telephone call. It was Zinovy. He was crying and yelling at me, "Why didn't you tell me that you were ill?"

I was shocked. But I kept my wits and responded, "I am fine. Believe me, if it was serious I would have let you know. Don't worry about me. If I tell you that I'm all right, then I am fine."

I couldn't believe that he knew about my hospitalization. My sister, Eva, came to New York from Israel to be with me and help around the apartment until I recovered. We made every effort not to let him know anything. I asked Zinovy, "How did you find out?"

He said, "It's a very small world now, you know."

EL PASO DEL NORTE
(THE PASS TO THE NORTH)

THE TORTILLA CURTAIN

Michael Teague
Border Patrol
U.S. Immigration and
    Naturalization Service
El Paso, Texas

MOJADOS (WETBACKS)

José and Rosa María Urbina
Illegal Immigrants from
    Juárez, Mexico
Farmworker and Domestic Maid
El Paso, Texas

CHUPPIES

Arnulfo and Cesar and
    Ana Caballero
Three Generations of Immigrant
    Family from Puebla, Mexico
Retired Entrepreneur and
    University Librarian and
    High-School Cheerleader
El Paso, Texas

THE TORTILLA CURTAIN

It was a scene more bizarre than my wildest dreams. As the first light of dawn warmed the raw desert air, thousands of Mexican men and women, in polyester and denim, light jackets and baseball caps, emerged from squalid shacks that cover the outlying hills of Ciudad Juárez. They began a rush across the shallow Rio Grande toward the Texas city of El Paso.

Some rode across the waist-high muddy river on the shoulders of human taxis. Others crowded into a flotilla of inflated rubber rafts. Hungry-eyed men filled railroad bridges, waiting for a lone Border Patrol van to pass in a cloud of dust before they began scaling a massive iron gate. Smaller groups of three or four squeezed through holes in a twelve-foot wire fence called the Tortilla Curtain, then sprinted across the highway. Throughout the day and night, hundreds of others invaded freight yards, hoping to hop trains headed for Dallas, Albuquerque, Los Angeles, Denver, or Chicago—fabled cities of riches.

Between the wayfaring masses and the promised land are a handful of American border patrolmen dressed in cowboy hats and green uniforms. Their police vans can hold at most six to eight migrants for a trip to a small station house where they are booked and held for a couple of hours. When the cells fill, they are bused back to Juárez. Within minutes, they cross the river again.

In 1986, Border Patrol officers in the El Paso sector, which covers West Texas and New Mexico, apprehended 312,892 illegal aliens. At least twice that many got through.

El Paso is the largest American city on the two-thousand-mile U.S.-Mexican border. Crisscrossed with transcontinental railyards, it is the midway point between San Diego, on the Pacific Coast, and Houston, on the Gulf of Mexico. The border region, called La Frontera, isn't really America or Mexico but an amalgam of both cultures, languages, and economies. The majority of El Paso's five hundred thousand population are of Mexican heritage, including, in early 1987, fifty thousand illegal residents. Many have relatives just across the border. Another sixteen thousand residents of Juárez work legally in El Paso. And maybe twice that number of illegals commute across the river as laborers, maids, and farm hands up the Rio Grande Valley. Their earnings bolster the merchants of both El Paso and Juárez, who thrive on cross-border shoppers.

The U.S. Immigration Act of 1986 has made a modest dent in the migratory traffic, but social conditions in Mexico are ominous. In 1950, Mexico's population was around twenty-five million. In 1982, when their economy collapsed, the population had rocketed to eighty million, more than half under sixteen years old. Mexico is projecting a population of a hundred million people by the turn of the century. Inflation has been hovering at a hundred percent annually. The peso, valued at 10 to the dollar in 1980, fell to 2,500 to the dollar in early 1988. Half of all workers are unemployed or underemployed, with few making above the minimum wage of $2.85 per day. If not for three to ten million Mexicans illegally employed in the United States, who send money home to impoverished relatives, the society would be near explosion.

The overwhelming flow of migrants to El Norte, the North, has severely strained health and education systems in American cities along the border area, already one of the poorest regions in the entire country. In some employment areas, such as construction, American workers have been undercut by the migrants. And there are crime problems. Although the vast majority of migrants seek an honest living, there are some troublemakers, and drug smugglers have learned to take advantage of porous border wastelands. A congressional narcotics study found that thirty-three percent of the cocaine, forty-two percent of the heroin, and thirty-five percent of the marijuana found in the United States came through Mexico.

A week before I arrived in the El Paso sector, border patrolmen made five different drug busts that netted fifteen hundred pounds of marijuana. A few months earlier, they intercepted a load of 1,997 pounds of cocaine near Las Cruces.

During my second day in El Paso, I accompanied border patrolmen on three shifts, covering a twenty-four-hour period. From the parched, barren foothills of Cristo Rey Mountain, just across the New Mexico state line, to the sandy riverbanks east of the Tortilla Curtain, I observed a phenomenal procession of illegal border crossers. Most are skilled at hovering patiently on the Mexican side to outwait a patrolman who must stay on the move to cover twenty miles of city line. An impossible task at best.

One of the officers I accompanied was Michael Teague, a seasoned veteran.

Just outside of El Paso, there's a triborder area where you can toss a stone into three different states and two countries. At this place, the only barrier that separates the U.S. and Mexico is a thin two-foot-high wire cable. It's the point where the Rio Grande stops being the international border and continues north through New Mexico, then to its mountain source in the Colorado Rockies. But from El Paso, 700 miles east to Brownsville, on the Gulf of Mexico, the river is the natural boundary between Texas and Mexico.

Here, in the El Paso sector, we have a private war all of our own. Illegal aliens are constantly sneaking across the border in droves, and a handful of border patrolmen try to catch them. I've been working in this sector long enough to tell the difference between Mexicans who are visiting along the border, having a picnic, and illegal entrants, by how they dress. If they are dressed for travel and carrying water bottles and small sacks with their belongings, like those guys on the hill . . . they plan to cross over the border right after dark.

Usually we catch young men, who are looking for work to support their families back in Mexico. But more and more we are seeing entire families. They start coming around 7:30 P.M. over the mesa near Cristo Rey Mountain. A steady stream of people all night. We use our night-vision "infrared" equipment to spot a lot of illegals who would otherwise go unnoticed.

Sometimes border patrolmen ride horseback to patrol these hills. It's an interesting contrast—high-tech infrared machines directing cowboys on horseback. Other times we patrol in small trucks, which provide maneuverability. Before we began using night-vision equipment, aliens had an easier time coming through this area without getting caught. Now we can sit on top of a hill, spot undocumented aliens, then radio for patrol vehicles to come apprehend the groups or individuals after they enter into Texas or New Mexico.

This time of year, in late winter, the aliens try to find work on farms in the Upper Rio Grande Valley. This is the time when farm laborers start pulling weeds and preparing the ground for planting. Between New Year and June, on the northbound highways to Las Cruces, many of the aliens we apprehend are usually agricultrual workers or people heading for cities further north, like Denver or Chicago.

Perhaps our greatest concern is the trafficking of drugs tied to the smuggling of illegal aliens. Smuggling of all sorts has become big business in the border regions. Some smugglers have set up networks that may start in Central America or Cuba. We catch illegal immigrants who come from as many as eighty-five countries around the world. Even people from Eastern Europe, who are smuggled in for large fees through South America and Mexico City. Narcotics and firearms aren't always packed on aliens, but the smuggling networks being set up are more sophisticated than ever before. Since the increase of drug trafficking along the southern border, we've seen more guns and incidents of violence.

Nations like Mexico have vowed to crack down on smuggling crimes. But in some areas, international drug trade and corruption is a way of life. And with such a high demand for drugs in the U.S., it's hard to remove the magnet.

Some aliens smuggle Mexican avocados. They carry between forty and two hundred pounds of the produce on their backs. We've caught tons and tons in the past couple of years. Recently we received a letter from the head of the U.S. Agricultural Department that said many of those avocados tested positive for fruit-fly larvae or other contamination.

Some illegal people coming into this country have exotic diseases. I was surprised when I first got here—I discovered a couple of people that we apprehended had leprosy.

It's a pretty lonesome feeling out here at night, alone or with a partner. We do get the feeling that we're outnumbered. [Laughs] I've jumped into a boxcar or a freight-train gondola, turned on my flashlight, and seen twenty-five or thirty aliens. What can I do? Surround them? I can only tell them to get off the train. If they want to fight, I'm in trouble.

That does happen from time to time but, fortunately, not very often. Most of the freight-yarders are from farther down south in Mexico. They're real docile. There have been times I've jumped off a moving train while chasing people, stepped in a hole, and fallen face down. The guy I was chasing stopped and came back to help me. He said, "Gee, did you hurt yourself? I'm sorry."

With people from the interior of Mexico—places like Durango and Zacatecas—the differences are like night and day from those who live along the border. The great majority of them are decent people coming here to look for work. Their families' economic conditions are pretty bad in Mexico. You have to sympathize with them to a point. But if you open the border wide up, you're going to invite political and social upheaval. Our job is to prevent illegal entry to our country, but we know that they're going to keep coming as long as our grass is greener. And we also know that we can't catch them all.

Mexico's population has grown from thirty million people in the early 1960s to some eighty million people today. The population is also projected to skyrocket to a hundred million by the turn of the century. Who is going to feed them and give them jobs? What's going to stop massive migration? For many of them, their only alternative is to go north and do whatever kind of labor they can find, whether that means cleaning toilets or stooping all day in the hot sun. Whatever it takes to buy a few more beans or some lettuce.

My sector chief, Mike Williams, likes to say, "The Statue of Liberty holds a torch for freedom. But she also holds a book of laws in her other hand." There're a lot of arguments from the heart and pocketbook about how illegal immigrants help this country, but there has to be a systematic order, or else we'll have anarchy.

In our sector, which stretches from the Arizona–New Mexico boundary to Sierra Blanca, Texas, we apprehended 312,000 illegals in 1986. This was a tremendous increase. For instance, in 1960, this sector arrested only 3,630 aliens; in 1970, 43,640; and in 1980, 127,428. Through 1986, all the sectors up and down the Mexican border have faced the same trend.

The message going out all over the world, not only in Mexico, is: "If you can get past the *thin green line*"—the Border Patrol—"you're home free."

After the new immigration bill passed, the number seemed to drop. That is not to say the numbers won't pick up again. Sometimes we catch the same undocumented alien twice or even three times in the same day. Because of the large volume of illegals in our sector, we voluntarily return them across the river, unless they have committed a prosecutable offense. There is no way to house each and every undocumented alien we pick up for very long. Many of them come across on a daily basis to find work, then return home to Mexico.

[*We drive in the patrol truck on a dirt road along the Rio Grande, toward downtown El Paso. Across the river, in Juárez, groups of Mexican youths jeer and yell insults. Officer Teague nods his head toward them without a change in facial expression.*]

You can tell they really love us Border Patrol people. [Laughs] Around here at night, it's like a game of cat-and-mouse. The aliens sneak around in the dark after they cross the river, trying to get away from us. And we sneak around trying to catch them.

We've also had agents overrun just like in San Diego. The gates of the Santa Fe Railroad bridge that extends across the river used to be welded shut, but Mexican train engineers got to where they would bust them down. Here at this point, dozens of aliens mass together throughout a twenty-four-hour period and wait for a chance to hightail it across the border. Even if a patrol unit is there.

Border Patrol officers had to sit at our end of the bridge twenty-four hours a day. In the summer, during daytime, two or three hundred aliens would mass at the bridge, just waiting for the patrolmen to go for lunch or to the bathroom.

If you didn't go, after a while the aliens would get tired of waiting. It would be like a banzai attack. The aliens knew good and well that the two patrolmen weren't going to get any reinforcement. How many could we grab as they came over us? Maybe two aliens apiece. That's just a drop in the bucket when a couple hundred are rushing you.

In the 85,000 square miles that make up the El Paso Sector, there are no more than six hundred agents. We are responsible for patrolling desert areas, mountains, and cities. Locally, twelve patrolmen work the line on each shift. We could use double or triple that number. Close to half our people are Hispanics. Many are from the El Paso area. And all the Border Patrol agents are fluent in Spanish. We receive several weeks of training at an academy in Glynco, Georgia, which includes language, immigration law, firearms, and physical training. The program is quite rigorous—about thirty percent of the recruits wash out.

Most of the illegal entrants in our sector come right through town. El Paso's got twelve miles along the river. Just about everything that happens, happens there. Across the border in Juárez are 1.5 million people. Like other major cities in Mexico, Juárez is growing in leaps and bounds, with a large number of transients from southern Mexico coming to the border. El Paso, its sister city, is the home of another half-million people. Across the international border, thousands of people commute every day. Many of the people from Mexico have legal work permits. Many of them return to their homes in Mexico at night. Others will stay on farms until the weekend, during the growing seasons.

When water is released from the dams up north for irrigation, the river levels get high. That means the currents are swift and quite dangerous to illegal crossers. You couldn't pay me to swim in that river— there are too many drownings. But every day and night, no matter how high it is, rain or shine, they keep coming.

The Tortilla Curtain is this multimillion-dollar boondoggle of a wire fence along one stretch of the river. Some of the local Hispanic groups got riled up and compared it to the Berlin Wall and Iron Curtain. They dubbed it "the Tortilla Curtain." It hasn't much stopped aliens from crossing. They've cut big holes in it and come right through. Once I drove along the Tortilla Curtain and counted the holes that Mexicans have cut into it. From one end to the other, there were more than thirty holes. The only thing it's been useful for is to protect us from rocks thrown from the other side of the river.

The majority of the people who come across the river don't try to cause trouble. But any time you have a large number of people, a certain percentage are going to be troublemakers. Like the group of glue-heads you see hanging around the bridge area. It appears like they're just drinking Coke, but in reality they're inhaling glue fumes from the can. That's the more socially acceptable way of doing it. Some, who don't care, just spray glue or paint into an old sock or rag. They walk around with it stuffed in their face.

They are the types you must watch, because they are unpredictable and can turn on you in a minute. The glue-heads are a large percentage

Puente Negra: The Black Bridge

of the gangs that rob aliens and other people. Some are hardened criminals. They might be armed with knives or pipes, anything that can be used as a weapon.

We've had knives and instruments like ice picks pulled on us. Patrolmen have been hurt by rocks or sucker-punched in the nose during an apprehension. We also get a lot of complaints about aliens being robbed or assaulted. At times like that I call fojr a backup team and try to catch the perpetrators. Sometimes we chase them down into the river, where their allies on the other riverbank, or on this side, start throwing rocks at us. Some advocates for immigrants' rights don't see that as a problem. But when you're hit upside the head with a two-pound rock, it gives you a different perspective.

Another concern is the amount of assaults and rapes that occur along the Santa Fe Railroad bridge, called the "Black Bridge," near Stanton Street. It's probably the most well-known crossing point throughout Texas. Aliens nabbed as far away as Florida or Chicago can identify this point here at the border. They call it Puente Negra.

Along the southern border from San Diego to Brownsville, there has been a tidal wave of aliens since 1982, when Mexico's economy really collapsed. Crime has also risen dramatically. Added to the problem in southern Texas is high unemployment, which varies between eleven and fourteen percent. Most economists say that the border regions have among the lowest per-capita incomes in the country.

Because of the scarcity of jobs, many aliens hop freight trains to other parts of the country. We try to spend time checking trains as they roll out of El Paso. At sundown, or the evening shift, is when we catch the most aliens on trains.

My personal record was on the Fourth of July, 1985. A Santa Fe Railroad freight train was rolling out of town at eleven o'clock at night. There were 110 boxcars on this train. We pulled off ninety-one aliens. I guess it was a good thing that we caught them. The train would've needed an extra engine to get up the hill with all that extra weight. [Laughs]

Freight-yard aliens will go wherever the train is going. Many of these people know the train schedules better than we do. The Santa Fe train, for instance, goes through small towns like Las Cruces, or agricultural areas. It ends up in the Albuquerque area, where the aliens can make connections to just about any destination.

The Southern Pacific line rolls out of there in three directions. One goes to Los Angeles and San Francisco. One goes east, toward Dallas. And one heads north, to Kansas City and Chicago—that's the most popular.

A favorite river-crossing point for freight-yarders is only a hundred yards from the tracks. They just hang loose until they see a train coming. Then they jump up and run for the overpass, where the trains are going around ten miles per hour. Many times, the aliens dash across the highway and jump onto moving trains. Just as you would imagine, some of them are injured and even killed. The chase is dangerous for patrolmen, too.

The aliens have burrowed a path under the highway that we call "the Ho Chi Minh Trail." They don't actually live there. They just crawl on that trail right into the freight yard. It's a well-beaten path.

Our freight-yard apprehensions can get as high as thirteen hundred a month. Our record for total apprehensions throughout the sector is more than thirty-four thousand in a month.

We also catch undocumented aliens at El Paso Airport. Some carry false documents, others don't have any papers. Our plainclothes agents can spot aliens by the way they dress, the way they act. Aliens wear brand-new clothes, and shoes or boots that are so new that they stick out like a sore thumb. Sometimes you can see the price tag still hanging. The aliens walk down the airport causeway and see all the people getting on an escalator, which is very rare in Mexico. They can't quite figure it out. So they stop. And they watch for a couple of minutes.

They finally think, "Okay, that looks easy enough." They walk up

with suitcase in hand. They step up to the bottom of the escalator, get
on it. And they go, "Whoa, Whhooa!," as they lose their balance and
stumble around. The agents just sit there watching them. When the
aliens finally get to the top of the escalator, an agent walks up and
escorts them away.

It's not only Mexicans that we find at the airport. We get a number
of illegal aliens from Europe and Central and South America. What we
call OTMs—Other Than Mexicans—which includes Salvadorans, Guatemalans, Chinese, and even some Iranians. The majority get a valid
visa to enter Mexico as a tourist.

They may fly from their native countries into Mexico City, then travel
north by bus, train, or by air to Juárez. We catch them coming across
the river or at the airport. The majority are assisted by professional alien
smugglers, at a stiff price. If we catch a Yugoslav smuggling other Yugos,
chances are they met in Europe. If we have a Mexican smuggling Yugos,
they probably met in Mexico City or somewhere closer to the border.
The smuggling of aliens and narcotics is a full-time profession.

Very few of the Europeans we catch speak English. We use volunteer
translators. The University of Texas has been a big help with people
from Korea and other nationalities that are outside of our language
capabilities.

Every time we catch someone from an East Bloc nation, we advise
the FBI. A few years back we heard about some people who were trained
in Mexico for some type of anti–U.S. terrorist operation. We never
caught anyone related to it; nor were there any incidents. But it's a very
real possibility—the idea of Soviets, Cubans, or Libyans coming here
to perform some act of espionage or terrorism. If they were to get across
this border, it would be difficult to catch them. Or, if we apprehend
them and they are Hispanic, and claim to be Mexican, we would just
send them back across the river—they could try again.

We're finding illegal entrants from the People's Republic of China,
Korea, Punjab in India . . . a whole variety of countries. It's not hysteria
when those of us who deal with this every day say, "Look, people, there
is a problem. And it's across the country, not only on this border."

People have a tendency to be very opinionated about the illegal
immigration problem, from "Stop them totally at the river" to "Just let
them all in." Until you've really had a bird's-eye view of what goes on
at border areas, it's hard to be objective.

The new immigration bill has made a dent in the flow of illegals. But
it's still too early to tell just how much of an impact will be made when
it's all said and done. From all indications, the legalization of qualified

residents, agricultural provisions, and employer sanctions of the new bill are a step in the right direction. The new bill isn't designed to solve Mexico's massive economic troubles, so it can't be considered a "magic wand." With 1.5 million people in Juárez, many living without running water or electricity, folks will continue to cross the river.

MOJADOS (WETBACKS)

Rosa María Urbina, age thirty-five, crossed the muddy Rio Grande in 1984 with the hope that she could earn enough money as a housecleaner in El Paso to take her three children out of an orphanage. A widow, she had to place her children in an institution because the $14 a week she earned on a factory assembly line in Juárez was not enough to feed them.

Each morning she joined hundreds of other young to middle-aged women from the hillside colonias, who walked down to the concrete riverbank and paid men called burros to ferry them across the river on their shoulders—and back to the squalor of Juárez in the evening. On one of these excursions, she met a handsome farm worker, José Luis, age twenty-six, with dark mestizo features. It was fate, they believe. Within months, Rosa's children joined them in a two-room apartment on the American side of the river.

I was introduced to José and Rosa during a tour of overcrowded tenement buildings in South El Paso that house many of the city's fifty thousand illegal residents. In Mexican slang, they are called mojados, or "wets," the river people.

My guide, Julie Padilla, a public-health nurse from the Centro de Salud Familiar La Fe clinic, visits the Urbinas to give their two-month-old baby, José Luis, Jr., a post-natal checkup. We walked up a dark stairwell to a dimly lit landing decorated with a colorful gold-framed mural of Our Lady of Guadalupe, the religious patron of all Mexican Catholics. There are sixteen apartments with ripped screen doors along a narrow graffiti-covered corridor. On the back fire-escape is a closet-sized communal toilet. Julie said, "There used to be one bathtub that every family on the corridor shared. But in the past year, that's been taken out. I don't know where they bathe now."

Rosa María, José, and the children have the luxury apartment. Half of the 12-foot-square room is taken up by a bed covered by a magenta Woolworth blanket. On the wall, above a calendar of the Good Shepherd, is a portrait of Pope John Paul II. A Winnie the Pooh blanket serves as a makeshift closet door. On a miniature two-tiered nightstand, alongside baby bottles and a green plant, are metal-framed elementary-school photos of the children. Their seven-year-old daughter's Honor Roll certificate is proudly displayed on a mirror above an all-purpose foldout table.

During winter months, José Luis is out of farm work. The baby is Rosa's full-

time chore. They survive on $58 a month in food stamps earmarked for the baby,
who is an American citizen by virtue of his birth in El Paso. And WICC, the Women,
Infant and Children Care program, provides a bag of groceries each week. Although
the children attend public school, José and Rosa seldom leave the apartment. They
fear that border patrolmen will send them back across the river to the squalor of Juárez.

JOSÉ: The majority of the people in our apartment building have the same problem as my family. All of us are in El Paso without legal papers. I have been living here since 1981.

ROSA: I came in 1984, to find work. After José and I were married and we found a place to live, I brought my children from a previous marriage. We lived across the river, in Juárez. But I was born further south, in Zacatecas.

JOSÉ: My hometown is Juárez. Since I was nine years old, I've been coming to El Paso to work. At first I did gardening in people's yards, but I have stayed in El Paso constantly since 1981, going out to the fields to do farm work. I used to go to Juárez to visit my relatives at least one day each month. But in the last year, I haven't gone, because of the new immigration law. To visit Juárez I have to swim across the river. I can't cross the bridge or the *"migra"* [Border Patrol officers] can catch me right there.

During the past few months, the river has been very high and fast. That's one reason why not so many people have been crossing lately. I am not working now, because it isn't the growing or harvesting season on the big farms. On February 15, we usually begin to plant onions. That is when the main agricultural season begins. But during a three-month period between planting and harvesting, there is no work.

We haven't paid our rent since December. If we're lucky, I can find some part-time work to pay for food. Our baby, José Luis, is two months old. Because he was born in El Paso, he is an American citizen. We can only get food assistance for him. Once in a while, I find a job as a construction laborer, house painter, whatever is available. We use the money to buy food for the baby and the other three children first.

ROSA: I haven't been able to work lately, because the baby is so small. My other children are all in school. Lorenzo is twelve years old, José Rubén is ten, and Miriam is seven. From the time I came to El Paso, I have worked as a housekeeper and minding homes for people. I am not used to staying in the apartment every day, but I have no other choice, because of my small baby.

I have known many changes in my life. I moved to Juárez from a farm in Zacatecas when I was seven years old. My mother and father were split up. After mother remarried, my stepfather took us to Juárez. We lived in an adobe house in the *colonias* [ramshackle housing projects] up in the hills.

When I was a teenager, I worked as a hairdresser in a beauty salon, cutting hair. My first husband was a mechanic, fixing cars. We made a good living. But my husband spent the money he made drinking in the *cantinas*. And after a while, he wouldn't let me work, because I had young children to take care of. When he died in 1984, he left me nothing at all. He drank too much and died from cirrhosis of his liver. I had no money . . . nothing. My children were nine, seven, and three years old. I had to find a way to pay rent and feed them.

At that time, the economy in Mexico had become horrible. Inflation was going crazy. The peso jumped to 500 per dollar. Today it is still climbing at 1,000 per dollar. I found a job working on an assembly line at a factory. We produced rubber gloves for hospitals and medical supplies like little caps for syringes. I would go into work at 4:30 in the afternoon and stay until 2:00 A.M. I was paid only 7,000 pesos [$14] each week. That was not enough to feed my kids. And I didn't have any relatives or friends to watch the kids while I worked. So I had no other choice but to put them in a special institution, like an orphanage, for children without parents. This upset me very much. But with my husband dead, and no other form of support, there was nothing I could do.

My only hope was to cross the river to the United States. If I could find a job that paid enough money, my children could join me. I wanted them to have an education and a proper life . . . to be someone.

After I made up my mind to cross the river, I met José Luis. It was like fate—we just found each other. You could say it was love at first sight. [Laughs] I had two young boys who needed a good man to learn from. When he asked me to live with him, I said yes.

JOSÉ: Before I met Rosa, I lived with my grandmother in Juárez. I would go back and forth across the river to work in El Paso or the farms in New Mexico. After Rosa and I fell in love, we decided to rent this apartment in El Paso and live together.

ROSA: Before I met José, I crossed back and forth across the river five days each week to my housekeeping jobs in El Paso. On weekends, I took my children out of the orphanage. Then I had to reluctantly

return them to the orphanage on Sunday evenings and prepare to go
back across the river.

For a while, I traveled alone, which can be dangerous. But after I
men José Luis, we crossed together. There are men who carry people
across the river on their shoulders. The water is kind of rough, but
that's what these men do to make a living. They charge passengers
1,500 to 2,000 pesos [$1.50 to $2.50]. The water is up to their
chests, but they manage to hold us up on their shoulders so we can
get to work dry.

JOSÉ: Crossing the river can be very dangerous, especially if you cross
alone. There are fast water currents, and sometimes the water is quite
high. If you don't know how to swim, the undercurrents can pull you
right down. And in places the bottom of the river is like quicksand
that can trap you. The water turns into kind of a funnel that can drag
you down. Some friends of mine have died.

ROSA: I don't know how to swim. I relied on José Luis, who is a good
swimmer. We were both very lucky. I can clearly remember an incident where we almost drowned. It began on a Sunday evening,
which is a customary time for crossing. At the time, a man was running
loose who was raping and killing women who crossed alone. So there
were a lot of American border patrolmen and Mexican police along
both banks.

After the sun went down and it became quite dark, José and I waited
for a while near the riverbank, but it seemed hopeless to try to cross
the river undetected. We waited until the next morning to try again.

When the sun came up, we saw that the men who carried people
across on their shoulders weren't working, because of all the police.
When we noticed that the border patrolmen had left the area, we
decided to try to cross by ourselves. That was a big mistake. The
current was very fast that day. In the middle of the river, we lost our
balance and began to be dragged downstream. I felt helpless and
began to panic. Fortunately, another man who was a strong swimmer
came to our rescue. He pulled us to the shore.

After José and I began living together in El Paso, I decided to bring
my children across the river. The water was too high and swift to
risk men carrying them on their shoulders. So I had the children
taxied across on a rubber raft.

JOSÉ: Another danger for people who cross the river is crime. Packs of
men hang around the riverbank like wolves. They try to steal people's
knapsacks or purses. Sometimes they demand that you give your wallet
or wristwatch. If you don't obey them, they will knife you.

Were we ever caught by the *migra* when we crossed the river to-gether? Oh, yes. [Laughs] Lots of times. But the patrolmen are really okay people. They arrest you, ask the usual questions. If you get rough, they will get rough, too. Otherwise they are fine. It all depends on the person who arrests you. If he has a mean personality, he will treat you rudely, whether you are impolite or not. But most of the time, it is a routine procedure.

When the *migra* catch us, they just put us in their truck and take us to their station. They ask our name, address, where we were born. They keep us in a cell maybe three or four hours. Then they put us in a bus and drive us back to Juárez. They drop the women off very near the main bridge. The men are taken a little further away from town.

Our favorite place to cross the river is close to the Black Bridge, which is not far from downtown El Paso. Many of us would stand on the Juárez riverbank and wait for the change of Border Patrol shifts. Each morning, the shift changes between seven-thirty and eight-thirty, sometimes nine-thirty. We learn by observing over long periods of time. And all of our friends have been held in the immigration station. We observed certain patrolmen coming in to work and others checking out after their shifts.

Experienced river crossers pass this information to new people who are just learning the daily routines. Over a period of time, we learn the shift changes by recognizing different officers' faces. Some Mexican people even know the *migra* by name.

ROSA: Suppose I am caught by the patrolmen at seven-thirty in the morning. They will take me to the station and hold me for a few hours, then bus me back to Juárez. I would walk back to a crossing point and try once again. It is like a game. I think the most times I was ever caught by the *migra* was six times in one day. No matter how many times they catch me, I keep coming back.

The majority of the people in the *colonia* where I lived in Juárez worked in El Paso, mostly as housekeepers, construction workers, or helpers in the fields. In the United States there is a lot of work, but in Mexico we have nothing.

JOSÉ: The men, like myself, who work in the fields come across the river at around 2:30 A.M. to meet the buses that take us to the fields from El Paso. The transportation is owned by the *padrone* of the farms, or by the labor-crew chiefs who hire and pay the workers. In the evenings, we ride the buses back to the river. Sometimes I work twelve hours in a day and earn $20. I've learned to check around to see which farms pay the best. Some pay up to $35 a day.

Farm-labor jobs are not very steady. We just grab whatever is open at the moment. I accept anything, any time, as long as it is work. But suppose I take a job that only pays me $12 a day. It would only be enough to cover my transportation and meals in the field. I must find jobs that pay enough to feed my family.

In order to make $25, I must pick seventy-two buckets of chili peppers. That could take me four or five hours; it depends on how fast my hands are. The total amount of buckets we pick depends upon the amount contracted by the big companies in California. For a big contract, we work as long as necessary to complete the order. But the most I can earn in a day is $35.

During the summer, it gets very hot in the fields, up to 110 degrees. We work for eight hours with a half-hour break for lunch. To save money, I bring my lunch from home. The companies usually provide us with a thermos bottle of cold water. The farthest we travel from El Paso is to Lordsburg, New Mexico. That is around three and a half hours by bus. We leave El Paso at 3:00 A.M. For Las Cruces we leave at 5:00 or 5:30 A.M.

ROSA: To my housekeeping jobs I can take a regular El Paso city bus at 7:00 or 8:00 A.M. I usually come home around 3:30 or 4:00 P.M. each day. For a long while, I worked at one house—a Mexican-American family. They started me at $20 a day. Eventually they increased my wages to $25. They live near a large shopping center in the eastern part of town. The job was a little bit easier than working in the factory in Juárez, and paid much better.

In the factory, a whistle blows to let us know when to start, when to stop, when to eat dinner, and when to resume work. Doing housecleaning, I can rest a little when I need to take a short break.

To compare our apartment in El Paso with where I lived in Juárez, I prefer it a little better over there, because in the *colonia* I had a place to hang my clothes after I washed them. The bathroom was outside of the house. But we don't have a bathroom in our apartment here, either. All of the apartments in this part of the building share a toilet on the back stairwell. But in this apartment we have electric appliances, which makes life better than my previous home.

JOSE: The landlord who owns this building is very generous. He lets us owe him rent for the months that I am not working. He understands how tough our life is. We pay whatever we can, even if it's only $50.

And he knows that, if the day comes where we are raided by immigration officers, we will run.

The rent for this apartment is $125 a month plus electricity. We all live and sleep in this one room. The two boys sleep on the couch. Our daughter, Miriam, sleeps with us on the bed. And the baby sleeps in a crib next to our bed. Fortunately, we have a kitchen, and a closet in this room. Living conditions in Juárez were better, but there was no work at all.

If it is possible, Rosa and I would like to become American citizens. I would have my documents, and the government wouldn't be after us. All we want is to be able to work in peace.

Our dream is to be able to give the children the best of everything. We know that, for them to have a better future and purpose in life, they need a good education. Of the three children in school now, Miriam is the fastest learner. She received an award for being an honor student, the best in her classroom.

We hope the children can finish high school and have the career of their choice. We are going to sacrifice for them, so that they can have the profession that they desire.

I was only allowed to finish grammar school. I am the oldest in my family, of five sisters and two boys. I had to stop going to school when I was twelve, to work with my father to support the family. I would have liked to finish school, but my parents needed me to work. They chose my sisters to study. So I gave up my studies to support my sisters.

At first, I liked working better than going to school. But after a while, I wanted to attend junior high school. But my mother told me that the family couldn't afford for me to go, and she said my sisters seemed to like the books better than I did. So I continued working. My father had a fruit-and-vegetable business. We sold from a pushcart in downtown Juárez, and I came across the river to do some gardening.

Even though I've come to work in Texas and New Mexico for many years, I've never learned to speak much English. I would like to learn, but I've never had the chance to study. I have a lot of responsibility now to provide for the children. It is more important that they have school, so I must work.

The dreams that Rosa María and I had of living in the U.S. and reality are not the same. We hoped to find a job and live comfortably. Now that we are here, our main purpose is to survive.

I worry about our status under the new immigration law. In the previous place where I lived, I paid the rent all the time, but the landlord threw away all of the receipts. So we have no proof that we have been living here enough years to qualify for amnesty.

On the farms where I worked, my employers or crew bosses didn't keep pay records, because I only worked temporarily at each place. And, besides, I was illegal. So what was the use? If the police showed up, we would be in trouble whether or not the employer had a record. And the employers wanted to protect themselves. They didn't pay us with checks; it was always cash.

Fortunately, the last farmer I worked for took taxes and Social Security out of our wages. He is sending me a W-2 form as proof. I am waiting for it now. But things are getting worse, because the immigration police are putting pressure on people who hire un-documented workers. If the police catch illegals on a job site, the boss can be arrested under the new law. So most places have stopped hiring illegals. For example, my last job in El Paso, I was fired because the *migra* would raid the construction site every day. We would have to stop working and run.

When the planting season begins on the farms, I hope the immi-gration police don't show up. They raid a farm with a truck and four or five police cars. They position themselves outside the entrance to the farm and wait for us to walk by. They ask us for identification. If we cannot show proof that we are legal, we've had it. They'll take us away.

On the farms where I work, some people are legal and others aren't. If you drive your own car, the police usually won't question you. But if you come to work in the employer's bus, they'll take you away.

ROSA: In town, we don't feel comfortable walking on the street. If the immigration officers see us, they will grab us. We are not afraid for ourselves, because we are accustomed to it. But I worry about the children. They have just begun studying in school here in El Paso. They like it very much. My sons are in the sixth and fifth grades, and Miriam is in second grade. They are learning English very quickly. My oldest boy, Lorenzo, likes social studies and mathematics; he would like to be a doctor. My other son likes the army a lot. He could probably be a good soldier.

JOSÉ: If we become citizens and the United States government asks them to spend time in the army, we would be honored if they are chosen to serve. We would be very proud of our children for doing their duty for their country.

ROSA: My daughter, Miriam, received a certificate from her teacher. You can ask her what she would like to do when she finishes school.

MIRIAM: [Big grin] I like to study English and mathematics. Some day I would like to be a teacher.

ROSA: In the buildings on this block, the majority of the people are families. In each apartment there are three or four children. This is the only area we found where the landlords don't mind renting to families with kids. The kids play outside, in the alley behind our building. Not many cars pass on this street at night, so it is pretty quiet. But other neighborhoods are more active and there is more crime on the streets.

We would like to have an ordinary life, but our problems with the *migra* are nothing new. If they catch me again and send me back to Juárez, I will just come back across the river.

CHUPPIES

In the sixties, Cesar Caballero was an angry young man. Born in Mexico and raised in Secundo Barrio on the American side of the Rio Grande, he helped lead the fight for equal rights at the University of Texas. Today, Cesar, at thirty-seven, is a director at the university library in El Paso. He is among a growing number of first- and second-generation Chicano young professionals who are rising to leadership roles in an evolving bicultural community.

On a Saturday afternoon, Cesar invited me to his house in the La Paz Estates, in the arid suburban hills overlooking the city. We are joined by his father, Arnulfo, a modest man in eyeglasses and a neatly trimmed mustache, who still chooses to live in a Spanish-speaking downtown barrio. Growing up, Cesar never associated with Anglo Americans until he entered college. Today his daughter, Ana, a lively sixteen-year-old in Levi's and an oversized blue sweater, is the only person without blond hair on her high school's varsity cheerleading squad.

CESAR: My father always talks about the first time he came to the United States and walked up to the top of the Statue of Liberty. He inscribed his name on the wall inside her crown. He put: "A. Caballero aquí." That means "Arnulfo Caballero was here."

The Statue of Liberty is the symbol of New York. Many of us in El Paso believe that the giant crucifix on the mountain of the triborder area between Mexico, Texas, and New Mexico is a similar symbol. It is the migration route for thousands who walk from Mexico. It's called Cristo Rey. On the crucifix is a figure of Christ, at least twenty to thirty feet high, that can be seen for miles around.

People say that the stories of El Dorado, the Spanish quest for gold, came from the golden sunsets in this area. They saw the gold-colored sky and said, "There's got to be gold in the mountains here."

When I first saw the United States, I was seven years old. It was all very strange. The superficial things jump out at you—people have a lot more money, they dress a little better. My mother would bring me across the border to shop in El Paso. We ate lunch downtown in some of the little restaurants or cafés, American food like hamburgers and french fries.

We had a TV in Juárez, so we watched American programs like the "Mickey Mouse Club." All of us in Juárez wanted to be Mouseketeers. That was our favorite program. We used to learn the little songs. We didn't know what they meant, because we didn't speak English. But we could sing, "M-I-C-K-E-Y M-O-U-S-E." [Laughs]

When my family moved to El Paso in 1958, legal immigration from Mexico was relatively easier than it is today. Fewer people were trying to come. Mexico had a much smaller population, and the social and economic pressures weren't as critical.

I was born in Puebla, Mexico, in 1949. It's a state capital, a hundred miles from Mexico City . . . a long way from Texas. My grandfather was a blacksmith of Spanish descent, and my grandmother was an Indian. That mix makes us a mestizo family. I still have fond memories of going to the blacksmith shop and playing, and I remember going to school to learn reading and writing in Spanish and nationalistic things about the Mexican flag and history.

My dad did a lot to encourage me when I was young. He is very philosophical. He always talked about the importance of education in getting ahead. And he always emphasized doing things for the community and achieving in life.

ARNULFO: The main reason I came to El Paso was to get a better education for my sons and to earn a better standard of living for the whole family. Because, when I came to work in the United States during World War II, I saw that people lived better than in Mexico. I saw the children were strong and tall. I wanted my sons to live that way.

I came to the U.S. in 1944 as part of the "Bracero" labor program. I went all the way up to New York City to work for the railroad company. The American government needed Mexicans to work, because so many of its men were in the military. The United States government advertised in Mexican newspapers, offering to pay for our travel if we would come work.

I was taken to New York City. I lived right on 42nd Street, close to Fifth Avenue, on the fourth floor of a small building. I'm sure that all of those apartments are gone now. The big library was there on the corner, with the big statues of lions in front. Another place I liked was the Empire State Building. I walked all the way up to the top, to view the entire city. The skyline of Manhattan is beautiful at night.

There were fifty-four of us who came to work in New York from

Puebla. Five or six friends and I worked together on the New York Central Railroad. We worked in the freight house, loading and unloading. It was a good job, but it sure was cold. There were huge blocks of ice in the river. I was very surprised to see that.

In 1945, when the war was over, my contract ended with the railroad. I went back to Puebla. But I liked this country. I thought all the time about coming back to the United States with my family. I really love this beautiful country.

Puebla is one of Mexico's most ancient cities, but, like Mexico City, it is also one of the most modern. My wife and I owned a cleaning-and-dry-cleaning shop and a restaurant. I had three sons by 1952, when I decided to come back to the United States. Cesar, who was born in 1949, is my oldest. I traveled alone to Juárez, right across the river from El Paso, and started working in a restaurant. Then I opened another cleaning shop.

In 1956, once I was established and had some money saved, my family joined me. We lived in Juárez for two years while I prepared my papers for residency in the United States. I've always been in the U.S. legally, never anything wrong. It took about six months to get my papers certified to start working across the border in El Paso. I spoke some English, which I learned in night school in Puebla.

The first place I worked in El Paso was as a waiter in the Eagle Café. It serves Mexican, Italian, Chinese, all kinds of foods. Then I found work in the Police Officers' Club, as a bartender.

Back then, El Paso was very small. The central plaza downtown, where people congregate to catch transportation, we called Lagartos, which means "Alligator" Plaza, because it had two or three real alligators that just used to sit there and bask in the sun. The real name is San Jacinto Plaza, but old people like me still call it Lagartos. Even back in the 1950s, the population in El Paso was around half Mexican. I sent Cesar to school here even before we moved to the States.

CESAR: I began school in El Paso at Sacred Heart School in the second grade. I would get in a trolley in Juárez with a little group of kids and come over the border to attend school. My father designed my bilingual program long before they became formally used.

I remember my first day of school. I was in a concentrated English class where all the kids only spoke Spanish. The teacher spoke to us in English. We all went, "What?"

But she was very good. She translated what she was saying. She told us, "I'm doing this so that you can get used to the English sounds." She was a real pretty lady, too. It was fun to have a very pleasant

*The Caballero family after their
1958 arrival in El Paso*

person teaching us, but the school was a little bit of a culture shock because of the American customs.

My mother made a lot of my clothes. And all of the Mexican kids wore khaki pants and solid-color or floral shirts. American kids wore semi-dressy pants and bright-colored rock-and-roll Elvis Presley shirts or pullovers.

The school was fifty percent Mexican children. We mingled pretty well with the kids from El Paso. They were of Mexican heritage but lived here. We all learned from each other. The idea in the school was for all of us to learn English.

At Sacred Heart School we were sometimes served American food. At first I felt that it was too bland, because Mexican food has a lot of spices and chilis. Some American food was completely strange to me, like asparagus. I got into eating pickles and drinking milk out of a carton.

ARNULFO: In 1958, my legal immigration papers were accepted, and I brought my whole family through the border into El Paso. My first daughter was born in Juárez. My wife had three more children after we were settled in El Paso—seven kids all together.

After six months, my wife and I opened a business, Caballero Cleaners. It was located on the corner of 7th and Lawrence, downtown, in South El Paso, close to the border. Very close to the Stanton Street bridge.

CESAR: The neighborhood is called Secundo Barrio, the Second Ward. It is one of the oldest communities in the United States. In 1982, we celebrated four hundred years of its existence. It's even older across the river. Before the Pilgrims crossed the Atlantic in the *Mayflower*, this community was already established.

In Secundo Barrio, we lived very near the Boys Club and Amigo Center. The neighborhood was mostly brick tenement buildings. We lived in one of those, with a small store on the bottom floor. Our tenement was two rooms. The front room was a kitchen and eating area for socializing, and the back room was for sleeping. We had seven kids in the two rooms. [Laughs] There were two or three beds in the sleeping quarters. We stayed cozy. We didn't need heaters in winter.

During the summers, our front porch was the sleeping quarters. It was a lot of fun, nice breeze. The veranda connected from one building to the next. And all the kids in the neighborhood would be sleeping out there. We'd visit with our neighbors until we got tired: "Hey, what did you do today?" "Oh, I went to the swimming pool."

We didn't feel like we were poor at all. Not knowing what the rest of the world was like, we felt real comfortable. My dad used to get around on a bicycle. He would take me to school on the bike, I still remember. Now my daughter just turned sixteen and is about to get her driver's license. [Laughs]

Later at another location, my family's cleaning shop was in a brick building near where we lived. It was two businesses—a cleaning shop, and in the store was a wall of shoes. People would bring in their dirty clothes and then possibly buy a pair of shoes or get their shoes shined.

ARNULFO: I worked all the time so that we had enough food and clothes for the children. Besides operating the business with my wife, I worked at the bar. My wife was a very hardworking woman, and the kids helped when they were old enough.

CESAR: We all learned the business and helped at the counter. At one point, my father bought a van. We would go around the neighborhood and solicit business. We all became pretty good salesmen. We learned how to talk with people, relate with people well. Dad gave us good training.

He instilled an entrepreneurial spirit in us kids by setting up our own business. We would get art prints from Mexico, the frames, everything separate. We assembled them at home and peddled the prints around El Paso. We felt like rich little kids. [Laughs] We had more money in our pockets than we knew what to do with.

After we were living in El Paso for five years, my father and then the kids who were born in Mexico became American citizens. My mother has never become a citizen. She is a die-hard Mexican. Even though we kids were picking up a lot of American traits, my family remained Mexican in our cultural traditions.

During Christmas, my mother would still have a Nativity scene, which many Mexican-American families have abandoned in favor of Santa Claus and all the commercial stuff. Mother would assemble a table full of ceramic Nativity statues of the baby Jesus. We combined the Mexican symbol of the Three Kings with Santa Claus, even though the Kings holiday is supposed to be in January. My father did Santa Claus for us, so we wouldn't feel bad. We received candies and toys. It was fun.

Mexican culture puts much more emphasis on family activity. If there is an event at the church or school, the whole family, parents and kids, go together. A lot of that is carried on in El Paso. I think it's healthy.

We didn't waste our time on streetcorners. My father wouldn't let us stand on corners and shoot the bull too long. He'd call us in and say, "Do you have something worthwhile to do? If you don't, I'll give you something to do. Don't waste your time." That didn't mean we didn't have fun. We played sports with our friends, we went to the swimming pool, and I've always been fond of reading. One of my best hobbies was to walk to the library.

I always wanted to be working or studying. When I got a little older, in my free time I practiced my trumpet. I played in the marching band in school. But a lot of my friends didn't finish high school. We had more than a fifty-percent dropout rate. It was mostly because of language problems. In the barrio and in homes, hardly anyone spoke English. At Jefferson High School, students couldn't read well, so they did poorly in their studies. A lot dropped out for that reason.

ARNULFO: I encouraged all my children to graduate from high school and go on to college. Always. My other kids liked to study, too, but not like Cesar. My wife and I would say, "I don't know why Cesar is like this." It made us happy to see him trying hard.

I never wanted my sons to have to work as hard as me. I liked my jobs, but they were hard work. Look at me—I'm sixty-four years old, but I look much older. I always told my kids, "Find jobs with good salary. Do better than me."

Around the time that Cesar was to graduate from high school, I asked my wife, "Does Cesar want to work or try college?" She said, "He wants to go to college." I said, "That's good."

CESAR: Right before I graduated from high school, my father closed his cleaning business. I didn't know where I would get the money for college tuition, so I got a job making hamburgers at one of the first fast-food joints in El Paso, called Mr. Quick. It was a forerunner of McDonald's. And I worked Sundays at a bakery shop, selling bread.

I love music. All through high school and college, I played in a semi-professional band called the Blue Diamonds. We played both American and Mexican music. Even jazz and country-and-Western. We had to be versatile in the types of music we played to be competitive, but we mostly played rock and roll—James Brown, a lot of Beatles, and the salsa music by Santana. It was great, because when I was in college I paid for part of my tuition with money I made playing music. We'd play on weekends at bars and dances. Fridays and Saturdays for sure. Weddings, parties, anywhere somebody would hire us.

I can remember taking my college books to gigs. I studied between breaks for tests that I would have on Monday. My friends thought that I was kind of weird. I was the only guy in the barrio who carried my horn in one hand and my books in the other. Instead of drinking beer and dancing, I sat in a corner reading. I was known as kind of a weird guy. [Laughs] People always wondered about me.

I met my first wife, Martha, in high school. We began dating. We both attended the university. I started at UTEP [University of Texas, El Paso] in the 1967 fall semester. Only a small minority of us from the barrio got to college.

When I first began attending classes, UTEP only had around fifteen percent Hispanic students, and only a small percentage of them graduated. I was in the ROTC program for a while. My father wanted his boys to be military officers. It was the middle of the Vietnam War.

Needless to say, I got caught up in the antiwar movement. I dropped out of ROTC. My father hit the ceiling. I thought he was going to kill me. [Laughs] We didn't speak for months. He said, "Long-haired hippie." My hair was short but was starting to get kind of long. It got worse as time went by.

In part, I was going through the process of questioning values and family relationships that most of America was going through. I became involved in the Chicano movement, too. I said, "I'm needed more in

El Paso to fight than in Vietnam." We were having a local revolution, rediscovering Mexican-American pride. We talked about cultural respect and self-development among our people.

Mexican-American students at the university felt prejudice, both subtle and overt. We labeled some professors as racists because they would openly say some very negative things about Mexican language or culture. And they would give Mexican students low grades in comparison to the other students, even if the Mexican students did the same level of work. Our student movement was mostly Chicano kids, but some blacks and Anglo kids were also involved.

Growing up in the barrio, I had very little contact with Anglo kids. I knew mostly Mexican kids. It was two separate worlds, the Mexican and Anglo communities. The only time that we had contact with Anglo or black kids was in high school. And that was a very small number, mostly kids who had mixed parents or whose families had stayed behind in areas that became barrios.

In high school I had incidents where I experienced direct discrimination. One night I went to a dance. I didn't know that it was a place with mostly Anglo girls. An Anglo policeman told me to leave the premises. At that point I questioned him, and he arrested me. I asked him why he was arresting me, and he uttered some very racist sentiments. At the station, they let me go. Nevertheless, I spent a very embarrassing and uncomfortable few hours in jail. Not to mention the physical abuse.

In college, there were times that I traveled around Texas with my music group, the Blue Diamonds, and couldn't get served in restaurants. I remember one incident in central Texas. Our whole band walked into the restaurant. The waitress cleaning the tables threw leftovers into our laps. She walked away. And we didn't get served.

Then in school, when some of the grades we received from professors exhibited their prejudice, we felt that we had to do something about it. I became active in setting up cultural things, like a folk-dance group. I tried to revive the idea that it is important to retain the language and the good things in Mexican culture. Philosophically it was a serious movement. The small number of us Hispanics at the university didn't want to forget who we were and where we came from.

We felt that it was important to instill among ourselves a strong cultural pride, so that we didn't develop inferiority complexes, and to remember to help our people as much as possible after we became professionals. We saw that some of our already successful people weren't doing that, because they felt ashamed of where they came from.

Perhaps I was going through an angry-young-man period. Now that I'm a little older and mellowed out, I'm more effective. I'm no longer a "young militant." [Laughs] I was involved in demonstrations. I belonged to one organization that was considered very militant— MECHA—the Chicano Student Movement of Aztlán. "Aztlán" is the Aztec Indian word for northern Mexico, meaning the southwestern United States. At one time it was considered a separatist movement, although not many of us particularly supported the radical separatists.

Nevertheless, we did push for immediate changes, like increased enrollment of Chicano students at the university, increased number of Chicano professors. We created an impact in reducing prejudice in the community. I feel that there has been a change in recent years, a lot of it due to the political and social movements which some of us were involved in. At UTEP, the Hispanic student population is now forty-eight percent and increasing. Some people, like myself, have earned our master's degrees.

Even after I got married, my wife and I performed with a Mexican folk-dance group at the university. Our baby daughter, Ana, would sit in the audience and watch. Later on she became a dancer, too. There used to be a Mexican children's folk-dance group that my wife, Martha, directed. We remained active in cultural activities for many years.

I became involved in library work almost by coincidence. I've always enjoyed libraries and books, but when I started college I majored in business and accounting. My intention was to eventually help my parents.

After my freshman year, I went into the college office and asked for student work. They said, "Why don't you work in the library?" I liked the job so much that I went from work-study to full-time staff. Following graduation, I realized that I wanted to make a career of library work. In 1973, I went to graduate school on a fellowship to the University of Texas at Austin. After a year of concentrated study, I graduated in 1974 with a master's degree in library science.

Living in Austin was another transition for me. It was my first prolonged experience away from El Paso and the border area. In Austin, I always kept extra money in my pocket, just in case I got into trouble. I heard that the Ku Klux Klan had been very active in the streets, and were giving blacks some trouble. In El Paso, the KKK never surfaced—probably because they would consider it dangerous to their physical well-being.

I think a lot of the Chicano radicalism of the sixties and early seventies was a direct result of people feeling abused. Gradually we found that it was hard to make changes by giving the system hell. We moved into the system, rather than trying to knock it down. We joined boards in the community and tried to get into positions of decisionmaking. That's bascially what a lot of us have done.

In a sense, it's a form of being co-opted, but a lot of us have clear goals as to what kind of changes we want to see in society. Most important is pluralism, having equal justice for all.

I've climbed the management ladder at the university library. I'm in charge of developing the collections on the history of Mexico, especially the Mexican Revolution. Scholars visit our library from universities in Mexico, the United States, and even from Europe. And we have a very good collection of early archival materials relating to northern Mexico, and the Southwestern United States when it was still under Spain and Mexico.

I provide reference service to visitors and show them where to find materials. I'm also in charge of evaluating and reviewing new materials that are donated to the library. Among our special collections are Western fiction, rare books, the history of printing and book pro-duction, Judaica, Chicano studies, and the S. L. A. Marshall Military History Collection. As if all those things weren't enough, I've been given the responsibility to develop the library's collection in account-ing and real estate.

At UTEP, the percentage of Chicano faculty is still pretty small, around seven percent. I've been on academic committees related to Chicano and Border studies programs. I've been acting director of that. I've also been on the advisory committee to the Center for Inter-American and Border Studies, and I've been asked to serve on various committees on the aspects of Hispanic studies and community affairs. I feel appreciative of what this community and the country have done for me. The least I can do is offer as much community service as I can.

In recent years, the society in El Paso has become very accepting of different nationalities. We don't have an extreme racial problem here. It's very subtle. For example, although there are a large number of well-educated Chicanos active in all areas of the community—in business, banking, communications—there are only a small percent-

Cesar Caballero in his office in the UTEP Library

age in the top management of these institutions. Even though around sixty-five percent of El Paso County is Chicano.

As for my situation, after I finished graduate school and returned to work at the UTEP Library, little by little my wife and I were moving up without realizing it. We moved out of the barrio and bought this brand-new house in the hills overlooking the city six years ago. The name of this housing development is La Paz Estates. We're in the Upper Valley of El Paso. A lot of new housing developments are still being built out here. Mostly upper-middle-class families are moving in, both Anglo and Chicano. See those barren hills? Pretty soon they'll be leveled and a new housing development will spring up. But city ordinances have been voted in to preserve the mountains.

A lot of our neighbors are Americans who have come from the North to manage the *maquiladora* industries that are being set up across the border in Juárez. The *maquiladoras* are factories or assembly shops that employ thousands of Mexican workers at $3 to $6 a day to do basic labor for American corporations. They do the basic production; final assembly of the products is done in the U.S. For every twelve *maquila* jobs created in Juárez, one job is created in El Paso. If there are ninety thousand new jobs in Juárez, then seven thousand related jobs are created here. Add to that the indirect jobs like corporate managers, truckers, and insurance and other services, and the number grows to twenty thousand jobs that we wouldn't have if it weren't for the *maquiladora* program.

El Paso has a strong business tradition with people in Mexico. If the Mexican economy stabilizes, it will create a golden opportunity for small-business people here. Many Mexicans come to El Paso to shop and trade, but the past few years there has been a downswing because of their economic problems. The popular feeling is that the *maquiladora* program is here to stay.

I have seen a lot of changes in the community during the thirty years that my family has been in this country. When I was growing up, I felt that the barrio was my place. We were pretty isolated from the Anglo community. An area like where we are sitting right now was off limits for me. We just didn't feel welcome. But today kids like my daughter, Ana, who is sixteen, are not isolated any more. Ana's a varsity cheerleader at her high school.

ANA: Most of the kids in my high school are Anglo. I'm the only Mexican-American girl on my cheerleading team. I'm the only cheerleader with black hair. [Laughs] Everyone else has blond hair and blue eyes. There's a lot of competition within the school, but other kids accept me for who I am rather than for my background or nationality.

CESAR: Busing had a lot to do with that. Ana was involved in one of the last phases of court-ordered integration of the schools.

When I was a university student, a friend of mine who is now a big-shot lawyer wrote a legal brief that was entered into court as a suit against the school district. He was still an undergraduate student when he wrote the proposal, but it resulted in changing El Paso's highly segregated school system.

There was resistance within the community at first. At PTA meetings, Anglo parents had never sat next to Mexican Americans in that kind of equal social context before. It was the same for us. There was some tension. But as time moved on, busing has worked really well. Occasionally there's some problems with established kids in a school segregating the new kids, but that's only natural. Any time a kid goes into a new place, it takes time to fit in and make new friends.

ANA: When I moved to this neighborhood, I felt strange getting started. My first day in fifth grade in the new school, it seemed so different. Not only because they were new kids, but the way they talked. There were so many blondes! Then, when I began to get used to everyone, I was bused to a new school. There were a lot of blondes there, too.

But they were the children of doctors and the rich. The way they looked down on certain styles was very upsetting for me. After seventh grade, I started to fit in with them. I became more relaxed. There are a few kids who come from Mexico, so I get to speak some Spanish.

CESAR: Ana can carry on a good conversation in Spanish. When she was small, under five years old, my wife and I encouraged her to speak Spanish as a first language. But school acculturation has turned that around. She is very outgoing. At school she likes to show newcomers the ropes, like she's their older sister.

ANA: I haven't visited Mexico very often. The last time we went down to Puebla, I was five years old. I remember that it was always raining. When I go to Juárez, it's just to shop. That's very different from visiting family.

I don't speak Spanish as fluently as I should. [Laughs] I'm studying Spanish in school now, because I don't write it well. I was born here, but I'll always feel part Mexican. I still like Mexican culture. Even though my mother and father aren't living together now, like Dad says, "We're always a family." For me especially, it's always been that the family comes first. We still celebrate Christmas some of the Mexican ways. I think I'll always have a little of both cultures.

CESAR: The neighborhood where my father lives, near downtown, is predominantly Mexican American. A lot of people there are new immigrants who are just learning the English language. But my youngest brother, Caby, who is twelve, speaks perfect English. When you hear him speak, you would never know that Spanish was his first language.

In 1978 and '79, when the wars of Nicaragua and El Salvador heated up, a number of refugees started coming into El Paso. And after the Mexican economy collapsed in 1982, a lot more women and children, undocumented immigrants, began crossing the river.

We've had all kinds of problems in El Paso with immigration people. Local courts have chastised INS officers for indiscriminately harassing Chicanos just because of our brown skin. Our organization sued the immigration people, and we won in court.

ARNULFO: When I first arrived, in the 1950s, immigration officers didn't stop people and ask a lot of questions as much as they do now. They work in teams, one immigration officer and one city policeman. They stop people who look Mexican. They never stop me. I don't know why. Maybe I'm a lucky man.

CESAR: The last two years, the INS has been very aggressive. Before we complained, they used to come onto El Paso buses and question

anyone. We also get harassed at the airport—even professionals going
to conferences.

A lot of the INS officers are Mexican Americans. We don't mind
them doing their job—it's just that we don't like being singled out
because we are brown. I've been stopped by Immigration. They asked
all kinds of questions to try to establish whether I live here or not. I
showed them my IDs and answered their questions politely. They
weren't discourteous. It's just a bother.

The airport isn't as big a problem as walking the streets in our
neighborhoods. I know Chicano doctors who were working in their
yards. INS officers came up to them and asked, "Do you have your
papers? Who do you work for?" The doctors told them, "I live here.
This is my house." A doctor's wife was walking to the store. She was
stopped by INS agents, who asked if she was a maid for one of the
local doctors. There are many other funny stories. When I was a kid,
we played games like "cowboys and Indians" and also "Immigration
and wetbacks."

We know that it is difficult for immigration agents on the border
to do their job. The problem is that sometimes they aren't as tactful
as they should be. Perhaps those of us who are first-generation immigrants believe more in the Constitution of the United States than
established Americans do. We appreciate its values.

The local Chicano community has mixed opinions toward all the
newcomers who have crossed the river in the past few years. I personally think that the stream of immigration has played a positive
rather than negative role. If we closed down the border, the economy
on this side of the river would go bankrupt. Many people here are
as dependent on people coming across to work as the Mexican people
are dependent on coming. If it wasn't for immigrant labor, the economy of the Southwest would have been hurt even more badly by the
economic crisis we face. What negative impact that has occurred is
perceived in terms of some immigrants' bringing in illegal drugs or
some radical philosophies.

There is a possibility that, if there is any big upheaval in Mexico,
it could spill over the border. But I think our military would be ready
to handle that. Not only that—most Mexican Americans are very
nationalistic in support of the United States and our government.
The proof is the number of Medals of Honor that Mexican Americans
have earned for heroism while serving in the U.S. military, the highest
percentage of any ethnic group.

My dad is fiercely patriotic. He had my little brother, Caby, dress up in a GI outfit, bought him a plastic gun, and borrowed an American flag. He took the most patriotic photo of Caby, looking like a mini-Rambo. Oh, man. If America is ever under attack, Dad is going to send his sons—dress us up in uniforms and give us machine guns to defend the country. [Laughs]

If a revolution ever occurred in Mexico, we would probably get many of Mexico's eminent personalities. Lately there've been more professional and middle-class Mexicans coming to El Paso. Some are businessmen with a lot of capital, pouring their money into our economy, setting up shops, and developing jobs here in El Paso. Some others are contributing to the professional and intellectual base of the community. You'd be surprised that the illegal immigrants don't only come from the rural areas. Many are from cities and fairly well-educated areas of Mexico.

These people look for jobs as maids or in the service industries—restaurants or doing gardening. If they cannot find work in these areas, they go out into the fields to do stoop labor, or into the canneries or construction sites. They take very menial jobs that many Americans don't want because the pay is little and it's hard work. And with the housing shortage in El Paso, they live in conditions that you would never suspect in this century. Poverty and the lack of opportunity, rather than ethnicity or ideology, are the greatest threats to both Mexico and the United States.

A serious problem in El Paso, and in barrios in many parts of this country, is that the Hispanic community is not well educated. That's a reason why some of us who have left the barrio to get an education are going back to tell kids, "Stay in school, develop a career, pursue an education."

The numbers are disappointing. Around fifty percent of junior-high Hispanic kids are dropping out. Part of the problem is language. Part is having to work for the family. Part is the parents' not placing emphasis on education, because they never had much schooling and are intimidated by institutions. Their poverty and material needs are so great that wage earning comes first. If a student is hungry, he or she can't learn on an empty stomach. And there are problems with drugs, pregnancies, and gangs.

All of those reasons combined create a high dropout rate. Hispanics can't expect America's major industries to come knocking on our doors to offer us jobs if we are not trained, skilled, and educated.

I've become involved in a voluntary community project called El Paso Adelante, which is a group of Chicano educators and professionals working together. We are attempting to raise the education level throughout the community, specifically targeting the high drop-out rate. Our goal is to develop model programs that can be used throughout Texas.

Our main focus is to find solutions: role models, positive-attitude development, and parental involvement. Reading education has been very lax in the schools, so we're sponsoring reading contests and providing free reading materials that students can take home. We're trying to develop the idea that "reading is fun."

Most of the members of El Paso Adelante are second- or third-generation Mexican Americans, with the exception of a couple of us. We have a good number of businessmen and women, educators, doctors, and media professionals. There is a Chicano yuppie community in El Paso. What we call "Chuppies"—Chicano upwardly mobile young professionals. Most of us are products of the local education system, graduates of UTEP or UT Austin. There are exceptions. For example, one of our women members went to Harvard after attending UTEP.

When I was a kid, there were some Chicano professionals, but they were so few in number that we didn't have them around as role models. Our group is trying to make ourselves available to kids and encourage other Chicano professionals to be role models for the youths. They can be speakers in the school system. And we are trying to establish a scholarship fund for young people to return to high school or attend college.

One of our members, Pablo Salcido from the Spanish-language television station, wants to produce public-service announcements for TV and radio, to encourage parents to motivate their children, and for teachers to motivate their students.

I'm involved in a literacy effort through the *El Paso Herald-Post* newspaper. I'm serving on the literacy board of El Paso Community College, which has a large Chicano student population. And I'm chairing the El Paso Book Distribution Project. This project has brought more than $1 million worth of free books into the El Paso area from New York publishers. We use them throughout the community, mainly in poor areas of the city, to try to encourage people to read in English. We also use them in schools where there are problems with kids dropping out. And I've been on the Board of Directors of the Public Library for six years.

All the time and effort that I've put into community work has taken a toll on my family life. I think that my ex-wife, Martha, felt that I didn't spend enough time with her and our daughter. I grew in one direction, and Martha was growing in another. We split up around ten years ago.

I don't really think that my community activities were the major factor, just a part of why Martha and I grew apart. I really don't think that anyone can analyze exactly why some marriages work and others don't. If our compatibility was strong enough, we would've worked through the problems.

When we split up, Ana was around six years old. At first it was hard for her. But, after a while, she accepted it and adjusted very well. I'm happy to see her in pretty good spirits. I try to be real close with her. I probably see her as much now as when I was married. But being involved in so many activities took its toll on the family.

Ana is excited about being selected for varsity cheerleading, for football and basketball. And she just found a job in a novelty store close to her school, where she works in the evenings.

Her grades in school haven't suffered. She's had some problems in math, but she's been on the honor roll. She's motivated to continue to do well, because in Texas, if a cheerleader gets a low grade in a class, she will be dropped from the team.

ANA: My dad has encouraged me to plan to attend a university. I would like to study public relations. I'm going to try to get a master's degree, hopefully. I'll major in business and go on from there.

CESAR: I hope that she gets a master's or even a Ph.D. I also aspire to become a Ph.D. at some point in my life—education should be a lifetime experience. But I haven't detached myself completely from business. I've been selling real estate for three years. I haven't made a lot of money, but I'm learning by doing a little bit on weekends. I feel that I have a career in the library field that is well developed. I've put in an application for the position of director of the public library. I'm still waiting for an interview. If I'm lucky and do well on my test and my interview, I will run the whole public-library system for the city of El Paso.

I always thank my father for teaching me to appreciate the value of doing good work: Being productive, self-development, and the concept of having goals.

ARNULFO: One of the main reasons why I came to the United States was for my family. I wanted all of them to make it. They are good kids. My son Carlos is a lawyer in El Paso and is now teaching at the Community College. My son Mario is a lawyer in the Legal Aid office in San Antonio. My son Gonzalo is a meat cutter at the Safeway in

El Paso. He's doing very well. My daughter Viviana is a computer operator in a bank in Albuquerque. My daughter Alicia is a housewife in Albuquerque, although she has an associate degree in fashion merchandising. And my daughter Gracie has worked as a technician for the city of Albuquerque for many years. I'm happy that they have tried hard and are succeeding. I say, "Thank you, United Sates. Thank you for everything."

I've always liked this country, from the time that I lived in New York during the war. I took a boat to the Statue of Liberty. And I walked all the way up the winding stairs to her crown. I wrote my name on the wall, right inside her crown, where thousands of people had done the same. Maybe you can still find it if you look.

THE APOLLO

Albert Santoli, Sr.
Born in Bisaccia, Italy
Quality Assurance Supervisor
Cleveland, Ohio

Generations of the Santoli and Roberto clans scratched a living from the volcanic soil of southern Italy, braving earthquakes—"Eartha Quakes," as my grandfather called them—eruptions of Mount Vesuvius, and cycles of drought. After returning from the trenches of World War I to find his papa had perished from exhaustion, my grandfather decided that America should be the place to raise his children. He joined nearly four million Italians, mostly pick-and-shovel farmers and craftsmen, who helped build and expand America's great Eastern and industrial Midwestern cities between the 1880s and early 1920s.

My father arrived in America as an infant cradled in his mother's arms aboard a steamship packed with Italian peasants. They endured a tumultuous three-week ocean voyage to join my grandfather, who had come through Ellis Island the previous year.

Most impoverished Italians clustered in ethnic neighborhoods or ghettos. Although a number of his cousins chose to settle in and around New York, my grandfather was lured by the promise of construction work in Cleveland. My father's childhood was shaped both by the travails of the Great Depression and by the traditional closeness of the family. Although the children spoke English with their friends at school, Italian was always spoken at home. And because a visit to the Old Country was always too expensive, my father grew up with a romantic nostalgia for his hometown from stories that he heard from his parents, which colored tales he later told his own children. Like many first-generation Americans, he was torn between two cultures.

My childhood idols were cowboys. I rode my rocking horse imagining myself with Hopalong Cassidy, the Cisco Kid, and Roy Rogers. But to visit my grandparents, who lived a few blocks away, was to enter an Italian village. In their small grassy backyard was a handcrafted stone table under an overhanging arch of grapevines, and pear trees, next to a small patch of tomatoes and green-pepper plants. My grandmother, who never learned much English, would cook up the best spaghetti, and my grandfather would ask me and my cousins to bring him a pitcher filled with homemade wine from wooden barrels in the basement.

On Christmas Eve, the house would fill with my uncle's and aunts' families. We feasted and played cards or Bingo until late in the evening, when we gathered around the lighted Yule tree to exchange presents, before my Uncle Sam and Aunt Babe went to sing at midnight Mass with their church choirs. Even though he never had much money, Grandfather always gave small envelopes containing a few dollar bills to each of his two dozen grandchildren.

Whatever his shortcomings, the greatest gift my grandfather gave his children was the encouragement to excel in school and achieve the education that he was denied in the mountains of Italy. A skilled craftsman who knew only sacrifice and hardship, he instilled in his sons a fierce pride in their work. Years later, my father applied these values when he became part of a history-making team, which included many other Americans of similar immigrant backgrounds, who helped to send the first astronauts to the moon.

When I arrived in this country from Italy in 1921, everybody came by boat. There were no transatlantic commercial airlines. We wouldn't have been able to afford the price of a ticket even if there was. My father came first, in 1920, to establish himself. He came through Ellis Island in New York Harbor with thousands of other immigrants from all parts of Europe.

The United States was still a very young country, still growing. Big cities like New York, Boston, and Cleveland needed the strong backs and craft skills of immigrants. My mother's father was a co-owner of his own construction business in Cleveland. Dad and all of the men from my hometown who were helping to build the city didn't make much money. But they sent enough back to Italy to support their families.

I was just a baby when my mother packed up all the worldly possessions she could carry to join my father in America. We made the boat journey with many other Old Country relatives who were leaving their farms behind for what they hoped would be a better life. We landed in Boston and took a train for six hundred miles through New York and Pennsylvania to Cleveland. This was my mother's first experience of a big industrial city. My four-year-old brother, Tony, and I were too young to have any real fear or expectations.

Until my father found a house of our own, we stayed in my Uncle Jim DeMateo's home, which was already crowded with his wife and kids, plus a few boarders. Can you imagine a dozen people in a single-family house? We only stayed a short while, until Pa rented a place on 105th Street near Cedar Avenue. In the neighborhood, the only people who spoke English were the black people and some Italian kids who had been living there for a long while. At home we spoke only Italian. But by the time I started kindergarten, I knew English from playing with kids on the street.

In 1927, when I was six, we moved to Angelus Street, on the Southeast Side. It was called the Corlett neighborhood, because the streetcar ran on Corlett Avenue. Very few people had cars. Our milk was delivered by large wagons pulled by horses. Fruit-and-vegetable peddlers and the "paper-rags" man also drove horse wagons. He would ride down the street shouting in a deep voice, "Paay-per rags, Paay-per rags!" He would take old papers, clothes, and scrap materials that people didn't need, then sell them to earn his living.

Cleveland was divided into ethnic areas. But a few neighborhoods, like Corlett, were a mixture of many immigrant nationalities. The block I lived on was mostly Italian. But going east was a mixture of Italians, a lot of Bohemians, some Polish families and Slovenians. Also in the neighborhood were some Americans—English, some Germans, and a few Irish. And a few blocks away was a small black community which had been there before we arrived. The Jewish neighborhood was up toward Union Avenue into the Kinsman area.

Most people in the neighborhood didn't speak English as a first language. On the street, nobody ever felt self-conscious about speaking in their own ethnic tongue. If I was out in public with my mother, I'd talk Italian. On the streetcar, you'd hear all these people—Bohemian, Slovak, or Polish—speaking their own language. The only time people used English was with somebody from a different ethnic group.

My father wasn't a millionaire. [Laughs] Are you kidding? We were paupers. Dad struggled all his life. When he died in 1983, he was surviving on Social Security. That's not what you call a rich man. And when I was growing up, my mother couldn't go to work. She had six kids plus my father. We were a handful!

At first my dad worked for my mother's father, doing heavy construction. They dug and installed water lines, sewers, and gas lines as the city was expanding. He also worked on the railroad—anything to make enough money to live. There was no mechanical equipment; the work was done by hand. In later years, in a cave-in at a construction site, Dad was buried alive and almost died. He suffered breathing problems from the accident for the rest of his life.

My relatives and neighbors were no strangers to hard work. Most were from small farm towns in Europe, except a few who lived closer to the sea and were fishermen. Most of the women, like my mother, never had an opportunity to attend school. They had to work on the farms.

Bisaccia, the town where I was born, is up in the mountains east of Naples, between the Mediterranean and Adriatic seas. Just about all of the town's ten thousand people worked on little plots of land in the valleys below the town. During the medieval centuries, when feudal lords fought among each other, my ancestors built stone houses high on a plateau around a duke's castle, for protection from rival lords.

My father never regretted leaving Italy. He always told me, "We worked and we worked, but had very little to show for all the work we did." He and our relatives came to America because they wanted to have a better life, better opportunity. Today Bisaccia is modernized, with electricity, television, and running water. But back then my mother had to carry water from a spring in a large pail that she balanced on her head. She cooked on a wood-burning stove. My great-grandmother lived in a small stone hut without windows. Dad said that when she cooked he'd have to stay close to the ground to breathe, because the house would fill with smoke.

The people in those mountains always live with the fear of natural disasters. My mother's mother and three of my cousins were killed in an earthquake in 1931. Their stone farmhouse collapsed on top of them. And the last big earthquake, in the early 1980s, devastated some of the towns surrounding my home area. Dad came to America to get away from that kind of life.

When World War I broke out, Dad and his brother, Angelo, were drafted into the Italian army and sent to the Alps to fight the Austrians. There was nobody left at home but his sisters, so his father had to work the farm alone. He died from overwork. Dad never forgot that, because he loved his father. It made him very bitter. That's what finally motivated him to come to America.

When I was growing up, as far as we were concerned, we were Italians but we were Americans, too. In the neighborhood, people still held on to traditions from the Old Country. There were all kinds of family and social gatherings. Like picnics where Dad and Uncle Angelo would slaughter a sheep or rabbits and roast them. We'd save the sheepskins down in our basement. I don't know what we kept them for. [Laughs] The old sheepskins would be sitting there, but we never used them for anything. Just like on a farm, we did a lot of our own butchering.

Father always had a garden in the backyard, and grapevines. The grapes were used mostly for eating or jelly. But making wine for our home was a necessity for Dad, because in Europe Italians drink more wine than water. In Bisaccia, Dad's family had a beautiful vineyard. In Cleveland, we didn't have enough property. Still, he tried. We always had grapes.

The Great Depression came in October 1929. I wasn't even ten years old. I remember when the stock market crashed and the banks closed. Father came home and said, "There's no more money."

Albert Santoli (left) in the late 1920s

During the Depression, Dad was always trying to make a buck for the family. He was a go-getter. If he didn't have construction work, he would do some bricklaying or stonework. He was hired under a federal WPA program as a stonecutter. You can still see some of his work on the beautiful sandstone garden walls in Gordon Park and Wade Park.

When he wasn't on other jobs, he dug basements. In those days, there weren't bulldozers or mechanical equipment. They used large shovels dragged by horses to dig the large hole. Then Pa and the other men would jump in with picks and shovels to square out a basement's walls. Dad was terrific with horses. He took care of them for the building contractors in our neighborhood.

My brothers and I would help Dad gather logs that we used in the furnace to heat our home, because we couldn't afford to buy coal. We'd walk five miles into a wooded area and used a two-handed saw to cut fallen trees—oak, maple, or whatever we found—into six-foot logs. Dad built a crude wooden wagon that sat very low to the ground. But it sure held a load. It took all five of us to pull that wagon home. It actually was a godsend. Before we had the wagon, we had to carry the logs on our shoulders. The logs were so heavy that, as we walked, it felt like our arms were breaking off.

When I was thirteen, I tried to help make money for the family by caddying at a golf course. All the money I made I gave to my mother. We made 35¢ for carrying a golfer's bag for eighteen holes, four hours of work. In those days, with 10¢ you could buy a loaf of bread. A can of beans was less than a nickel. Sometimes there was a sale and we could get three cans for a dime. Whenever we could get flour from the government, which was donated to people in need, Mother made bread or spaghetti. Otherwise, she would shop at the Italian store, because she couldn't speak English. She made macaroni so many different ways— with tomato sauce, or oil, or beans.

Because of the Depression, most people in the neighborhood went out of their way to help each other. In the small towns they came from in Europe, it was the tradition for neighbors to pitch in. Nobody expected to get paid. Because we only had enough money for rent and food, we seldom bought new clothes. Coats were handed down from one child to another. Mother was always patching up the few shirts and pants we had.

We made our own fun. We built scooters out of an apple or orange crate, a two-by-four of wood, and an old pair of skates. And we loved to go to the movies to see cowboys. Tom Mix, Hoot Gibson, and Buck Jones were our heroes. We'd play cowboys and Indians at the schoolyard. To imitate horses, we would crush metal canned-milk containers with our heels, so they stuck to our shoes. Then we'd gallop down the street— clippety-clop, clippety-clop—sounding just like a horse.

I went to Paul Revere, and then Corlett School. The kids were from all parts of Europe, mixed with American whites and blacks, but there weren't many problems of newcomers being accepted. During my childhood, I never saw a racial confrontation. The first time I ever tasted mayonnaise was when a black classmate invited me to his house for lunch. His mother gave us mayonnaise sandwiches. I couldn't get over it, because Italians never used mayonnaise. My friend's family was large, like my own, with the grandparents at home. They lived in a large house, with the family's grocery-store business downstairs.

At home, we still spoke only Italian. But we considered ourselves to be Americans, too. The government wasn't rushing immigrants to become citizens. People like my dad did that gradually, as they became more adjusted to American life. He wanted to study, to learn about his new country and be prepared. He went to a night class to study for his citizenship test. He took me with him to translate; then he would study at home. I was thirteen years old when Dad got his citizenship papers in 1933.

My brother Tony and I automatically became citizens when my father was sworn in. My brothers Sam, Ray, and Pat and my sister, Elvira, were born here, so they were Americans from birth. My mother was required to get her own separate citizenship papers, but she never did, because she never learned to read or write in English. It never bothered her. She was just as American as we were.

In Italy, children were encouraged to begin working on the farm as soon as they were strong enough to walk. But my father always wanted us to stay in school. He had some education when he was a kid, so he knew how important it was to learn. I wanted to quit school after ninth grade to help support the family. I had just finished at Nathan Hale Junior High. Some of my friends had already dropped out and were working. I told my father, "Dad, I'm going to paint the house, and then maybe I'll go to work." He kept telling me, "I think you should go back to school. I don't expect you to drop out."

I finished painting the house anyway, but three weeks later I reluctantly started classes at John Adams High, which was right across the street from my home. Today I'm thankful that Dad convinced me to change my mind.

After graduation, I couldn't afford college. It was 1939, the tail end of the Depression. Work was still hard to come by. I put in applications at stores and factories all over town . . . and I mean *all over*. But I couldn't find work. Finally I was hired by an optical company. I went from the mail room into the shop, where I learned to be an eyeglass-lens cutter and grinder. But Pearl Harbor was bombed, and the United States entered the war. Right away, I volunteered into the service. In my neighborhood, most young men went into the military. I never saw one ethnic family take exception. Everyone wanted to do their part. Regardless if they had to go overseas to fight against their own people.

I found that, once immigrants like my dad took the citizenship oath, they were sincere. When they say, "I pledge allegiance to the United States," they meant that. When the American army invaded Italy, many of our soldiers were Italian Americans. They went right in and did what they had to do.

My cousin Pete came to America from Italy when he was around five years old. He died during the Normandy landing on D-Day. The army sent his body back to Cleveland. He was the only son, and his mother took it very hard.

Pete had come to see me when we were in the same training area in Kansas. I was in the army air force and he was in the infantry. He and my brother Sam were on their last training maneuvers. Later on, Sam was badly wounded in Germany. He drove a tank under General Patton's command.

I had a strange twist of fate when I enlisted that colored the rest of my life. I originally volunteered for the horse cavalry. I loved horses. When I was a kid, the cowboys and Indians always stuck with me. But Uncle Sam had another idea. He said, "I want *you* . . . in the air force."

The army sent me to the Aeronautical Institute in Lincoln, Nebraska, to learn airplane-engine mechanics. After I qualified on B-17, B-24, and B-29 bomber aircraft, I was sent to Guam Island in the Pacific. I was made a crew chief and inspector in the 20th Air Force. Our planes did bombing missions against Japan. In my unit, there were people from all over the United States. I learned a lot about life from my buddies. The whole experience greatly expanded my ideas about what I could do in life.

World War II changed a lot of things for my generation of immigrants. Not the old folks so much, but the young. We came home from the military with much higher confidence and expectations. We all bought cars and branched out away from our ethnic boundaries.

I was discharged from the service on Christmas Eve, 1945. My steady girl, Fay [Serafina Ambrogio], was waiting for me. We were married three months later, on March 2, 1946. We were twenty-five years old. Like many of my friends and relatives, I broke with the old Italian tradition of living close to my parents and moved to another area of Cleveland, which was closer to where I worked. Convenience was only part of the reason. Most young couples wanted to live in better neighborhoods, where their kids would have a better environment.

I found a job at Cleveland Airport as a mechanic and inspector for the Air Force Reserve Training Command. In the postwar years, the government maintained a pretty good-sized reserve, because nobody knew what would happen in various parts of the world. When the Russians blockaded Berlin, some of my buddies were called back into active duty. The air force had to drop supplies into Berlin to break the siege. And later on, the Korean War broke out.

At the airport, I worked on aircraft and engine maintenance five days a week. I worked overtime whenever I could. My first child [the author of this book] was born in June 1949. And in 1950, just before the air base was closed, my second child, Gloria, was born. Because of the kids, my wife and I decided to move to a larger home back in my old neighborhood. When my air-force reserve job was phased out, I was offered a position in the Navy Department's Bureau of Aeronautics.

I was assigned to a massive factory, Thompson Products, which became a branch of TRW in Cleveland. My job was the inspection and quality control of aircraft parts. My supervisors were naval officers, but TRW was making aircraft equipment, like jet engines, for all branches of the military. My responsibility to the government was to assure that all parts manufactured met contract requirements. My ultimate concern was the safety of our boys in the service, who would use these items in their aircraft. Without my division's signature to guarantee quality, nobody at that shop would get paid.

For the next thirty years, I worked as a representative of the Defense Supply Agency in private industry. I attended eighteen different colleges and schools and earned the equivalent of degrees in chemical and mechanical engineering, and in industrial management. In my job, I had to follow the manufacturing process from the acquisition of raw materials to the finished assembly of the product. I had to be able to inspect the entire process.

Even though I was moving up in education and job responsibility, my wife and I and our three children—Albert, Gloria, and Donna— stayed in the old neighborhood until 1961. By that time, just about everyone I grew up with had moved to the new suburbs that were being built just outside the city. Cleveland's ethnic neighborhoods were breaking up. My family was becoming part of the American melting pot.

My brother Sam and I both married Italian girls. But my brother Tony married a Hungarian, and my brother Ray married a Polish girl from the neighborhood. All of our wives came from first-generation families from the Old Country. Their parents were strictly ethnic.

My sister, Elvira, married a Polish refugee named Stanley. He worked in the steel mills. And my youngest brother, Pat, was the first in our family to earn a college degree. He met his wife, Mary, a red-haired Irish nurse, while he was getting his master's degree at the Chrysler Institute in Michigan.

My dad didn't object to who we married, as long as the couples were happy together. He said, "We all struggle, but the main thing in life is health and happiness." That's how it went. The family is no longer a hundred percent Italian; we're a mixed group. My son, Al, married a Vietnamese. I accept that. As long as they get along, that's fine.

Actually, my son's marriage was agreed upon similar to the way it used to be done in the Old Country. Phuong's parents and I exchanged letters to introduce ourselves and our families. They were concerned because their daughter met my son in a refugee camp in Thailand while he was working on a book. Their marriage seemed to Phuong's parents like an irrational decision. So, after talking it over with my son, I assured them that we would love Phuong like our own daughters. Even though she didn't have any close relatives in the United States, she was welcome in our family. They've been married three years now. We made the right decision. Al and Phuong complement each other beautifully.

My wife and I have been living in the same house here in South Euclid for twenty-six years now. This suburban area was a forest when I was a kid. When we decided to move from the old neighborhood, it was because the three kids were becoming teen-agers and they were still sleeping in the same room. We needed a bigger house, and the neighborhood was going downhill.

Financially, the move was a leap of faith. I was paid a government salary, which in those days was not more than $12,000. We looked at a number of housing developments that were being built before we decided on South Euclid. When we moved in, the street wasn't even paved. The whole area was covered with mud. Each house on our street was painted white, with six rooms and a basement. But each buyer could choose their own style of roof and interior design. We told the builder, "Make ours look exactly like the model house," with a pink roof. And the contractor did us two favors. First, he lowered the kitchen cupboards, because we are short people. And, to save us some money, he allowed my father and Uncle Angelo to help me put in our own concrete driveway and build my own garage.

The house cost $19,000. That doesn't seem like much today, but on my small salary, and with three growing kids, there were many months when we weren't sure if we could make our payments. What saved us was that my wife is a terrific bookkeeper. She knows how to budget and make every dollar stretch. And I never spent money on vacations. During the summer, I'd take a couple weeks off from work to paint the house and do whatever repairs were needed. Any extra money usually went for the kids' needs. I think that sometimes my wife and I were a little high-strung because of our financial pressures. The kids were still too young to understand our situation, and they had to make new friends. In many ways, moving to the suburbs was a difficult adjustment for all of us to go through.

In 1963, NASA began the Apollo Program to send a spacecraft to the moon. In this new phase of space exploration, I was assigned to the Space Program Division at TRW. NASA reviewed my background and assigned me to be their representative. I started working by myself, but in a short period of time I became the supervisor of a whole division. We were doing research development and production for items and systems to be used in lunar spacecraft in the Apollo Program.

The work was incredibly challenging both in the areas of scientific progress being made and in the speed and demands of our production schedule. My division's responsibility was to make sure that quality wasn't sacrificed. Each and every item that came from our shop had to be at least 99.9 percent reliable. As you know from the recent space-shuttle tragedy, we couldn't afford even the slightest error in any item that went into a spacecraft.

During my five years in the program, we participated in the development and production of three major items that made space travel and the lunar landings possible. One item we produced was the attitude-control rockets, which are very small—around eighteen inches long—but they perform the critical task of keeping a spacecraft on its flight path to the moon.

The second item we produced was the cooling pump for the spacecraft's instrument ring—which was produced by General Electric. The instrument ring controlled all of the functions of the spacecraft before the lunar-capsule separated from the booster rocket.

The TRW shop where I worked was a huge manufacturing and assembly factory that was built in an old farm field. Some of the old farmhouses were still used as office buildings. The noise level from all of the giant machinery used to manufacture and assemble a wide range of items, from jet-aircraft engines to the spacecraft parts, was a continual roar. My team workers and I had to practically shout to hear each other over the sound of the mechanical noise. There were rows and rows of giant lathes that cut iron bars and sheets of metal. Enormous pressing and stamping machines, fifteen to twenty feet tall, weighing many tons. And equally tall broach machines were used for cutting slots in jet engines for rotor blades.

When I came home from work at night, my wife and kids always asked me why I was talking so loud at the dinner table. I couldn't help it. I was so conditioned to the noise level at the shop that I had a hard time controlling my voice. And because a lot of the work we did was top secret, I couldn't discuss anything from work with the family.

Just this week, after many years away from the shop, I went to see the doctor because I've lost a lot of my hearing. It's what I call "shop ear." The doc says I probably need to wear hearing aids. I guess that was one of the occupational hazards. But, looking back at what we accomplished during those years, I have no regrets.

During the Apollo Program, many factories around the country were developing items needed to make space travel possible. To build a spacecraft, many scientists, engineers, and ordinary factory workers all perform their own assignments and specialties. It took real teamwork to make the program a success.

NASA was the ultimate prime mover. Their planners would tell TRW what was needed. My job was to make sure that the factory made each part according to the original drawing. From the acquisition of raw materials until the finished product came off the assembly line, I had to inspect the quality every step of the process. As the science and technology were rapidly moving forward, NASA sent me to a number of schools, like the NASA Space Flight Center and the Air Force Institute of Technology, to keep up to par. The greatest obstacle in a complex technological program is the concentration it takes to prevent the slightest error. Once a spacecraft lifts off, we get no second chance.

All of us in the program realized that we were on the cutting edge of history. Whenever a spacecraft went up successfully, we were elated. I felt a deep pride that, to this day, I have a difficult time expressing.

As the Apollo Program advanced toward the first manned flight to the moon, we didn't have time to savor our previous accomplishments. I remember being invited down to Florida to observe one of the space shots. But I was a supervisor of both inspection and quality assurance in my division. The program was charging ahead. So I wasn't allowed to go. Instead, I chose one of my team members to go to Florida in my place.

To prepare for the moon landing, the third item we produced was the exhaust cone that allows a space capsule to land on a planet. The cone, which is around four feet long, is located on the bottom of the space capsule. It contains the rockets necessary for descent onto a planet's surface.

On July 20, 1969, it was an incredible feeling to watch the Apollo 11 space shot on television as our astronaut Neil Armstrong walked on the moon. I thought of the small farm town I came from in the mountains of Italy, where people were lucky to attend elementary school and didn't even have plumbing or running water in their homes.

THE SACRED DRUM

Shoua (center right) and Nhia Vang (far right) in their Hmong store in Saint Paul

Shoua and Nhia Vang
Hmong Refugees from Laos
Farm Manager and Student Computer Genius
Saint Paul, Minnesota

A family farm in the rolling grasslands of Minnesota. An abandoned farmhouse. A storybook red barn. An empty sixty-foot corn silo. Here ten hardworking cousins who lived in the poorest inner-city area of Saint Paul decided to invest their savings for one last attempt to preserve their ancestral heritage and to teach their children self-sufficiency. Like many independent farmers under the finance gun of the farm crisis during the '80s, half of the cousins had lost a similar cooperative venture less than eighteen months earlier. In October 1985, they made a down payment on seventy-three acres of rich brown soil, fresh rainwater ponds, and hardwood-covered ridgelines. This time they were determined not to fail.

These men were no ordinary farmers. Although they had grown up planting corn and vegetables, they had never seen a tractor until ten years ago. Instead of rotating crops, spraying pesticides, and spreading chemical fertilizers, they used machetes to slash and clear bamboo thickets on the dizzying chimney-shaped peaks of the Annamite mountain chain of Laos. And they offered prayers and animal sacrifices to implore the ghosts of ancestors and local spirits to protect their subsistence crops from the ravages of nature.

The word "Hmong" means "free people." With origins in China four thousand years ago, the Hmong people had no written language until the 1950s. But for countless generations, village storytellers and balladeers have passed down tales of how their ancestors moved from mountain to mountain, defending their independence and culture from more powerful invaders. Although many Hmong can still be found in remote areas of China, hundreds of clans fled south from the conquering Han Dynasty in the early nineteenth century. In Laos, the crossroad of Southeast Asia's diverse cultures, isolated hill tribes form the majority of the country's three million people. Some 450,000 Hmong farmed in peace until the late 1950s, when the North Vietnamese began building the Ho Chi Minh Trail through Laos to invade South Vietnam.

Throughout fifteen years of direct American involvement in Indochina, the Hmong were our most loyal and self-sacrificing ally. Thousands of courageous young Hmong perished while attempting to block North Vietnamese forces marching south. Unknown to the American public, the "secret war" in Laos prevented countless American casualties from occurring in Vietnam.

Shoua Vang, forty-three, is under five feet tall. For six years, he was a member of special search teams who rescued sixty downed American pilots in the rugged jungles along the North Vietnam border. Within range of enemy rifles, he was lowered by rope from hovering helicopters into crash sites to carry disabled flyers to safety or to retrieve casualties.

In 1975, after the fall of Laos, the Vietnamese Communists and their Pathet Lao surrogates began a brutal revenge campaign against the Hmong, who stubbornly held on to their traditions and refused to be collectivized. An estimated hundred thousand Hmong have been slaughtered in their beloved mountains or trying to flee across the Mekong River to Thailand, where almost sixty thousand were still in refugee camps in 1988. Frustrated Thai authorities threaten to evict them like thousands of new arrivals who are being pushed back to certain persecution and death.

Shoua Vang and his family are among eighty thousand Hmong resettled in the United States. For most, the transition has been a nightmare. Displaced from a primordial life style, the Hmong were scattered into city ghettos. Confronted with cars, telephones, rent payments, and bills, they became paralyzed with confusion. Some searched for friendlier surroundings. Close to forty thousand Hmong traveled to the Central Valley of California, hoping to reunite the clans and re-establish their traditional beliefs and way of life. Today at least seventy percent of them continue to languish on welfare.

Other Hmong communities in Texas, North Carolina, Nebraska, and Minnesota have been more successful in their struggle to adapt. Encouraged by American friends, they are finding ways to integrate their ancestral beliefs into the computer age.

After the first Hmong farm project in Minnesota failed, Shoua attended courses to learn modern farm-management techniques. He actually invented a hand-held computer calculator to simplify bookkeeping for small businesses. He and his cousins realize they may never be able to depend exclusively on their farm earnings. They invested in the land to supplement their city jobs and to remain connected to their ancestors.

Shoua's oldest son, Nhia, age fourteen, is learning to conduct ancestral ceremonies. A few inches taller than his father, he is powerfully built, like a football linebacker. Weekends on the farm, he wears a hooded sweatshirt and soiled corduroy slacks while cleaning the chicken coop and chasing cows out of the corn patch. But during the week he is an elite student in advanced classes at his junior high school. A computer genius, he has taken university-level courses in electronics. At thirteen, he invented and built "Herbie," a walking, talking robot that responds to voice commands.

SHOUA VANG: Centuries ago, when all Hmong people lived in China, large wooden drums were used to signal through the mountains when Chinese raiders were coming. Villagers would band together to defend their homes. A famous and much-loved Hmong king was killed by the Chinese. The sound of the drums recalled memory of the King and gave people courage to resist against powerful armies.

For generations, while the Hmong were persecuted and scattered through the mountains of Southeast Asia, the drum evolved as an important part of funeral ceremonies for every clan and family. Playing the drum helps to liberate the souls of loved ones.

When my family fled Laos in 1975, we prayed that, if everyone was protected on the journey and we reached a safe place, we would rebuild our sacred drum. The drum in our home was too big to carry, so we only took the ceremonial hoop that framed its wooden barrel-shaped body.

After my family came to the United States, for six years we were always trying to work and survive in this new society. We didn't have time to keep our spiritual promise. My parents had many bad dreams. They thought this was because we hadn't rebuilt our sacred drum.

In 1982, after my father and I discussed his dreams, we decided to rebuild the drum. Keeping with our traditions, we brought together a group of thirty or forty Hmong elders in Minnesota. Using the hoop, we framed a new wooden body. Then we slaughtered a cow and stretched the hide for the drum's head.

Since that time, we have used the drum in spiritual ceremonies. In the city, we feel self-conscious, because we don't want to disturb our neighbors with music or many people praying. So now we have a Hmong cultural center on our farm near White Bear Lake. Hmong people come from all parts of Minnesota, Wisconsin, Iowa, and even California to perform religious ceremonies and preserve our important traditions.

Our religious beliefs and traditions are tied to nature and agricultural work. We believe that there are two or three worlds, including spirit dimensions, going on at the same time. Even after death, life is ruled by how a person is buried. It is very important to bury a relative in a beautiful location, near a river or stream with mountains in the background. We believe that, if the dead are not comfortable, the new generation might have bad fortune because the ancestor is unhappy.

When my aunt was very ill in the hospital in Saint Paul, we started looking for a place to bury her. We found the process to be very expensive. And the way we like to be buried isn't suitable with the local cemetery system.

In Asia, the Hmong live in mountains apart from society. America is the first time we have to live in cities. This presents radical readjustment problems. In Asia, our children are born in our houses, which have dirt floors. In Hmong tradition, we bury the baby's umbilical cord under the middle post of our homes. We call it "the ghost pole," or "the ancestral pole." But in this country, people live in apartments, and babies are born in the hospital. Doctors throw the umbilical cord away.

In Laos, we have legends about everything—stories about ghosts, giants, and demons. Those legends are diminished for Hmong children in the United States because of technology. There are no ghosts, because we have electricity.

In the home country, if people get sick, we automatically see the spiritual doctor. He does a ritual to rescue the soul from malevolent spirits. Even now, if one of my children gets sick, we call a Hmong spiritual person. We will get the medicine herbs for tea or do a ceremony in the house. If that doesn't stop the fever, we take the child to an American hospital.

I have six children. My oldest son, Nhia, who is fourteen, and my daughter You, thirteen, were born in Laos. My daughter Youa, who is nine, my son Kou, seven, daughter Mae, five, and my baby daughter, Plua, are all born in this country. My wife, Mee Xiong, is thirty-six years old. I was born in 1944, during World War II. At that time, the old generation was very afraid of the Japanese fighting in China. So they called me Shou-ta which means "the Chinese war."

My home village, Nagnang, in Khammouane Province, is in central Laos, near the Vietnam border. Our community of five hundred people was built in a forest plateau between high green mountains. Each family's one-room house was surrounded by a bamboo fence to hold in our livestock. We had pigs, chickens, ducks, goats, cows, and even some horses, which carried large loads of tools or seeds, or harvested crops on the mountain trails.

Our rice and corn fields were a short distance from the village, on steep hillsides or in sloping valleys. Each year, before planting, we cut the foliage and burned the fields. The ash was good fertilizer, but allowed monsoon rains to deplete the soil through erosion. So, every couple of years we had to move our fields deeper into the mountains.

I have ten brothers and sisters. My father's first wife had three children before she died. Then he married my mom and they had five children. I was born in the middle, before my father died. Then my mother married my uncle, and they had another three kids.

It is Hmong custom that, when a man dies, his wife should marry one of his brothers, because in Hmong society we don't like to break up a clan. And it is important to keep all children within the extended family, to help with the farm work. I began working in the fields when I was six. Survival is very difficult, so all family members have interdependent responsibilities. Hmong clans descend from the father. When a son gets married, he expands his clan. When a daughter marries, she leaves home to join her husband's clan, but her parents receive a dowry, which helps the family. A boy and girl from the same clan are not allowed to marry. The constant infusion makes Hmong extended-family relations quite large. Sometimes we have a thousand or two thousand cousins.

Big trouble began in Laos around 1947, when Ho Chi Minh's North Vietnamese began to form the Pathet Lao Communist army. At first, most Pathet Lao soldiers were actually Vietnamese and Laotian tribal people. There was a rivalry between the two Hmong governors, Faydang and his cousin Touby Lyfong. After the chief Hmong died, they fought for the top position. When Touby was chosen, Faydang and his people went with the North Vietnamese. The Communists promised Faydang power.

In 1953, my family moved further north, to Xieng Khoang Province. We were still too close to the North Vietnam border. A month after we arrived there, the Vietnamese Communists troops began pouring into Laos to fight the French in the Plain of Jars. I never saw so many soldiers in my life.

There are seven roads that go through Xieng Khoang. For three days and nights, we saw the Viet Minh on every road. In the fighting in Laos, the Vietnamese lost, but the offensive overextended the French and drew them into Dien Bien Phu, just across the Lao border. This was where the Viet Minh won the important victory in 1954 that caused the French to leave Indochina.

When I was ten years old, I was allowed to begin school. But I still had responsibilities at home. Early in the morning, when my parents left for the fields, my chore was to feed our horse and the chickens. In the evenings, when I returned from school, I gathered firewood for dinner. Before bedtime, I prepared rice and dried corn for the pigs.

After third grade, to continue my education I had to walk a full day to Xieng Khoang town, the regional capital. Though I came from a big village—more than a hundred families—only seven or eight children were able to further our education. Most families needed the kids at home to help work, and they couldn't afford the extra expense. Though school was free, families had to pay for students' living expenses. Every two or three weeks, I would walk home to get a supply of rice, which I carried back to the city.

I helped to build a little hut near the capital where I lived during the school year. We didn't have electric lights, so I collected wood to build a fire to study by in the evenings. This sounds like a lot of hardship, but for a Hmong it was a rare privilege to be in school.

Hmong people didn't even have an alphabet or a written language until 1959, when some Christian missionaries began to create one. In school we learned by writing the Laotian alphabet, which is like a Sanskrit script, with French letters alongside. By sixth grade, I could speak Hmong, Lao, and French pretty well.

In 1960, when I was finishing elementary school, the Communist Pathet Lao came to Xieng Khoang. They tried to catch students for their army, especially to measure their maps for artillery. I was sixteen years old and didn't want to leave school.

The ethnic Lao in the lowlands didn't want to lose their land, so they tried to make a deal. They sent one or two members of a family to join the Communist forces.

The Hmong people were nervous and started asking each other, "What should we do?" Our elders tried to negotiate with the Pathet Lao and North Vietnamese, to find out how we could be neutral.

At first the Communists came to our villages to persuade the people with sweet talk. Then they came more and more often . . . more forcefully. They pressured young people to join their army. So the Hmong began fleeing. Maybe twenty-five to thirty percent of the Hmong stayed with the Communists. The rest of us joined the government side.

Before the war, there was very little fighting between Hmong people—occasional quarrels between individuals, but no weapons. But when the Vietnamese and Pathet Lao moved into our area, Hmong people began to fight to protect their land. I was seventeen when I joined the army, in 1961.

After four weeks of training, I went on several missions to fight the Communists in the Xieng Khoang area, on the Vietnam border. In one battle, my brother fired a machine gun and I handed him the ammunition. My cousin was the leader of our unit. In this particular battle, we caught the Hmong leader in the area who worked for the Vietnamese and Pathet Lao.

I started as a rifleman. But I was the only person in my unit who could read or write, so I had to measure map coordinates for firing the mortar—the small cannon.

Through 1962, the intensity of the fighting varied. I heard that a few Americans became involved, but I never saw any. At one point, a peace agreement was signed, but the North Vietnamese ignored it, and the fighting continued. During heavy fighting in 1964, we lost our village. So we were moved to Nam King, where there was a short airstrip. Our unit became part of a small battalion, five hundred soldiers, recruited from many villages and clans. We were like a national guard for our home area. Unfortunately, Laos has always been central for North Vietnamese strategy, because our land is in the center of Southeast Asia. Our territory was the main infiltration route for the Communist army into South Vietnam. North Vietnamese soldiers never stopped coming. Many of my relatives and friends were killed . . . women, kids. The Communists would go into villages and wipe out everyone who didn't support them.

We were fighting to protect our families, our traditions, our land. It wasn't until after I came to this country that I realized that our efforts saved a lot of Americans in South Vietnam. The Hmong were the only soldiers on the North Vietnamese infiltration route trying to stop the Communist soldiers and supplies from entering South Vietnam. Of course, we suffered horrible casualties, the highest of any ethnic group during the war. The Communists are continuing to persecute the Hmong even today because of our friendship with Americans.

During 1966–67, I was commissioned as a lieutenant and transferred to the headquarters base at Long Tieng. It was in the Phu Bia mountain area, a hundred miles north of the capital, Vientiane, and the Thailand border. Because of my ability to speak three languages, I was assigned to work with American pilots in old glider airplanes. We would fly over target areas and then radio for support from jet fighters.

Another one of my jobs was to help rescue downed American pilots in the Vietnamese border areas. If an American plane was hit while making a bombing run against Communist troops and supplies on the Ho Chi Minh Trail, our rescue team was called.

I was on continuous alert, twenty-four hours a day, seven days every week. On a rescue mission, I kept radio contact with the air base or friendly troops near the crash site. When a plane crashed, if a pilot was still alive, he would signal with a small radio or beeper that he carried. If the pilot was presumed dead, we still searched the jungle for the crash site. Often, while our "Jolly Green" helicopter hovered at a low altitude, we took fire from the Pathet Lao or Vietnamese. I could follow the tracer bullets zipping past our helicopter.

It was very dangerous flying at treetop level through the mountains, searching through dense foliage for a crash site. When we spotted a site, if there was a chance that a pilot was alive, we wouldn't hesitate to go in. Even if Communist troops were nearby. The American crew would tie me to a rope sling from the hovering aircraft and lower me down, between trees, right into the crash. At times I only found bodies. If a pilot was wounded, I would have to carefully carry him up on a rope sling. I am less than five feet tall, so I had to be very careful how I balanced the Americans, who were much taller.

There were times when I thought I would be killed. But my attitude was that I must try to rescue the people, even if I die. I didn't care if they were Hmong or American.

All together, our unit rescued around sixty downed American pilots and recovered a number of dead bodies, not only air-force people, but CIA and commercial pilots as well.

During that time, I got married to Mee Xiong, who joined me at Long Tieng. We didn't have a happy family, because she was afraid every time I went on a rescue mission. She was very young, only seventeen when we were married.

I met Mee after I was transferred to Long Tieng. My parents went through the traditional matchmaking process with her family. The town where Mee lived was a two-hundred kilometer journey away, through forests and mountains. No way I could see her except by helicopter or small airplane.

Mee agreed to marry me, but I was afraid her parents would object, so we eloped. Afterward, I visited the parents and made friends. As is our custom, I gave them a dowry gift of silver bars. The reason for the dowry is to assure the family that the husband will take good care of the daughter. There were hardly any divorces in our culture.

In 1968, when I married Mee, I was twenty-four years old. That is old for a Hmong, but I was a soldier and always moving around. My family was living in Long Tieng with many other people from my province who had to migrate because of the fighting. My first son, Nhia, was born in 1972. And our oldest daughter, You, was born the following year.

I continued doing rescues until the Americans left Laos in 1974. Then I went into the [Hmong] 2nd Brigade of the Lao army. With the rank of major, I helped to deliver supplies by aircraft to villages throughout northern Laos. There was a cease-fire treaty between the government and the Communists after the Americans moved out. A coalition government was formed. I hoped that there would be peace and we all could have normal life again. I had been in the service since childhood. I wanted time to develop my family. They were always worried about my safety and their own fate. We lost many relatives during the war. My brother was killed, shot right through the eye. I was lucky. Even though I was in a few aircraft crashes, I was never really hurt. One time our aircraft crashed in the trees, but we climbed down the branches with only minor injuries.

Believing that there would be peace, my dad bought some land at Ban Xon, near Long Tieng. I was going to plant some rice fields there. But in 1974, after the American bombing stopped and a coalition government began, the North Vietnamese started a surprise offensive in Laos. This was to prepare their supply lines to conquer South Vietnam.

The Hmong were thrown into the heavy fighting. We were at a terrible disadvantage. The Communists were receiving a tremendous amount of new weapons from the Soviets and China, and their armies had never demobilized. But many Hmong had already returned to their home villages. We only had eight battalions. All of our supplies had to go through the capital, where the coalition was being manipulated by the Pathet Lao. So American ammunition meant for us was being taken by the Communists.

When we realized that the Americans had abandoned us and we would get no more supplies after we used up what we had, even our most dedicated fighters began weeping and weeping. The Vietnamese and Pathet Lao didn't attack Long Tieng, but Hmong in many other areas fought for their lives until they ran out of ammunition.

By mid-1975, the Vietnamese and Pathet Lao dominated the country. I remember the morning that we left. General Vang Pao called a meeting with our last American adviser, Jerry Daniel. Vang Pao told Jerry, "For the past ten years, we have worked together. Now you are leaving us behind. Please help us with one more evacuation flight."

Then Vang Pao asked, "What are you going to do about Snoopy?" That was my radio call name. Jerry said, "Let me call Udorn [the American base in Thailand]." An aircraft was sent. A lot of people were fighting to get on. So I put my wife and two young children on that morning flight. I got out later, on the last flight. But our parents were left behind.

As the airplane left Laos, I sadly reflected on my life. When we landed at an air base in Thailand, I was still wearing my military uniform. The Thai police took my pistol. A couple days later, they checked if we still had any military clothes. They were very impolite and took everything.

My wife and I were destitute. In the confusion of trying to get out of Laos, I lost all of our money. My wife brought a few clothes for the kids, that's all.

The Red Cross gave us some clothes. Weeks later, when my brothers escaped across the Mekong River, they brought a small amount of money. So we went shopping for supplies in a nearby town. Thai police saw us shopping and made a plan. They locked us up in jail and said that they would kill us if we didn't give all our money to them.

The refugee camps were tough places. My younger brother, who was fourteen, became ill with meningitis and lost his hearing. I think that his illness motivated our family to hold together despite all the stress in the camps. At first there were three thousand Hmong refugees. But by early 1976, the number reached twelve thousand. People continued to flee across the Mekong. So we were moved to a new site, Ban Vinai, a few kilometers from the river.

Ban Vinai was all jungle. Each family lived in a small tent for six or seven people. We were very afraid, because we were in an unsafe border area. Food was brought by the Red Cross or the United Nations. But it was never enough, only rice with a small bit of meat or fish. We were very concerned about our small children's health.

Thai soldiers in charge of the camp robbed the refugees. Sometimes they raped women. They had guns, so they could do anything. We didn't know what was going to happen. The Thai wouldn't give any answers. We just sat there for months, waiting.

In December, a U.S. Immigration team came to interview us. They were accepting people who used to work with the Americans. A month later, camp officials brought forms for us to sign. They said, "You have been accepted to resettle in the U.S. Here is your sponsor's name and address."

Our sponsor was Saint Paul Lutheran Church in Menominee, Wisconsin. When we arrived, in March 1976, there was still snow on the ground. We arrived at night, cold and exhausted from the long trip. The next morning, I woke up and looked out the window. I shouted to my family, "Look at the white thing on the ground over here!" My children were four and three years old. We walked outside and followed behind a truck that was plowing snow. It was so much fun to play in the snow pile.

We came from a tropical climate, and even in the mountains it was never very cold. Our sponsors provided us with warm clothes and furniture for our house. Two days after we arrived, I started work. I was a janitor at the church for only $2.81 an hour. It was a shock, because as an officer in Laos I had a lot of responsibility to make life-and-death decisions. To come here to clean up a church was a real letdown.

My first day on the job, my face turned red. I felt that I was losing respectability. I got depressed and thought, "This will be the end of my life." But I had a second thought: "I have to do a good job, in order to feed my relatives."

The hardest obstacle was language. In Laos, I communicated with Americans, but with few words. We used mostly hand signals. Here, I had to learn new words and language concepts every day. For example, in Hmong language we don't have verbs in past tense. We say, "Last year I go," instead of "Last year I went." And I have a lot of problems with sounds like "th" and "ed."

Hmong language is so different from English, because it is tonal. Every vowel has eight different tones; each vocal inflection will give a word a totally different meaning. It's a lot like music.

The first month here, when my wife and I went into a supermarket we thought that people must buy something any time they go into a store. When I saw everybody standing in line and a girl running everything by a machine, that really surprised me.

In Laos, at Long Tieng Base, we had a generator for electric lights and telephones. When I looked in American store windows and saw household appliances, TVs, and coffee machines . . . everything looked so perfect.

But after six months, I started getting tired out by all the things we couldn't do. We could look in a store window any time, but it takes a certain amount of money to make your dreams come true. Even if you are a penny short, the store will not sell to you. I thought, "Stupid store."

My children adapted very quickly. They watch television and see advertising. When I took them to a store they asked for things I never heard of. I was very frustrated. We had no contact with other Hmong. We didn't know what happened to our relatives in the refugee camps, or if they would ever join us. Being among the first of our people in this country was a very lonely experience.

I remember our first full winter in Wisconsin, in 1976–77. I had bought a car. The first time that ice formed on my car window, I couldn't believe it. I ran into the house and put boiling-hot water into a coffee thermos bottle, then poured it onto the car window. I was shocked when it turned into big icicles.

I worked a year and a half as a janitor at the church, until I found a better job, at an iron foundry in La Crosse. My job was to break molds and inspect motors that the foundry made. But after four months, I was laid off.

After three months on unemployment, I decided that moving to a big city would be better for job and school opportunities. In mid-1978, we took the chance and moved to Saint Paul, Minnesota. There were only around ten or twelve Hmong families already there. None were close relatives. But a distant cousin introduced me to a subsidized housing project, where I registered for an apartment.

My first job in Saint Paul was as an interpreter in the Model City Health Clinic. It provided services for the black community and a large number of refugees. My wife began to study English for the first time. Even though her language ability was limited, she took a job on an assembly line at Control Data Corporation. Her factory makes electronics components for computers, microwave, and machines for hospitals.

More Hmong began arriving in the Twin Cities. There wasn't an adequate social-services system to handle the large influx. For most Hmong, coming to America was the first time they saw a modern society. They didn't have experience with rent or taxes. They didn't understand their telephone and electricity bills. Some people told me, "When we lived in wartime, the thing I feared was death. Now, in peacetime, the fear I have is bills."

I was very frustrated to see the refugees unable to cope with all these problems in their new life. I helped to organize a basic health project. Then, in the summer of 1978, I began working at the International Institute, a nonprofit community-service organization. We initiated a program to collect warm clothing and basic home needs for the refugees through the local churches. Even though we are of different religions, Christians and non-Christians, our humanitarian goal is the same. When the first Hmong families arrived, the church groups may have seen us as strange. But after they got to know us, we overcame any differences.

After 1980, when more Hmong arrived from the refugee camps, I was a translator for American sponsors. We had to show the refugees how to turn on electric lights, how to open and close curtains, and how to turn on water, because the Hmong had never seen a bathtub or shower.

Most Hmong men had been soldiers. It was depressing for them, after having a lot of responsibility, to enter a society where they don't speak the language and feel totally helpless. In war and as a refugee, it's day-to-day survival. You don't think about a year from now or long-term planning. But in American society, people need goals. People have to take the initiative to make decisions that will determine whether or not they get ahead in the future. For the Hmong, the freedom in this country is overwhelming.

The Hmong are amazed by the material conveniences and the speed and mobility of this society. We miss the mountains. Every time I go to the zoo, where there are bamboo and banana trees, I just stand there and stare as if in a trance.

We are fortunate that in the Twin Cities there are Americans at local universities who are familiar with Hmong culture. They have helped to create assimilation programs. For instance, in Saint Paul, when Hmong people are ill they see both American doctors and traditional healers. The two styles of medicine have become integrated. At local hospitals, American doctors recognize our need for both. Sometimes they allow us to bring herbs and do our ceremonies in their facilities.

If the shaman advises a sacrifice is needed, people buy a chicken, pig, or goat at the farmers' market. They bring it home to their basement for slaughter. Then, after the ceremony, they cook and eat it, so nothing is wasted.

There are close to twenty-five thousand refugees in the Twin Cities area, from Indochina, Eastern Europe, and Ethiopia. Around thirteen thousand are Hmong. I've learned that refugees are like tape recorders: they pick up good or bad habits, depending on the environment they're placed in.

We had a problem in Minnesota not long ago. Senator Durenberger wrote an editorial in the newspaper against Hmong refugees. It reflected the resentment, among some Americans, that the government has given handouts to the refugees and benefits that other citizens don't receive. And some people resent what they see as a foreign intrusion into their community.

Congress is already cutting back support for refugees. Most of the refugees have family members who worked with the Americans during the war. These people are still fleeing Laos, because of persecution by the Vietnamese Communists and Pathet Lao. If they are forced back, many will be shot. I find that hard to explain to Americans, who don't think about Asia. They only see people coming here and taking welfare. I try to tell the Hmong refugees, "If you want to see your relatives again, you have to get working."

Around fifty-five percent of the Hmong in Minnesota are still on some type of public assistance. Many don't have the education or skills to compete in the job market, and if they start at the bottom, they can't earn enough to support a large family. So they stay on welfare, which guarantees medical coverage.

I try to encourage the adults to go to school, even though many have never been in a classroom before, and find some type of job, even if it is menial. I say, "If you are on welfare, you don't have to get up early to go to work, but it's no hope. You don't know if your case will be cut off because of some technicality, so you worry all the time. It's better to try to work at some job for at least six months. If you do well, you can jump to a better job."

I encourage them, "Buy your own home" or "Start your own business." In Laos, Hmong were either farmers or soldiers. Only a few were merchants or had business experience. In Xieng Khoang there was a market, but not many people used it. Families grew their own food, made their own clothing. People in the clan helped each other without pay. Land in the mountains was free; we built our own homes. Most trade was done through barter. In Hmong society, to borrow money was disgraceful.

In Laos, if you know a merchant who trusts you, they'll say, "Okay, pay me when you can afford to." Any deal was a gold or silver exchange. In American credit system, you don't see cash—only piles of paperwork.

It is very difficult for Hmong refugees to adapt to these new terms. Very few have tried to open businesses, because they don't have training in financial management. There are not even any Hmong restaurants, because our traditional dishes are very simple: boiled sticky rice, a few types of chicken or pork, and boiled vegetables. Our soup is just vegetables with a little salt for flavor.

My cousin and I taught ourselves how to run a business. The Oriental Grocery Store in Saint Paul is owned by our extended family. Everybody earns a little bit of the profit, like buying stocks. My brother is the cashier, and other family members help out. My cousin is the manager. We used to have two stores. But, because one manager could not run both at the same time, we sold the store in Minneapolis.

Our store in Saint Paul is now turning a decent profit. If customers we know say, "I don't have money now; can I take some rice and canned items?," we write down their bill and give them a copy. If they don't pay in thirty days, we call them up and say, "Your payment is overdue."

Recently my wife's cousins opened a wholesale food-distribution business that supplies Asian food stores in the Midwest. One of the cousins earned a business degree in a local college. He uses a computer to manage their accounts.

I believe that it has been a mistake to send refugees into job training before they understand English or anything about the job market. The refugees become frustrated and confused. Some social-service agencies try to explain these things to new refugees. But others promote certain programs only because they want to receive government funding.

In 1981, Church World Service surveyed six hundred Hmong families in the Twin Cities. More than half said they would like to go back into farming. So I got together with CWS to find some land for a Hmong farm. We asked Hmong community leaders to choose ten men to attend a one-year program at Hennepin Vocational School. They learned all about farm machinery, herbicides and pesticides, irrigation systems, identification of plants, and specialty crops.

The Hiawatha Valley Farm Cooperative began in the summer of 1983. We found a thirteen-hundred-acre farm in Homer Ridge, around 140 miles southeast of Saint Paul. The hills and woodland areas reminded us a little of our home country. Initially, fourteen families—close to a hundred people, including fifty-seven children—were involved. Six families moved out to the land, and the others traveled back and forth from Saint Paul.

The first season, we planted crops and raised hogs, cattle and dairy cows. I became one of the farm's managers. To prepare for the job, I took courses in management, bookkeeping, computer programming, and small-engine repair through the Church World Service. And each Hmong project leader had an American partner to learn from.

The Church World Service provided the technical assistance, equipment, livestock, and financing. The CWS contract on the land was for two years. If the Hmong could become self-sufficient, we could have the whole farm. But if we did not succeed, everything would be returned to the CWS.

When we first moved in, the local people were very upset. They thought, "Why have the refugees received federal funds?" And they heard rumors that we were going to be wild and hunt everyplace and catch all of their fish. But I studied books on the hunting and fishing and traffic laws. I translated them into Hmong and showed that to local officials. I told them, "When we move to the farm, we want to be good citizens."

We began planting in late May, which was too late for many crops. But we put in a hundred acres of corn, thirty-three acres of cucumbers, and small plots of cabbage, broccoli, pumpkins, squash, cauliflower, and string beans. By the end of the season, most of these vegetables came up well. Everyone was working hard.

We earned a little over $125,000 selling crops and hogs. We invested that into repairs. We put a whole new floor in the barn, built a new fence, and repaired the gate. We remodeled the whole business, so we didn't have any money left over. I felt pretty good about our progress, so I moved my children from Saint Paul.

But right after our first harvest, in October 1983, we began having money problems. Checks weren't coming. The problem was that, even though the CWS had made a $100,000 down payment on the farm, the original owner hadn't paid taxes. The county went after him. He began to blame the CWS for his problems. The CWS director told us about this. We hoped that, after two years of assistance, we would become responsible for our own affairs, but we didn't know anything about business.

For extra income for my family while the children and I lived on the farm, my wife spent most of her time in Saint Paul, working at Control Data. She stayed with my cousin until the subsidized housing that we had earlier applied for came through. She moved into that apartment complex.

My four oldest children went to elementary school near the farm. The teachers thought the kids wouldn't know any English and prepared for the worst. But on the first day of school, they were impressed by how much the kids already knew. And the kids seemed to enjoy living in the countryside.

The following spring, we received permits to build five more houses and put in drainage and sewage systems to accommodate fourteen families. We went to work trimming the shade trees along the hillside. It took us a month to pick a couple tons of rocks out of the ground, to expand our planting area. But at the end of April, we received word from the state that because of the financial problems, we had to leave. I stayed until the kids finished out the school year in June 1984.

Before I left the farm, I got a call from the International Institute inviting me back to work. And I also received a call from Washington. The U.S. Department of Health and Human Services asked me to be a consultant.

For one year, I periodically traveled around the country helping to evaluate forty-seven different community-development programs for refugees. My fieldwork took me to Utah, Kansas, Michigan, and Washington State.

A Hmong community near Salt Lake City applied for a grant for farming. I spent a day at their farm. I estimated the cost to remodel their housing would be at least $50,000. Livestock supplies would be another $50,000. The land and buildings had already cost them $265,000. I figured their request for a $365,000 grant wouldn't work out, because the prices were so high and they were too far away from livestock suppliers and markets. These were things I learned from the failure of my first farm.

The Office of Refugee Resettlement saw that I was serious about developing the community's needs, so they sent me—through the Rural Development Network—to a four-week community-economic-development school in Davis, California. I was the only refugee among students from six different states. We each had a different goal, based on our communities' needs. My goal was to research farming and business.

When I returned to Saint Paul, the government sent a team of economic experts to the Twin Cities to conduct a four-week conference. They talked about housing, business development, and management, and how to use computers.

Then, in the summer of 1985, I joined a group of Hmong from other parts of the United States to attend a two-month course in Arkansas, to study small family farming. My main concern was to learn about business planning, tax calculation, and new trends in farm production.

At the school, I created a computer program to make accounting easier for small-business men with limited education. When I came home, I tried to set up a class to help Hmong businesspeople and consult for them. Some people were interested, but many weren't. They didn't want to open their problems to an outsider, and they think a computer is too difficult. They are afraid to take a chance, because they don't want to fail. Their self-image is very fragile.

For refugees like myself, with some education and knowledge of American language and culture, our adjustment is easier. But most Hmong refugees arrive without education . . . it's very hard for them.

At the Institute, we do a lot of counseling. The Hmong have many family problems, because of the conflict of cultures. Every stage of assimilation into this society has its own unique conflicts. Many problems among husbands and wives, parents and children.

In our home country, most of the heavy work is done by men. When Hmong come to this country and have to go on public assistance, the husband's role is diminished. Federal welfare rules add to the problem. To qualify for Aid for Dependent Children (ADC), you have to be a single parent. Every government check comes under the wife's name. So the husband feels that he doesn't have any usefulness.

The children go to school and become more independent. They don't listen to the father. This creates tension in the family, especially if the husband and wife don't get along. The husband feels frustrated, loses control. If he beats up his wife, she calls the police. They come right away. But if the refugees are robbed or are victims of some other crime, the police never come. So the husband feels that the police take the wife's side right away but don't care about stopping real criminals.

Some Hmong women would like to copy American women, who have much more social mobility and independence from their families. Back in the home country, I didn't have to do any cooking or housecleaning. Not only that—my wife had to wash my feet. But now I help do the laundry, cook, and do housecleaning, because my wife is working in the factory. That was a big adjustment for me, but I understood her situation. My children don't see me as less of a man because I help with housework. They understand what responsibility is.

My wife and I work at different places, different shifts. Sometimes we sleep in different rooms, because I don't want her to wake me when she comes home from work in the middle of the night. I have to get up at 6:00 A.M. to prepare for work and see the children off to school. I don't want to wake her, because she needs rest to manage as both a mother and a full-time factory worker. You can imagine the stress that this creates. Our children don't have enough time with us. In Laos, families are very close, because everyone works together as a team. That's the reason that, after the first farm failed, I decided that we should try again.

In 1985, I found a nice piece of land just outside Saint Paul, past White Bear Lake, near Hugo Township. It's seventy-three acres, with an old farmhouse and a big red barn. Ten families bought into the farm cooperatively. Some were members of the first farm; the rest were new members. We all used money that we saved from working. Some of the members worked in factories, and others in social services. At first we were really scared, because of what happened at the other place. We said, "The mistake we made at the other farm was that we depended on the federal dollar. We must pay the money from our own pockets and work very hard." To support our families, all of us kept our jobs in Saint Paul. We only took one state grant of $40,000 for equipment and building repairs.

The farm is in a very beautiful area, rolling hills, a few small lakes. The road leading to it is lined with pine trees. There's a lot of grazing land. One of our neighbors breeds thoroughbred horses.

One family lives on the farm full-time. The rest of us commute from the city. We have a schedule for members to do farm work, drive the truck, and deliver cucumbers, our main cash crop, to a produce company twenty-five miles away. The smallest cucumbers are worth the most, for pickles. Machines can't harvest those, so we pick by hand. At least twenty to thirty people from the twelve member families come out to work on the farm each day.

Besides the cash crops, every family has their own small plot for whatever vegetables they want to grow. My dad planted some eggplants.

Shoua Vang at the cooperative farm near White Bear Lake, Minnesota

We have ten acres of corn for everyone, and we have a big cauliflower-and-pepper field. Overlooking a small lake are a lot of raspberry bushes that are ripe in mid-July.

We now have six cows and a good-sized chicken coop behind the farmhouse. I'm doing research to see if it is economical for refugees to raise their own livestock. And I'm trying to research which Asian crops can be grown in Minnesota. I tried to grow rice and Chinese eggplant, which sells for $2.50 a pound in the store. But the outdoor growing season is only from June until August. So I'm trying to research how to use a greenhouse or hydroponics.

What we earn from the farm is not sufficient, but we use the income to supplement our other jobs. And the crops we take home reduce the cost of family groceries. If we can raise some chickens, pigs, and a fish pond, our food budget will be significantly reduced.

To be successful, we need people to weed and care for crops, especially during cucumber harvest. To help the refugee community, we hire Hmong from the city for part-time jobs. We split with them the profits on what they pick, fifty-fifty. And if they help with weeding, we give them seventy percent of the profit from what they pick. For example, this weekend one woman picked $101.60 worth of cucumbers per day. She took home $71.60 each day.

Our co-op members decided that for the first three years we are not going to touch any of the farm's profits. Instead, we are investing it to improve the farm. By not using federal or state dollars we have a lot more freedom.

I do the co-op's bookkeeping. The little hand-held computer system I invented at the Arkansas farm-management school makes accounting very easy. Keeping with Hmong tradition, I teach my children responsibility at a young age. I have them help me with the bookkeeping. Even my daughter Youa, who is nine, and my son Kou, seven, can help me to separate stacks of checks that I have to pay. They enjoy it as family activity and kind of a game.

I would like my children to advance in this society, but I am also concerned that, for the young Hmong in America, their traditional beliefs will never be strong. In Laos, we performed many ceremonies to pray for successful crops. Even here, we can't control nature. But we have better chance for success because of chemicals and technology. This alters traditional Hmong beliefs. The children become much more materialistic and don't pray as much.

On our farm, we set up a cultural center for Hmong to have the chance to carry on and learn our traditional ceremonies. In Hmong society, youngsters learn by watching older people and repeating their words. Hmong come to our center from Wisconsin, Iowa, California, even from France, because they live in cities and have no place in the countryside. They perform ancestral remembrances, and other ceremonies for good fortune or thanksgiving.

I would like to get some tropical plants for the farm, so that, when refugees come to visit, it will remind them of home. There are not many types of plants or trees in the Midwest that are similar to Laos. Only pine trees and oak are the same.

More than half of our refugee population are under eighteen years old. Many were born in refugee camps, maybe half were born here. If the Hmong kids stay in school, they do very well. The problem is early marriage. This is one aspect of the old culture that hurts our young people, particularly the girls.

In Laos, without medicine and modern conveniences, Hmong life expectancy was much lower and infant mortality was very high. So people married at a very young age. Because of the lack of educational opportunities and the need for help on the farm, girls seldom went to school. But I tell my daughters, "You should try hard at school. If you cannot get a degree, have at least two years of college." And Hmong community leaders in Saint Paul have tried to discourage kids from getting married too young.

But some Hmong teen-agers still want to get married. Some are as young as thirteen or fourteen years old. In the Saint Paul area, fifteen percent of Hmong students get pregnant during school age. For blacks school-age pregnancies are ten percent, and eight percent for Mexicans. Hmong still have the highest percentage.

My oldest daughter is thirteen years old. In a couple years, if a Hmong boy comes to me and asks to marry her, I will say, "Get out of here. I'm going to call the police." I want her to have a good education. My wife feels the same way.

I experienced many difficulties when I was young. That is why I encourage my children to study hard. I make a schedule for my two oldest. I say, "Okay, eight o'clock you have to be doing homework before going to bed early." If they like to watch TV, they can stay up a little bit longer than usual. But they keep to the schedule without me having to force them.

The kids also have responsibilities around the house. My wife works second shift five days a week, and on some weekends. When the children come home from school, she leaves for work. Our daughters take turns caring for the baby. Each day I make a plan for one of the older kids to be in charge of the house while the others do their homework. They share chores—each has a job to do. Even the five- and seven-year-old do some sweeping and mopping. But I let the older children share the harder work and rotate being the boss. If only one is always the boss, the others will never know how hard that responsibility is. If I find out that the youngest don't listen, I get after them.

My oldest son, Nhia, who is fourteen years old, loves to practice on the computer and read. His room is packed with boxes of books. Nhia was born in Laos. He was only four when we came to the United States. So he is very American.

NHIA VANG: I still remember when we left Laos. Our village was on a plateau between two hills. The Vietnamese were bombing us with rockets. They'd hit the hillside, but they never hit the village. I was glad that they weren't too good at aiming.

When we arrived in the United States, I thought the airports were really neat. All these big planes were flying in and out, tall buildings. In Laos, all the houses we lived in were just huts.

I started in kindergarten right away. At first the teacher might have thought that I didn't have too much interest: I just sat there, because I didn't know any English. But in first grade, schoolwork became quite easy, once I knew the language. All of the kids around me were American, so I learned faster.

We were the only Hmong family in Menominee. The American kids had stereotypes about Asian people, because of stories they saw on TV. But after a few days, we got used to each other and learned each other's names. Maybe if there were more Hmong around I would not have learned English very well. My family had to relate to the community around us. I also think it depends on your personality. If you are shy or self-conscious, you will never meet anybody. I've always believed, "Do it now. Why put it off for later?"

In America, children have a lot more independence from their parents. Hmong parents are pretty strict. My younger brother and sisters see all the kids playing outside, and they aren't allowed to go out as much. They have to study. They feel mad, but in the end it's all for their own good.

I was only five and my sister was four when my mother had our second sister. We helped take care of the baby. So at a young age we learned responsibility. My dad always tells us stories about when he was four or five and had to carry a baby and feed the pigs and chickens. Now we go out to our farm usually every second night during the summer, and on weekends during the school year.

At the farm, I help to drive the tractors and plant corn. Every year, flocks of birds come to eat our corn. My uncle asks us to shoo away the blackbirds so they won't eat the crop.

Last year, I was in the accelerated class at school. So was my sister. I'm going into the ninth grade and she's in the eighth. We competed in citywide and statewide competitions in computers, poetry, and essay writing. I won a poetry contest. The cash prize was twenty bucks. Then I won an essay contest. And I've won three computer competitions statewide, and one was national. The contests encouraged students to develop computer learning programs.

The national contest was in Washington, D.C., during July 1986. My dad had to be in Washington at the same time, to attend a refugee leadership conference. So we spent a week in Washington together and crunched everything in. I brought my fishing pole, hoping there was a lake or clean river. But I didn't see a single lake. And I didn't want to fish in the Potomac.

The computer competition was held at the University of Maryland campus. There were around three thousand students involved, representing forty-six states. The theme was "Tragedies and Triumphs." The computer programs we developed had to have those things involved.

So I thought, "What better way to symbolize both of these than a war." Because you have tragedy to begin with, and suffering, and in the end there's triumph, because it's over. I chose World War II, because it was the biggest war yet.

I developed a game like computerized chess, where you must use all of your abilities against the computer's. You could take any side, the Allies or the Japanese. You had battles on staging fronts, like the Pacific Ocean, Burma, or China. I think this was the only game that really got the judges involved.

In Minnesota, I do a lot of fishing and hunting. When you hunt, you have to kill; that is just a part of the cycle of nature. And I enjoy playing video games that involve adventure themes. So I put this factor into my game. There were always four choices a player could make, but only one choice would let you survive.

A lot of the American kids thought that you have to be nice to the judges—don't let them die in any games. But the judges loved my game. They gave it an "Excellent" rating. All of the students in the competition received memberships to the Historical Foundation in Washington. Any time I need historical data, I can just send them a letter.

I started learning computers two years ago, when I was in sixth grade. My school bought this Apple computer. Nobody knew how to use it. I went over and started reading the users' manual. I began programming all by myself.

In the whole state of Minnesota, out of forty thousand refugees, I'm the only student who has ever won any prizes. When my father and I visited the Center for Applied Linguistics in Washington, the lady who was interviewing us remarked, "It seems like you're paving the road for others." I told her, "Yes, but it's a lonely road. I want to pull someone along with me." If you're on the road all alone, it's not too much fun.

I have three cousins who have gotten married in their teens. I tried to tell them, "You're going to ruin your life. All you're going to do is go on welfare. You won't have a chance to fulfill your potential." That was two or three years ago. Now they can't go back to school, because they already have two or three children.

There are quite a few Hmong kids at my junior high school, but my sister and I are the only minority students in the advanced classes. This year, in ninth grade, I start college preparation. The curriculum goes at a faster rate of learning.

Last year, I was the assistant teacher in the computer classes. I've taken all the computer and electronics courses there are. I completed

Nhia and Youa Vang

around twelve of those courses in two years. I don't like to take breaks or study halls. I thrive on work and taking classes.

I'm always thinking about what will help me later in life. It's surprising that, out of all students, only my cousins and I—six of us—have advanced computer training. The American kids are all at the basic level. It's amazing that Hmong are paving the way into a new field.

In one electronics course, we had to build little robots. I kind of went overboard and built a big robot. My teacher and I attended a seminar for robotics at the university. I demonstrated mine. It had remote control, was about three feet tall, and could walk. I computer-programmed it and put in a voice synthesizer, so it could talk. For hands, it had screwdrivers. And I put magnets in its feet so that when it walked it wouldn't tip over. His name was Herbie.

His voice synthesizer had a thousand words. He'd introduce himself: "I'm Herbie. How are you?" His voice sounded totally robotic. He could distinguish words spoken to him and respond through a tape loop in his speaker. Like if someone asks, "How are you?," Herbie responds, "I am fine." Everyone enjoyed him.

I thought of Herbie as a living thing. My teacher at the college has him now. I was the only junior-high kid in the class. I just keep jumping all the courses at my school. I know six different computer languages now.

Last year, when I was twelve or thirteen, my father bought our first home computer. But I'm learning a lot from my uncle, who's studying electronics in college. At his house, everything is covered with circuit boards, electronic switches, and wires. He's always working on projects and has little gadgets everywhere. He's twenty-four years old and is graduating this summer.

My uncle became deaf in the refugee camp, from an illness. If my family pitied him, he would sit around feeling sorry for himself, watching television all day. He's the only man in our clan over twenty-two years old who isn't married. But he's quite an achiever.

Sure, I'm a workaholic. But I don't work so hard that I drop dead. I like to go fishing. In Minnesota there are so many lakes. And our family is pretty big. So at home there's always something going on with my brother and sisters.

A lot of Hmong kids are lost between cultures. I still get homesick when I hear my parents talk about life in Laos. I can't escape those feelings. But I don't let them overwhelm me.

At home, I speak Hmong with my parents. But my younger brother and sisters, who were born in America, really don't have much of an idea of what Hmong is. We try to teach them the rituals and culture, but slowly they lose their identity. Their introduction to the world is through TV—"Gobots," "He Man," "Mr. T," or "Punky Brewster." They want to be like that.

My cousin, who is fifteen, dresses all punk and goes skateboarding everywhere. He can't decide if he is Hmong or American. He's going to get into a lot of trouble that way, because he can't be either one. He's a small kid, but he's got the eyes, the gaze, to make you feel unsettled.

He doesn't have the Hmong sense of responsibility and kindness. His younger brothers and sisters are all like him. In most Hmong families, the oldest son inherits everything from the father. As the father gets older, the oldest son is supposed to look after the family affairs. The younger children always look up to him. If the oldest child is a rebel, the others will follow suit.

The oldest son is also responsible for preserving the ancestor ceremonies. My father has passed that on to both myself and my younger brother. If anything ever happens to me, Kou will be responsible to carry on the tradition to our children.

I don't feel confused about who I am. Being American is great. I enjoy going to football games, eating hot dogs, and cheering the team on. But with my relatives I go to ceremonies at the farm. I know that I am Hmong. I have black hair and speak a certain dialect. But my ideals are American.

AN EXECUTIVE
DECISION

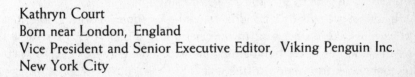

Kathryn Court
Born near London, England
Vice President and Senior Executive Editor, Viking Penguin Inc.
New York City

P eople violently uprooted by war, revolution, or nature's wrath have contributed heart and grit to America, as new waves of immigrants arrive each generation. But from the days of the first English colonists in 1607, among the adventurous voyagers have been a large number of well-to-do businesspeople seeking to expand their fortunes. Intellectuals and inventors have been lured by the promise of an experimental society free of rigid Old World convention. Others have sought to exploit a dynamic marketplace, open to new ideas and innovations.

New developments in transportation and technology are reshaping the world into a more homogeneous "global village," especially in communications and other intellectual professions. Academicians, scientists, and artists from all parts of the globe have come to study and work in America. Among them are the cream of Great Britain's universities and thousands of top scientists and engineers who enjoy higher pay and more stimulating facilities in the United States. And some of Britain's most distinguished knights of commerce have joined the legions of Wall Street's corporate raiders.

Kathryn Court, at thirty-nine, is one of the most brilliant and successful literary editors in New York. She arrived from London as an unknown junior editor in 1976. After struggling to land a job in the fiercely competitive book-publishing market, she quickly moved up the corporate ladder to become the editorial head of Viking Penguin's U.S. company.

But, unlike most foreign-born executives, who migrate in pursuit of wealth and become obsessed with "making the deal," Kathryn was motivated at first by love.

I came to New York in the fall of 1976. It was a very emotional decision. I had been living in England, married to a student doctor, and hadn't been very happy. In London, I met a young American named Jonathan Coleman. A friend recommended that he come see me because I was editing fiction at Heinemann, a British publishing house, and he worked at an American publishing company.

Jonathan was visiting London for only a couple of weeks. We met three times during his trip, for lunches and a drink. After he returned to America, he started bombarding me with letters saying, "I really want to come back to London to see you."

It was all rather awkward because I was married. But Jonathan persevered. Finally he said, "If you really want me to go away, tell me. I'll understand." I didn't know what to say. We finally agreed that he should come back to London. We spent a week together. A couple of weeks after he left, I decided to go to America.

I said yes mostly because of my attraction to Jonathan. But it also had to do with my dissatisfaction with my life in London. My husband was a very dedicated student doctor. He spent a lot of time away from home, undergoing grueling training. I don't think that is an excuse for what happened between us, but it made our relationship more difficult.

I left England very quickly after I made my decision. I said yes to Jon in October and arrived in New York in November. I didn't stop to think about it. I was twenty-seven years old, and it just felt like the right thing to do. I didn't realize how difficult it was going to be.

Jonathan was a publicity writer at Alfred A. Knopf, Inc., and wasn't earning very much at all. His salary was only around $11,000 a year. I wasn't earning very much at my job in London, either, and I was covering most of the living expenses while my husband was in medical training.

What I found especially attractive about Jonathan, which I've come to see in many Americans, is his fantastic intensity, a real drive. My first husband had some of that. But deep down, most English people don't really admire ambitious character. They believe that people who are too concerned with success are not fully rounded. In English eyes, that makes them lesser people. That is hard for New Yorkers to comprehend, because life here is based on setting goals, achieving, and moving up.

When I first arrived in New York, it was quite difficult on a professional level. It was just the opposite in terms of the people I met, who were enormously kind and generous. I was very involved in my romance with Jonathan. But I had to find a job to help pay the rent on our apartment, which we could barely afford. We were living on East 35th and Park Avenue, in a nice old prewar building.

My problem was with Immigration. Because I left London so quickly, I came on a tourist visa. When I started looking for work, I had to explain my immigration status any place I applied, since any potential employer would be required by law to undergo the complicated process of filing specific work-permit papers for me with the Immigration Service.

I was offered two jobs in publishing that I wanted. When both employers discovered how difficult the immigration process was, they withdrew their offers. I was much too junior a person for them to invest a lot of lawyer's time and expense. I understood their position, but it was pretty distressing. I had no money and really needed a job.

Before I arrived, Jonathan borrowed our first two months' rent from his father. He was living in a dismal apartment on 93rd Street. His mother told him, "If you bring that girl into your apartment, she'll go right back to London." [Laughs]

When we moved in, it was unbelievable. There was nothing but a bed, one chair, two knives, and two forks. We had to start from scratch. It all seemed very exciting.

I grew up in a middle-class suburb just outside London in the years following the war. My mother, who came from a working-class Wiltshire family, and whose own mother had been in service, was a happily married woman and traditional housewife. In those days, most women only worked if there wasn't enough money in the family. She did that on occasion.

My father, who was born in Vienna, a Jew who had converted to Catholicism in the mid-'30s, came to England in 1939 via Holland. He was the son of a very successful father. Very disciplined, with a lot of demands put upon him. My father was much less ambitious. During his career he never wanted to be managing director of the company he worked for. As an engineer, he took work that paid well and interested him, but he was equally concerned about spending time with his family.

I was born in December 1948. Both of my parents were very loving toward my sister, Jo, and me. They were very supportive as we were growing up, and they spent lots of time with us. I had a lovely childhood.

I suppose that the war had a great effect on my parents. After surviving the bombing of London and suffering losses in their families, people were perhaps more reflective in the postwar period. My father lost quite a few members of his family. He and his parents were lucky to have got out of Austria. My father always felt very grateful to England. He never expressed a desire to return to Austria.

I suspect that, for my parents, having a happy marriage and two healthy children was most of what they wanted out of life. Adventure for my father was in foreign travel. He would take my mother, my sister, and me on these extraordinary automobile trips through Europe every summer. We went all over the place . . . Austria, Germany, Yugoslavia, Portugal, Spain. Many of the fondest memories of my childhood are of those trips, which I can remember vividly. Those trips were a real goal every year. We planned them together . . . maps would be laid out on our living-room floor. We'd mark out our routes with red pencil. But none of our overnight stops were ever booked in advance.

It was always an adventure. My father worked overtime to save extra money, and my mother would take a part-time job. The joy of those trips is still a part of me. I continue to have an absolute love of going somewhere new. I felt the same about going to live in New York.

My parents encouraged my sister and me in our schoolwork, sending us both to a Dominican convent school from the age of five to the age of eighteen. But they never said, "You *must* go to university." There was no pressure. When I decided to apply for university, their basic view was "That's fine. If you want to continue your studies, fine." Jo wanted to attend secretarial college. That was fine, too.

In a funny sort of way, after I had grown up a little bit I would've welcomed a little bit of pushing. Someone to challenge me: "Why don't you do this?" Or "Why don't you do that?"

In England, going to university is a very strict, selective process. We had to apply to six places and hope for interviews. If all six universities turned a student down, that was pretty much the end of it. You had to wait another year to apply, or give up on the idea. A lot of students were refused. And it's not like in America, where there are a lot of community and junior colleges. The English are very snobbish. It's hard to get a good job if you don't attend the "right" schools.

I went to a university in the Midlands, the University of Leicester, which has a very good English department. I attended Leicester from 1966 to 1970. Although I was a diligent student and did well, I didn't take advantage of opportunities to do more than what was required. To take more classes seemed too restrictive. I was trying to get away from the school mentality.

I met my first husband, David Court, on the last day of my first year. I was waiting for a friend. We were going home together. David was sitting on a wall, reading a *Playboy* magazine. It turned out that we were going to the same destination. His family lived very near my parents. He was leaving Leicester to study at a big teaching hospital in London. I spent some time with him that summer. The next school year, we were constantly going back and forth from London to Leicester to see each other. When I graduated in 1970, David was very involved in his medical studies and we were making plans for marriage.

I graduated without any job prospects. One day my mother said to me, "You can't just hang around the house complaining. You've got to find a job." So I went to an employment agency, thinking I'd find something temporary.

The woman in the office said, "Well, there's a job open in the investment department in a huge insurance company in the City." I said,

"I don't think that I'm very qualified." But she said, "Why don't you go for an interview?" I applied at the bank, and they offered me the job. Becoming an investment analyst—researching mining companies—was quite a challenge, because I knew nothing about economics.

The City of London in the early 1970s was, as now, a very male business environment. Very proper, very sexist. The men in the office had to wear white shirts. I enjoyed the work, but I felt uncomfortable in a department of thirty or so people where there was only one other woman. I decided to leave after six months and took a short secretarial course.

I began job hunting in earnest and saw a funny little ad in a London newspaper; I think it was the *Times*. The ad said something like: "Mainstream English publisher wants graduate with absolutely no experience." I thought, "That's strange. There must be a typo in the ad." I dialed the phone number. The first question the woman asked me was "You don't have any experience, do you?"

I said, "No, I don't have any. Except I had a job at an insurance company." She said, "No, no, no, no. That's fine. You can come in for an interview."

I had three interviews, actually, at that publishing house, Heinemann. Their choosiness was incredible, considering the pay they were offering was only £900—a year. That's around $2,250. The job was as editorial secretary for the managing editor of the company. One of the three interviews was in an Italian restaurant. They wanted to see if I could eat my spaghetti properly!

English publishing in the seventies expected you to come from a certain background. If you didn't have a degree from Oxford or Cambridge, that was a real problem. In my first interview at Heinemann, they asked me, "Do you have a private income?" They meant "Do you have family money?" In other words, "Do you have to live on this pathetic salary we're offering?" I found that to be pretty insulting.

When they finally gave me the job, I found out the mystery of the ad. The company was part of a publishers' training program, to which they contributed and from which they received grants. If they hired someone with no experience, fifty percent of the salary would be reimbursed by the program. So my salary only cost them £450 a year, or $1,100. [Laughs] I was expected to work hard full-time, plus make China tea with fresh lemon every afternoon. My boss had been through a couple of secretaries within the year before I was hired. But she and I got on all right, and I enjoyed my work.

I married David in 1972. We moved into an apartment in central

London, a short bicycle ride from my job. David was receiving a grant that just covered his studies, and I had that miserable salary. But we never felt terribly poverty-stricken. London was very inexpensive in those days. We were only paying £11 rent each week, around $105 a month. Our apartment had two bedrooms, an eat-in kitchen, and a nice sitting room with a view over gardens in the back.

After one year as a secretary at Heinemann, I was promoted to an editorial job. I was assigned to edit mostly mainstream women's fiction. I had an author named Constance Heaven who wrote romantic novels. I didn't have much training, so I learned by experience. It was a frustrating, overly paternalistic place to work. Young people weren't encouraged very much or taken very seriously.

The attitude toward women in the office was quite patronizing: "These women are in these jobs waiting to find a husband. Once they get married, they'll leave. So we really don't want to take them too far into the company."

The women's movement, as we know it in America, hadn't really taken root in England, at least not to the same extent. It still seems far behind America, though not living there may give me a skewed view. One of the things I love in America, in New York particularly, is that women can be financially independent; we can make our own choices. I look at some of my friends and relatives in London, who are still having a horrid time. They can't find job opportunities that are more than basic.

Before I came to live in New York, I had been in America once before. I came on a three-week holiday when my husband was finishing a medical training course in Arizona in 1974. I found America especially surprising because I grew up without a television. My English friends always had a romantic view of America. They'd tell me about the American movies they'd see. Because I was unfamiliar with all these images, it was a very fresh experience for me to come here.

I remember thinking that New York was stunningly beautiful. And the West was quite extraordinary . . . the Arizona desert, southern California, and Yellowstone Park, in Wyoming. I truly loved it. But I never thought that I would live here.

After I made my decision, I remember Jonathan calling me from New York and saying, "I've found us a place to live." I asked, "How much is it?" He said, "Four hundred dollars." I said, "Oh, my God, you're going to bankrupt us. How are we going to pay for this?"

Nineteen-seventy-six was the year when Penguin, a paperback publisher in London, bought The Viking Press, an American hardcover company in New York. The two companies merged. When I was job hunting, a person at Viking said, "We can use somebody to improve the relationship between the Penguin editorial people and those at Viking and make it function better." It seemed like a ridiculously difficult job. However, I was desperate for work, and the people were very nice. So I took the job.

When I was hired, in the spring of 1977, I was the only British employee in the New York office, which was run by Americans. Subsequently one or two other English people went to work there. The company agreed to file for all of the immigration papers I needed to work legally in this country.

Living in New York didn't feel like being in a strange place. This country and England share so much history and tradition. Other ethnic groups may tend to cluster closer together, because of cultural and language differences. But from the time I arrived, I've felt quite at home. And there were things in English society I was happy to get away from—the kind of snobbiness; the English are very class-conscious.

One of the things that amazed me when I was job hunting here was that nobody asked about my university degree. And when the subject came up, no employers emphasized, "*Where* did you get your degree?" In this country, people's main concern is "Can this person do the job? And do it very well? If they can't, we'll fire them."

In England, there are very strict rules about how an employer can or cannot fire people. A very complicated process of verbal warnings and written warnings. Then six months must go by before re-evaluating the employee. So America is better for most people, because they are given the chance to prove themselves. People can accomplish an awful lot when their employer has confidence in them. In a purely working environment, people here have a better shot to be what they *think* they want to be. It's a great country for confidence building.

In my job at Penguin, I reported to Richard Seaver, the editorial director. After a few months, I said to Dick, "I'm really pleased to be working here, but I would like to be an editor." Without hesitating, Dick said, "Yes. That's fine."

The responsibility of a paperback-book editor is to buy the rights of books published by hardcover companies. One of the first books I purchased was called *One L* [*One L: An Inside Account of Life in the First Year of Harvard Law School*]. It was the first book by a writer named Scott Turow. *One L* is the story of a young man at Harvard studying to be a lawyer. I loved it. I had no experience of Harvard Law School, but the book made me think, "This is what it must be like." A wonderfully lively story about friendships and competition. It didn't matter that I wasn't brought up in this country, because the quality of the story was universal. It became very successful in paperback. A very lucky start for both Scott and me.

I began in American publishing by choosing books that I found to be fabulously well written, books that I really wanted to finish reading. And I had some projects that just seemed like basically good ideas. For instance, an agent came to me with a little self-published book about the importance of reading aloud to children. The author had already sold twenty thousand of this booklet out of his garage in Massachusetts for $2 each.

I thought, "Of course, it's wonderful to read aloud to your children." I read the book and the tone was wonderful, it was very nicely done. So I got in touch with the author and said, "Can you expand this into a full-size book for Penguin?" He said yes. The first edition of *The Read-Aloud Handbook*, now going into a second revision, has sold more than a half-million copies.

I really enjoyed being a junior editor at Penguin. My professional experience in England was helpful, and I also had terrific colleagues. Within the space of two years, every one of those editors who were more experienced than I had left the company. One went to law school, one got a better job somewhere else—they all disappeared. Finally, I was in an office next to Dick Seaver. Then he announced that he was going to leave.

I went home that night and said to Jonathan, "God, Dick's leaving." And Jonathan's first words were "Apply for the job." I said, "C'mon, I've only been in this country for two years. And I'm only thirty years old. I've never worked in paperback before. I don't think I'd get the job."

Jon said, "It's true, you probably won't get it. But you've got to show that you're serious."

The man running Viking Penguin was Irving Goodman. I went into his office and asked if I could have the Penguin editor-in-chief job. He said there were a lot of people he wanted to talk to, but he asked me to run the editorial department until he made a decision. So I ran the department for three or four months while he was looking. Then one day Irv called me into his office and said, "Kid, the job is yours." I nearly died of panic.

I felt a bit shaky when I started, but after six months of being rather nervous, I had some wonderfully successful projects. I hired some very bright, energetic people, and we had a ball. We made that company grow from a tiny trade paperback house with a few American books into a major American trade paperback publisher.

I'm a firm believer in having people working for you who are as good as or better than you are. If you're lucky enough to hire them, first of all, as head of the department you get all the credit. [Laughs] But I learned a tremendous amount from my colleagues.

I'm quite an instinctive person in everything I do. I think that too many people analyze things to death, whether it be at their jobs or in their relationships. I've trusted my instincts. And I've always had confidence in the people who've worked for me.

It's not that I've never had problems. Three times I fired people who I'd hired. I believed it was the right decision in each case, but it was without a doubt the most difficult part of my job. And there have been some projects I believed in that didn't work out. But, overall, I've had terrifically good luck with my colleagues and our publishing choices.

I remember an editorial meeting where one of my editors, Gerry Howard, wanted to do a book called *More Fun with Dick and Jane*. All of my colleagues at that meeting immediately understood what that was. They began chuckling. I said, "Well, who are Dick and Jane?" [Laughs] Gerry explained, "They are characters that all American schoolchildren learn to read by." Then he showed me this humor book, where Dick and Jane have become West Coast yuppies.

I told Gerry, whose opinion I valued, "It seems very funny. If you think it will work, we should do it."

I tended to rely on my colleagues' judgment in areas of American culture. Having grown up without a television in my home, I didn't have a stereotypical view of America. I didn't come here influenced by Hollywood. And I didn't know much about American sports and entertainment personalities, or comic strips that kids enjoy. When someone like Chuck Verrill, an editor who is very knowledgeable about sports, would say, "I've got this great baseball book about this great baseball player," I would go completely blank and say, "Who the hell is that?" Everybody at the meeting would laugh and say, "You don't know who Willie Mays is?" I would respond, "No, I don't." And they would tell me, "He's a famous baseball guy from the fifties."

I relied a lot on my colleagues' judgment because I believe most successful books begin as projects that editors really believe in. My lack of cultural knowledge forced the editors to have to work hard to convince me about a book. If they did a good selling job and said, "This is a wonderful, brilliant book, we can sell the hell out of it," I would say, "Fine, let's do it."

It all comes down to choosing books that we feel strongly about. I like to do funny books. Humor is subjective, I know, but sometimes my colleagues would say to me, "Are you getting carried away? What's funny about this?" But it wasn't my job to take a poll of the company. You have to trust your own instincts.

In our business, the key to success is to get people to notice a book. Every year, an awful lot of good books are published that, for good and bad reasons, don't get enough attention. From this perspective, I try to make sure that all of my books are something that everybody involved can be proud of, and that all of us have done our best possible job for.

I had a colleague, Martha Kinney, who listened to a radio show called "A Prairie Home Companion" all the time. One day she came to me and said, "Atheneum has just published a collection of pieces by a man named Garrison Keillor, who you must have heard on the radio."

I said, "No, I'm afraid that I haven't heard of him." She said, "Well, there's a fifty-thousand-dollar floor bid in the paperback auction for his book." I told her, "That's quite a lot of money for a collection of pieces." She asked me to take the book home and read it.

I started reading the book, bit by bit. I thought, "This guy is fabulous. We have to publish this." So Martha and I went to Irv Goodman's office. We wanted to clear a hundred thousand bucks to buy Keillor's book. That was a lot of money at the time. Fortunately, Irv happened to be "A Prairie Home Companion" listener. He said, "Yes, I love that show."

Another publisher had made the floor bid in the auction. So we followed with a bid of $70,000. Nobody else came in, including the floor holder, and we got the book. We published Keillor on the Penguin list, and the book did very well.

Garrison decided on a new project, *Lake Wobegon Days*, and we acquired it for Viking and Penguin. I loved that book, because it deals with the most basic concerns, like marriage and raising children, with wonderful humor, but a real edge. It seems to me that Keillor's great gift as a writer is to write about the little epiphanies in all our lives. I was thrilled by Garrison's success.

One of the big differences I've seen between English and American culture, especially in New York, is that people here are much more obsessed about work. The British are much more reserved and loath to talk about their emotional life. In America, the first time you meet people, they will sit down at dinner and tell you more than you ever wanted to know about who they are and what the state of their marriage is. I find that kind of openness refreshing.

I believe the reason that many Americans are so open is because from a very young age it's instilled in people to stand out, to be successful. I've met a lot of people in New York, compared to my experiences in

London, who want to be famous. That motivates them to say to some-body they don't know, "I want you to understand who I am. Not just who I am on the outside, but who I am as a person."

I don't think the British really understand American ambition. When I visit England, I don't see quite the same energy and drive I'm used to in New York, which often makes people here excel at what they do. It gives them an edge that a lot of English people in the same types of jobs don't have. It's not that they don't have the ability. Work is simply not considered such a high priority.

There is a major problem for English people, like myself, and perhaps other Europeans who move to America, which can be quite upsetting. I don't just mean the growing social problems that we have in New York, which are difficult for everyone. It's more the discrimination among professionals toward others who aren't as successful. That upsets me. Partly because I find that so impolite, but more so because too much respect is given to those who are successful, as if that automatically makes them super people. What does that say about real friendship?

In New York, competitiveness in the workplace is quite intense. In the larger publishing companies, the pressure to be profitable is very great. Most editors have their jobs on the line every season. And in this town there aren't too many of those jobs around.

At the lower levels of publishing, there are few financial rewards, and New York is a very tough, expensive place to live. Many people move into the city to establish their career without family nearby. If they earn even a middle income, they can't afford a decent-size apartment. To succeed, a tremendous amount of work is involved. It is easy to develop a kind of tunnel vision, which puts people under a tremendous amount of pressure.

Publishing is much less glamorous than it is perceived to be. If people don't want it very badly, they move on. That leaves the rest of us working very energetically in our jobs.

I've sometimes woken up at six o'clock in the morning to start reading manuscripts, gone into the office at 8:30 A.M., and stayed until 7:30 at night, then gone to a business dinner with an author or literary agent, come home at midnight, and been up again the next morning to be in the office early. I did that for years. And still do, to some extent.

One reason I was able to withstand the pressure was the confidence my husband, Jonathan, had in me. He was amazingly kind and sup-portive. When I was going through a difficult period, he would tell me, "You'll get over these problems. Let's talk about what's bothering you." Without his kindness, I couldn't have done what I accomplished.

Jonathan also rose quickly through the book-publishing ranks. As an editor, he moved from Knopf to Simon and Schuster, where he quite quickly became a senior editor and member of the editorial board. All by the age of thirty. That was quite an achievement professionally. But one day he said to me, "I've had enough of publishing. I want to work in television." And I remember responding in a very English sort of way: "Why would anybody offer you a job? You never had any training in television." Well, he was determined and he got a job with CBS News. The offer was $10,000 less than he was currently making, but he wanted to accept it and I agreed.

After two years at CBS, he decided to write a book based on a crime story he had researched and done a piece on. Again, we talked about it, because it was unlikely he would be able to get more than a modest advance. I had my worries about it, but I believed in him. For almost two years, that's pretty much what he did, seven days a week, mostly inside our small apartment. I mean, we were both working excessively hard.

At Penguin, my department continued to have great success. In my five years as editor in chief, our sales volume increased fivefold. We bought a number of very good American books. Some became big sellers. It was quite heady—wonderful, actually. I can see why people who do well in these kinds of jobs become intoxicated. We had a fabulous time.

Peter Mayer, the chief executive of the Penguin group in London, kept looking at us and saying, "These people are doing amazingly well." In January 1984, Peter came to New York to evaluate what was going on at Viking, and decided to make some changes in the company.

He called me into his office one day and said, "Listen, I've got some wonderful news for you. I want you to be editor in chief of Viking, in addition to continuing to run Penguin." I was stunned, but I had learned from previous experience. I said, "Peter, I'm not sure that I want to do that." He said, "Okay, think it over. You have until tomorrow afternoon to give me your answer."

He made it quite clear that if I didn't want the job, he would find somebody else, and Penguin would also be run by the new person. The reason he wanted one editor in chief for both imprints was because of a trend in publishing to make both hardcover and paperback deals for certain books. That was one of the main reasons why Penguin bought Viking in 1976.

Though I understood his rationale, what caused me to hesitate before I accepted the promotion was that we were talking about an enormous number of books. For example, in 1986 I was responsible for six hundred books. That included two hundred hardcover originals and four hundred paperback books, including some two hundred imported Penguin titles. I'm very keen on detail. I like to see every book jacket, every publicity campaign scheduled, all the reviews. And I had to give the okay for the acquisitions, I signed every contract.

I was only thirty-five years old when I took over as editor in chief for all the adult books at Viking Penguin. In retrospect, I think that I made a rather female mistake. I never felt that I could say, "I can't do this much work." I felt absolutely compelled to prove that I could do the job.

Maybe a man would've said, "This job, the way it's structured now, can't be done by one person. We'll have to reallocate certain responsibilities." But my initial reaction was "I've been given this prestigious but perhaps undoable job. Nevertheless I'll prove that I can do it." I don't know if that's a female response, or the response of somebody who never had that big a job before and couldn't come to grips with how immense it was.

In publishing, there are quite a few women in top positions, particularly in editorial jobs. Many people consider publishing to be a female-oriented business today. Traditionally, women have accepted lower salaries in higher-level jobs than men would accept, and salaries in publishing are low across the board. The range for senior editors at most houses is between $35,000 and $60,000 a year. But junior editors begin at much lower salaries, barely subsistence in this town.

Part of my difficulties when I took over at Viking was trying to merge two completely separate editorial departments. There were a lot of personality differences between the Penguin and Viking editorial staffs. When I look back, I don't know how I managed. The constant pressure did take its toll on my personal life. Both Jonathan and I were so consumed by our work that we lost touch with each other.

In any marriage or close relationship, pressure has to shift so that one person or the other can play a more supportive role. We were always supportive of one another, but not in all the ways we should have been. When both people can't give any support, the relationship falls apart. I've often talked with Jonathan in retrospect: "After eight years of living together, why didn't we realize our lack of communication? How did it happen?" The intensity of our career pattern made us lose track of everything else—and ourselves. Our work became like tunnels that we couldn't escape from.

The amount of time I had to put into my job, combined with the intense concentration that Jonathan was putting into his book project, led to our separation. I can't blame his book for what happened to us, but that period definitely contributed to the end of our marriage. The two incidents that crystallized our decision to separate—at least on my part—seem kind of funny now.

One evening I came home from the office quite late. I was always working late. It was after 8:00 P.M. I walked into the apartment and fell over a bicycle that was in the hallway. It wasn't mine or Jonathan's. I came into the living room to find this girl sitting at the word processor with Jonathan.

I walked into the bathroom and found someone's laundry dripping all over. I said to Jonathan, "Whose laundry is this?" He said, "It's Susan's," or whatever her name was. She was a student he was paying to do some of his typing. We had a launderette in our building's basement, and she didn't have one where she lived, so she washed her laundry in our basement and hung it in our bathroom. I mean, we had a tiny apartment; the place was complete chaos.

I had piles of manuscripts that I took home from work. I often spent all weekend at home editing and reading through my authors' work. The pace that Jon and I were keeping was crazy. I don't know how we stayed together as long as we did. [Laughs] It was only because we had an absolute desire to make our relationship work.

The last straw came on a Sunday. I told Jonathan, "We're living such an uncivilized life now. This is ridiculous. I'm going to cook Sunday dinner. We're going to have a homemade meal."

I went to shop and came home to make roast lamb with all the trimmings. I spent the afternoon cooking it all. As we were about to have the meal, I looked around the apartment and said to Jonathan, "There's no place for us to sit and eat."

The dining-room table was covered with the computer. The sofa was covered with interview tapes. And there were pages of transcripts and manuscripts everywhere. If you can imagine, we had this dinner sitting on our bed.

I said to Jonathan, "This is it. I've had enough of this sort of life." That was the moment I realized, "We must really be mad to live this way. We can't even sit down as husband and wife and enjoy a meal."

Our marriage ended in June 1985. The irony is that, toward the end, when people would look at us, they would say, "Oh, what a wonderful couple. Kathryn is the editor in chief of Viking Penguin. And Jon's book is doing so well and he's made quite a bit of money at it. That's great." Everybody thought that we were so successful. We had everything that people in this town are scrambling to achieve. Jonathan's book, *At*

Mother's Request: A True Story of Money, Murder and Betrayal, was a best seller, and it was made into a CBS television miniseries.

By the end of our relationship, I felt very sad. I had been hooked into the American dream, in a way, but I didn't have the experience to know what I was doing. I was so bowled over by my achievements, as if they were terribly important. I needed to learn how to understand when to stop it. How to say, "I don't want to have this sort of life. I don't care if I don't make this much money. I don't care if my friends think I'm a failure."

After Jonathan and I split up, I eventually came to terms with my feelings. I decided that, even if I worked twenty-four hours each day, my job wasn't doable by one person. In early 1987, I decided that I wanted to spend more time with my authors and less time sitting in long meetings worrying about things like a new union contract or how our warehouse distribution was working out. And I was also sitting on the company's executive committee and board of directors. These are all very important in running a successful business, but I decided that I no longer wanted to deal with all that.

And I had become involved with a man named Michael Stephenson. He decided to move to New York from London so that we could live together. We had been at the same university together in England. But after not seeing each other for many years, we bumped into each other quite by chance in an elevator in San Francisco. He was the publishing director of Guinness in London. We were both attending the American Book Sellers' Association meeting.

I feel very strongly that I won't make the same mistakes as before. I don't want my job to destroy my relationship because I'm working twenty-four hours a day. I'm a person who wants to have a real life with someone else. Just the chance to go to a movie together in the evening without feeling guilty—something that simple sounds ridiculous, but after years of constantly working, the ordinary luxury of going out together or having friends over for dinner seems so precious.

My parents have visited me in New York at least three times, and I go back to London on business a few times a year. So I have a close relationship with my family, even though we live so far away.

After eleven years in this country, I suppose I still consider myself as being British. But not terribly strongly. Perhaps I don't identify completely with England because my father wasn't born there and during my childhood many of my relatives spoke German and I wasn't brought up on English food.

I have two English friends in New York who I met through my job, and I had an English landlady. But I don't seek out the company of other English people, even though there is a large English population here. I enjoy spending my time with American friends.

When I decided to step down from the top editorial job, I wasn't sure that Viking would be receptive. I had a feeling that they would say, "We employed you to do this particular job. If you're not prepared to continue doing it, then maybe you should look somewhere else. We'll give you six months to find another job."

I was very fortunate that they were understanding of my needs. When I went in to talk with my boss, Alan Kellock, he said, "Fine." He agreed that I could have my own list of authors of books published under the regular Viking imprint.

After I changed my job, some people's first instinct was that I'd probably been pushed out. One or two people who didn't know me terribly well called up and said, "Are you all right? What's this all about?" I told them, "You've got the wrong idea. This is something that I initiated for reasons that are important to me." It was as if I'd given up status. People were just amazed. Even a couple of my close friends said, "Are you sure you know what you're doing? You're giving up a great job. And you got it when you were so young. You've been so lucky."

In their view, perhaps I was backing away from success. Especially in New York, where people fight tooth and nail to get to the top. It's hard for many people to imagine somebody taking a step away from a position of power.

LITTLE HAITI

Paulette Francius
Born near Saint Marc, Haiti
Unemployed Single Parent
Miami, Florida

I've seen several young single mothers with malnutrition, right here in Miami. They can't work, because day care isn't available, and women without legal immigration documents are ineligible for work permits or public assistance. Paulette Francius is a brave lady. She's managed to survive on her own with four young kids."

These words of Gerard Jean-Juste, the fiery activist director of Miami's Haitian Refugee Center, led me to visit a tall gaunt woman with café-au-lait skin wearing a loose-fitting Caribbean peasant skirt. Paulette Francius, twenty-seven, is a devoted mother to her two-and-a-half-year-old son, one-and-one-half-year-old twins, and four-month-old daughter. Their world is a pastel-green stucco building on a run-down side street lined with weathered palm trees. She is one of thirty thousand residents of Little Haiti, a sixty-block-long area that straddles Miami's roughest black ghettos. They have fled a continual cycle of bitter poverty and bloody dictatorships that has ravaged their island homeland. In Little Haiti, most remain in abject poverty.

In the spring of 1980, South Florida was recovering from the sudden arrival of 125,000 boat people from Cuba's Mariel Harbor. No one was prepared for what happened next. Ramshackle sailboats jam-packed with wretched survivors of an arduous one-to-two-week journey across six hundred miles of stormy Caribbean waters began landing along the Miami coast. Those lucky enough to run blended into northeastern Miami's black neighborhoods. Thousands more, unable to speak English or Spanish and too ill to move, were taken into custody by U.S. Immigration officials. An abandoned missile site near the Everglades, twenty-five miles from downtown Miami, was turned into a steel-fence-enclosed holding center.

Officer Michael Teague thought that he had seen the depths of human misery on the Mexican border. When he saw the Haitians, he shuddered. "When I arrived at Krome Avenue Detention Center outside of Miami," he recalls, "I couldn't believe what I saw. Almost half the Haitians had tuberculosis. Virtually one hundred percent had all kinds of scabies, crabs, and other types of parasites. Many had some type of venereal disease. A few had leprosy. One poor guy even had rabbit fever. It looked like little chunks of him were falling off onto the floor.

"During '80 and '81, there were twelve to fifteen hundred Haitians in the camp at any given time. They lived in a large two-story concrete building filled with bunk beds. The Public Health Service practically ran the place for us. Before we could release any of them or send them to another detention facility, we had to scrub them down and smear them with Quell, an antibacterial goo.

"Outside of the building was a wall of portable johns. They didn't have the vaguest idea what those things were. Haiti being one of the poorest countries in the world, they just didn't know any better."

Large groups of Haitians were transferred to detention centers in other parts of the country until they were sent back to Haiti. Others were assisted by human-rights lawyers and the Haitian Center run by Jean-Juste, the first Haitian priest ordained in the United States. Haitian entrants who filed for asylum were released for a small bail bond, to the custody of local relatives. Before 1980, around fifteen thousand Haitians lived in the Miami area. In 1987, sixty thousand were estimated. While the legal process for each case drags on in appeals courts for years, Little Haiti has grown.

Fearing a perpetual flotilla of Haiti's destitute six million people, the U.S. Coast Guard was assigned to patrol the waters around Haiti. Since late 1981, around ten thousand potential migrants have been intercepted and turned back. Immigration and naval officials estimate that an equal number have perished in unseaworthy vessels. Still, between 100 and 150 Haitians continue to land on the Florida coast each month. In April 1983, one of these survivors was Paulette Francius.

Having spent five months in Krome Avenue Detention Center, she met Jean-Juste after her lover smuggled out a cassette tape begging for help. Paulette had all the physical symptoms of being pregnant, but immigration officials refused to believe her. Jean-Juste recalls the controversy: "I went to Krome to talk with immigration officials about Paulette. They told me, 'No, she can't be pregnant. Men and women here are under strict supervision.' So I sneaked into the hospital and took a photograph of her swollen stomach. I gave the story to the media. After public controversy about Paulette's case, the immigration people got tired of her. All of a sudden, late one afternoon, they kicked her out the front gate. All by herself."

In Haiti, where traditions are strongly influenced by ancestral African cultures, there are few formal marriages in the countryside. A man will have as many families as he can afford. If a woman believes her man is unsupportive, she will change partners. It's not unusual for a woman to have children by different men. Relatives help care for the children while a mother works in the marketplace or tries to grow rice or corn on a small plot of eroded soil. But in Miami, separated from her extended family, a single mother can languish in hunger and despair.

With no babysitter to watch her children, Paulette spends most of her days inside her musty three-room apartment. On a humid afternoon, Paulette's cotton-candy hair is tightly pulled back into a bun with slender plastic clips. Barefoot, she reclines on an overstuffed sofa, surrounded by her four diaper-clad toddlers collapsed in an *afternoon nap. They sleep undisturbed by a neighbor's stereo, which rattles the walls with disco drums, in competition with booming rhythmic raps that harangue empty sidewalks from a teen-ager's ghetto-blaster tape box.*

In the midst of ongoing urban chaos, Paulette radiates serenity and effortless charm. In her musical patois of Creole, a fusion of French and African dialects, she tells me about her life in Little Haiti. A mutual friend, Marise Piverger, an associate of Jean-Juste who was born in Port-au-Prince but educated in American schools, translates while gently rocking Paulette's infant daughter in her arms.

In this neighborhood, you can live your life without needing to know English: everyone speaks Creole. Sometimes friends have tried to teach me a few words or useful American phrases, but after a while I forget.

I shop at a market on 54th Street where they accept food stamps. The store is run by a Cuban named Tony who speaks Creole. He's a good businessman. The store has the kinds of food I need—rice, beans, fruit, and Beechnut baby food.

I have been in Miami almost four years, but I don't have a car. To get around, I use a shopping cart that I push. When I go shopping, I load all four kids into the cart. If I'm lucky, I can go out while they are sleeping. I quietly slip outside and try to get back before they wake up. [Laughs] My oldest child, Paul, is two and a half years old. The twins, Gerard and Gerald, are one and a half. The baby, Tanya, is only four months.

One time I took them all to the immigration office. That was like a revolution. They were crying and screaming. The judge and other officers came out into the hall to look at that circus. I had such a headache by the time we got home.

The children keep me so busy that I seldom feel lonely. I'd rather be alone with the kids than have men come by to give me trouble. Sometimes the father of the three youngest has fought with me when I asked him for support, or to help me send a little money for my mother and my oldest son in Haiti. Sometimes I am depressed about my situation. When I go to the clinic or to Immigration, I've met many Haitian women, single mothers, in the same situation as myself.

In Haiti, life is different: you can leave your children with your relatives or your spouse's relatives while you work. Here I don't have anyone to watch my kids so I can look for a job. Even if I was working, most of the money I could earn would go to pay a babysitter, and any small income would disqualify me for state help. I would be worse off: they would take away my food stamps; I wouldn't qualify for Medicaid;

I wouldn't have anything. And now, with the new immigration law, it is illegal for someone to hire me.

My home in Haiti is Saint Marc, a beautiful port city on the central coast, a two-hour drive north of the capital, Port-au-Prince. There are mountains outside of the town. My house was near the sea. We could see the water and the palm trees on the sandy beach. Wild banana and papaya trees grow along the streets and in the yards of private homes. People from small villages in the countryside come into town for school, to find work, or to do small business. I lived on the outskirts of the city, but we still say Saint Marc.

I left Haiti in November 1982. My friend Eliphete said, "Let's go." I wasn't sure where my friends were going, but I went on the boat with them. I didn't know very much about Miami or the United States. But I knew that I would have freedom of speech. I thought that I could have a better job. In Haiti, if you say the government is no good, the Macoutes would beat you up.

The Tontons Macoute were President Duvalier's security force. They didn't answer to anyone but him. The government didn't give them regular pay, so they were free to take whatever they wanted from the people. They kept their loyalty to "Papa Doc" and his son, "Baby Doc" Duvalier.

In Miami, you can talk with the police. But in Haiti, when a man joined the Macoutes, he would turn against his neighbors and even his own relatives. Sometimes Macoutes cut off people's heads. In the countryside, the Macoutes are worse, because they have even fewer restrictions.

I wasn't involved in politics, but when the Macoutes seized my mother's land, we couldn't do anything about it, not even talk about finding justice. And in town, at the market, the Macoutes would take people's merchandise without paying. There was no legal process. If people's business wasn't good and they told the Macoutes they didn't have money to pay taxes, the Macoutes beat them.

In my family, there were six children. Most of them lived in the countryside with my mother. But I grew up in Saint Marc with my oldest sister, who only had two children at the time. The great difference in our age is because in Haiti women bear children many years apart. In many families, the oldest children help to raise the youngest. There isn't much money or food for any of the children.

My father was a farmer. He died when I was a baby, so I never knew him. My mother had to work alone in the farm field every day. Haiti is very mountainous, and the soil is very rocky. The main crops are sugar cane, rice, sweet potatoes, beans, and corn. Rice, our staple food, needs a lot of water. Some years there is not enough rain. Other times it rains so hard that much of the good soil is washed down the hillsides. We cannot stop erosion, because the land that was forest is now very barren. People cannot live without firewood.

Homes don't have electricity, so we use charcoal or wood in portable iron stoves. Sometimes the fire filled our house with smoke, so I carried the stove outside to finish cooking the meal.

Countryside houses are made from thin strips of wood or young bamboo trees tied together. They are very lightweight. A strong wind easily damages the homes or knocks them down. Roofs are made from dried straw from rice plants. People with money use sheets of corrugated tin. There's no indoor plumbing. Just a bare floor with everyone sleeping on it.

In Saint Marc, houses have wooden frames covered with adobe mud or cement. In our house, there was no electricity or running water. I hear that now the neighborhood has a pipe with water running in the street that everyone goes to. Most Haitian people still use public wells. We carry water home in pails for washing or cooking. Houses in Miami that poor people live in have electricity, running water, a toilet—only a wealthy person would have such a home in Haiti. To take a bath or wash clothes, we went to the river or carried water in a pail to wash at home.

If you live in the countryside, you have to carry a sick person many miles on your back, because there are few doctors, and medicine is hard to find. There are few cars and no government hospital care like in Miami. Many poor people die because they don't have money to see a private doctor. So people go to voodoo doctors, who cannot really help them.

In Haiti, people are Catholics but practice the African religion also. We are born into loa [voodoo] spiritualism. For instance, most families respect their ancestors' spirits. At ceremonies, people dance and go into trances so the gods can enter their body and speak.

Special voodoo holidays or celebrations are not done in the open, because the church has tried to suppress these beliefs. Still, most people, like my own family, have both Catholic and voodoo beliefs. Even in Miami, Haitians go to church but also believe in loa.

Most voodoo holidays are held around the same time as Catholic holy days. Where I come from, the voodoo celebrations are held every year between November and January. For example, November 1 and 2

[All Souls' Day and All Saints' Day] are big holidays for both religions. People go to the church and cemetery to pray for deceased relatives. And in the evenings, at home, we celebrate the *guedés* spirits—gods of the dead—in the voodoo tradition.

At parties, people eat and dance and tell jokes that make fun of death. The reason is to remind ourselves that, even though we eventually must die, we celebrate that we are alive.

In my hometown, there are many *boko* [voodoo priests], but only one highly respected priest in each town. If people are sick and a medical doctor cannot help or says that nothing is wrong, the sick person will go to the *boko*. A voodoo priest does rituals and prayers to communicate with the spirits. In *loa* there are many types of spirits, male and female. Some are ancestors, some are higher spirits. Different priests have their own special spirit guide. The *boko* can be a man or a woman.

The *bokos'* spirit healing is special, but there are also herbalists, who are not voodoo priests. For instance, in Miami there are Haitian herbalists who make all types of natural medicines. In Haiti, I knew what kind of trees or plants to use for medicinal teas. But in Miami, I take my children to the clinic or the hospital. They were born here, so they should see American doctors.

One of my favorite times as a child was Christmas. I remember receiving gifts from my godmother. She would make rice bread. And my mother would make treats with fruit or sweet yams to send to her. Families don't have much money, so they exchange gifts, such as farm animals.

We would go to midnight Mass on Christmas Eve, then on Christmas Day have a big party for all of the family and friends. This year, I can't even see Christmas coming. It is just like any other day. If only my mother were here, I would feel like celebrating.

Mother would visit my sister and me in Saint Marc quite often, and I would often visit Mother in the countryside. Because of the poverty, many people have left their land to try to survive in the cities. Natural disaster and poor government planning have made things worse.

On my mother's farm, a few years ago, all the pigs had to be slaughtered, because Duvalier made that law throughout the entire country for fear of some disease. All Mother had left were some chickens. Pigs have always been important to the farmers' economy, like money in the bank. Selling a pig pays for seeds for the coming season's crops, medical expenses, weddings, and funerals. When it's time for a child to go to school, the parent sells a pig to provide money for tuition, books, and uniform. That's what my mother did when I started school.

Whenever I asked my mother if I could stay in the countryside with her, she always told me, "Stay in town and go to school." My six years of education aren't considered to be very much in the United States. But in Haiti, few people go to school at all, because of the poverty, and first priority will usually be given to a boy. Most Haitian people's choices in life are limited, hopeless.

At the all-girl school I attended, I learned basic reading and writing. I was sick very often, so I had to quit school when I was fourteen. A doctor said that I have problems with my eyes. I can see things far away, but not close up. There was no way for me to get eyeglasses.

Shortly after I left school, I became pregnant. Yes, I was shocked. Many of my friends told me to get an abortion. But I refused. I wanted to have the baby, even though I wasn't formally married. Traditionally in Haiti, marriages are just common-law relationships. People don't have enough money for a wedding party; a man and woman just start living together. But you take your spouse to meet your family. I took my spouse to meet my older sister before we found our own house.

After the baby was born, I breast-fed him for five months. When my son was old enough to eat, I gave him to my spouse's mother, so I could work. I built a small food stand in the market, which is located in the center of a large street. I wove a tent out of dried palm leaves between the stands of vendors who sold fruit, vegetables, and many other things. I set up a large table and straw chairs and provided bowls.

I woke up at six o'clock every morning to go to the market. I would carry a large cooking pot onto a public bus. At the market I would buy provisions before I built a small cooking fire. In the mornings I made cornmeal with salt and beans. And at midday I would cook boiled rice with beans and peas. I sold a bowl of food for a gourde and a half [1 gourde equals 20¢]. Some customers would sit around the table and use my bowls; other people would bring their own bowls to carry food out. I worked alone all day, usually until around 5:00 P.M.

The Macoutes were always in the marketplace, strutting around in their blue uniforms with open-collar shirts. They always carried weapons. They gave everyone tickets to pay tax on our merchandise. It was unfair, because the big stores didn't have to pay if the owners were friends of the government. The Macoutes leaned heavily on poor people. There was too much corruption.

On a good day, I could earn around 100 gourdes. Out of that I subtracted the amount I paid for provisions, transportation, and tax to the Macoutes. Most of what was left I gave to my mother-in-law to help care for her and my son.

My spouse worked on a government truck. When he was out, he didn't want me to be alone in the house. So he asked a friend, who was his co-worker, to stay with me. Unfortunately, this man had taken something from the truck. When the Macoutes came for him, they arrested me, too. I didn't understand what was going on. They beat me and kept me in jail for three days. I had to sleep on bare concrete, without even a mat. When the Macoutes released me from jail, they didn't explain anything. They just said, "Go."

I stopped working in the market and began cleaning wealthier people's houses. I could make better money at the market, but I was getting sick from the smoke and heat of the cooking fires. I couldn't stand it any more.

Around four months after the Macoutes arrested me, I was still feeling a little nervous. One day my friend Edith sent a man named Eliphete to ask me to leave Haiti with them. I wasn't sure where they were going, but I said yes. I asked my spouse to come with us. He said that he didn't want to leave, but he told me to go.

It was dark night when we left. All together seventy-two people walked down to the harbor. We took turns getting into a small rowboat that quietly ferried us to a sailboat in poor condition, owned by Eliphete. Our departure turned quite frightening. The Macoutes saw us and came after us, shooting.

The Macoutes have their own patrol boats. Even on the ocean, they continued shooting. Our sailboat was too crowded and could hardly float. Everyone was crammed together on the boat's deck because there was no bottom compartment. There was only a small cabin where the captain's wife stayed.

The weather turned bad—the wind became fierce, and there were very high waves. Our food and drinking water were lost overboard. While we were in the narrow passage between Haiti and Cuba, the boat tipped over on its side. The boat was sinking quickly. We all dove into the sea. I was a strong swimmer and was able to keep my head above water. A Cuban patrol boat saw what was happening and came to rescue us. We were taken to an isolated place in Cuba called Femme Haiti, on the coast. A short time later, the Cuban government sent a large boat. Sailors pulled us up by rope, and we were taken to a place of exile called Antillote, which means "small island."

Only the people from our boat stayed on this island. We stayed in cement houses, with regular beds to sleep on. We were not allowed to leave the compound to work or visit any Cuban people to buy food, but some people came to see us, and we were permitted to gather firewood for cooking.

My friends and I didn't want to stay in Cuba. After eight months of isolation, we were fortunate that another Haitian refugee boat landed at our place to make minor repairs. When they left for Miami, they took us with them.

During the week it took to sail to Miami, I was not feeling very well. I was so seasick, because the waves constantly rocked the boat. Some people thought I wouldn't survive.

It was April 6, 1983, when we finally reached the Florida coast. The night was so dark that we couldn't tell we were just outside of Miami. Some people said, "We are in Nassau, Bahamas." But other people on the boat, who knew Miami, said, "No, this is Florida." When an American coast-guard boat approached, we knew that we were in Miami. I didn't know whether to be happy or afraid.

The coast guard came with other police. They took our names and gave us something sweet to eat. People who were very sick were taken to a hospital. A woman who worked for Immigration told the rest of us that we were being taken someplace comfortable, where our families would come to pick us up. That was a lie. The next morning, we were taken in a big bus to Krome prison. They gave us uniforms to wear.

The Krome Center is built like a regular prison for illegal immigrants. All the detainees live in big white cement buildings. There is barbed wire surrounding the compound. Men and women are separated by a large steel chain-link fence, but we were allowed to socialize certain times of the day. The women's quarters was one huge room lined with bunk beds. There were around a hundred women from different countries. Most were Haitians. I cried all the time.

Every day, we would just sit there. Women who knew how to sew kept busy on machines. I met a Haitian man in Krome who I came to love. It seems unbelievable, but I became pregnant in Krome. I became very ill and asked the authorities for permission to go to a hospital. They told me that I was insane and refused to accept my pregnancy, even though my stomach and breasts were obviously swelling with all the clear symptoms.

The authorities said that they always had guards watching us, so it was impossible for me to be pregnant. But my boyfriend and I found ways to have private time together, such as when everyone went to the cafeteria for meals. He and I planned to get married when we were released from Krome.

In September, five months after we had been imprisoned, my stomach was so swollen that the authorities had to send me to the hospital for a checkup. I had dizziness and was vomiting, as well as swelling breasts—

Paulette Francius and Father Gerard Jean-Juste at the Haitian Refugee Center, Miami, Florida

all the signs of pregnancy. But they kept saying that I wasn't pregnant. I got into a big argument with them in the hospital, because they said my condition was just an infection.

My boyfriend was desperate, so he sent a tape-recorded plea to Father Jean-Juste at the Haitian Refugee Center in Miami. I spoke in Creole, and he did an English translation. We explained that we were afraid that the Krome officials were concealing my pregnancy in order to give me an abortion and then deport us. My boyfriend said, "I am the father of the baby. Paulette will be my wife when we get out of this jail. That is something we planned before she became pregnant."

Father Jean-Juste came to visit me at the hospital. He photographed my large stomach and gave the picture to a newspaper. I was shocked when the immigration officers released me from Krome. I stood outside the huge steel fence and said, "Thank God, I'm free."

Because I have no relatives here, I was put under the responsibility of the Haitian Refugee Center, pending an asylum hearing. I moved in with relatives of my boyfriend and waited for him to be released. I looked forward to getting married and began looking for work right away.

I applied for jobs at many hotels and restaurants in the Miami Beach area, but every place only wanted to hire women who spoke some English. During that time, I had a miscarriage and lost the baby. Then I got the news that my boyfriend had been sent back to Haiti. My dreams were shattered.

I realized that there was no work for me in Miami. I met people who were going to work on farms in another part of Florida, but I didn't have close friends or relatives there, so I was afraid to go on my own. I met another man, who I began to spend time with. We moved into an apartment on 58th Street in Little Haiti in January 1984, when I was again pregnant. My son Paul was born one year after I arrived in Florida.

I didn't have a good relationship with Paul's father. So, although I was kind of afraid, I began to look for a place of my own. I felt very insecure and took up with a man who was working. Paul was not even a year old when the twins, Gerard and Gerald, were born.

While I was in the hospital giving birth, the twins' father took care of Paul. It was a very difficult time for me. In Haiti, when a woman has a baby, her mother or sister helps take care of the other children. Even a friend might help. Here I felt so isolated and alone. I cried so much because of that. I had a Cesarean operation, and when I came home from the hospital, there was nobody to help. Right away I had to take care of the children, do the housework, everything by myself, even though the doctors at the hospital had warned me to take it easy. The father worked during the day. I was home by myself with the children. We lived in an upstairs apartment.

Occasionally one neighbor, an American woman married to a Haitian, came by to help with the children. Sometimes other neighbors would stop by. But they thought my husband was there, so they didn't come very often.

For two and a half years, ever since I moved back out on my own, I have just stayed home with the kids. I can't socialize, because I don't have anyone to leave the kids with. In Haiti, especially in the country-side, women work hard. Here, because of the lack of jobs, women don't work as much as men. This gives the man more power in the household. He tells the woman, "You're not working. You take what I give you."

In Haiti, if wives don't hold a job, they find other ways of making money by doing small home-style business. They sell food that they cook or bake at the marketplace or outside of their homes. Some women buy and resell small quantities of rice or canned food, others sew or make clothes. This is a way of life for Haitian women.

In Miami, some women have been able to find similar ways to make a little money from their homes. Some cook and open their home like a small restaurant for a few hours each day. If I had a sewing machine, I would try to do some work for friends. First I need to learn how to sew well. And with the kids, I have no time to make money. I just stay home.

A woman down the street has six children. The other day she became angry and threw boiling water on two of them. The police came and took them away.

After the birth of the twins, when I regained my strength, I decided that it would be better if I had my own place. I found this apartment even though I don't speak English, because the landlord is Haitian. I've learned how to get around, because people I've met give me advice. And there is a Haitian radio station, newspapers in Creole, and a pretty active grapevine.

When Americans talk to me, I can understand some words, but I cannot comprehend exactly what they are saying. If I had someone to watch the kids, I would take English class. At home, I can't even learn English from watching television, because the kids are usually running around. I know how to count in English, and the days of the week. That's about all.

In the four years I've been in Miami, I've had limited contact with Americans. I only see Haitian people. I am afraid of Americans. Robbers come into people's houses with guns and say, "Give us everything you have, or we will kill you." It's happened many times on this street. A thief came into my next-door neighbor's apartment just this week, but the lady was home and heard the noise. She ran outside, yelling for help.

Many times, thieves come when everyone is asleep and steal even decorations on window ledges. That is why we all have iron bars on our windows. And I make sure to lock my door every night. The robbers are both Haitians and black Americans. The Liberty City neighborhood is seven blocks away. That's a pretty rough area. What can we do? The white police can beat us up, and the blacks come in and rob us.

In Haiti, there wasn't this kind of problem with robbery. The problem was the Tontons Macoute bullying people all the time. They controlled everything. And after Duvalier, social chaos.

Since I've been in Miami, I never received a letter from my former spouse in Haiti. Only once, I received a letter from his mother asking why I don't keep in touch. But my former spouse has given messages to me through other Haitians who have come here by boat. He always asks me to buy things for him, but he hasn't provided for our son. First his mother, and now my mother have raised the child.

Even if I wanted to send a letter to Haiti, the mail system is very slow. Sometimes letters never get through. Maybe everything would have been different for me if I had married my boyfriend in the Krome Center. . . .

I still see the father of the twins. I know this sounds unbelievable, but he fathered my little girl, Tanya, who was born only four months ago. But he has given me little support. I get Aid for Dependent Children from the government. I receive $344 each month. My rent is $340. I get by on $283 in food stamps. But it is barely enough to eat, because the kids are growing. The father of the children has given a little furniture—like the stereo, the televisions, and the tape recorder. A lot of Haitians make cassette recordings to send to relatives, because many don't read or write.

My whole world now revolves around my kids. In Haiti, women know about birth control but we don't like to use it. And when we go to public clinics here, the first thing we're told about is birth control. I've never tried to get pregnant. After my second child, I asked the clinic to insert an IUD in me. But the doctor said that I could get sick and the clinic wouldn't do it. After my last child, they asked me if I wanted an IUD. I said no. Instead, I asked to be sterilized.

Haitians are very religious. We believe that birth control is against God's will. Even people who aren't Catholic believe they shouldn't do anything. Sterilization is different, because it's not seen as birth control. In Haiti, I went to Mass every Sunday. But now I have nobody to watch my children.

Here in my house there are mice. They eat my rice and bread, though they have never bothered the kids. The landlord doesn't take very good care of problems. When there's no hot water, I call him, but he doesn't come. He only shows up when he feels like it.

I don't know what will happen to me. My immigration case is still on appeal before the judge. Periodically I am called into the INS building for the judge to ask if what I have already told them is true. But they still haven't scheduled my final hearing. If my plea fails, they can send me back to Haiti. My children are American citizens, because they were born in Miami. They would leave with American passports and could come back any time. But I wouldn't be able to come with them. My hope is for the children to go to school, so they can become *someone*.

I am very worried about my status, but I don't like to complain while I am in this country, because the American government has given me food to eat. They provide medical care and enough money to pay the rent. In Haiti, there is no welfare program or American-style clinic for the children.

I worry. Not about these children's future: I believe that nothing bad will happen to them. But I worry about my son in Haiti. He is eleven years old now. I would like to send money to my mother to take care of him or to send for him, but I cannot afford to. And my mother is very poor. She sent me a letter recently and asked me to take him. The government took some of her land and left her without anything. In Haiti, there is no justice.

I have no regrets about coming to Miami. Even though my life is uncertain, I have food. I can say anything I want to say. There are no Macoutes or police who bother me. Still, I miss my relatives and wish that I could do more for them.

If I could find work now, I would be happy. Any type—on a farm, in town—it doesn't matter. But I can't look for work, because in this neighborhood there is only one day-care center, on 22nd Avenue. You have to sign a waiting list. It takes two years; sometimes they forget about you. And a requirement for day care is that you must already be working. They won't take children if the parent is trying to find a job. Where does that leave me?

THE BLUE-EYED CUBAN

Pedro Reboredo
Refugee from Havana, Cuba
Mayor
West Miami, Florida

Sun-splashed Miami. A dazzling zigzag of silvery skyscrapers and Art Deco flats. Coconut palms. Nouveau-riche condo-lined marinas sporting yachts and festive cruise ships. Just twenty-five years ago, this star-spangled fusion of can-do American work ethic, Roaring Twenties–style crime, and showy Latin panache was a glittering oasis for "snow-bird" tourists and retirees on the backwater of Old Dixie. Then came the Cubans.

The first wave made the 150-mile journey from Havana after Fidel Castro seized power in 1959. They were the cream of Cuba's middle class—doctors, lawyers, businesspeople, technicians—whose progression into the American dream began by washing dishes and busing hotel restaurant tables, driving taxis, and setting up storefront-café Cubano stands on Southwest Eighth Street. Now Calle Ocho ("Eighth Street" in Spanish) is the heart of a thriving Little Havana, where in 1986 more than twenty thousand Hispanic-owned Miami businesses generated around $2.5 billion worth of sales.

Transformed by an energetic coterie of Cuban-American entrepreneurs, Miami's Gold Coast has become headquarters for hundreds of multinational corporations, as well as the banking capital of Latin America. Neighboring Coral Gables has become the center of the second-largest international banking community in the United States. Miami's air- and seaports handle around $7.5 billion in Latin-American trade annually. Its manmade harbors have made Miami the largest cruise-ship port in the world. Sandy white beaches and the hypnotic beauty of Biscayne Bay are preserved by humid Atlantic breezes and the absence of heavy industry.

Although South Florida has experienced phenomenal revitalization through the presence of close to seven hundred thousand Cubans, there is underlying tension. The "Latinization" of Dade County, where the city of Miami is the largest of twenty-seven municipalities, has alienated many native residents, white and black, who now feel like foreigners in their hometowns.

Spanish is the dominant language on the streets, on the media airwaves, and in City Hall. After suffering decades of corruption and then totalitarianism in their homeland, Cubans have passionately embraced the American political system. Miami's mayor, Xavier Suarez, a Harvard Law School graduate, was born in Cuba. And in neighboring West Miami, where seventy percent of six thousand residents are Hispanic, *the mayor is a tall, broad-shouldered man, with thick grayish-black hair and blue eyes, Pedro Reboredo.*

When he first arrived in Miami on April 4, 1962, a nineteen-year-old refugee without family, his first act was to borrow $1 from a friend, so he could buy a $12.90 pair of shoes.

I got involved in politics because my godchild's house was always flooded. In 1979, the South Florida Water Management raised our underground water table from one foot above sea level to three feet. This caused flooding after heavy rainfalls. Stagnant water would be in the streets for two weeks, like a lake.

I'm an engineer. With two or three friends, I measured the water levels in the canals that surround the city. It was obvious that a new drainage system would solve the problem. So I went to the City Council. I said, "Hey, guys, we have to do something about this problem." But the engineer who they hired said that the city had to spend $2 million to fix the system. I said, "No, that's too much money."

We debated back and forth on this for three or four months. I decided that the only way to convince these people was to get into government. So, in April 1982, I ran for City Council. And I was elected.

A month later, another downpour came—three inches of rain. Once again the city was flooded. I told the Council, "Please, let's rent a pump. We'll buy some pipe and solve the problem temporarily." In one day we emptied the water from the city.

During the following months, one thing led to another, and I was able to solve the drainage problem. Instead of spending $2 million, I only spent $85,000—twenty times less than the original estimate.

During this period, as the Cuban population in the Miami area was becoming established, there was some disunity in the overall community. I experienced some animosity regarding "the Cuban issue." So my reasons for running for Council were to solve the water problem and to prevent a break in the community. In 1984, I received the highest vote in that year's Council election, ninety percent, which according to city rules made me the mayor of West Miami.

The face of Miami and South Florida has changed during the past twenty years. Especially after 1965, when Cuban refugees, who had begun arriving in 1959, realized that we wouldn't be going back to Cuba. We began to really buy into the American dream. Most are decent middle-class people who come from Havana. Like myself, almost all arrived here penniless.

The Southwest Eighth Street area [Calle Ocho] is known as Little

Havana. Cubans have renovated that section of Miami very nicely. And much of the high-rise buildings that have made Miami's skyline famous have been designed by Cuban architects. Many buildings in the area are owned by Cubans who are not involved in anything illegal. Miami has become the trade center for Latin America. Our ports have become the center for U.S. export to all of Central and South America.

Miami was revitalized because of the Latin trade. Before, it was a low-key "snow-bird" town for winter vacationers. Now it is becoming a regional metropolitan center. Some local people fear this. We are trying to convince the Anglos that the new economic and political power must be shared. It belongs to everybody who lives here.

I have seen that it is difficult for the Anglos to adapt. For instance, any local politician must now speak a little Spanish. I try to convey that bilingualism is a way to improve the community, because so much of Miami's commerce is with Spanish-speaking peoples, from other countries and local residents.

Like any city undergoing rapid growth, we do have some crime problems. We absorbed around a hundred thousand new people in two months during the Mariel boatlift from Cuba in 1980. It would be impossible not to have some negative results. Especially because there were at least five thousand criminals and psychiatric cases that Castro placed among the refugees.

We've been able to take care of problems created by Cubans pretty well. You can see by the development in the neighborhood and public places like José Martí Park. With many Americans, if their neighborhood begins to change a little bit, they leave. They move to a suburb or someplace else. But Cubans, rather than abandon our neighborhoods, decided to stay and make them better. Moving from Cuba was very painful. We have very strong family ties. In our culture, houses are usually passed from one generation to the next. We have pride in the place where we live.

I didn't leave Miami after I graduated from college, when I was offered a good job by Procter & Gamble. In 1968, they would've paid me a lot of money. But I decided to stay near my family. I didn't complain. Like many other Cubans, I have given all of my energy to help improve the community. Ironically, our success has created some friction with non-Hispanics, who are resentful of our size and independence. In turn, this creates an attitude in some Cubans: "If the Americans don't like us, we can be by ourselves." That is very bad for the community. I try to bridge that gap.

My family has assimilated well, but I have mixed emotions. As we

A café mural on Calle Ocho in Little Havana

get closer to our fellow American brothers, I don't want to lose our ties to Cuba. The danger is that we will also lose the incentive to remember what happened to Cuba.

Maybe if more people had stayed in Cuba and fought back, Cuba would not be Communist today. Miami would still be a quiet backwater town. . . . Maybe. But now that I step back and reflect, the problem we had was always the paternalistic attitude of the U.S. government toward Cuba: "Don't worry, Cubans, we'll take care of your problems. You just keep producing sugar."

On the one hand, the American companies were the best in Cuba. They gave the best salaries, the best working conditions. On the other hand, other Americans brought the most corrupt gambling casinos to Cuba. The almighty dollar bought everything—and some Cuban people sold themselves. During the last two years of the Batista dictatorship, corruption was rampant. The overwhelming display of dirty politics destroyed people's faith in the government. Even though Cuba had a democratic constitution established in 1940, it was never effective, because of corruption and public apathy.

The mafiosi—gangsters like Lucky Luciano and Meyer Lansky—practically owned the Cuban government. This made a lot of people want a revolution to reclaim our national spirit and lost freedoms. Then Castro emerged, showing a good nationalistic front. He awoke people who wanted to be Cuban again, not dependent on Americans. But we did not want to be Communists. Castro became subservient to an even worse power, the Russians.

I'm not putting the blame on the United States. The blame is on Cuban people, for having accepted the corruption. We did not have a government under Batista to stand up and say, "No more. I won't sell myself."

After Castro took power, decent American people felt that, by supporting Fidel, they were making up for all the mistakes the U.S. and the Batista governments ever made: "Batista was a bad dictator. Sorry. Now we support Castro to solve Cuba's problems." But Fidel double-crossed everybody.

I was sixteen years old when Castro took over in Havana on January 1, 1959. My first direct experience with the Communists was two years later, on January 28, 1961. It was the holiday of José Martí's birthday. [Martí is Cuba's national hero. A poet and leader of the independence movement against Spain, he was killed in battle in 1895.] It is customary on this holiday for students to sing the national anthem at school. But in our high school, Instituto de Havana, the Communists tried to make the students sing their 26th of July anthem or the Communist "Internationale." Two friends and I refused. We sat down in our seats silently.

Some Communist students in the classroom began to harass us. They warned, "You have to sing." These boys were members of the Association of Students, which was controlled by the Communists. But we refused.

They took us down to the principal's office, where they again tried to force us to sing. They put a gun to my friend's head. He told them, "We don't sing." They threatened, "We're going to kick you out of school. You're going to be on our list."

These students carried guns into school, because they were militiamen, Communist soldiers. But they never called themselves Communists at first. I would say, "You're Communist." They would say, "No, we're socialists. I haven't perfected myself. When I am perfect I will be a Communist."

I had never been involved in politics. I was only concerned with studying to make a career. My father was well respected but not wealthy. He worked in a sugar-mill office in Havana for thirty-five years. His whole family worked there. But his brothers had gone back to Spain.

I was the only child. We lived in an apartment in downtown Havana. Our extended family was very close. My uncle lived right on the corner. His wife is my godmother. She is the sister of my mother.

Up to the sixth grade, I went to a Catholic school taught by Saint

Augustinian fathers. It was not a rich school, but clean and in the central part of Havana. I was one of those kids who received a lot of awards for schoolwork. By the end of a school year, I was decorated with more medals than a general. Wilfredo Rodríguez and I, from first grade, would alternate as first in our class. One year he would be top student, the next year I would be. I still remember walking home from school. We didn't have a car, but the bus system was great. You could ride anywhere for 8¢.

Havana in the 1950s resembled a city in the United States more than any other place in Latin America. The city was larger and more dynamic than Miami. Baseball was the number-one sport. In the 1950s, Cuba was the first overseas country to receive the World Series on television. A broadcasting station was set up in Key West, Florida, so that Cubans could watch American programs. I remember the "Ed Sullivan Show."

When the revolution happened, there were strikes in the schools, a lot of violence. The police would club students involved in antigovernment actions. They might disappear. But I was never in trouble. In a dictatorship of the right, people still had some breathing room. For instance, one time a policeman told my father, "We have the son of your friend in jail. Go tell his father." And they were able to get the boy out of jail.

In reality, it was not the Communists who toppled Batista. It was good Catholic people who were trying to solve the country's problems. The main theme of the revolution was to re-establish the 1940 democratic constitution. There were priests in the mountains who fought alongside Fidel. Castro himself had studied in a Jesuit school. But after his Communists took power, he started cracking down on the church, because he feared potential rivals to his power. Fidel and his close circle didn't reveal that they were Communists until after Batista was toppled. They imprisoned or killed many of the non-Communists who had fought alongside them. These victims were not prepared to defend themselves against this betrayal.

My friends and I were branded as troublemakers or "counterrevolutionaries" by the Communists, because we refused to sing their anthem. Teachers would not even talk to us, except to give classroom assignments. We felt separate from the world. Some teachers, like Dr. Barrios, our biology teacher, were Communist. He would still talk with me, but he let me know that he didn't approve of my attitude.

I would overhear when some of the Communist kids or sympathizers talked with him and pointed their fingers at me. Dr. Barrios's attitude toward me changed. All of my teachers acted this way, except the *gusano* teachers. *Gusano* means "worm." That's what the anti-Communists were called.

On April 17, 1961, some friends and I were at a buddy's house near La Beneficencia, an old part of Havana, studying for our high-school exams. We heard on a neighbor's radio that Cuba had been invaded. We decided, "Let's not go to our homes." We knew that we would be targets of the Communists.

I went to my godmother's home, where I hid for more than a month. My parents' house was checked all of that time by the Committees for the Defense of the Revolution, neighborhood committees used by the secret police. During my time in hiding following the Bay of Pigs incident, more than a hundred thousand people were jailed. The Communists turned amphitheaters and stadiums into jails and filled them up.

My friends Agustín, Mayito, Negro, and Mulatto were picked up by the police. Mayito was arrested because of the incident where we refused to sing. He died in jail from an infection in his liver. And later my friend Roque, who was sixteen years old, spent sixteen years in prison for passing out leaflets against Castro. He was arrested by one of the guys working for the Communists at the school, who, ironically, lives in the U.S. now. Roque is still in Cuba.

After a couple months, things calmed down. Thousands of people were being released from jail, little by little. Many, though, remained in prison for years. After my parents checked out the situation through the local underground and determined it was safe, I surfaced from hiding. I went back to high school to take my exams. Fortunately, some of the teachers were friendly—I passed the tests. But the authorities wouldn't give me a diploma. Surreptitiously, I received my grades through an underground network.

I didn't know that my father was preparing to send me out of the country. I never planned to leave. I was in love with a girl named Norma. We met in high school through mutual friends. We had a teacher, a very nice woman, who was an anti-Communist. Her father had fought alongside José Martí for Cuba's independence. She had a great influence on us. She would instruct the boys to be polite with the girls. She'd say, "Never touch the hand of a lady in public." The old rules of courtship. My wife is from that kind of family. The first time I went to visit Norma's home was on March 4, 1960. I rode all the way to her house standing on the fender of a bus because it was so crowded. That day a large boat full of ammunition, the *Coubre*, exploded in Havana Port.

In the old Cuban tradition, when you visit a girl at her home, her parents act as chaperones. By the time I graduated from high school, Norma and I were serious about each other.

After my friend Mayito died in jail, I knew that I might have to leave the country. But on the day my father said to me, "You're leaving," it came as a shock. I said, "What?" I was very unhappy. When I let Norma know, she was stunned. We made plans to reunite. My idea was, "I'm going to Venezuela to study and find work. I'll prepare to send for you. We'll write to each other every day."

On August 29, 1961, I found myself on a boat heading for Venezuela. In Caracas, I looked up a friend of my father who owned a mattress factory. He gave me a break working there. I lived in a rooming house alone, but I wrote to Norma every day.

My experiences in Venezuela were tough, like going through the army. The adversity made me a man. I saw corruption; there were criminals. I had to live among Cubans who had murdered people for Fidel and then were persecuted by him. They also escaped to Venezuela. I learned to become a diplomat to survive.

My original plan was to study in Caracas, then work in the petroleum industry or chemical field. I walked into the university's student union to ask for a curriculum schedule. They gave it to me, with a printed border of thoughts by Mao Tse-tung, Fidel Castro, and Che Guevara. I said, "This is not the place for me."

People in Venezuela were still pro-Fidel. His "agrarian reforms" in Cuba received a lot of publicity. Fidel was very clever. His collective-farming policies were ruining the Cuban economy, but while people in Cuba were lining up to buy groceries, Fidel was sending large plastic bags of vegetables to Venezuela, labeled "Surplus of the Agrarian Reform." This gave the appearance that his policies were successful.

Venezuelans had never suffered under a Communist regime, so they wouldn't listen to what we tried to tell them. They called us "Batistianos," accusing us of supporting the former dictator. It was ridiculous.

I moved from the rooming house to the *maicara*, where many refugees lived, to save money. Around forty families lived in this large old house with many rooms. My first night there, six of us slept in a room with bunk beds. There was one empty upper bed in front of a window. I was so tired that I climbed up, put a couple towels over the window, and fell asleep.

In the morning, I opened my eyes and saw many holes in the wall directly across from the window. I walked outside and saw that the front of the building was full of holes, and dark, like there had been a fire.

I learned that occasionally the leftists would throw Molotov cocktails or small bombs at the building. I immediately went back into the room and took the mattress off of the bunk. Thereafter, I always slept on the floor.

On January 28, 1962, President John F. Kennedy visited Venezuela. That was my first life-threatening situation. Cuban refugees prepared a ceremony to bring flowers to Kennedy. But there was a *paro*, a strike. All transportation was stopped by the leftists, to disrupt Kennedy's visit.

We went to greet President Kennedy with a large Cuban flag, thirty feet long by ten feet wide. The leftists threw ink at us from the tops of buildings. We placed floral wreaths at the José Martí monument. Then we walked to the monument to the Venezuelan hero Simón Bolívar. I was a young kid, eighteen years old, but I was tall, so I was chosen to be one of the guards for the march. I believed in what we were marching for. I had seen the injustices in my country and was fed up.

When we reached the Simón Bolívar monument, the park was surrounded by soldiers, who disbanded our procession. We didn't argue. Everybody was in a quiet mood. All of a sudden, I heard things crash around me. Leftists were throwing Coke bottles at us from the top of a hill. They had a crowd of about a thousand people, mostly students who had just come out of school. They were encouraged by agitators. I could easily pick out Communist militants in the crowd by the way they dressed, their attitude, their smile.

This was the first time a policeman fired toward me from close range. The Communists were throwing rocks and bottles over the policemen's heads to hit us. A policeman spun around 180 degrees and fired over our heads. But I wasn't afraid. I just kept throwing rocks and bottles back at the Communists. I was so angry. For the first time in my life, I was rebelling against persecution.

As the bottles crashed around us, we knew that we might not get away. But some black Venezuelans were working on a construction site nearby. They cut pieces of pipe and shouted, "Hey, Cubanos, here! Defend yourselves." It still sends shivers up my spine when I think about it. There were only fifteen of us. We took the bars and charged after the agitators. I hit a few guys, and then we pulled back. We heard the sirens of the National Guard. They carried machetes. And they would really whack you with them. We didn't want to go to jail, so when we heard the sirens we dropped everything and began walking very slowly.

I was the last person in our group. I looked back and saw twenty militants running after me. I dashed toward the troops and said, "Hey, those guys are Communists. And they're after me." But the Guard just drove away. I was standing in front of these twenty guys. I said, "Oh, shit."

The first guy that charged me was a fat guy who had a broken Coke bottle, who I had hit during the previous encounter. I'll never forget this. He said, "You *coñomadre* (you mother . . .). You're going to die."

I put my hand inside my jacket and said, "That will be the last thing you do, you son of a bitch."

They stopped, looked at each other. . . . It was the grace of God. Another Cuban, who was hiding behind a tree a hundred feet away, decided to run. They said, "Hey, there goes another one," and chased after him. I just walked home.

Months later, when my mother and I reunited in the United States, she asked me, "What happened to you on January 28, last year? I dreamed that you were in trouble." When I was standing in front of those Communist guys, I thought of the Virgin Mary. My prayer was answered.

After the riot, I applied for U.S. resident status through the American embassy in Caracas. On April 4, 1962, I arrived in the States on the boat *Santa María*, a cruise ship. I came off the boat with $12 in my pocket. I bought a $12.90 pair of shoes. So right away I owed my friend Ramón Ferrer around $1.

Ramón let me stay at his family's house in Fort Lauderdale, around thirty miles north of Miami, and he found me a job at the Governor's Club Hotel. I started out as a busboy. Though it was a step above washing dishes, it was a difficult experience. Though I had studied some English at school in Cuba, my ability to speak or comprehend the language was very poor. And I was too eager to do things right.

My first day at the restaurant, I tried so hard that I attempted to carry a pile of the most expensive dishes. I broke around twelve of them. The hostess made fun of me by saying all kinds of silly things in English that I couldn't understand: "You dumb Cubans are good for nothing." I kept saying, "Yes, yes." I didn't understand her. But I was so nervous, and I wanted to please her. My friend was standing next to her, laughing his head off.

But the people at the hotel were very nice. Newly arrived Cubans had such a warm reception from Americans in South Florida, we felt like we were at home. Although we thought a lot about our families, who were still in Cuba.

Among the first things I did was go to the marines' recruiting station at the post office. Orestes Romero and I wanted to join. I said, "We

will join if you guarantee that we will fight in Cuba." It was silly. The
sergeant said, "Well, no. You join for four years, nothing guaranteed."
I said, "No. We want action right now."

A few months later, during the Cuban missile crisis, Orestes and I
went to Freedom Tower in Miami to enlist in the army for a special six-
month program. I said, "I want a guarantee that I'm going to fight in
Cuba." They said, "No, no, no. No guarantee." I told myself, "I'm going
to college. There is too much indecision on the part of Americans, even
when this crisis is going on with Russian missiles in Cuba." I don't know
if I was being unpatriotic or just careful. I had seen many other people
suffer the betrayals of war and American indecision—like the Bay of
Pigs survivors.

My parents arrived in Miami in September 1962, shortly before the
Cuban missile crisis. I was still working at the hotel in Fort Lauderdale
from 5:00 A.M. until 2:00 P.M. I went to afternoon classes at Broward
County Community College. In the evening I would drive to Miami to
see my parents and attend classes at Dade College, finishing at 10:00
P.M. I made that round trip daily in my run-down 1955 Plymouth that
used a gallon of oil a day. I had to put in a half-gallon in the morning,
and a half-gallon before I returned to my apartment in Fort Lauderdale.

Finally, in 1963, I moved to Miami to live with my parents, where
the Cuban community was evolving. In the early 1960s, there were
between fifty and a hundred thousand Cuban refugees here. Mostly
middle-class folks, who continued to sponsor their family and friends.
We had to start from scratch, living in the more depressed areas of town.

On weekends, when I didn't have work, my father and I worked in
the sugar fields in Belle Glade. We harvested sugar cane, making piles,
then hitched trailers to the backs of tractors. I did this to earn a little
extra money to bring my fiancée, Norma, from Cuba.

Norma and I continued to write letters to each other every day from
the time I was in Venezuela. There was a lot of hardship for both of
us, but we were true to each other. I had to convince her parents to let
her join me. In 1965, I was so fed up with waiting that I had a talk with
her godfather, who lived here. I said, "Look, if she doesn't come soon,
I have friends who are in the underground. I can get into Cuba at any
time. If you don't tell her parents that I really love her, I'm going to
bring Norma here myself."

That got the message across. Her godfather wrote to her family:
"You'd better do what he asks. He's crazy enough to go in a boat and
show up at your front door. That's going to get you in trouble."

Norma's parents made arrangements for her to go to Mexico. Then, after three or four months of red tape, I brought her to Miami legally in September 1965. We were married on November 25, on Thanksgiving Day.

Our first home was near Norma's godparents, in a poor section of town, on Drexel Avenue, in the South Beach area. The rents were pretty cheap, so many Cubans started out there. South Beach is the entry area of Miami. It used to be old Jewish, then Cuban, but now it's a lot of Haitians, Colombians, Puerto Ricans, and Mariel Cubans. It's not the best atmosphere—a lot of prostitutes—but the beach is still enjoyed by all kinds of people. We used to have all of our picnics there when the children were born.

When I was married, I kept working while I was a full-time student. I had an associate degree of arts from Miami-Dade Community College. I started at the University of Miami in September 1965, when Norma first arrived. I majored in chemistry, so I landed a job in a laboratory as an assistant to its director, cleaning beakers and sterilizing the lab. All through college, I took twelve credit hours of classes and worked forty hours each week. My employers allowed me to work a schedule that accommodated my studies. I also found a part-time job in the *Miami Herald* mailroom.

My first daughter, Norma, was born in April 1967. At that time, my wife's parents were about to arrive from Havana. Her brother, a doctor who had been held for many years in one of Castro's prison camps in the jungle, managed to escape and departed with them. I had to come to grips with the realization that I wouldn't be going back to Cuba. Up to that time, I didn't wish to become an American citizen, because I was afraid to lose the ties with my native country. Sometimes I thought about going back to Cuba and joining the underground. But after I got married . . .

By the late 1960s, the attitude in Miami's Cuban community changed. We realized how quickly we were being absorbed into the American melting pot. All of the optimism we had about defeating the Communists in our country fizzled out. In 1968, I became an American citizen.

More than a hundred thousand Cubans were living in Miami. Many of us knew that we could probably make more money in other parts of the United States. But many of us decided to stay in Miami, because at least we had the sun and the Cuban atmosphere. Cuba was only ninety miles from Key West, and 150 miles from Miami. We used to go on excursions to Key West to have picnics, just to feel closer to Cuba. We visited Club San Carlos and other historic places used by our patriots before Cuba's independence in 1902.

When I graduated from the university in 1968, I wasn't drafted into the army, because I had children. I had a bachelor's degree in engineering and a major in chemistry. Right away, Florida Power and Light Company gave me a job in a power plant. I worked as an engineer in charge of water treatment. I wanted to improve my business skills, so I began a master's-degree course in business administration. I only completed half the credits, because I started designing homes and doing a little contracting work part-time. It was a way of making enough extra money so that Norma could take care of our young children and not have to worry about finding a job. Two years after our daughter Normita ["little Norma"], our second child, Maggie, was born on July 29, 1969. And our youngest, Elizabeth, on February 26, 1971.

When I was a refugee in Venezuela, I learned about survival. But after finishing the university, I learned about providing material things. We bought a house in West Miami, the one we still live in. I built new rooms as my children were born.

We were a churchgoing family, but perhaps I became too concerned with material things. I worked obsessively, overtime, at the Power and Light Company, and evenings and weekends with the construction company. Just trying to make a few bucks to buy a house and a piece of land, and increase the family savings. But I was forgetting everything else.

I still had respect for family unity and our traditions. We spoke Spanish at home, because we wanted our children to know the language. But I was becoming a part of the melting pot too fast. Then, on November 26, 1976, I lost my arm. That was the kick in the butt that woke me up. Being close to death made me look at things a lot differently.

I was going hunting. My .22-caliber rifle was upright next to me in the car. As I bent over for a cigar, I accidentally set the rifle off. The blast blew a hole through the lower arm bone, bursting both arteries below the elbow. When the doctor put my arm in a cast at the hospital, he forgot about the arteries. I kept complaining about the pain, but nobody paid attention. The lack of circulation caused an infection that nearly killed me.

I remember the doctor came to my hospital bed and said, "Pedro, we have cut your arm off." I said, "What?" For two weeks, I had been in and out of the hospital. I had a feeling that things were bad. A friend of mine, who was a priest, stood by me throughout that whole time. He helped me to realize, "Maybe I don't need to work so much. Maybe I need to look after other things."

They cut off my arm on November 26. On the 27th, the doctor came to me and said, "Pedro, I need your help." I asked why. He said, "A kid in the next room has lost his hand in a shark attack. I want you to talk with him." I asked, "Why me? What can I contribute to the kid?" He said, "You'll understand."

When I walked in the room, the boy was in pain, because they stopped giving him morphine. He was going through a slight withdrawal. He was alone, without family there, around nineteen years old. I spoke with him several times. That was good, because it gave me confidence that I could help somebody. At first I thought, "How can I help somebody else when I am in such bad shape?" But it dawned on me that God had helped me to live. It made me look at the direction I was going.

Three months later, my father, who was disgusted by what the doctor had done to me, died of a heart attack. Before my accident, we had gone to Spain with the whole family. It was the first time my father and mother, who were both born in Spain, had the chance to return. My cousins in Germany and France all joined us in the house where my father was born. We had a wonderful time.

On February 11, 1977, my whole family went to church together in Miami on a Friday, something we had never done. We gave thanks for being all right. On Sunday, for no particular reason, we met and had a tremendous lunch. On Monday, my father died. It was the way I had hoped he would go when his time came, in the garden with his flowers.

The entire series of events made a better person of me. The priest who stayed with me at the hospital, I had known since we were in the Squires, a Catholic youth organization, as students. His influence, having my life spared, and seeing my family together helped to open my eyes.

In 1979, we had a situation in West Miami where developers wanted to throw a bunch of people out of a trailer park to build some high-rise low-income apartment buildings. I didn't mind the buildings, as long as they would include the four hundred families who were going to be thrown out. They were American families, not Cubans. I went to the county and said, "Why not give first choice for an apartment to the folks who are being displaced?" They said no.

Because of this, I started a homeowners' association in West Miami. I called for a meeting. It was the first time that I had spoken in public since my student days. We got enough signatures to stop the project.

Eventually, after five years, the county tore down the trailer park. A shopping center is being built there now, but at least it gave those poor people a little more time.

Nobody in Miami could foresee the events in 1980 that dramatically altered the perception of the Cuban community by Americans. And for Cubans, it was the jolt that revitalized our determination to become more involved in politics. The event was the Mariel boatlift from Cuba. It brought back to us the reality of Cuba that we wanted to forget, like a slap in the face.

Through the 1970s, even though Cubans in Miami wanted to go back to our homeland in our hearts, we cared more about the material things that we earned here. Because of homesickness, the idea of having a dialogue with Castro evolved. Some Cuban Americans went on short trips to Cuba to visit their families. They'd bring a few pairs of pants, dresses, or some shoes and give them a few dollars. They'd brag about how much money they had here in the States. And they'd return to Miami and tell their friends, "Cuba was nice."

But we saw the reality of Cuban Communism in the Mariel. Castro's police forced convicts into boats with ordinary refugees. When we saw how nasty and corrupt Castro's government was, many of us woke up.

When the boatlift began, my wife's grandmother asked us to get her out of Cuba. Norma's aunt, uncle, and little niece also wanted to leave. So Norma's father and I borrowed a friend's boat. I spent $5,000 to buy a small dinghy and a few tanks of gas. My father-in-law and I headed for Cuba.

I was not familiar with how to operate the boat. We were bouncing around on the waves. Cuba is only ninety miles from Florida, but the trip took fourteen hours. I heard many other Cubans on the boat's radio pleading for help. One guy was lost. It was four o'clock in the morning. He was crying over the radio, "Lord, I'm lost." I picked up the transmitter and asked him, "Do you have a compass?" He said, "Yes, I have it here on deck." I knew that it was worthless. So I told him, "Look, the sun is going to be coming up from the east. Keep going with it on your left and you'll find land." I asked him to look for my boat's flashing light, so that he wouldn't feel alone. When the sun came up, he found land.

By mid-morning, we neared Havana Harbor. I spoke with the captain of the port on my radio. I could hear him speaking fluent Russian to other ships. I recognized the area, because it was near where I used to live. It was a popular fishing place for generations.

My father-in-law was feeling seasick. He had a heart condition. And our engine was breaking down. I don't know how we made it. I was praying the whole trip. We had to land somewhere. Fortunately, the Cuban government was allowing boats into the Mariel area to pick up refugees. Soldiers pointed to us to go forward. We were the third boat to arrive in Cuba on April 24, 1980. As we approached Barlovento, thirteen kilometers west of Havana and thirteen kilometers east of Mariel Harbor, I became very emotional. This was the first time I was seeing Cuba in almost twenty years. I only saw one new structure in the port. Everything else was unpainted and in such bad condition. This used to be a high-class area where American tourists came for fishing tournaments.

As we entered the canal, I saw a little girl in rags standing on a small pier. She was nine or ten years old, the same age as my own children. She waved hello, hiding her hand at her waist, so that no one would see her waving to me. It dawned on me: "Gosh, this is not my country any more."

When we got into Barlovento port, I asked the police to help me fix the boat. They said, "Okay, you've got to leave it with us." I said, "Wait a minute." I didn't know what to expect.

My father-in-law and I stayed behind on the dock, with my briefcase and $5,000 in cash. I heard a big sound, *whoom, whoom, whoom*. Into the canal comes this 150-foot-long patrol boat. I thought, "Oh, no." This happened to be a military base. The Soviets I saw looked kind of fat.

Then I watched a Fiberglas boat come in. Officials filled it with ice, beer, and rum. It was funny. They had forty people doing work that two or three could have done. Then they bring this lawnmower to cut the grass. A Russian machine—red, of course. It was full of watches and dials. They crank it up and it goes *zzzzzz*. The weeds are about a foot tall. The guy pushes the mower over the weeds, flattening them down. And after the machine passes—*boing*—they pop right back up.

My father-in-law watches this for a while. Then he went up to the workers. He says to them, Lord rest his soul, "Wait a minute, son. Do you have a machete?" The worker said, "Yes." Dad said, "Let me show you how this is done." And he bent down and demonstrated: "You hold the weeds, and chop them like this." The worker looked at him like, "Who is this guy?" He left the awesome machine there, still running, and he walked away. We never saw him again. [Laughs]

In this port they also had some kind of youth academy. The kids, teen-agers, were tough-looking boys, muscular. But their facial expressions were like that of zombies. They were moving back and forth in small kayak canoes but not doing anything.

I tried to mingle and find out what was on people's minds. Around three o'clock in the afternoon, I brought a beer for a police officer and started talking with him. I said, "What a shame that Jimmy Carter is such a son of a bitch, that we cannot visit my country, where I was born, more often."

The officer looked at me and said, "Look, friend, an SOB is what we have here in Cuba."

I felt so embarrassed that I wanted to disappear. I couldn't understand why this navy lieutenant was risking his neck to tell me that Fidel is an SOB. I didn't want to keep talking with him, because, if somebody overheard or was watching, he would be in trouble. And if he wanted to defect, I couldn't help him, because I was alone in a harbor filled with Cuban and Soviet ships.

That night, around 10:00 P.M., the police brought our boat back to us. They couldn't fix it, because it needed parts that they didn't have. I had to pay them $100 anyway, for doing nothing. I put gasoline in the boat and said, "Thank you for trying."

Before we left Barlovento, the same officer came back to see me. He said, "When you get back to the U.S., tell our brothers up north that the Cuban people are dying of hunger."

That night my father-in-law and I departed for Mariel Harbor. The sea was calm, like glass. We could see Havana just beyond the curve in the horizon. From the opposite side of the boat, we could see Mariel. Lights were glittering on the horizon, of fishing boats out at sea. It was beautiful.

The next morning Cuban immigration officers came on board. They were in uniform, guns, the whole shebang. I gave them our papers. A number of Miami Cubans chartered boats and went to Mariel to try to pick up their relatives. By the time that Jimmy Carter issued a proclamation not to go, it was too late: there were two thousand boats in Mariel Harbor.

I lowered my ten-foot dinghy with an outboard motor, and rode all through the harbor. I saw the military with their guns . . . the sadness on the people's faces . . . the refugees and the prisoners from jails or insane asylums that Castro was loading onto big and small refugee boats. The whole scene washed over me. I thought, "These people don't look Cuban to me. This is not the Cuba I left. Their mannerisms—everything is different. This is not my Cuba."

During the next few days, we helped people by exchanging spare parts to fix up their boats. A community feeling developed. But when authorities told me that only one person of the family of four that we had come for could leave, I said, "No way. That's it. We're going. We've already been here one week wasting our time." It was May 1, 1980, in the middle of Castro's May Day speech, one that goes on for hours, when we escaped.

The police wanted each boat to go through customs as it left Mariel.

We didn't. We pretended like we were broken down. I passed a barge that I had seen all day going back and forth to a huge ship that had an open back, where smaller fishing boats entered. As we went past, the smell of processed fish was so strong that I couldn't breathe. I realized what was happening to Cuba's fish. It goes to feed the Russians, not Cubans. I remembered the face of the officer and his words: "The Cuban people are dying of hunger."

The Mariel program backfired on the U.S. government and caused a lot of trouble for the Cuban-American community. A Communist defector estimated that, out of the 125,000 Mariel refugees, around three thousand were Castro's agents, besides the criminals and mental cases sent by Castro to make Cuban refugees look like bad people.

It's true that the previous waves of Cuban refugees were better educated and better accepted by Americans. But toward the late 1970s, even those Cubans were feeling friction. Local people began to feel that maybe we weren't adaptable. Perhaps we didn't break our ties to Cuba as fast as people who came to America from other countries. Then the Mariel people forced a more drastic separation between the Anglos and the Cubans. In response, people like myself said, "We have to demonstrate to our American neighbors that Castro's rule made these Marielitos what they are. And we have to show that Cuban Americans are just as American as anybody else. We love this country. Just because the bad among the Marielitos came here, other people shouldn't have to move away from Miami."

We became more involved in community affairs. Some people participated in the United Way and other charities to show the American people, "No matter what my last name is, I am American."

Around the same time that I started the homeowner's association, there was the flooding problem in West Miami which led to my being elected to West Miami's city council.

The next political crisis was the Christmas Nativity scene in front of City Hall. Every year, the city traditionally displayed a Christmas tree and a Hanukkah menorah. In December 1982, some friends and I donated money out of our own pockets to add a Nativity scene to the holiday decorations. But a man came to a City Council meeting with the ACLU [American Civil Liberties Union] and demanded that we take the Nativity scene down. They threatened, "We're going to sue you." The other City Council members, who were mostly Jewish, said, "Pedro, we'll remove the Hanukkah decoration if you remove the Nativity scene." I said, "I'm sorry, the Nativity scene stays. I'm going to fight for the cradle and your menorah as well."

Before the next City Council meeting, I got signatures from many residents, and we filled City Hall with four hundred people. They demanded that we fight to keep the holiday decorations. We had to go to court. A friend of mine became our attorney for free.

The ACLU's position was that we couldn't use city funds for a holiday scene. But at the City Council meeting I had already told them that all expenses came out of our own pockets. On December 24, we won the case. Hanukkah decorations and the Nativity scene stayed.

It wasn't a matter of church and state. It was in keeping with a tradition. Like I started a Christmas-caroling chorus. On Halloween we have a pumpkin patrol to protect the kids and neighborhood property. And we have other community activities.

In 1983, I started a hot-lunch program for the elderly, because, when I walked the street campaigning to be elected, I found many old folks alone in their homes. When they opened their door, I could tell that their houses weren't being cleaned, and I knew that they weren't eating well. All they have from retirement is a few dollars to pay taxes. So in the City Council we discussed how to serve the elderly better. We started a program to bring them trays of hot lunches.

I obtained $150,000 from the county to expand the program, and provide a new building. We have classes for the older folks, Bingo games, and other social events to keep them busy. And we organize bus trips to take them shopping.

I was elected mayor in 1984. My salary is $140 a month, so I keep my job as a full-time engineer at Florida Power and Light. City Council meetings are held twice a month. But I have to attend other meetings at least four times a month. I don't eat lunch at work; instead I go to City Hall to check my mail and messages.

I still do construction contracting work, to be able to earn an independent living. I am building three houses in the Keys now, besides my own, where we can go to relax. I do the design, pay a contractor to do the building; then I sell them. But there isn't consistent money in construction. It depends on bank interest rates. To do well, you have to be really big into it. Even then you could lose money, but it keeps me busy. And I earn enough money for my children's college education. My wife does my business administrative work. This way she can still keep a close relationship with our kids.

No matter how busy I am, each night between six and seven o'clock I always manage to be at the kitchen table to have dinner with my family. I like to see the kids' faces and talk about their activities.

My oldest daughter, Normita, won a full scholarship to Miami-Dade College. She's an artist. All of the paintings decorating our walls—she did them. My middle daughter, Maggie, is the president of the student union in her high school. She's also very active in the youth group at the church. My youngest, Elizabeth, is a character. She's always a lot of fun around the house, and she has a tremendous memory.

My daughters consider the U.S. to be their homeland. They were born here. It would be very hard for them to make a transition to move to some other country. They have never seen Cuba. But they know Cuba—not only the geographical picture, but the history. They are highly motivated by the experiences my wife and I have told them about. So at least my experiences have not only had a positive influence in my work with other people, but also in my own house. That is the first place where communication is most important, among my own family. Otherwise I would be a failure.

I truly appreciate to have the opportunity as a mayor to get people involved in charitable programs. People say, "What have I been doing all these years? I didn't realize it was so easy to get involved." Motivating people is what my job is all about.

Besides being involved in community programs in West Miami and the greater Dade County area, I've sent $250,000 worth of donated medical supplies to El Salvador this year. I'm trying to help start a program to provide artificial legs for people who have been banged up by antipersonnel mines and booby traps. Right now I'm in the process of bringing a little girl to Miami who lost her right arm above the elbow. First I have to raise some money for her operation and rehabilitation. There are so many children like her. I hope we can get a prosthetics clinic to be set up down there, where people can get affordable arms and legs. A doctor in Miami has been very helpful. He went down to Salvador and fixed a few legs.

The problem is eliminating bureaucratic red tape. I've found that in Miami many people are willing and able to give. I got a call yesterday from a dental company who donated two complete dental offices. I've just got to get to their warehouse in central Florida, to pick the materials up and bring them down to Salvador. I do this in my private time and pay for my expenses from my own pocket. As mayor, I have credibility to do these types of things. That company wouldn't donate those materials to just anybody. That's what is so nice about being in politics sometimes.

When I bring the donated materials to Latin America, I give the local leaders a piece of my mind about the imbalance in those societies. But I try not to be too harsh. Otherwise, they would kick me out, and I wouldn't accomplish anything.

Last October, I was invited to speak at the Rotary Club in San Salvador. I told them, "Fellows, in my experience as a Cuban refugee, I learned that, when you lose your motherland, there is no coming back. You might go to the United States to live, enjoy freedom. But here is your home. You had better get down on your knees and pray that you never lose it. And you must act responsibly and democratically to solve your country's problems."

Miami is the gateway to Latin America. It is important that we do whatever is possible to help the people down there. Not only with material things, but with democratic principles and ideals.

In late 1984, the governor from Quiché, Guatemala, came to Miami looking for a sister city. So he was sent to me. The governor, who is an Indian and a Christian, invited me to visit. So I paid my own money for my wife and me to travel there in 1985.

Quiché is near the border of Mexico, inhabited mostly by Mayan Indians. It is a very poor, mountainous area plagued with Communist guerrillas. The guerrillas, whose leaders are trained in Cuba and Nicaragua, stage in camps in Chiapas, Mexico. They come back across the border to do raids and assassinations in Quiché. And they do radio broadcasts in Indian languages from Cuba. I felt that this was a good place to help people. As long as their government didn't abuse them, they wouldn't be swayed out of desperation by the Communists' promises.

I got deathly sick from dysentery there. I learned that the city Santa Cruz del Quiché didn't have potable water. So I helped them to design an aqueduct for safe drinking water. A friend of mine in Florida donated two kilometers of pipe, another friend donated the freight cost, and another the container to ship it in. I went back to Guatemala to make sure they received the materials and supervised the installation. On December 19, 1985, they inaugurated the new aqueduct system.

In West Miami, the schools are donating all the desks and materials that nobody wants for me to send to Santa Cruz del Quiché or San Miguel in El Salvador, or to a priest friend in Honduras who has a mission. They refurbish the run-down materials, then use them. Otherwise those communities would have no school supplies whatsoever.

By sending aid, the city of West Miami shows that we Americans care. We are not involved in sending war materials, only items that improve their basic living conditions and, most important, to give them a little hope. There's always a tendency in those countries for people to say, "Give me, give me." But we don't send them anything but the tools to help themselves.

In a recent cultural exchange, twenty-three mayors from El Salvador were brought to the Miami area under an AID program. I was one of the Cuban-American mayors in Dade County who were chosen to communicate with them and show them how municipal government works, and about the concept of democracy. They were all from towns around the size of West Miami, not more than ten thousand.

These mayors observed the way city governments function, how we deal with problems like garbage pickup, water meters, cleaning streets, and other basic community activities. These mayors weren't used to democracy, wheeling and dealing in a group process. I brought them to a City Council meeting in West Miami so they could see the discussion and arguing.

At that particular meeting, there was a pretty hot debate. I proposed a straw ballot, nonbinding, to find out if people in the community were offended by movies that desecrate religion. This all began with the showing of a movie at a nearby movie theater that most Catholics felt was denigrating to their religion.

A group of citizens came to the Council meeting to complain about the straw ballot. They had the support of one Council member, who was very adamant and argumentative about his position. The debate dealt with whether or not the straw ballot meant censorship, and the separation of church and state. But because the ballot was nonbinding, it couldn't stop a movie from being shown, nor could it change any laws. All it could do was express the opinion of the community.

I asked, "Does a film company have more rights than millions of people of a particular religion to make public mockery of their faith? In Cuba, when the government ridiculed religion, people were not able to say anything about it. Neither could Jews in Nazi Germany or in the Soviet Union." Within a democratic society, I believed that the best way for ordinary citizens, who don't have access to the media or movie corporations, could express ourselves was through the straw-ballot action. If people vote with their hearts, it sends a message. And if they don't agree with the ballot, they can vote it down.

There were people on the Council who disagreed and expressed their disapproval strongly. But at the same time, we all were respectful of the parliamentary process. We kept control, even though the debate was very hot. The Salvadoran mayors watched all of this.

The Council room is not large: it seats around sixty. There were around fifteen or twenty local people present who supported the straw-ballot proposal. There were a dozen or so people who opposed it. And the twenty-three Salvadorans with a translator. Everyone was packed in pretty tight.

The Salvadorans felt unwelcome. They couldn't speak English. There was a translator for them. But sometimes you don't need a translator to know that you are unwanted. They related to me as their friend. They saw a group of hostile people against me. And they took that to mean that this group was also against them. It was at least partly true. Some of the oppositionists made comments like, "Look, Pedro brought all his church members." They didn't realize that these were guests from abroad.

We took a vocal vote among the five Council members at the end of the meeting to determine whether to proceed with the straw ballot. We debated back and forth, everyone arguing. My proposal won by a three-to-two vote.

Afterward, I explained to the Salvadorans what had happened in the meeting. I assured them that it was the citizens' right to speak out when they disagreed with their elected officials.

The mayors had a lot of questions. They asked, "How were you being so patient?" They couldn't understand why people were opposed to trying to protect religion. Maybe what they were asking was, "Why didn't you shut them up?"

In El Salvador, in the past, there could never be a meeting like this. The mayor was the sole authority in the town; he did whatever he pleased. If somebody challenged him, that person probably wouldn't last very long.

I tried to convey to the Salvadorans, "Yes, I was having trouble. But I tried not to raise my voice or be malevolent in making my point. As a mayor, I have a certain clout, but I am not entitled to any extra power." I explained, "If we had lost on the proposal, it would have been either because I didn't prepare our position correctly, or my position might not have been proper." This gave them a better understanding of democratic government. It was good for them to experience the process directly.

Later, when the straw ballot was also introduced in the cities of Hialeah and Miami, the issue was strongly debated in the local media. I knew that I might have lost votes for re-election because of my position. But I feel that what cheapens any politician as a human being is making decisions only because you are thinking about re-election. Still, it hurts when people criticize me in the newspaper. It hurts to read name calling by a columnist. But I cannot let unfair statements get under my skin.

They have their freedom of speech; they are entitled to it. But I have my freedom of speech, too. I feel that people will respect me for doing what I believe.

Some local radio shows really put supporters of the ballot down. In a way, I'm glad it surfaced, because I don't like hypocrites. Certain news columnists or radio commentators talked nice about me when I did certain activities. But all of a sudden I'm a "dirty Cuban." I'm not the blue-eyed Cuban any more.

Some people still see me, a Cuban, as a second-class citizen. I prefer that their prejudice surface, because that is the only way that I can work with it. I do not see, in being an American, the need to lose ties with the country I was born in. Sometimes I feel that has been demanded of me. It hurts.

There are Cubans who have been here for a long time. They've gone to college and are successful in business. We are asked, especially if we are between the ages of thirty and fifty, "Where do you stand? Are your dreams in Spanish or English? Are they taking place in Cuba or here?"

I could become "Peter" Reboredo. Why do I still call myself Pedro? Because that is the name my father gave me. But I named my daughters Maggie and Elizabeth. I didn't say Margarita or Isabela. What's wrong with keeping my name and still telling people that I am American?

I have my roots. I want you to respect them the same way that I respect your roots. You cannot break away from your traditions. I am an American, and I would die for this country. Sometimes people don't understand that I can love two countries, one as much as the other. I am a hot-blooded American, but I am also a hot-blooded Cuban.

I try to fight prejudice from a position of love. I've got to say, "You have your position; I respect it. But you have to respect mine, for this reason or the other." I don't respond like, "I'm going to lose votes, so I'm going to watch what I say."

The straw ballot won by a large margin in the election. In West Miami it won with sixty-eight percent of the votes, in Hialeah with sixty-nine percent. And in Miami it won with fifty-eight percent. The reason was the community's right to express itself.

In a pre-election rally to discuss the issue, the Omni Hotel ballroom in Miami was packed with white Protestants, black Baptists, Cuban and American Catholics, and a letter of support from the president of the Jewish Orthodox rabbis. It was a coming together of many elements in the community. That's what democracy is all about.

But in a postelection editorial, a newspaper said, "Reboredo has won." They said that like twenty times in the same article. That didn't sit well with me. Because the paper didn't give credit for the success of the straw ballot to the people who voted. The *people* won.

Cynics would say that the reason I got involved in controversial issues is to gain something political for myself. But I don't get involved for an egotistical trip. I'm involved in politics because it's one way that I can give back to the community. I want to show gratitude and be part of America.

The future can seem so gloomy when we look at all of the problems in our society. But on the other hand, if we ignore them and don't try to do something about those problems, the future will become gloomier. Sometimes I criticize myself: "Is my effort really worth it?" I realize that one person cannot resolve the whole picture, but we can look at what is close to us and try to make it better.

ABOUT THE AUTHOR

Al Santoli was born in Cleveland, Ohio, the son of an Italian immigrant. He now lives in New York City with his wife, Phuong, a Vietnamese refugee.

His first book, *Everything We Had*, was nominated for the American Book Award, and *To Bear Any Burden* was the first multi-culture oral history of the Vietnam War and its aftermath.

Mr. Santoli is a contributing editor at *Parade* magazine, and his articles have also appeared in *The Atlantic*, *The New Republic*, *Readers Digest*, *Insight* and other publications. He remains active in refugee affairs as a consultant for the Lawyers Committee for Human Rights and has testified before Congress on refugee protection.